Other Books by Stephanie Coontz:

The Way We Never Were:
America's Families and the Nostalgia Trap

The Way We Really Are:
Coming to Terms with America's Changing Families

The Social Origins of Private Life

American Families:
A Multicultural Reader

Marriage, a History

From Obedience to Intimacy
or How Love Conquered Marriage

Stephanie Coontz

Viking

VIKING
Published by the Penguin Group
Penguin Group (USA) Inc., 375 Hudson Street,
New York, New York 10014, U.S.A.
Penguin Group (Canada), 10 Alcorn Avenue,
Toronto, Ontario, Canada M4V 3B2
(a division of Pearson Penguin Canada Inc.)
Penguin Books Ltd, 80 Strand, London WC2R 0RL, England
Penguin Ireland, 25 St. Stephen's Green, Dublin 2, Ireland
(a division of Penguin Books Ltd)
Penguin Books Australia Ltd, 250 Camberwell Road, Camberwell,
Victoria 3124, Australia
(a division of Pearson Australia Group Pty Ltd)
Penguin Books India Pvt Ltd, 11 Community Centre, Panchsheel Park,
New Delhi - 110 017, India
Penguin Group (NZ), Cnr Airborne and Rosedale Roads, Albany,
Auckland 1310, New Zealand
(a division of Pearson New Zealand Ltd)
Penguin Books (South Africa) (Pty) Ltd, 24 Sturdee Avenue,
Rosebank, Johannesburg 2196, South Africa

Penguin Books Ltd, Registered Offices:
80 Strand, London WC2R 0RL, England

First published in 2005 by Viking Penguin,
a member of Penguin Group (USA) Inc.

3   5   7   9   10   8   6   4

ISBN 0-670-03407-X
CIP data available

This book is printed on acid-free paper. ∞

Printed in the United States of America

Set in Bembo
Designed by Elke Sigal

For the three generations of men in my family:
Bill, Will, Kris, and Fred

Acknowledgments

A book covering this many centuries and geographical regions requires an author to rely heavily on the work of many other researchers. I acknowledge my debts to them in my extensive endnotes, but I want to highlight here some of the colleagues, friends, and complete strangers who were astonishingly generous with their time in allowing me to pick their brains.

I owe a special debt to the hundreds of my students over the years who have taken oral histories of their own families and neighbors as part of their work with me. I draw on their stories in this book. Many chose to remain anonymous, but a few have written up their work as extensive oral histories, which are available in the libraries of their respective institutions. I thank Susan Collins at the University of Hawaii at Hilo and Maggie Sinclair, Mary Croes-Wright, and Ben Anderson at The Evergreen State College, as well as all my students in programs called "What's Love Got to Do with It?" and "Growing Up Global."

The library staff at The Evergreen State College has always gone way beyond that extra mile for me. Reference librarians Ernestine Kimbro, Liza Rognas, Sarah Pedersen, Randy Stilson, Sara Huntington, Don Middendorf, Jules Unsel, Caryn Cline, and Carlos Diaz have always been there to help. Equally vital to my work have been the patience and kindness of the circulation staff: Mindy Muzatko, Jason Mock, Joel Wippich, and Jean Fenske. Thanks also to my successive research assistants, Jacyn Piper, Jesse Mabus, Nat Latos, and Jesse Foster for tracking down sources and hard-to-find papers. I

Acknowledgments

am grateful to the deans and provost at The Evergreen State College, who allowed me extra leaves of absence when this book took twice as long as I'd originally estimated. My colleague Charles Pailthorp has my gratitude for his patience and his active intellectual support, and my former student and colleague Maya Parson stepped up to the plate to take a teaching assignment I couldn't do myself. I am especially grateful to my friend and colleague Peta Henderson, who has generously shared her anthropological and archaeological research over the years and who came through once more as I struggled with new material for chapters 2 and 3.

When I was trying to summarize the material on the origins and evolution of human society, I wrote to four prominent anthropologists, none of whom knew me, to ask if they would review my first stabs at these chapters. To my grateful surprise, each agreed to look at a total stranger's early drafts and then patiently explained what sources I should and should not use and what mistakes this novice was making in interpretation. Several read two or more drafts, and all were extraordinarily generous with their time. My sincerest thanks to Adrienne Zihlman of the University of California at Santa Cruz, Allen Johnson of the University of California at Los Angeles, Brian Hayden of Simon Fraser University, and Thomas Patterson at the University of California at Riverside. Of course they are not responsible for any errors I have made, but because of their input, I was able to correct many errors before this book went into print.

My colleagues at the Council on Contemporary Families have been extremely generous with their time and resources. I would like to thank especially Philip Cowan and Carolyn Cowan for their careful reading and thoughtful comments on several chapters, Paula England for calculating several of the figures I use in chapter 17, Pamela Smock for her close reading of chapter 17, and Scott Coltrane, Nancy Folbre, Constance Ahrons, Virginia Rutter, Donna Franklin, Pepper Schwartz, Steven Wisensale, and Steven Mintz, who have been unfailingly generous with sources. Frank Furstenberg, Jr., shared several chapters of an early draft of this book with his graduate students; his feedback was very helpful. Barbara Risman, cochair of the Council on Contemporary Families, was always available to bat ideas around, as were Judith Stacey and Larry McCallum.

I thank Paul Amato for a careful, critical reading of my data on contemporary family changes and Sandra Wagner-Wright for feedback on my chapters on European history. Janet Gornick, Alexis Walker, Thomas Bradbury, John Gottman, Judith Seltzer, Stacy Rogers, Dorion Solot, Marshall Miller, Ted Brackman, Doug Foster, Sarah Raley, and Arloc Sherman gave me sources and suggestions. Joanna Radbord of the Epstein Cole law firm provided me with several of the affidavits in *Halpern v. Canada*. I called on Suzanne Bianchi and Andrew Cherlin several times for data on contemporary family trends and appreciate how patient they were with each request. Steven Nock kindly responded to personal communications to clarify recent trends in divorce. Therese Saliba directed me to resources on women and marriage in Islam. Pam Udovich did an amazing job getting my manuscript ready for publication and finding ways to make my word processing system compatible with my editor's. I just wish I could personally thank all the individual students and participants in workshops or discussion groups across the country whose questions and comments have challenged and inspired me over the years.

This book would never even have gotten off the ground if Gay Salisbury had not helped me find Susan Rabiner as my literary agent. Susan combined unsparing criticism with warm personal support to help me focus my changing ideas about my subject and get me through several crises of confidence. My editor, Wendy Wolf, believed in this book even when it was such a ponderous manuscript that a lesser woman would have despaired. I thank her and Hilary Redmon for their careful editing and strict insistence that I get this down to a manageable size, as well as for the sense of humor they managed to maintain throughout the project.

Finally, I don't know what I would have done without the help of my husband, Will Reissner. He patiently edited and improved every successive draft of the manuscript and was always ready to build me a spiffy new bookcase to store my ever-growing piles of notes and manuscript drafts.

Contents

Contents

PART FOUR:
COURTING DISASTER?
THE COLLAPSE OF UNIVERSAL AND LIFELONG MARRIAGE

CONCLUSION:
BETTER OR WORSE? THE FUTURE OF MARRIAGE

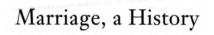

Marriage, a History

Introduction

———◦❈◦———

Writing this book about marriage over the last several years has been a lot like adjusting to marriage itself. No matter how well you think you know your partner beforehand, the first years are full of surprises, not only about your spouse but about yourself. The struggle to reconsider preconceived notions often takes you in directions you never anticipated when you began.

This is not the book I thought I was going to write. I have been researching family history for thirty years, but I began focusing on marriage only in the mid-1990s, when reporters and audiences started asking me if the institution of marriage was falling apart. Many of their questions seemed to assume that there had been some Golden Age of Marriage in the past. So I initially decided to write a book debunking the idea that marriage was undergoing an unprecedented crisis and explaining that the institution of marriage has always been in flux.

I soon changed my approach, but this was not an unreasonable starting point. After all, for thousands of years people have been proclaiming a crisis in marriage and pointing backward to better days. The ancient Greeks complained bitterly about the declining morals of wives. The Romans bemoaned their high divorce rates, which they contrasted with an earlier era of family stability. The European settlers in America began lamenting the decline of the family and the disobedience of women and children almost as soon as they stepped off the boats.

Worrying about the decay of marriage isn't just a Western habit. In the

1990s, sociologist Amy Kaler, conducting interviews in a region of southern Africa where divorce has long been common, was surprised to hear people say that marital strife and instability were new to their generation. So Kaler went back and looked at oral histories collected fifty years earlier. She found that the grandparents and great-grandparents of the people she was interviewing in the 1990s had also described their own marital relations as much worse than the marriages of *their* parents' and grandparents' day. "The invention of a past filled with good marriages," Kaler concluded, is one way people express discontent about other aspects of contemporary life.[1]

Furthermore, many of the things people think are unprecedented in family life today are not actually new. Almost every marital and sexual arrangement we have seen in recent years, however startling it may appear, has been tried somewhere before. There have been societies and times when nonmarital sex and out-of-wedlock births were more common and widely accepted than they are today. Stepfamilies were much more numerous in the past, the result of high death rates and frequent remarriages. Even divorce rates have been higher in some regions and periods than they are in Europe and North America today. And same-sex marriage, though rare, has been sanctioned in some cultures under certain conditions.[2]

On the other hand, some things that people believe to be traditional were actually relatively recent innovations. That is the case for the "tradition" that marriage has to be licensed by the state or sanctified by the church. In ancient Rome the difference between cohabitation and legal marriage depended solely upon the partners' intent. Even the Catholic Church long held that if a man and woman said they had privately agreed to marry, whether they said those words in the kitchen or out by the haystack, they were in fact married. For more than a thousand years the church just took their word for it. Once you had given your word, the church decreed, you couldn't take it back, even if you'd never had sex or lived together. But in practice there were many more ways to get out of a marriage in the early Middle Ages than in the early modern era.

However, as I researched further and consulted with colleagues studying family life around the world, I came to believe that the current rearrangement of both married and single life is in fact without historical precedent. When it comes to any particular marital practice or behavior, there may be nothing new under the sun. But when it comes to the overall place of marriage in society and the relationship between husbands and wives, nothing in the past is anything like what we have today, even if it may look similar at first glance.

The forms, values, and arrangements of marriage are indeed changing dramatically all around the globe. Almost everywhere people worry that marriage is in crisis. But I was intrigued to discover that people's sense of what "the marriage crisis" involves differs drastically from place to place. In the United States, policy makers worry about the large numbers of children born out of wedlock. In Germany and Japan, by contrast, many planners are more interested in increasing the total number of births, regardless of the form of the family in which the children will be raised. Japanese population experts believe that unless the birthrate picks up, Japan's population will plunge by almost one-third by 2050. So while federal policy in the United States encourages abstinence-only sex education classes for young people and the media tout teenage "virginity pledges," Japanese pundits lament the drop in business at Japan's rent-by-the-hour "love hotels." One Japanese magazine recently pleaded: "Young People, don't hate sex."[3]

The United Nations kicked off the twenty-first century with a campaign to raise the age of marriage in Afghanistan, India, and Africa, where girls are frequently wed by age twelve or thirteen, often with disastrous effects on their health. On the other hand, in Singapore the government launched a big campaign to convince people to marry at a younger age. In Spain, more than 50 percent of women aged twenty-five to twenty-nine are single, and economic planners worry that this bodes ill for the country's birthrate and future growth. In the Czech Republic, however, researchers welcome the rise in single living, hoping that will reduce the 50 percent divorce rate.[4]

Each region also blames its marriage crisis on a different culprit. In Saudi Arabia and the United Arab Emirates, governments criticize women's families for demanding such high bride-prices that it is impossible for young men to marry, even though they are eager to do so. But in Italy, commentators are concerned about the growing numbers of *mammoni,* or "mamas' boys," who choose not to marry. These are educated men in their twenties and thirties with good jobs who stay in their parents' homes, where their mothers continue to cook, clean, and shop for them. More than one-third of single Italian men between the ages of thirty and thirty-five live with their parents.[5]

Two Canadian authors, a physician and a psychiatrist, recently argued that the crisis in family life is caused by too much gender equality. In societies with high degrees of gender equality, they predict, birthrates will fall until the culture eventually collapses and is replaced by a society that restricts women's options in order to encourage higher fertility. But in Japan, many women say they are avoiding marriage and childbearing precisely because of the lack of equality between the sexes. In China, traditional biases against women could end up making it impossible for many men ever to find wives. Because of China's strict policy limiting family size to one child, many parents abort female fetuses, with the result that there are now 117 boys born in China for every 100 girls. By 2020 China could have between 30 million and 40 million men who cannot find wives.[6]

Reviewing the historical trends behind these various concerns, I began to see some common themes under all these bewildering differences. Everywhere marriage is becoming more optional and more fragile. Everywhere the once-predictable link between marriage and child rearing is fraying. And everywhere relations between men and women are undergoing rapid and at times traumatic transformation. In fact, I realized, the relations between men and women have changed more in the past thirty years than they did in the previous three thousand, and I began to suspect that a similar transformation was occurring in the role of marriage.

My effort to understand the origins and nature of that transformation forced me to go much farther into the past than I originally intended. Along the way I had to change many other ideas I once had about the history of marriage. For example, like many other historians and sociologists, I used to think that the male breadwinner/full-time housewife marriages depicted in 1950s and 1960s television shows like *Leave It to Beaver* and *Ozzie and Harriet,* the kinds of marriages that actually predominated in North America and Western Europe during those decades, were a short-lived historical fluke. In writing this book, I changed my mind.

It is true that 1950s marriages were exceptional in many ways. Until that decade, relying on a single breadwinner had been rare. For thousands of years, most women and children had shared the tasks of breadwinning with men. It was not unusual for wives to "bring home the bacon"—or at least to raise and slaughter the pig, then take it to the market to sell. In the 1950s, however, for the first time, a majority of marriages in Western Europe and North America consisted of a full-time homemaker supported by a male earner. Also new in the 1950s was the cultural consensus that everyone should marry and that people should wed at a young age. For hundreds of years, European rates of marriage had been much lower, and the age of marriage much higher, than in the 1950s. The baby boom of the 1950s was likewise a departure from the past, because birthrates in Western Europe and North America had fallen steadily during the previous hundred years.

As I continued my research, however, I became convinced that the 1950s *Ozzie and Harriet* family was not just a postwar aberration. Instead it was the culmination of a new marriage system that had been evolving for more than 150 years. I now think that there was a basic continuity in the development of marriage ideals and behaviors from the late eighteenth century through the

1950s and 1960s. In the eighteenth century, people began to adopt the radical new idea that love should be the most fundamental reason for marriage and that young people should be free to choose their marriage partners on the basis of love. The sentimentalization of the love-based marriage in the nineteenth century and its sexualization in the twentieth each represented a logical step in the evolution of this new approach to marriage.

Until the late eighteenth century, most societies around the world saw marriage as far too vital an economic and political institution to be left entirely to the free choice of the two individuals involved, especially if they were going to base their decision on something as unreasoning and transitory as love. The more I learned about the ancient history of marriage, the more I realized what a gigantic marital revolution had occurred in Western Europe and North America during the Enlightenment.

This led me to another surprising finding: From the moment of its inception, this revolutionary new marriage system already showed signs of the instability that was to plague it at the end of the twentieth century. As soon as the idea that love should be the central reason for marriage, and companionship its basic goal, was first raised, observers of the day warned that the same values that increased people's satisfaction with marriage as a relationship had an inherent tendency to undermine the stability of marriage as an institution. The very features that promised to make marriage such a unique and treasured personal relationship opened the way for it to become an optional and fragile one.

The skeptics were right to worry about the dangers of the love match. Its arrival in the late eighteenth century coincided with an explosion of challenges to all the traditional ways of organizing social and personal life. For the next 150 years, societies struggled to strike the right balance between the goal of finding happiness in marriage and the preservation of limits that would keep people from leaving a marriage that didn't fulfill their expectations for love. The history of the love-based marriage from the late eighteenth to the mid-twentieth century is one of successive crises, as people surged past the barriers that prevented them from achieving marital fulfillment and then pulled back, or were pushed back, when the institution of marriage seemed to be in jeopardy.

The *Real* Traditional Marriage

To understand why the love-based marriage system was so unstable and how we ended up where we are today, we have to recognize that for most of history, marriage was not primarily about the individual needs and desires of a man and woman and the children they produced. Marriage had as much to do with getting good in-laws and increasing one's family labor force as it did with finding a lifetime companion and raising a beloved child.

Reviewing the role of marriage in different societies in the past and the theories of anthropologists and archaeologists about its origins, I came to reject two widespread, though diametrically opposed, theories about how marriage came into existence among our Stone Age ancestors: the idea that marriage was invented so men would protect women and the opposing idea that it was invented so men could exploit women. Instead, marriage spoke to the needs of the larger group. It converted strangers into relatives and extended cooperative relations beyond the immediate family or small band by creating far-flung networks of in-laws.

As civilizations got more complex and stratified, the role of marriage in acquiring in-laws changed. Marriage became a way through which elites could hoard or accumulate resources, shutting out unrelated individuals or even "illegitimate" family members. Propertied families consolidated wealth, merged resources, forged political alliances, and concluded peace treaties by strategically marrying off their sons and daughters. When upper-class men and women married, there was an exchange of dowry, bridewealth, or tribute, making the match a major economic investment by the couple's parents and other kin. In Europe, from the early Middle Ages through the eighteenth century, the dowry a wife brought with her at marriage was often the biggest infusion of cash, goods, or land a man would ever acquire. Finding a husband was usually the most important investment a woman could make in her economic future.[7]

Even in the lower classes, marriage was an economic and political transaction, although on a much smaller scale. The concerns of commoners were more immediate: "Can I marry someone whose fields are next to mine?"; "Will my prospective mate meet the approval of the neighbors and relatives on whom I depend?"; "Would these particular in-laws be a help to our family or a hindrance?"

Moreover, farms or businesses could rarely be run by just a single person, so a prospective partner's skills, resources, and tools were at least as important as personality and attractiveness. In those days there were few two-career marriages. Most people had a two-person, married-couple career that neither could conduct alone.

Traditionally, marriage also organized the division of labor and power by gender and age, confirming men's authority over women and determining if a child had any claim on the property of the parents. Marriage was the most important marker of adulthood and respectability as well as the main source of social security, medical care, and unemployment insurance.

Certainly, people fell in love during those thousands of years, sometimes even with their own spouses. But marriage was not fundamentally about love. It was too vital an economic and political institution to be entered into solely on the basis of something as irrational as love. For thousands of years the theme song for most weddings could have been "What's Love Got to Do with It?"

Because marriage was too important a contract to be left up to the two individuals involved, kin, neighbors, and other outsiders, such as judges, priests, or government officials, were usually involved in negotiating a match. Even when individuals orchestrated their own transitions in and out of marriage, they frequently did so for economic and political advantage rather than for love.

As a result, many of the greatest love stories of the ages, such as the tale of Antony and Cleopatra, had more to do with political intrigue than romantic passion. The marriages of the rich and famous in the ancient and medieval worlds can be told as political thrillers, corporate mergers, military epics, and occasionally even murder mysteries. But they were not the tales of undying love that I imagined when I was a teenager, and they often make modern marriage scandals seem tame in comparison.

The system of marrying for political and economic advancement was practically universal across the globe for many millennia. But the heritage of Rome and Greece interacted with the evolution of the Christian church to create a unique version of political marriage in medieval Europe. As early as the sixteenth century the distinctive power struggles among parents, children, ruling authorities, and the church combined with changes in the economy to create more possibilities for marital companionship in Europe than in most other regions of the world.

But only in the seventeenth century did a series of political, economic, and cultural changes in Europe begin to erode the older functions of marriage, encouraging individuals to choose their mates on the basis of personal affection and allowing couples to challenge the right of outsiders to intrude upon their lives. And not until the late eighteenth century, and then only in Western Europe and North America, did the notion of free choice and marriage for love triumph as a cultural ideal.

In the nineteenth century, most Europeans and Americans came to accept a new view of husbands as providers and of wives as nurturing homebodies. Only in the mid-twentieth century, however, could a majority of families in Western Europe and North America actually survive on the earnings of a single breadwinner.

The 1950s family, then, was not so new a development as we used to think. Rather, it was the culmination of a package of ideals about personal life and male-female relations that emerged at the end of the eighteenth century and gradually became the norm across Western Europe and North America. These ideals gave people unprecedented opportunities to get more personal satisfaction from their marriages, but they also raised questions that posed a fundamental challenge to traditional ways of ordering society.

If marriage was about love and lifelong intimacy, why would people marry at all if they couldn't find true love? What would hold a marriage together if love and intimacy disappeared? How could household order be maintained if marriages were based on affection rather than on male authority?

No sooner had the ideal of the love match and lifelong intimacy taken hold than people began to demand the right to divorce. No sooner did people agree that families should serve children's needs than they began to find the legal penalties for illegitimacy inhumane. Some people demanded equal rights for women so they could survive economically without having to enter loveless marriages. Others even argued for the decriminalization of homosexual love, on the ground that people should be free to follow their hearts.

There was a crisis over these questions in the 1790s, and another in the 1890s, and yet another in the 1920s. Then, in the 1950s, everything seemed to calm down. More people than ever before embraced the ideals of love and marital companionship without following them to the dangerous conclusion that loveless marriages ought to end in divorce or that true marital partnerships should be grounded in the equality of men and women.

Still, even as people became convinced they had at last created the perfect balance between individual desires and social stability, and even as virtually all of North America and Western Europe finally embraced this marital model, it was on the verge of collapse. When people remarked on the stability of marriage in the 1950s and early 1960s, they were actually standing in the eye of a hurricane.

For years, historians and public-policy makers have debated why lifelong marriage and male breadwinner families began to unravel in the 1970s. The real question, I now believe, is not why things fell apart in the 1970s but why they *didn't* fall apart in the 1790s, or in the next crisis of the 1890s, or in the turmoil of the 1920s, when practically every contemporary observer worried that marriage was "on the rocks." And the answer is not that people were better partners in the past or better able to balance the search for individual self-fulfillment and the need for stability. The reason is that for the most part they could not yet afford to act on their aspirations for love and personal fulfillment.[8]

This book explains why the revolutionary implications of the love match took so long to play out and why, just when it seemed unassailable, the love-based, male breadwinner marriage began to crumble. The final chapters describe "the perfect storm" that swept over marriage and family life in the last three decades of the twentieth century and how it forever altered the role that marriage plays in society and in our daily lives.

For centuries, marriage did much of the work that markets and governments do today. It organized the production and distribution of goods and people. It set up political, economic, and military alliances. It coordinated the division of labor by gender and age. It orchestrated people's personal rights and obligations in everything from sexual relations to the inheritance of property. Most societies had very specific rules about how people should arrange their marriages to accomplish these tasks.

Of course there was always more to marriage than its institutional functions. At the end of the day—or at least in the middle of the night—marriage is also a face-to-face relationship between individuals. The actual experience of marriage for individuals or for particular couples seldom conforms exactly to the model of marriage codified in law, custom, and philosophy in any given period. In this book we shall meet many people who rebelled against the rules of marriage over the centuries and others who simply evaded or manipulated them for their own purposes.

But institutions do structure people's expectations, hopes, and constraints. For thousands of years, husbands had the right to beat their wives. Few men probably meted out anything more severe than a slap. But the law upheld the authority of husbands to punish their wives physically and to exercise forcibly their "marital right" to sex, and that structured the relations between men and women in *all* marriages, even loving ones.

For the thousands of years that marriage was more about property and politics than personal satisfaction, this reality also shaped people's expectations about love. People have always fallen in love and have suffered when their feelings have not been reciprocated. But for most of history the institutional norms of marriage required women to suffer in silence if their hopes for love inside marriage were thwarted and permitted men to seek love outside marriage. People have always loved a love story. But for most of the past our ancestors did not try to live in one. They understood that marriage was an economic and political institution with rigid rules.

Today most people expect to live their lives in a loving relationship, not a rigid institution. Although most people want socially sanctioned relationships, backed by institutional protections, few would sacrifice their goal of a loving, fair, and flexible relationship for those protections. This book traces how men and women achieved fairness and flexibility in marriage and the unanticipated consequences that accompanied their victory.

Can we learn anything from the history of marriage that can guide us in dealing with those unanticipated consequences? Can knowing where we came from help us figure out where we ought to go from here?

The study of history doesn't offer cut-and-dried answers to questions about the changes in modern marriage or the emergence of alternative ways to organize family life. Life is not a court of law, where precedent is key. No historical "logic" requires us to respond to change in a particular way.

In fact, precedent is a poor guide for the choices we face today in personal life and public policy. Throughout most of history a key function of marriage was to produce children and organize inheritance rights. Marriages were often nullified if a couple did not produce a child. But in our modern world no one suggests that couples who don't have children should not have access to the legal benefits of marriage.

Precedent doesn't help much on the controversial question of same-sex marriage either. Some people argue that because at various times in history same-sex marriages have been accepted in some societies, such marriages should therefore be legal now. But should precedent also apply to other alternatives to the heterosexual nuclear family? On the basis of historical precedent, dissident polygamous Mormons in the United States have an open-and-shut case. Polygyny, whereby a man can have multiple wives, is the marriage form found in more places and at more times than any other.[9] If precedent is our guide, shouldn't we legalize polygyny, bring back arranged marriages and child brides, and decriminalize wife beating?

But if history can't give us specific instructions, it can help us decide which precedents are relevant to contemporary situations and which are not. While I was working on this book, attorneys in Canada were preparing for the same-sex marriage case whose outcome led to recognition of gay and lesbian marriages in 2003. Both sides were soliciting affidavits for or against recognizing same-sex marriage. Although many of these drew on contemporary research about how children fare in gay or lesbian families, some also debated the historical precedent for such unions.[10]

I was particularly struck by one exchange in the depositions. One historian testified that same-sex marriage had been recognized in several historical periods and places, citing ancient Rome as an example. A second historian challenged the relevance of that precedent by pointing out that such marriages were exceptional in Roman times and were regarded unfavorably by contemporaries.

I happen to believe the evidence from Roman history supports the second interpretation. But the Romans made a very different argument against same-sex marriage than the one we hear in today's political debates. The ancient Romans had no problem with homosexuality, and they did not think that heterosexual marriage was sacred. The reason they found male-male marriage repugnant was that no real man would ever agree to play the subordinate role demanded of a Roman wife. Today, by contrast, many heterosexual couples aspire to achieve the loyal, egalitarian relationships that Greek and Roman philosophers believed could exist only in a friendship between two men.

If we can learn anything from the past, it is how few precedents are now relevant in the changed marital landscape in which we operate today. For thousands of years, people had little choice about whether and whom to marry and almost no choice in whether or not to have children. Death ended many marriages much sooner than divorce does today. A husband owned his wife's property, earnings, and sexuality and had the final word on all family decisions.

A man who fathered a child out of wedlock was seldom responsible for its support, and a woman who bore a child out of wedlock could often survive only by becoming a concubine, mistress, or prostitute. Kin, neighbors, and custom exerted far more control over people's choices and behaviors than is possible today. Most important, people's political rights, jobs, education, access to property, and obligations to others all were filtered through the institution of marriage.

Between the mid-eighteenth and the mid-twentieth century, the social functions and internal dynamics of traditional marriage were transformed. The older system of arranged, patriarchal marriage was replaced by the love-based male breadwinner marriage, with its ideal of lifelong monogamy and intimacy. New expectations came to structure marriage. Then, in just the last thirty years, all the precedents established by the love-based male breadwinner family were in turn thrown into question.

Today we are entering uncharted territory, and there is still no definitive guide to the new marital landscape. Most of what we used to take for granted about who marries and why, or how to make a marriage work, is in flux. But perhaps reading this book will do for you what researching it has done for me: help you understand how we got where we are today, how our choices have changed, what old options have fallen away, and what new ones have opened up.

Part One

—⇒◉⇐—

In Search of
Traditional Marriage

Chapter 1

—◦◉◦—

The Radical Idea of Marrying for Love

George Bernard Shaw described marriage as an institution that brings together two people "under the influence of the most violent, most insane, most delusive, and most transient of passions. They are required to swear that they will remain in that excited, abnormal, and exhausting condition continuously until death do them part."[1]

Shaw's comment was amusing when he wrote it at the beginning of the twentieth century, and it still makes us smile today, because it pokes fun at the unrealistic expectations that spring from a dearly held cultural ideal—that marriage should be based on intense, profound love and a couple should maintain their ardor until death do them part. But for thousands of years the joke would have fallen flat.

For most of history it was inconceivable that people would choose their mates on the basis of something as fragile and irrational as love and then focus all their sexual, intimate, and altruistic desires on the resulting marriage. In fact, many historians, sociologists, and anthropologists used to think romantic love was a recent Western invention. This is not true. People have always fallen in love, and throughout the ages many couples have loved each other deeply.[2]

But only rarely in history has love been seen as the main reason for getting married. When someone did advocate such a strange belief, it was no laughing matter. Instead, it was considered a serious threat to social order.

15

In some cultures and times, true love was actually thought to be incompatible with marriage. Plato believed love was a wonderful emotion that led men to behave honorably. But the Greek philosopher was referring not to the love of women, "such as the meaner men feel," but to the love of one man for another.[3]

Other societies considered it good if love developed after marriage or thought love should be factored in along with the more serious considerations involved in choosing a mate. But even when past societies did welcome or encourage married love, they kept it on a short leash. Couples were not to put their feelings for each other above more important commitments, such as their ties to parents, siblings, cousins, neighbors, or God.

In ancient India, falling in love before marriage was seen as a disruptive, almost antisocial act. The Greeks thought lovesickness was a type of insanity, a view that was adopted by medieval commentators in Europe. In the Middle Ages the French defined love as a "derangement of the mind" that could be cured by sexual intercourse, either with the loved one or with a different partner.[4] This cure assumed, as Oscar Wilde once put it, that the quickest way to conquer yearning and temptation was to yield immediately and move on to more important matters.

In China, excessive love between husband and wife was seen as a threat to the solidarity of the extended family. Parents could force a son to divorce his wife if her behavior or work habits didn't please them, whether or not he loved her. They could also require him take a concubine if his wife did not produce a son. If a son's romantic attachment to his wife rivaled his parents' claims on the couple's time and labor, the parents might even send her back to her parents. In the Chinese language the term *love* did not traditionally apply to feelings between husband and wife. It was used to describe an illicit, socially disapproved relationship. In the 1920s a group of intellectuals invented a new word for love between spouses because they thought such a radical new idea required its own special label.[5]

In Europe, during the twelfth and thirteenth centuries, adultery became idealized as the highest form of love among the aristocracy. According to the Countess of Champagne, it was impossible for true love to "exert its powers between two people who are married to each other."[6]

In twelfth-century France, Andreas Capellanus, chaplain to Countess Marie of Troyes, wrote a treatise on the principles of courtly love. The first rule was that "marriage is no real excuse for not loving." But he meant loving someone outside the marriage. As late as the sixteenth century the French essayist Montaigne wrote that any man who was in love with his wife was a man so dull that no one else could love him.[7]

Courtly love probably loomed larger in literature than in real life. But for centuries, noblemen and kings fell in love with courtesans rather than the wives they married for political reasons. Queens and noblewomen had to be more discreet than their husbands, but they too looked beyond marriage for love and intimacy.

This sharp distinction between love and marriage was common among the lower and middle classes as well. Many of the songs and stories popular among peasants in medieval Europe mocked married love.

The most famous love affair of the Middle Ages was that of Peter Abelard, a well-known theologian in France, and Héloïse, the brilliant niece of a fellow churchman at Notre Dame. The two eloped without marrying, and she bore him a child. In an attempt to save his career but still placate Héloïse's furious uncle, Abelard proposed they marry in secret. This would mean that Héloïse would not be living in sin, while Abelard could still pursue his church ambitions. But Heloise resisted the idea, arguing that marriage would not only harm his career but also undermine their love.[8]

"Nothing Is More Impure Than to Love One's Wife as if She Were a Mistress"[9]

Even in societies that esteemed married love, couples were expected to keep it under strict control. In many cultures, public displays of love between husband and wife were considered unseemly. A Roman was expelled from the Senate because he had kissed his wife in front of his daughter. Plutarch conceded that the punishment was somewhat extreme but pointed out that everyone knew that it was "disgraceful" to kiss one's wife in front of others.[10]

Some Greek and Roman philosophers even said that a man who loved his wife with "excessive" ardor was "an adulterer." Many centuries later Catholic and Protestant theologians argued that husbands and wives who loved each other too much were committing the sin of idolatry. Theologians chided wives who used endearing nicknames for their husbands, because such familiarity on a wife's part undermined the husband's authority and the awe that his wife should feel for him. Although medieval Muslim thinkers were more approving of sexual passion between husband and wife than were Christian theologians, they also insisted that too much intimacy between husband and wife weakened a believer's devotion to God. And, like their European counterparts, secular writers in the Islamic world believed that love thrived best outside marriage.[11]

Many cultures still frown on placing love at the center of marriage. In Africa, the Fulbe people of northern Cameroon do not see love as a legitimate emotion, especially within marriage. One observer reports that in conversations with their neighbors, Fulbe women "vehemently deny emotional attachment to a husband." In many peasant and working-class communities, too much love between husband and wife is seen as disruptive because it encourages the couple to withdraw from the wider web of dependence that makes the society work.[12]

As a result, men and women often relate to each other in public, even after marriage, through the conventions of a war between the sexes, disguising the fondness they may really feel. They describe their marital behavior, no matter how exemplary it may actually be, in terms of convenience, compulsion, or self-interest rather than love or sentiment. In Cockney rhyming slang, the term for *wife* is *trouble and strife.*

Whether it is valued or not, love is rarely seen as the main ingredient for marital success. Among the Taita of Kenya, recognition and approval of married love are widespread. An eighty-year-old man recalled that his fourth wife "was the wife of my heart. . . . I could look at her and no words would pass, just a smile." In this society, where men often take several wives, women speak wistfully about how wonderful it is to be a "love wife." But only a small percentage of Taita women experience this luxury, because a Taita man normally marries a love wife only after he has accumulated a few more practical wives.[13]

In many cultures, love has been seen as a desirable outcome of marriage but not as a good reason for getting married in the first place. The Hindu tradition celebrates love and sexuality in marriage, but love and sexual attraction are not considered valid reasons for marriage. "First we marry, then we'll fall in love" is the formula. As recently as 1975, a survey of college students in the Indian state of Karnataka found that only 18 percent "strongly" approved of marriages made on the basis of love, while 32 percent completely disapproved.[14]

Similarly, in early modern Europe most people believed that love developed after marriage. Moralists of the sixteenth and seventeenth centuries argued that if a husband and wife each had a good character, they would probably come to love each other. But they insisted that youths be guided by their families in choosing spouses who were worth learning to love. It was up to parents and other relatives to make sure that the woman had a dowry or the man had a good yearly income. Such capital, it was thought, would certainly help love flower.[15]

"Woman's work is never done." There they say: "Without cowives, a woman's work is never done." A researcher who worked with the Cheyenne Indians of the United States in the 1930s and 1940s told of a chief who tried to get rid of two of his three wives. All three women defied him, saying that if he sent two of them away, he would have to give away the third as well.[22]

Even when societies celebrated the love between husband and wife as a pleasant by-product of marriage, people rarely had a high regard for marital intimacy. Chinese commentators on marriage discouraged a wife from confiding in her husband or telling him about her day. A good wife did not bother her husband with news of her own activities and feelings but treated him "like a guest," no matter how long they had been married. A husband who demonstrated open affection for his wife, even at home, was seen as having a weak character.[23]

In the early eighteenth century, American lovers often said they looked for "candor" in each other. But they were not talking about the soul-baring intimacy idealized by modern Americans, and they certainly did not believe that couples should talk frankly about their grievances. Instead candor meant fairness, kindliness, and good temper. People wanted a spouse who did *not* pry too deeply. The ideal mate, wrote U.S. President John Adams in his diary, was willing "to palliate faults and Mistakes, to put the best Construction upon Words and Action, and to forgive Injuries."[24]

Modern marital advice books invariably tell husbands and wives to put each other first. But in many societies, marriage ranks very low in the hierarchy of meaningful relationships. People's strongest loyalties and emotional connections may be reserved for members of their birth families. On the North American plains in the 1930s, a Kiowa Indian woman commented to a researcher that "a woman can always get another husband, but she has only one brother." In China it was said that "you have only one family, but you can always get another wife." In Christian texts prior to the seventeenth century, the word *love* usually referred to feelings toward God or neighbors rather than toward a spouse.[25]

In Confucian philosophy, the two strongest relationships in family life are between father and son and between elder brother and younger brother, not between husband and wife. In thirteenth-century China the bond between father and son was so much stronger than the bond between husband and wife that legal commentators insisted a couple do nothing if the patriarch of the household raped his son's wife. In one case, although the judge was sure that a woman's rape accusation against her father-in-law was true, he ordered the young man to give up his sentimental desire "to grow old together" with

21

his wife. Loyalty to parents was paramount, and therefore the son should send his wife back to her own father, who could then marry her to someone else. Sons were sometimes ordered beaten for siding with their wives against their father. No wonder that for 1,700 years women in one Chinese province guarded a secret language that they used to commiserate with each other about the griefs of marriage.[26]

In many societies of the past, sexual loyalty was not a high priority. The expectation of mutual fidelity is a rather recent invention. Numerous cultures have allowed husbands to seek sexual gratification outside marriage. Less frequently, but often enough to challenge common preconceptions, wives have also been allowed to do this without threatening the marriage. In a study of 109 societies, anthropologists found that only 48 forbade extramarital sex to both husbands and wives.[27]

When a woman has sex with someone other than her husband and he doesn't object, anthropologists have traditionally called it wife loaning. When a man does it, they call it male privilege. But in some societies the choice to switch partners rests with the woman. Among the Dogon of West Africa, young married women publicly pursued extramarital relationships with the encouragement of their mothers. Among the Rukuba of Nigeria, a wife can take a lover at the time of her first marriage. This relationship is so embedded in accepted custom that the lover has the right, later in life, to ask his former mistress to marry her daughter to his son.[28]

Among the Eskimo of northern Alaska, as I noted earlier, husbands and wives, with mutual consent, established comarriages with other couples. Some anthropologists believe cospouse relationships were a more socially acceptable outlet for sexual attraction than was marriage itself. Expressing open jealousy about the sexual relationships involved was considered boorish.[29]

Such different notions of marital rights and obligations made divorce and remarriage less emotionally volatile for the Eskimo than it is for most modern Americans. In fact, the Eskimo believed that a remarried person's partner had an obligation to allow the former spouse, as well as any children of that union, the right to fish, hunt, and gather in the new spouse's territory.[30]

Several small-scale societies in South America have sexual and marital norms that are especially startling for Europeans and North Americans. In these groups, people believe that any man who has sex with a woman during her pregnancy contributes part of his biological substance to the child. The husband is recognized as the primary father, but the woman's lover or lovers also have paternal responsibilities, including the obligation to share food with the woman and her child in the future. During the 1990s researchers taking life histories of elderly Bari women in Venezuela found that most had taken lovers during at least one of their pregnancies. Their husbands were usually aware and did not object. When a woman gave birth, she would name all the men she had slept with since learning she was pregnant, and a woman attending the birth would tell each of these men: "You have a child."[31]

In Europe and the United States today such an arrangement would be a surefire recipe for jealousy, bitter breakups, and very mixed-up kids. But among the Bari people this practice was in the best interests of the child. The secondary fathers were expected to provide the child with fish and game, with the result that a child with a secondary father was twice as likely to live to the age of fifteen as a brother or sister without such a father.[32]

Few other societies have incorporated extramarital relationships so successfully into marriage and child rearing. But all these examples of differing marital and sexual norms make it difficult to claim there is some universal model for the success or happiness of a marriage.

About two centuries ago Western Europe and North America developed a whole set of new values about the way to organize marriage and sexuality, and many of these values are now spreading across the globe. In this Western model, people expect marriage to satisfy more of their psychological and social needs than ever before. Marriage is supposed to be free of the coercion, violence, and gender inequalities that were tolerated in the past. Individuals want marriage to meet most of their needs for intimacy and affection and all their needs for sex.

Never before in history had societies thought that such a set of high expectations about marriage was either realistic or desirable. Although many Europeans and Americans found tremendous joy in building their relationships around these values, the adoption of these unprecedented goals for marriage had unanticipated and revolutionary consequences that have since come to threaten the stability of the entire institution.

Chapter 2

━━●━━

The Many Meanings of Marriage

We know of only one society in world history that did not make marriage a central way of organizing social and personal life, the Na people of China. With that exception, marriage has been, in one form or another, a universal social institution throughout recorded history.

So it ought to be easy to cut through all the historical and cultural differences to find marriage's common features and explain why the institution is so ubiquitous. But talk about opening a can of worms! Long before legislators and judges, under pressure from gay rights activists, began to debate the definition of marriage, anthropologists and sociologists had been passionately debating the same question. After half a century there is still no definition everyone accepts.

Some people argue that marriage is universal because it simply expresses the biological urge to mate and reproduce. When I was a child, a pair of white geese showed up each spring on the lake at my grandparents' farm. Every summer my sister and I fed them, then watched them glide off together, nodding their graceful necks as if engaged in an intense conversation. Then one year only one goose showed up. All that summer he swam around the lake, honking plaintively, obviously missing his mate, or so it seemed to us.

Such animal behavior looks so much like our current idealized notions of courtship that it is easy to imagine a common biological impulse lies behind

24

both. Remember "Muskrat Love," the 1971 hit from The Captain and Tennille? "And they whirled and they twirled and they tangoed/Singin' and jingin' the jango/Floatin' like the heavens above/Looks like muskrat love."

Muskrats, along with beavers, wolves, gibbons, and the vast majority of bird species, do in fact form long-term relationships with single mates. Many of these animals also have elaborate courting rituals that bear a remarkable resemblance to the cooing and cuddling of human lovers. Just watch two pigeons on a window ledge, touching beaks, rubbing each other's necks, and making soft, gurgling sounds that can't mean anything but contentment.

These animal behaviors are not just about sex. Tree shrews, for example, take turns methodically licking and grooming each other's faces and necks before lying down for a friendly nap. In more than two hundred bird species, male and female mates sing complicated duets together, perform intricate dances, or "kiss" each other repeatedly with their beaks, even when sex is not on the agenda. When the female sea horse spots her mate each morning, they engage in an elaborate greeting ritual, wrapping their tails around a branch of coral or a blade of sea grass and rubbing their snouts together, seemingly quivering with joy over their reunion. Then they entwine tails and glide across the ocean floor.[1] A biologist friend of mine once remarked that she wished *her* husband would be half that affectionate when he didn't want sex.

Some people believe that human marriage is simply an extension of the same biological processes that produce pair-bonding among animals.[2] But if it were that simple, we would not be discussing the future of marriage today.

Clearly there is a biological basis for love and even, perhaps, for long-term pair-bonding, although one scientist who believes there is such a biological base in humans claims that it is limited to about four years. But primates, our closest evolutionary relatives, do not organize their social life around pair bonds.[3] And when we move beyond the most superficial similarities, we find nothing in the animal kingdom that remotely resembles human marriage.

For thousands of years, in human society, the question of who paired off with whom was not decided solely by the two individuals who ended up together. Families and neighbors almost always had a say. Nowhere in the animal world do relatives and other community members influence an individual's choice of a mate (except to try to get there first).

Moreover, through most of human history, marriage united not just two mates but two sets of families. When pairing off unites two kin groups instead of two individuals, that is much more than an expression of the biological functions of mating and reproduction. It is a transformation of those functions.

Finally, no other animals have elaborate rules about whom one should, must, or cannot marry. By contrast, notes anthropologist Meyer Fortes, marriage practices among humans "are universally subject to rules."[4] For most of history, those rules have been much more complex and far-reaching than simple prohibitions against incest, rudimentary forms of which may also exist among some primates. The rules governing who can marry whom have varied immensely from group to group. In some societies, marriages between first cousins have been prohibited. In others, such unions have been preferred. Some societies have encouraged polygamy. Others strictly prohibit it. Such a contradictory hodgepodge of social rules could not have sprung from some universal biological imperative.

The same holds true for the wide gamut of beliefs over the ages about how marriage should be organized and what its main purpose should be. So once we get past the seeming universality of marriage and examine the tremendous variations in the role it plays in different societies, it becomes much harder to define marriage and its reasons for existence.

In 1949 the eminent anthropologist George Peter Murdock defined marriage as a universal institution that involves a man and a woman living together, engaging in sexual activity, and cooperating economically.[5] At first glance, this seems a commonsense definition. In fact, however, there are many exceptions to this kind of marriage arrangement.

For example, in many times and places, husbands and wives routinely lived in separate residences. Among the Ashanti of Ghana and the Minangkabau of Indonesia, men traditionally live with their mothers and sisters even after marriage. Men of the Gururumba people in New Guinea sleep in separate houses and work separate plots of land from their wives. The only time husbands and wives are together on a daily basis is when the main meal is being cooked and eaten.[6]

In Zambia, Bemba husbands and wives traditionally do not even eat together. Men and women eat separately, as do boys and girls, in a variety of meal-sharing groups organized by gender, age, kinship, and friendship. In Austria in the eighteenth century, lower-class married couples commonly lived apart for many years as servants in other people's houses, taking their meals with their employers rather than their spouses. All these people would be puzzled by our periodic panics about how rarely contemporary families sit down to dinner together.

If living together is not always what defines a marriage, neither is economic cooperation always the rule. Among the Yoruba and many other African societies, husbands and wives do not pool resources in a common household fund. Sometimes a couple doesn't even share responsibility for their children's economic welfare. The child is supported by one parent's lineage rather than by the married couple. If the couple divorces, the child may not even be viewed as biologically related to the parent whose lineage isn't economically responsible for him.[7]

Faced with so many "exceptions" to Murdock's 1949 attempt to define marriage, the Royal Anthropological Institute of Britain took a stab at it. The institute, focusing on marriage's role in determining the status and rights of children, defined marriage as "a union between a man and a woman such that children born to the woman are the recognized legitimate offspring of both partners."[8] This definition also proved to be too restrictive.

There are West African societies in which a woman may be married to another woman as a "female husband." In these cultures, if the wife brings children with her to the marriage or subsequently bears children by a lover, those children are counted as the descendants and heirs of the female "husband" and her extended family. And numerous African and Native American societies recognize male-male marriages.[9]

What about traditional Chinese and Sudanese ghost or spirit marriages, in which one of the partners is actually dead? In these societies a youth might be given in marriage to the dead son or daughter of another family, in order to forge closer ties between the two sets of relatives.

For most of Chinese history the decision to arrange a ghost marriage was made by two sets of parents, without regard to the youth's wishes. But in the early twentieth century some women actively sought such marriages. This was common practice among female silk producers in the Canton delta, who wanted to maintain their economic independence but whose families wanted in-laws. Most parents would not allow more than one daughter to remain unmarried. So if one daughter had already declared herself a spinster, her sister had to conduct a marriage ceremony with a dead man, called marrying a tablet, to retain her independence. These women later told historians that "it was not so easy to find an unmarried dead man to marry," so when one did become available, they vied with one another "to be the one who would get to marry him."[10]

Over the millennia the preferred form of marriage in many cultures was that between a man and several women. More rarely, marriage might unite a woman and several men. Among the Toda of southern India, a girl was married off at a young age, sometimes as early as two or three. From then on she was considered the wife not only of the boy to whom she was married but of all his brothers as well. When the girl was old enough to have sex, she usually had sexual relations with all her husbands. When she became pregnant, one of the brothers gave her a toy bow and arrow and promised her the next calf from his herd. That man was henceforth seen as the father of all subsequent children the woman bore—unless she performed the bow ceremony with someone else.[11]

These forms of marriage are rare, at least in the modern world. So anthropologist Suzanne Frayser sampled sixty-two societies from around the world to calculate which functions marriage performs most frequently. On the basis of her statistical analysis, Frayser defined marriage as "a relationship within which a society socially approves and encourages sexual intercourse and the birth of children."[12]

But marriage has taken so many different forms in history that trying to define it by its most frequently encountered functions does not really help us understand what any particular society's marriage system is or how and why such a system changes over time. We also can't claim some groups did not have "real" marriages just because their marriage practices were not "typical."

Three prominent anthropologists recently argued that while "there are a few exceptions to virtually any definition," the point is that "there are commonly stable, mated relationships between females and males in every human society."[13] That is certainly true. But it is only part of the picture. For example, many societies prohibit some people from marrying even if they have stable, mated relationships that produce children, but allow other people to marry even if they do not engage in sexual intercourse or cannot bear children.

Throughout history and across the globe the huge majority of marriages have been between heterosexuals, even in societies where same-sex marriages have the same legitimacy as heterosexual marriages. But in most societies not all heterosexual relationships count as marriage. Few societies in history have given heterosexuals who live together outside marriage the same legal rights as married persons, even if the cohabiting couple is in a long-term, stable relationship with several children. In fact, in societies that recognize same-sex marriages, such unions, though numerically rare, have a firmer legal standing than the relationships of unmarried heterosexuals who live together and have children.

A different approach to defining marriage is taken by anthropologist Edmund Leach, who suggests that marriage should be seen as being more about regulating property than regulating sex and child rearing. He argues that marriage is "the set of legal rules" that govern how goods, titles, and social status "are handed down from generation to generation."[14]

In most complex civilizations, inheritance rights have indeed been at the center of marriage. This meant that the definition of a "legitimate" marriage was a burning and often a disputed question. However, in some societies, inheritance rights do not depend on marriage. A child born out of wedlock among the Kachin of northern Burma was counted as legitimate if the father paid a fine to the girl and her family. Among the Kandyan of Sri Lanka, by contrast, a child's legitimacy derived from the mother. As long as the presumed father was not from a caste lower than the mother's, his actions, intentions, and marital status had no impact on the child's status.[15]

Another wrinkle in the relationship between marriage and inheritance is found in those Middle Eastern societies that recognized the pre-Islamic tradition of mut'a, or temporary marriages. These were designed to allow sexual outlets for men and women under certain circumstances without subjecting them to the otherwise harsh penalties for nonmarital sex. Mut'a was condemned by Sunni Muslims but accepted by Shi'ites and by Babylonian Jews, who allowed a sage entering a new town to request a "wife for a day." In these temporary marriages the man and woman had no obligation toward each other once the contract was over. But if the woman bore a child as a result of the relationship, that child was legitimate and was entitled to share in the father's inheritance.[16]

Some societies pay no attention at all to "legitimacy" in determining a child's rights. When Jesuit missionaries from France first encountered the North American Montagnais-Naskapi Indians in the early seventeenth century, they were shocked by the native women's sexual freedom. One missionary warned a Naskapi man that if he did not impose tighter controls on his wife, he would never know for sure which of the children she bore belonged to him. The Indian was equally shocked that this mattered to Europeans. "You French people," he replied, "love only your own children; but we love all the children of our tribe."[17]

The concept of illegitimacy is completely foreign to matrilineal societies, such as the Navajo people of North America, in which descent and inheritance pass through the female line. But even some patrilineal societies give inheritance rights to the child of an unmarried woman. Among the LoWiili people in Africa, if a household needed more members, the head of the household might encourage an unmarried daughter to bear a "house child," who would become a member of its maternal grandfather's descent group.[18]

Japan had no equivalent to the English word *bastard* until the Meiji Restoration in 1868. Only then did Japanese reformers adopt Western distinctions between legitimate and illegitimate children. Prior to that time, the language had a word to indicate that a child had been born to a concubine rather than a wife, but such a child was not necessarily denied inheritance rights or legal recognition. Indeed, the Taishō Emperor, who ascended to the throne in 1912, was the son of a concubine of the last Meiji emperor.[19]

In societies where inheritance rights depend upon legitimacy, marriage is usually an elaborate ceremony that confers a whole package of rights and obligations on the partners—but only if all the procedures and social exchanges required by law or custom are carried out. In these cases, people have traditionally been enormously concerned to prove that their marriages were legally binding or to prove that someone else's marriage was not. A person's future could ride on whether the authorities declared that the marriage had been contracted in the proper manner and conducted with all the necessary rituals.

In other cultures, marriage may be nothing more than a public acknowledgment that a man and a woman have become a regular couple or are raising a child together. Among the Mbuti Pygmies of the Congo, a couple is considered married if they have lived together for two seasons.[20]

In some small-scale societies, if a man and woman are seen eating together alone, they are considered married. Among the Vanatinai of the South Pacific, studied in the 1970s by Maria Lepowsky, unmarried couples may sleep together, but until they intend to move their relationship to a new stage, they do not eat together separately from their kin or other social groups. "The act of marriage consists of the new husband's staying in the house with his wife after dawn and eating the breakfast his bride prepares."[21]

Anthropologist Edmund Leach, working in Sri Lanka, was startled to be told by villagers that a nineteen-year-old woman had already been married seven times. When he asked how that could be, he was told "that if a girl was seen to be cooking a meal for a man this was evidence that she was 'married' to him." Often the corollary is that when a woman stops cooking for a man, the marriage is considered over. And among the Gururumba of New Guinea, males and females who are not married to each other never eat meals together, because eating cooked food together is considered the equivalent of having sexual intercourse.[22]

Despite all these variations in the social role and meaning of marriage, through most of history marriage has generally involved a societally approved division of labor between the partners, with each sex doing different tasks. If a man went out on long hunting trips, which always ran the risk of his coming home empty-handed, it was good to have a woman gathering plants and nuts or tending crops. If a male was trapping animals, it helped to have a female manufacturing pottery and clothes. For millennia, one reason people married was that an individual simply could not survive trying to do everything on his or her own.

But sometimes the division of labor within marriage has been determined by the social role an individual *chooses* to play rather than by the person's actual biological sex. In many Native American groups, for example, the rare person who chose to do the work of the other gender could marry someone who shared the same biological sex but played the opposite role in the division of labor. A man doing "woman's work" could marry a man doing "man's work," and a woman doing "man's work" could marry a woman doing "woman's work."[23]

These social gender roles completely overshadowed the actual biological sex of the partners. As a result, sexual relations between two people of the same sex, when one had chosen man's work and the other woman's work, would not have been considered homosexual, had an equivalent of that label even existed. But eyebrows would certainly have been raised at the idea of a man and a woman living together if both were playing the same work and gender roles.

Probably the single most important function of marriage through most of history, although it is almost completely eclipsed today, was its role in establishing cooperative relationships between families and communities. In Anglo-Saxon England, women were known as peace weavers because their marriages established ties of solidarity between potential enemies or feuding kin groups. The Luo of Kenya defined their preferred marriage partners this way: "They are our enemies, we marry them." Anthropologists working in Africa and New Guinea have recorded many variations of the saying "We marry those whom we fight."[24]

Marriage also allowed families to pool labor and resources or to establish some kind of partnership between two different kin groups. When anthropologist Margaret Mead asked a New Guinea villager why people didn't marry inside their own families, what scandalized him was the question's violation of economic sense, not sexual morals: "Don't you realize that if you marry another man's sister and another man marries your sister, you'll have at least two brothers-in-law, while if you marry your own sister you will have none? With whom will you garden? Who will you go to visit?"[25]

The Bella Coola and the Kwakiutl societies of the Pacific Northwest provide a striking example of how establishing connections between kin groups sometimes took precedence over sexual or reproductive issues in determining marriage. If two families wished to trade with each other, but no suitable matches were available, a marriage contract might be drawn up between one individual and another's foot or even with a dog belonging to the family of the desired in-laws![26]

The Importance of In-Laws

By now you may be muttering some version of the old adage about art: "I may not know how to define marriage, but I know a marriage when I see one." Indeed, despite their differences, there are clear similarities among all the institutions that have been defined or celebrated as marriages throughout history. Marriage usually determines rights and obligations connected to sexuality, gender roles, relationships with in-laws, and the legitimacy of children. It also gives the participants specific rights and roles within the larger society. It usually defines the mutual duties of husband and wife and often the duties of their respective families toward each other, and it makes those duties enforceable. It also allows the property and status of the couple or the household head to be passed down to the next generation in an orderly manner.[27]

But marriage does not serve all these functions in any one society. Moreover, almost every single function that marriage fulfills in one society has been filled by some mechanism other than marriage in another.

In the 1970s anthropologist Ernestine Friedl pointed out that most of the functions of marriage could in theory be performed by a group of brothers and sisters. "Procreation," she wrote, "could be accomplished by irregular sexual encounters with men and women of other sibling groups, with each set of brothers and sisters supporting the children of the sisters only." The only thing such a system could not do, she said, was allow individuals to acquire in-laws. She suggested therefore that the effort to acquire in-laws was as vital a purpose of marriage as the organization of reproduction or the enforcement of the incest taboo.[28]

Friedl's comments were mere speculation before the recent publication of a huge and fascinating study of the Na, a society of about thirty thousand people in the Yunnan Province of southwestern China. Among the Na, the only society we know of in which marriage is not a significant institution, brothers and sisters live together, jointly raising, educating, and supporting the children to whom the sisters give birth.

Reports about this group's social practices have circulated for more than eighteen centuries, and a detailed description was drawn up during the Ming Dynasty (1368–1644). Now we have access to the work of Cai Hua, a trained anthropologist who was able to study the records and live with the Na people. We also have a personal account of growing up in a "society without husbands," in the autobiography of Yang Erche Namu, a woman who was raised in this region.[29]

Among the Na, sibling relationships are much more meaningful and long-lasting than love affairs or sexual relationships. Cai Hua found that some of the sibling-based households among them remained together for ten or more generations, with brothers and sisters practically inseparable—"companions for life." Yet these are not incestuous relationships. Indeed, the incest taboo is so strong that brothers and sisters are not supposed to talk about sexual or even emotional issues in front of one another.

So where do Na babies come from? In most cases, from casual romantic encounters called *nan-sese,* meaning "to visit furtively." The furtive visit, a sexual rendezvous that occurs at night, is the most common form of sexual relationship in Na society. Its conventions demonstrate how much less important sexual relationships are in this society than sibling and parent-child bonds. The visitor typically arrives too late in the evening to take part in meals or social interactions and sits out of the way in the corner until the household retires.

Some couples practice a more public relationship, the conspicuous visit. Here the man comes to the woman's home earlier in the evening, more openly and more regularly than in the usual sexual affair. Even in this relationship, however, the partners owe each other nothing. It is siblings, not spouses, who pool economic resources and cooperate in child rearing. If a woman's family needs more children of either sex, the group of siblings usually adopts them from another sibling set.

Even in the very rare cases where a couple lives together, that does not change the legal relations or identities of the two individuals, and most strikingly, it does not establish any in-law relationships. The families of the couple do not consider themselves linked in any way.

The Na are a startling exception to what otherwise seems to be the historical universality of marriage. But this society makes one thing clear: Marriage is not the only way to impose an incest taboo, organize child rearing, pool resources, care for elders, coordinate household production, or pass on property to the next generation. It is, however, the only way to get in-laws. And since the dawn of civilization, getting in-laws has been one of marriage's most important functions.

Only very recently have parents and other relatives ceased to have substantial material stakes in whether individuals get or stay married. As a result of this world-historic change, modern couples no longer have to let either partner's kin tell them how to run their lives. This unprecedented independence of the married couple from their relatives and in-laws has allowed many husbands and wives to construct more satisfying marriages than those of the past. But it has also played a critical role in creating the "crisis" of modern marriage.

Chapter 3

———— ✦ ————

The Invention of Marriage

Marriage is a social invention, unique to humans. Of the hundreds of theories, stories, and fables explaining its origins, my favorite is a Blackfoot Indian tale recorded in 1911. I love this story not because I think it's any "truer" than the others but because it makes such a wonderful change from the equally fanciful theories most of us were taught in high school and college during the 1950s and 1960s.

Before marriage was invented, according to the Piegan, or Blackfoot Indians:

> The men and women of the ancient Piegans did not live about together in the beginning. The women . . . made buffalo corrals. Their lodges were fine. . . . They tanned the buffalo-hides, those were their robes. They would cut the meat in slices. In summer they picked berries. They used those in winter. Their lodges all were fine inside. And their things were just as fine. . . .
>
> Now, the men were . . . very poor. . . . They had no lodges. They wore raw-hides. . . . They did not know, how they should make lodges. They did not know, how they should tan the buffalo-hides. They did not know, too, how they should cut dried meat, how they should sew their clothes.[1]

The Invention of Marriage

In the Blackfoot legend, it was the men, not the women, who needed marriage. Hungry and cold, the men followed the women and found out where they lived. Then they gathered on a nearby hill and waited patiently until the women decided to choose husbands and allow them into their lodges. The female chief selected her mate first, and the rest of the women followed suit.

This is only a folktale, of course, but it is no further off the mark than the story that some anthropologists and sociobiologists have told for years. Before marriage was invented, according to an Anglo-American anthropological theory,

> The men hunted wild animals and feasted on their meat. Their brains became very large because they had to cooperate with each other in the hunt. They stood upright, made tools, built fires, and invented language. Their cave art was very fine. . . . But the women were very poor. They were tied down by childbearing, and they did not know how to get food for themselves or their babies. They did not know how to protect themselves from predators. They did not know, too, how to make tools, produce art, and build lodges or campfires to keep themselves warm.

In this story, as in the Blackfoot tale, the invention of marriage supplies the happy ending for the hapless sex. Here, however, women were the weaker gender. They initiated marriage by offering to trade sex for protection and food. Instead of the men waiting patiently on the hill for the women to pick their mates, the men got to pick the women, and the strongest, most powerful males got first choice. Then the men set their women up by the hearth to protect them from predators and from rival males.

The story that marriage was invented for the protection of women is still the most widespread myth about the origins of marriage. According to the protective or provider theory of marriage, women and infants in early human societies could not survive without men to bring them the meat of woolly mammoths and protect them from marauding saber-toothed tigers and from other men seeking to abduct them. But males were willing to protect and provide only for their "own" females and offspring they had good reason to believe were theirs, so a woman needed to find and hold on to a strong, aggressive mate.

One way a woman could hold a mate was to offer him exclusive and frequent sex in return for food and protection. According to the theory, that is why women lost the estrus cycle that is common to other mammals, in which females come into heat only at periodic intervals. Human females became sexually available year-round, so they were able to draw men into long-term relationships. In anthropologist Robin Fox's telling of this story, "The females could easily trade on the male's tendency to want to monopolize (or at least think he was monopolizing) the females for mating purposes, and say, in effect 'okay, you get the monopoly . . . and we get the meat.'"[2]

The male willingness to trade meat for sex (with the females throwing in whatever nuts and berries they'd gathered to sweeten the deal) was, according to Fox, "the root of truly human society." Proponents of this protective theory of marriage claim that the nuclear family, based on a sexual division of labor between the male hunter and the female hearth keeper, was the most important unit of survival and protection in the Stone Age.

People in the mid-twentieth century found this story persuasive because it closely resembled the male breadwinner/female homemaker family to which they were accustomed. The male breadwinner model of marriage, as we shall see later, was a late and relatively short-lived way of organizing gender roles and dividing work in human history. But in the 1950s, 1960s, and 1970s most people believed it was the natural and "traditional" family form.

In 1975, sociobiologist E. O. Wilson drew a direct line from the male hunter marriages that he imagined had prevailed on the African savanna at the dawn of human history to the marriages he observed in the jungle of Wall Street: "During the day the women and children remain in the residential area while the men forage for game or its symbolic equivalent in the form of money."[3] The protective theory is still periodically recycled to explain why women are supposedly attracted to powerful, dominant men, while men seek younger women who will be good breeders and hearth keepers.

But since the 1970s other researchers have poked holes in the protective theory of marriage. Some denied that male dominance and female dependence came to us from our primate ancestors. Among baboons, they pointed out, a female who pairs up with a male does not get more access to food than females outside such a relationship. Among chimpanzees, most food sharing occurs between mothers and their offspring, not between male and female sexual partners. Adult female chimps give food to other females (even unrelated ones) just as often as males give food to females, and female chimps are often more protective of other females than males are. A female chimp who wants food from a male may make sexual overtures, or a male chimp who has meat to spare may use it as a bargaining chip. But males cannot control the sexual behavior of the estrus females. And when members of the group, male or female, want food from a female, they hold or play with her infant, in effect offering babysitting for handouts.[4]

Studies of actual human hunting and gathering societies also threw doubt on the male provider theory. In such societies, women's foraging, not men's hunting, usually contributes the bulk of the group's food. The only exceptions to this rule are Eskimo and other herding or hunting peoples in areas where extremely hostile climates make foraging for plants difficult.[5]

Nor are women in foraging societies tied down by child rearing. One anthropologist, working with an African hunter-gatherer society during the 1960s, calculated that an adult woman typically walked about twelve miles a day gathering food, and brought home anywhere from fifteen to thirty-three pounds. A woman with a child under two covered the same amount of ground and brought back the same amount of food while she carried her child in a sling, allowing the child to nurse as the woman did her foraging. In many societies women also participate in hunting, whether as members of communal hunting parties, as individual hunters, or even in all-female hunting groups.

Today most paleontologists reject the notion that early human societies were organized around dominant male hunters providing for their nuclear families. For one thing, in the early phases of hominid and human evolution, hunting big game was less important for group survival than were gathering plants, bird eggs, edible insects, and shellfish, trapping the occasional small animal, and scavenging the meat of large animals that had died of natural causes.

When early humans began to hunt large animals, they did so by driving animals over cliffs or into swamps. These activities involved the whole group, women as well as men. That is what happens in the surrounds conducted by modern-day foragers, where the entire band encircles the game and gradually herds it into a trap.[6]

We cannot know for sure how the earliest hominids and humans organized their reproduction and family lives. But there are three general schools of thought on the subject. Some researchers believe that early humans lived in female-centered groups made up of mothers, sisters, and their young, accompanied by temporary male companions. Younger males, they suggest, left the group when they reached mating age. Other scholars argue that the needs of defense would have encouraged the formation of groups based on male kin, in which fathers, brothers, and sons, along with their female mates, stayed together. In this view, the female offspring rather than males left the group at puberty. A third group of researchers theorizes that hominid groups were organized around one male mating with several females and traveling with them and their offspring. [7]

But none of these three theories, not even the male with his harem, suggests that an individual male provided for "his" females and children or that the male-female pair was the fundamental unit of economic survival and cooperation. No one could have survived very long in the Paleolithic world if individual nuclear families had had to take primary responsibility for all food production, defense, child rearing, and elder care.[8]

A division of labor between males and females certainly developed fairly early and was reinforced when groups developed weapons effective enough to kill moving animals from a distance. Such weapons made it possible for small groups to hunt solitary, fast-moving animals. Hunting with projectile weapons became the domain of men, partly because it was hard for women to chase swift game while they were nursing. So wherever humans organized small hunting parties that left the main camp, they were likely to be all or mostly male. However, this did not make women dependent upon their individual mates.

Women, keeping their children near, were more likely to specialize in gathering and processing plants and shellfish, manufacturing clothing, trapping small animals, and making digging or cooking implements. This gender specialization led to greater interdependence between males and females. As these productive techniques became more complicated, people had to invest more time in teaching them to children, providing an incentive for couples to stay together for longer stretches.

Having a flexible, gender-based division of labor within a mated pair was an important tool for human survival. One partner, typically the female, could concentrate on the surer thing, finding food through foraging or digging. The other partner could try for a windfall, hunting for food that would be plentiful and filling if it could be caught. Yet this division of labor did not make nuclear families self-sufficient. Collective hunting and gathering remained vital to survival.[9]

Couples in the Paleolithic world would never have fantasized about running off by themselves to their own little retreats in the forest. No Stone Age lovers would have imagined in their wildest dreams that they could or should be "everything" to each other. That way lay death.

Until about twelve thousand years ago, say archaeologists Colin Renfrew and Paul Bahn, nearly all human societies were comprised of bands of mobile hunter-gatherers who moved seasonally between different sleeping camps and work sites, depending on the weather and food supply. Humans lived in these band–level societies and small, semipermanent hamlets far longer than the few millennia they have lived in more complex villages, cities, states, and empires.[10]

Reconstructions by archaeologists suggest that bands were made up of anywhere from a handful to as many as a hundred people, but commonly numbered around two dozen. Bands lived off the land, using simple tools to process a wide range of animals and plants for food, medicines, clothing, and fuel. They typically moved back and forth over a home territory until resources were depleted or other environmental changes spurred them to move on. Periodically they might travel longer distances to find valued raw materials and take advantage of seasonal game or fish runs.[11]

Sometimes the band would break down into individual family groups that foraged alone. But the archaeological record shows that families regularly came back to a main camp, or hooked up with a new one, for protection and to cooperate in communal hunts. Regional networks of camps routinely came together at water holes or to collectively exploit fish runs or seasonally abundant plants. During those times, dances, festivals, and other rituals took place, building connections between families and bands that were dispersed for much of the year. On such occasions, people might seek mates—or change them—from within the larger groups.

No one suggests that prehistoric bands existed in utopian harmony. But social interactions were governed by the overwhelming need to pool and share resources. The band's mobility made it impractical for people to accumulate significant surpluses, which would have to be lugged from place to place. In the absence of money and nonperishable wealth, the main currency in nomadic foraging societies would have been favors given and owed. Sharing beyond the immediate family or local group was a rudimentary form of banking. It allowed people to accumulate personal credit or goodwill that could be drawn on later.[12]

Using computer simulations and mathematical calculations to compare the outcome of different ways of organizing the production and consumption of food, economic anthropologist Bruce Winterhalder has established the decisive importance of prehistoric sharing. His calculations show that because the results of hunting and gathering varied on a daily basis, the surest way for individuals to minimize the risk of not having enough to eat on a bad day was not to save what they gathered or killed on good days for later use by their "own" nuclear family, but to pool and divide the whole harvest among the entire group every day.[13]

With few exceptions, hunting and gathering societies throughout history have emphasized sharing and reciprocity. Band-level societies put extraordinary time and energy into establishing norms of sharing. People who share gain status, while individuals who refuse to share are shunned and ostracized. Ethnographer Lorna Marshall reports that for the Dobe !Kung Bushmen of the Kalahari Desert in Africa, "the idea of eating alone and not sharing is shocking. . . . It makes them shriek with uneasy laughter." They think that "lions could do that, not men." In seventeenth-century America, William Penn marveled that the Indians always redistributed the gifts or trade goods that European settlers brought, rather than keep them for their own families. "Wealth circulateth like the Blood," he wrote. "All parts partake."[14]

Many simple hunting and gathering societies place so much emphasis on sharing that a person who kills an animal gets no more of its meat than do his companions. A review of twenty-five hunting and gathering societies found that in only three did the hunter get the largest share of his kill. In most, the hunter was obliged to share the meat equally with other camp members, and in a few he got *less* than he distributed to others. Anthropologist Polly Wiessner observes that these customs create total interdependence among families: "[T]he hunter spends his life hunting for others, and others spend their lives hunting for him."[15]

The idea that in prehistoric times a man would spend his life hunting only for the benefit of his own wife and children, who were dependent solely upon his hunting prowess for survival, is simply a projection of 1950s marital norms onto the past. The male/female pair was a good way to organize sexual companionship, share child rearing, and divide daily work. A man who was a skilled hunter might have been an attractive mate, as would have been a woman who was skilled at foraging or making cooking implements, but marrying a good hunter was not the main way that a woman and her children got access to food and protection.

Marriage was certainly an early and a vitally important human invention. One of its crucial functions in the Paleolithic era was its ability to forge networks of cooperation beyond the immediate family group or local band. Bands needed to establish friendly relations with others so they could travel more freely and safely in pursuit of game, fish, plants, and water holes or move as the seasons changed. Archaeologist Brian Hayden argues that hunter-gatherers of the past used a combination of five strategies to create such ties with other groups and to defuse tensions: frequent informal visits, interband sharing, gift giving, periodic large gatherings for ritual occasions, and the establishment of marriage and kinship ties.[16]

All these customs built goodwill and established social networks beyond a single camp or a group of families. But using marriage to create new ties of kinship was an especially powerful way of binding groups together because it produced children who had relatives in both camps. The Maori of New Zealand say that "a gift connection may be severed, but not so a human link."[17]

However, a kin group that sent its daughters or sons to other groups as marriage partners also needed to make sure that it received spouses in return. Moreover, to create lasting links among groups, the exchange of spouses had to be renewed in later generations.

Sometimes such marriage exchanges would be very direct and immediate, a sister from one group being exchanged for a sister from the other. The exchange need not occur simultaneously, as long as the obligation to pay back one person with another was acknowledged. In other cases, spouses were not exchanged directly. Instead several lineages or clans would be linked in a pattern in which the sisters always married in one direction around the circle while the brothers always married in the opposite one. Lineage A would send its sisters and daughters as wives to lineage B, which sent wives to C, which sent them to A. As practiced among one present-day hunter-gatherer group, the Murngin of Australia, the circle of wife exchange takes seven generations to complete.[18]

Some people believe that from the very beginning, marriage alliances led to strict controls over a young person's choice of mates, especially a woman's. Among the Aborigines of Australia, one of the few places where hunter-gatherer societies lived completely untouched by contact with other societies for thousands of years, marriages were traditionally arranged when girls were still in their childhood and were strictly controlled by elders. Because of the scarcity of food and water in that harsh environment and the need to travel over long distances to ensure survival, Aboriginal elders had to ensure that their community's children were distributed in ways that gave the community family connections to the land and resources wherever they traveled. No rebellion against this system was tolerated.[19]

But the Indians of northeastern North America, who also lived for thousands of years in a "pristine" setting similar to the environment in which many of our Stone Age ancestors operated, traditionally took a very different approach toward marriage, divorce, and sexual activity from that of the Australian Aborigines. Among the Chippewyan people of Canada, the main function of marriage was also to build far-flung personal networks that gave people access to hunting, natural resources, or water holes in other regions. But in this more forgiving environment, individuals tended to make their own marital choices, and no one interfered if a couple decided to part.[20]

Nevertheless, many people argue that marriage originated as a way of exchanging women. Marriage alliances, the eminent anthropologist Claude

Lévi-Strauss declared, were "not established between men and women, but between men *by means of women.*" Women were merely the vehicle for establishing this relationship.[21]

In the 1970s several feminist researchers built on this idea to turn the protective theory of marriage on its head. They suggested that marriage originated not to protect women but to oppress them. These researchers argued that because women probably played a leading role in the invention of agriculture through their experimentation with plants and food preservation, and because women were certainly responsible for the physical reproduction of the group, the origins of marriage lay not in the efforts of women to attract protectors and providers but in the efforts of men to control the productive and reproductive powers of women for their own private benefit.[22]

According to this oppressive theory, men coerced women into marriage, often using abduction, gang rape, or wife beating to enforce their will. Brothers essentially traded their sisters for wives. Fathers gained power in the community by passing their daughters out to young men, who gave the fathers gifts and services in return. Rich men accumulated many wives, who worked for them and bore more daughters who could be exchanged to place other men in their debt.

Like the protective theory of marriage, the oppressive theory still has defenders. Philosopher Iris Marion Young maintains that the historical function of marriage was "to use women as a means of forging alliances among men and perpetuating their 'line.'" Even today, Young says, marriage is "the cornerstone of patriarchal power." Christine Delphy and Diana Leonard argue that marriage is one of the primary ways that "men benefit from, and exploit, the work of women."[23]

In today's political climate, in which men's power over their wives and daughters has greatly diminished, it is tempting to write off the oppressive theory of marriage as a product of 1970s feminist excesses. But there is strong historical evidence that in many societies marriage was indeed a way that men put women's labor to their private use. We can watch this process develop as recently as the eighteenth and nineteenth centuries among the Plains Indians.

In the Blackfoot legend about the origins of marriage, the men got dried meat and berries, warm robes, soft moccasins, and fine lodges only after the women chose to take them as husbands. In real life, men began to accumulate buffalo hides, large lodges, and other "fine" things, including, often, more than one wife, in a process that involved far less female choice.

Before the Europeans introduced the horse to the western United States, the Blackfoot and other Plains Indians hunted buffalo on foot, using surrounds. The entire group—men, women, and children—took part in driving the animals into traps or over cliffs. The men clubbed the buffalo to death, and the women dried the meat and tanned the hides. Although the men took on the more risky, up-close killing tasks, the work was evenly divided, and it was episodic; a good hunt could provide meat and clothes for a long time.[24]

But once Europeans introduced the horse, the gun, and the fur trade to North America, everything changed. Indian men were able to hunt buffalo individually. They had both the opportunity and incentive to kill more buffalo than they needed for their own subsistence because they could trade their surplus to whites for personal gain. This hugely increased the number of hides to be tanned and the amount of meat to be dried. The most successful hunters could now kill far more buffalo than one wife could process, and having more wives suddenly meant having more wealth. Richer men began to accumulate wives by offering horses to girls' fathers.

The expansion of the trade in buffalo hides brought a sharp increase in the number of wives per hunter. It also caused the age of marriage for women to drop to preadolescence, and it greatly multiplied social restrictions upon wives. According to nineteenth-century observers, the practice of keeping multiple wives was most common among groups that traded with the fur companies, and in these groups women's labor was much more intensive. These tribes too were more likely to practice forms of punishment such as cutting off a woman's nose for adultery.[25]

There are many other examples of societies in which men have exchanged women without consulting them and in which husbands have used the labor of their wives and children to produce surpluses that increased the men's prestige and power. It is also true that many more societies exchange women in marriage than exchange men, and there are some disadvantages to being the sex that moves after marriage. But in small-scale societies these disadvantages were not necessarily severe. Women could return home to their parents or call on their brothers for protection. Furthermore, in some societies men were the ones who moved at marriage. In these cases, one could just as easily argue that men were being exchanged by women.

In a current example, the Minangkabau of Indonesia, where marriage perpetuates the female line, refer to a husband as "the borrowed man." In traditional Hopi Indian marriages, a woman's kin made "a ceremonial presentation of cornmeal to the groom's household, conceptualized by the Hopi as 'paying for him.'" There is evidence that marriage systems in which men rather than women were circulated may have been more common in kinship societies of the distant past than in those observed over the past several hundred years.[26]

Even in cultures where women move at marriage, there has always been a huge variation in how much male dominance accompanies this arrangement. There are also enough exceptions to the practice of controlling women through marriage to call the oppressive theory into question. In the early eighteenth century a French baron, traveling among hunting and gathering peoples in what is now Canada, was scandalized to find that native parents believed "their Daughters have the command of their own Bodies and may dispose of their Persons as they think fit; they being at liberty to do what they please."[27]

In many hunting and gathering and simple horticultural societies, parents are likely to arrange a first marriage. They may even force a woman into a match. However, in most societies without extensive private property, marriages tend to be fragile, and women whose families have arranged their marriages frequently leave their husbands or run off with lovers without suffering any reprisals.[28]

I do not believe, then, that marriage was invented to oppress women any more than it was invented to protect them. In most cases, marriage probably originated as an informal way of organizing sexual companionship, child rearing, and the daily tasks of life. It became more formal and more permanent as groups began to exchange spouses over larger distances. There was nothing inherent in the institution of marriage that protected women and children from violence or produced the fair and loving relationships that many modern couples aspire to. But there was also nothing inherent in the institution of marriage, as there was, say, in slavery, that required one group to subordinate another. The effect of marriage on people's individual lives has always depended on its functions in economic and social life, functions that have changed immensely over time.

It is likely that our Stone Age ancestors varied in their behaviors just as do the hunting and gathering societies observed in more recent times. But in early human societies, marriage was primarily a way to extend cooperative relations and circulate people and resources beyond the local group. When people married into new groups, it turned strangers into relatives and enemies into allies.

That changed, however, as societies developed surpluses and became more sedentary, populous, and complex.[29] As kin groups began to assert permanent rights over territory and resources, some families amassed more goods and power than others. When that happened, the wealthier families lost interest in sharing resources, pooling labor, or developing alliances with poorer families. Gradually marriage exchanges became a way of consolidating resources rather than creating a circle of reciprocal obligations and connections.

With the growth of inequality in society, the definition of an acceptable marriage narrowed. Wealthy kin groups refused to marry with poorer ones and disavowed any children born to couples whose marriage they hadn't authorized. This shift constituted a revolution in marriage that was to shape people's lives for thousands of years. Whereas marriage had once been a way of expanding the number of cooperating groups, it now became a way for powerful kin groups to accumulate both people and property.

The Transformation of Marriage in Ancient Societies

Wherever this evolution from foraging bands to sedentary agriculturalists occurred, it was accompanied by a tendency to funnel cooperation and sharing exclusively through family ties and kinship obligations and to abandon more informal ways of pooling or sharing resources. In the American Southwest we can trace this transition through changes in architectural patterns. Originally surplus grains were stored in communal spaces in open, visible parts of the village. Later, storage rooms were enclosed within individual residences and could be entered only from the rooms where the family or household actually lived. Surpluses had become capital to be closely guarded, with access restricted to family members.[30]

As some kin groups became richer than others, they sought ways to enhance their own status and to differentiate themselves from "lesser" families. Excavations of ancient living sites throughout the world show growing disparities in the size and quality of dwellings, as well as in the richness of the objects buried with people.

Greater economic differentiation reshaped the rules of marriage. A kin group or lineage with greater social status and material resources could demand a higher "price" for handing over one of its children in marriage. Within the leading lineages, young men often had to borrow from their seniors in order to marry, increasing the control of elders over junior men as well as over women. A lineage that couldn't pay top prices for spouses had to drop out of the highest rungs of the marriage exchange system. Sometimes a poorer lineage would forgo the bridewealth a groom's family traditionally paid and give its daughters away as secondary wives or concubines to the leading lineages, in order to forge even a second-class connection with a leading family. But in other cases, lower-status kin groups were not allowed to intermarry with those of higher status under any circumstances.[31]

As dominant kin groups became more wealthy and powerful, they married in more restricted circles. Sometimes they even turned away from exogamy (the practice of marrying out of the group) and engaged in endogamy (marriage with close kin), in order to preserve and consolidate their property and kin members.[32] The more resources were at stake in marriage alliances, the more the relatives had an interest in whom their kin married, whether a marriage lasted, and whether a second marriage, which might produce new heirs to complicate the transmission of property, could be contracted if the first one ended.

In many ancient agricultural societies, if an heir was already in place and the birth of another child would complicate inheritance and succession, a woman might be forced to remain single and celibate after her husband's death. In a few cultures the ideal was for a widow to kill herself after her husband died.[33] More often, the surviving spouse was required to marry another member of the deceased's family in order to perpetuate the alliance between the two kin groups.

In India, early law codes provided that a widow with no son had to marry her husband's brother, in order to produce a male child to carry on his lineage. The Old Testament mentions several examples of the same custom. Indeed, it seems to have been preferred practice among the ancient Hebrews. A man who refused to marry his brother's widow had to go through a public ceremony of *halizah,* or "unshoeing." This passage from the Torah shows how intense the social pressure was against making such a choice: "Then shall his brother's wife come unto him in the presence of the elders, and loose his shoe from off his foot, and spit in his face, and shall answer and say, so shall it be done unto that man that will not build up his brother's house. And his name shall be called in Israel the house of him that hath his shoe loosed."[34]

As marriage became the primary vehicle for transmitting status and property, both men and women faced greater restrictions on their behavior. Men, like women, could be forced to marry women chosen by their parents. But because women could bear a child with an "impure" bloodline, introducing a "foreign interest" into a family, their sexual behavior tended to be more strictly supervised, and females were subject to severe penalties for adultery or premarital sex. The laws and moral codes of ancient states exhorted men to watch carefully over their wives "lest the seed of others be sown on your soil."[35]

Distinctions between legitimate and illegitimate children became sharper in all the early states. Children born into unauthorized liaisons could not inherit land, titles, or citizenship rights and so in many cases were effectively condemned to slavery or starvation.

The subordination of wives in the ancient world was exacerbated by the invention of the plow. Use of the plow diminished the value of women's agricultural labor, because plowing requires greater strength than women were believed to have and is less compatible with child care than gardening with a hoe. Husbands began to demand dowries instead of giving bridewealth for wives, and daughters were devalued to the point that families sometimes resorted to female infanticide. The spread of warfare that accompanied the emergence of early states also pushed women farther down in the hierarchy.[36]

As societies became more complex and differentiated, upper classes sometimes displayed their wealth by adopting standards of beauty or behavior that effectively hobbled women. Restrictive clothing, heavy jewelry, or exceedingly long fingernails, for example, made a public statement that the family had slaves to do the work once done by wives and daughters. By the second millennium B.C. the practice of secluding women in special quarters had become widespread in the Middle East. This was done not just to guard their chastity but to signify that a family had so much wealth that its women did not even have to leave the home.

Much later, in China, binding the feet of young girls became a symbol of prestige. Upper-class girls had their feet bound so tightly that the small bones broke and the feet were permanently bowed over, making it excruciatingly painful to walk.[37]

In many societies, elaborate ideologies of purity grew up around the women of the highest-ranking classes. A man who courted a high-ranking woman outside regular channels faced harsh sanctions or even death, while women who stepped out of their assigned places in the marriage market were severely punished.

Assyrian laws from the twelfth and eleventh centuries B.C. guarded women's premarital virginity and condemned to death married women who committed adultery. Married women were required to wear veils, but concubines were forbidden to do so. A man who wanted to raise the status of his concubine and make her his wife could have her veiled. But a woman who veiled herself without the authority of a propertied husband was to be flogged fifty times, have tar poured over her head, and have her ears cut off.[38]

Women's bodies came to be regarded as the properties of their fathers and husbands. Assyrian law declared: "A man may flog his wife, pluck her hair, strike her and mutilate her ears. There is no guilt." The Old Testament suggests that a bride whose virginity was not intact could be stoned to death.[39]

Centuries later in China, Confucius defined a wife as "someone who submits to another." A wife, according to Confucian philosophy, had to follow "the rule of the three obediences: while at home she obeys her father, after marriage she obeys her husband, after he dies she obeys her son."[40]

But men too faced new controls over their personal behavior. If a woman could no longer choose her mate, this also meant that a man could not court a wife on his own initiative but needed to win her father's permission. And in many states, the confinement of wives to household activities "freed" their husbands to be drafted into the army or dragooned into backbreaking labor on huge public works projects.[41]

By the time we have written records of the civilizations that arose in the ancient world, marriage had become the way most wealth and land changed hands. Marriage was also the main vehicle by which leading families expanded their social networks and political influence. It even sealed military alliances and peace treaties.

With so much at stake, it is hardly surprising that marriage became a hotbed of political intrigue. Families and individuals developed elaborate strategies to create unions that furthered their interests and to block marriages that might benefit their rivals. Elites jockeyed to acquire powerful in-laws. If, after they had agreed to seal a match, a better one presented itself, they maneuvered (and sometimes murdered) to get out of the old one.

Commoners could no longer hope to exchange marriage partners with the elites. At best they might hope to have one of their children marry up. Even this became more difficult as intricate distinctions were created between the rights of primary wives, secondary wives, and concubines. Formal rules detailed what kinds of marriage could and could not produce legitimate heirs. In some places authorities prohibited lower-class groups from marrying at all or made it illegal for individuals from different social classes to wed each other.

The right to decide who could marry whom had become an extremely valuable political and economic weapon and remained so for thousands of years. From the Middle Eastern kingdoms that arose three thousand years before the birth of Christ to the European ones fifteen hundred years later, factions of the ruling circles fought over who had the right to legitimize marriages or authorize divorces. These battles often changed the course of history.

———◇———

For millennia, the maneuvering of families, governing authorities, and social elites prevailed over the individual desires of young people when it came to selecting or rejecting marriage partners. It was only two hundred years ago that men and women began to wrest control over the right to marry from the hands of parents, church, and state. And only in the last hundred years have women had the independence to make their marital choices without having to bow to economic need and social pressure.

Have we come full circle during the past two centuries, as the power of kin, community, and state to arrange, prohibit, and interfere in marriages has waned? Legal scholar Harry Willekins argues that in most modern industrial societies, marriages are contracted and dissolved in ways that have more in common with the habits of some egalitarian band-level societies than the elaborate rules that governed marriage in more complex societies over the past 5,000 years.[42] In many contemporary societies, there is growing acceptance of premarital sex, divorce, and remarriage, along with an erosion of sharp distinctions between cohabitation and marriage and between "legitimate" and out-of-wedlock births.

Some people note this resemblance between modern family relations and the informal sexual and marital norms of many band-level societies and worry that we are throwing away the advantages of civilization. They hope to reinstitutionalize marriage as the main mechanism that regulates sexuality, legitimizes children, organizes the division of labor between men and women, and redistributes resources to dependents. But the last century of social change makes this highly unlikely.

Yet if it is unrealistic to believe we can reimpose older social controls over marriage, it is also naive to think we can effortlessly revive the fluid interpersonal relationships that characterized simpler cultures. In hunting and gathering bands and egalitarian horticultural communities, unstable marriages did not lead to the impoverishment of women or children as they often do today. Unmarried women participated in the work of the group and were entitled to a fair share, while children and other dependents were protected by strong customs that mandated sharing beyond the nuclear family.

This is not the case today, especially in societies such as the United States, where welfare provisions are less extensive than in Western Europe. Today's winner-take-all global economy may have its strong points, but the practice of pooling resources and sharing with the weak is not one of them. The question of how we organize our personal rights and obligations now that our older constraints are gone is another aspect of the contemporary marriage crisis.

Part Two

———⊷●⊶———

The Era of Political Marriage

Chapter 4

— ⁐◉⁐ —

Soap Operas of the Ancient World

For the past two hundred years, Europeans and Americans have seen marriage as an oasis of privacy and affection, where individuals are shielded from the scheming and self-seeking that take place at work and in public life. But in the ancient world, marriage provided no such respite from political and economic rivalries. It was at the very center of the fray.

More than four thousand years ago a few regional chiefdoms and small-scale warrior societies grew into mighty states in and around the Tigris-Euphrates Valley of the Middle East and the Nile Valley of Africa. Over the next two thousand years other states and empires arose along the Indus and Yellow rivers in India and China respectively, and by 800 B.C., military aristocracies in the Mediterranean region had established several powerful kingdoms there as well. A thousand years later the Mayan empire spread out across Central America. The Aztecs of Mexico and the Incas of South America were relative latecomers, but they developed in ways similar to their predecessors.

These societies were separated from one another by thousands of years and a myriad of distinctive cultural practices. But in all of them, kings, pharaohs, emperors, and nobles relied on personal and family ties to recruit and reward followers, make alliances, and establish their legitimacy. Marriage was one of the key mechanisms through which such ties were forged.

Would-be rulers justified their authority on the basis of their ancestry.

Whether they claimed descent from the gods or from an earlier king or legendary hero, their legitimacy depended on the purity of their parents' bloodlines and the validity of their parents' marriages. In a world where most of the upper class was busily establishing pretensions to noble blood, the best way to bolster one's legitimacy was to marry someone who also had an august line of ancestors.

In addition, aspiring rulers needed a powerful network of living kin who could throw their economic and military resources behind their claims. In the absence of an international economy and legal system, rulers used marriage to establish diplomatic, military, or commercial ties. Whereas heads of state today ratify treaties with a signature and ceremonial stamp, rulers—or aspiring rulers—of the past often sealed their deals with a marriage ceremony.

Since few rulers had the means to equip or maintain large standing armies and police forces, power was tied to a leader's ability to recruit followers on the basis of kinship, marital alliances, and other intensely personal ties. For thousands of years, despite periodic experiments with alternatives to the politics of kinship and marriage, marriage alliances remained central to governance throughout the world.

In the kingdoms of the ancient world, marriage was important for the common folk as well. In the millennia before the development of banks and free markets, marriage was the surest way for people lower down the social scale to acquire new sources of wealth, add workers to family enterprises, recruit business partners, and preserve or pass on what they already had. People who aspired to even the lowest rungs of government office often found it crucial to contract a marriage with the "right" set of in-laws. Intensified demands for tribute and taxes forced peasants to choose mates and in-laws who could help them increase agricultural production.

But the stakes of marriage were much higher for the ruling and upper classes. For them, marriage was crucial to establishing and expanding political power. In consequence, the marriages of aristocrats and rulers were marked by intense negotiations, rivalries, intrigues, and, very often, betrayal.

In the eighteenth century B.C., King Zimri-lim retook the city of Mari from the Assyrians, who had seized it from his ancestors. Mari, a prosperous kingdom that occupied a critical position in the trade routes between Syria and Mesopotamia, was a tempting prize. Zimri-lim, needing allies to protect himself from the many rulers who coveted his land, immediately married the daughter of a powerful neighboring king and, in a common maneuver, repudiated his queen in order to elevate his new bride to the position of principal wife. Zimri-lim subsequently married off eight of his daughters to rulers of vassal cities. A document of the day described succinctly what the king expected from a son-in-law: "He is the husband of Zimri-Lim's daughter and he obeys Zimri-Lim."[1]

Few rulers took account of their children's desires when they arranged such political marriages. When one Syrian princess threatened to kill herself if she was not allowed to marry the prince she loved rather than another man preferred by her father, the scribes found it extraordinary that the king relented.

Zimri-lim was not so indulgent. After he conquered the city of Aslakka, for example, he married off a daughter to the king there, installing her as the queen and principal wife of his new son-in-law. But as soon as her father returned home, her husband brought back his first wife to serve as queen. The new bride wrote to her father complaining that the first wife "made me sit in a corner holding my head in my hands like any idiot woman. Food and drink were regularly put in front of her, while my eyes envied and my mouth watered."[2] She begged her father to be allowed to return home, but to no avail.

Seventeen hundred years later and a world away, Liu Xijun, of the royal family of Chu'u, on the Yangtze River, was sent to marry the ruler of the Wusun, a nomadic Central Asian society. The feelings she expressed in a poem she wrote in 107 B.C. would have been instantly recognizable to Zimri-lim's daughter in Mesopotamia so many centuries earlier. Liu Xijun wrote:

> *My family has married me*
> *In this far corner of the world,*
> *sent me to a strange land,*
> *to the king of Wu-San [Wusun]. . . .*
> *My thoughts are all of my homeland,*
> *My heart aches within.*
> *Oh to be the yellow crane*
> *winging home again.*[3]

Moving forward fourteen hundred years, to sixteenth-century Europe, we hear a similar lament from the sister of the Holy Roman Emperor: "It is hard enough to marry a man . . . whom you do not know or love, and worse still to be required to leave home and kindred, and follow a stranger to the ends of the earth, without even being able to speak his language."[4]

Political marriages, like diplomatic treaties, had to be periodically renewed, especially if one of the parties died. The ancient records are full of successive (and sometimes simultaneous) marriages between one king and the sisters or daughters of another, as well as the establishment of new marriages between the descendants of each. Several years after Liu Xijun wrote her plaintive poem, her fellow countrywoman Liu Jieyu, the granddaughter of the Chu'u king, was sent to Wusun to marry the next ruler. When he died shortly after the marriage, she was promptly remarried to his cousin, who became regent. After this husband's death, Liu Jieyu was married to her stepson, to whom she bore an heir. When this third husband was murdered, their son became ruler of the largest segment of the kingdom. After her son died in 51 B.C., Liu Jieyu, at age seventy, was finally allowed to return home, where the emperor rewarded her with houses, estates, and slaves.

Marital "treaties" were sometimes thinly disguised forms of domination. In the fourteenth century B.C., for example, the king of Egypt commanded the ruler of a city on the Nile River to "send your daughter straightaway to your king and lord; also send your presents: twenty healthy slaves, silver-coated chariots [and] fine horses." This was followed by the not-so-subtle warning that "the king is as well as the sun god in the sky; his soldiers and his chariotry are in very, very good condition."[5]

Many families voluntarily offered their daughters or sisters to rulers with the aim of gaining a useful family connection. An upper-class woman would arrive at her new husband's home with a rich dowry and her own retinue, furnished by her family in the hope that her future son would inherit the throne or estate of the husband's family and show favor to his mother's kin. A lower-class woman might bring only her beauty and charm, hoping to become a favorite consort or even eventually to supplant the primary wife.

But this was a dangerous game. A secondary wife or concubine who found favor with the ruler might well be murdered by a primary wife or her kin. Sometimes the primary wife had the political or legal clout to ensure that the secondary wife remained subordinate even if the husband personally preferred her. One Babylonian marriage contract specified that the second wife had to prepare the first wife's daily meal and carry her chair to the temple.[6]

Even a princess from the highest royalty was vulnerable when sent as a bride to her husband's city, far away from her customary support networks. In the fourteenth century B.C., Amenhotep III of Egypt wrote to the king of Babylon, asking that a princess be sent to him as a wife. The Babylonian ruler wrote back indignantly that his father had already sent his sister to Egypt several years earlier: "Indeed, you want my daughter to be a bride for you even while my sister, whom my father gave you, is there with you, although no one has seen her now or knows whether she is alive or dead."[7]

Amenhotep didn't bother to reassure the Babylonian king that his sister was alive and well. He merely noted slyly that since the last Babylonian emissaries to Egypt did not know the princess personally, they would not have been able to recognize her. Egypt was far more powerful than any Mesopotamian state, and the king of Babylon did not press the issue.

In the modern world, we tend to think that "marrying up" is something only women do, as when a woman snags a rich husband or handsome prince. In many ancient societies, however, it was often *men* who sought wealth and power by marrying women higher up the social scale. "Someday my princess will come" could have been the theme song of fairy tales and male fantasies in the ancient Middle East and in Homeric Greece.

New kings or dynasties tried to validate their claims to power by marrying the widow or daughter of a previous ruler. Lower-ranking nobles competed to win wives from higher-status households. In some societies, a commoner had a shot at marrying a princess if he could bring enough wealth or fighting men to her father's household.[8]

In China, even a lowly scholar with no fighting skills could gain higher status by marrying a highborn bride. In the eleventh century, when the Chinese state began to determine entry into the governing bureaucracy through rigorous examinations, a lowborn man with exceptional scholarly talents might have a wife bestowed on him by a noble family that hoped the son-in-law had enough talent to rise through the ranks and keep the family in the governing circles.[9]

The marriage jackpot for a man was to wed the daughter of a deceased or soon-to-die king and to live with her in her father's household, where he might inherit the throne. Legends and folktales from ancient kingdoms are full of such marital rags-to-riches stories, in which a man gains fame and fortune by winning the hand of a noble lady or an emperor's daughter. In Greek mythology, Pelops won the princess Hippodamia—and her throne—after he had defeated and killed her father in a chariot race. An even more satisfying fantasy for would-be Cinderfellas was the legend of how Hippomenes won Atalanta for his bride. He defeated *her* in a footrace, simultaneously winning a kingdom and establishing the proper power relations between husband and wife.

Not all men who married princesses were so lucky. Those who married into the imperial house of China in the first millennium A.D., for example, had no chance of inheriting the empire or seeing their sons inherit. Neither the sisters of the emperor nor their descendants were eligible for the throne. But the status and privileges of Chinese princesses thoroughly overshadowed their husbands'. Imperial princesses were exempted from many of the rules that governed wives in China, and only the emperor could discipline them. During the rule of the Southern Dynasties (A.D. 317–589), one Chinese princess argued that she, like her brother the emperor, was entitled to a harem. Her wishes prevailed, and she was assigned thirty male "concubines."[10]

When a powerful ruler sent his daughter to be the primary wife of a lesser king or prince, he expected that she would represent his interests in her new husband's household. In places as far apart as Assyria, the Inca empire of the Andes, and the African state of Dahomey, princesses who became wives of their fathers' vassals wielded great power over their husbands as their fathers' agents. They frequently had their own independent retinues and were answerable only to their fathers. One Egyptian king's wife arrived with 317 attendants that he had to incorporate into his court.[11]

As we saw with the daughters of Zimri-lim and the sister of the king of Babylon, these women were very vulnerable if their fathers would not or could not enforce their authority over resentful or arrogant husbands. On the other hand, a husband who slighted the sister or daughter of a mighty ruler might live to rue the day. In the eighteenth century B.C., the king of Assyria wrote a worried letter to his son admonishing him to be more discreet with his "women-friends," so as not to humiliate the daughter of the powerful king of Qatna, with whom the king had contracted a diplomatic marriage alliance on his son's behalf.[12]

In pre-Columbian Mexico, Moquiuixtli, ruler of the city-state of Tlatelolco, could have used similar advice. Moquiuixtli had married the sister of the highest ruler in the land, the Aztec emperor Axayacatl. According to the chronicles, however, the bride "was skinny, and she had no flesh, and because of this her husband never wished to see her. He took all the presents that her brother Axayacatl sent her and gave them to his secondary wives. . . . And king Moquiuixtli would not sleep with her: he spent his nights only with his concubines." When the emperor learned of this, he "grew furious" and attacked Tlatelolco, destroying the kingdom.[13]

When a king neglected a royal wife for a concubine or secondary wife of lower status, contemporaries sometimes lamented that personal emotions had prevailed over self-interest. Roman historians reporting on the origins of the war with Egypt asserted that Cleopatra had bedazzled Mark Antony, clouding his judgment so that he left his Roman wife, infuriated her powerful brother, and thus wrecked his political future. Similarly, in Aztec Mexico, a chronicler reported in consternation that the secondary wife of the king of Texcoco had somehow brought the king "very much under her domination," even though she "was only a merchant's daughter."[14]

Yet there were logical reasons for a king to prefer the charms of a concubine or a merchant's daughter over those of his highborn wife. A commoner had no powerful kin to dilute her loyalty to the king.

A highborn wife and her in-laws, by contrast, had a greater interest in the well-being of her son than of her husband. There are many examples of a wife and in-laws plotting to displace a royal husband so that either a son might succeed to the throne or the widow and her family advisors could rule as regents for the minor. Sometimes, because of his ties to his father's family, even a woman's own son was considered an obstacle to be removed. So the political marriages of royalty and aspiring royalty were always fraught with danger as well as opportunity. The benefits of having wealthy and powerful in-laws had to be weighed against the possibility that they would try to usurp power or tilt policy in their favor.

Rulers tried many strategies to cope with this threat. Powerful kings whose social status and military might did not need bolstering by dynastic marriage sometimes took commoners for their primary wives. Amenhotep III of Egypt (1417–1379 B.C.) had wives sent to him by the king of Babylonia and other fellow rulers. But he chose the commoner Tiy, daughter of his high priest, to be his "Great Royal Wife." Their son, Amenhotep IV, followed his father's example and chose the elegant commoner Nefertiti for his primary wife.[15]

To rule out conflicts of interest between in-laws, an Egyptian pharaoh sometimes married a sister or, more frequently, a half-sister—a woman born by a different wife to the same father. This bolstered the claim to dynastic continuity both for the rulers and for any children they produced and eliminated the risk that husband and wife would be torn in different directions by the machinations of their respective kin. But it did not always prevent brother and sister from falling out, as we shall see in the story of Cleopatra.

Ancient Chinese emperors also tried to restrict the influence of their in-laws and prevent wives from putting the interests of their kin or sons before those of their husbands. During the Ming dynasty, rulers purposely chose women from weak or low-status kin groups as their wives. The Manchu dynasty took this one step farther, choosing the emperor's successor from among his consorts' sons so that the empress would not be tempted to poison her husband to hasten her son's succession.[16]

Egyptian kings, in their long campaign to bring Thebes under their control, created a different kind of political marriage. They set up a marriage alliance with the gods rather than with potentially troublesome human beings. During the eighth century B.C. the king of Egypt revived an old Theban practice of elevating a priestess to be the "divine wife of Amun," an Egyptian god very popular in Thebes. But the king filled the position with his own daughter rather than a lady of Thebes. From then on, the Divine Wife was always a daughter of the Egyptian king. Residing in Thebes, she managed great estates and made major political decisions but was expected to remain celibate to prevent her from founding a rival dynasty to undermine the king's power. The Divine Wife was required to adopt as her successor the daughter of the next king who ascended the Egyptian throne. That king then appointed a chief steward to administer the new Divine Wife's estates and help her carry out his wishes.

Even this strategy could backfire if daughters entertained their own political ambitions. One Divine Wife, Nitocris, outlived her father without adopting a successor and managed to maintain her independence from the next three kings by appointing her own men as stewards, making her essentially the independent ruler of Thebes. The Egyptian kings, left out of the loop, were in a tight spot. It was one thing to send your advisers and agents as the invited guests of the Divine Wife. But if she refused to recognize them, the city of Thebes might well rally behind her. Not until 594 B.C., when she was in her eighties, did Nitocris finally adopt her great-niece as her successor, giving the Egyptian king of the time the chance to send his own representative to serve in the retinue of the heir apparent.[17]

Alexander the Great of Macedonia conquered Egypt in the fourth century B.C., and merged it with Greece and most of Asia Minor to form a massive Greco-Macedonian empire. Thus began the Hellenistic Era, marked by the spread of Greek settlers, language, and culture into the East and the incorporation of Greeks and Macedonians into the upper circles of the Egyptian ruling class. But after Alexander's death in 323 B.C. the empire broke apart. Syria and the lands to the east were taken over by the Seleucid dynasty and Egypt proper by the Ptolemaic dynasty. Both dynasties relied heavily on polygamy as a diplomatic tool.

By taking more than one wife, kings could establish a network of alliances with several other rulers. But polygamy also yielded many potentially competing heirs, each with a different set of maternal kin, which helps explain the many intrigues and murders for which the Hellenistic dynasties were famous. No modern soap opera could compete with the goings-on among the ruling families of Egypt and Asia Minor. Wives plotted with sons to murder husbands, rival wives, and children. One queen, fearing her new husband might prefer her daughter to herself, tied the girl in a chariot and stampeded the horses over a cliff. Fathers killed sons by one wife in order to elevate sons of another or murdered their wives' children by previous husbands.[18]

The Ptolemies of Hellenistic Egypt tried to skirt this problem by reviving the old Egyptian practice of taking sisters or half sisters as wives. The children of a sibling marriage were viewed, in effect, as superlegitimate because they came from the same bloodline in both parents. This was meant to reduce the conflict between the children of the kings' other wives. But if a brother-sister marriage produced no heir, a sister's children by other men might vie for the throne, further multiplying the number of rival claimants. And sometimes married brothers and sisters turned on each other.[19]

Ptolemy II of Egypt established a diplomatic marriage between his daughter Berenice and King Antiochus of Asia Minor in 253 B.C. Antiochus had supposedly repudiated Laodice, his original wife as well as half sister, in order to cement the marriage. But he later resumed their relationship. Before the disgruntled Berenice could mobilize her own kin, however, Laodice took action on her own. Not trusting her husband/half brother to hold firm in his commitment to her as primary wife and to their son as heir, she poisoned Antiochus and arranged the murder of Berenice and her child. Berenice's brother, Ptolemy III, arrived too late to save his sister and her heir. However, he launched a war against the Seleucids and eventually conquered Syria and the south coast of Asia Minor.[20]

Not a Love Story: The Marriage of Antony and Cleopatra

The love affair between Antony and Cleopatra has been the subject of books, films, and a play by Shakespeare. As Plutarch tells it, the great Roman general Mark Antony fell hopelessly in love with Cleopatra after she dressed as the love goddess Aphrodite and sailed to meet him on a golden barge. The oars were made of silver, and the rowers kept time to the music of flutes and violins. Little boys dressed as Cupid were positioned on each side of Cleopatra and fanned her face and hair. Her ladies were costumed as mermaids, and the boat was furnished with precious metals, ornaments, and gifts. But, says Plutarch, despite all these delights to the senses, she relied above all on "the charms and enchantment of her passing beauty and grace" to secure Mark Antony's protection, keep him in Egypt, and divert him from his duties to Rome.[21]

According to most stories, Cleopatra soon returned Antony's love and the two married before the war with Rome broke out. After their defeat, believing that Cleopatra was already dead, Antony tried to commit suicide. He lived just long enough to die in her arms. Cleopatra followed her beloved husband into death by allowing a poisonous asp to bite her breast.

Marriage, a History

The real story is more complicated, because both Cleopatra and Antony were playing for stakes that had little to do with undying love. Their saga can be understood only in the context of the role of princesses in conferring legitimacy in Hellenistic Egypt and their active participation in struggles for political power. Sexual passion may indeed have existed between Cleopatra and Antony and, prior to that, between Cleopatra and Julius Caesar. But on everyone's part this was a calculated, even ruthless, political intrigue.

Before the Egyptian emperor Auletes died, in 51 B.C., he designated his ten-year-old son, Ptolemy XIII, and his seventeen-year-old daughter, Cleopatra, joint heirs, with instructions that they marry. Instead, they went to war, each seeking sole control of the kingdom.

The war between Cleopatra and her brother may have been started by ambitious advisers, certainly on the side of the ten-year-old. But Cleopatra, an educated, intelligent woman who spoke several languages, was no slouch when it came to intrigue and power plays. She first met the Roman general and ruler Julius Caesar in 48 B.C., when he was trying to effect a reconciliation between the warring siblings. Cleopatra immediately grasped the strategic advantage of allying herself with a Roman general. Even as she participated in the political and military negotiations designed to reconcile her with her brother, Cleopatra began a love affair, or at least a sexual liaison, with Caesar. Chroniclers of the day believed that Caesar was enraptured with the young woman. But that did not prevent him from officiating over a marriage between Cleopatra and her brother, confirming their joint rule of Egypt. Nor did any attachment she felt to Caesar prevent Cleopatra from agreeing to the match.[22]

A year later Cleopatra's brother/husband, Ptolemy XIII, died, and Cleopatra married Ptolemy XIV, who succeeded to the throne with her. That same year, Cleopatra also bore Caesar a son, whom he acknowledged as his own and whom she named Caesarion. Whether or not Caesar and Cleopatra were in love, Cleopatra was glad to have a child with a claim to Caesar's inheritance, and Caesar welcomed the birth of a son with a claim to the Egyptian throne.

In 44 B.C. Cleopatra's second husband died. Some sources suggest that she had him killed. Cleopatra then elevated her son, Caesarion, to the throne as her coruler. After Caesar was assassinated in Rome that same year, the question of what to do about Cleopatra and her son became central to Roman politics. The triumvirate set up to rule Rome after Caesar's murder was unstable and riven by rivalry between two of its members, Mark Antony and Octavian. Octavian, Caesar's designated successor, was Caesar's adopted son. The existence of a biological son in Egypt, acknowledged by Caesar himself, was a major worry for Octavian and an intriguing opportunity for Octavian's foes.

Initially, Cleopatra did not take sides in the escalating rivalry between Octavian and Mark Antony, although the military resources at her command made her a potentially valuable ally for any contender for Roman power. This was the situation when Mark Antony summoned the Egyptian queen, hoping to gain her support, and she arrived in her golden barge.

Within a year, Cleopatra bore Mark Antony twins. But if he was by then besotted with Cleopatra, as Plutarch claimed, Antony still managed to conduct his political and marital life in Rome in a very tough-minded, unromantic way. The same year his twins were born, 40 B.C., he and Octavian made up their differences. Antony took responsibility for the eastern part of the Roman Empire and sealed the deal by marrying Octavian's sister Octavia in Rome.

But Mark Antony did not repudiate his relationship with Cleopatra. Just a few years later he was issuing coins in Egypt with his likeness on one side and Cleopatra's on the other. Eight years after marrying Octavia, he formally notified her of his intention to divorce her and commit to his Egyptian marriage with Cleopatra, even though Roman law did not recognize marriages contracted with foreigners. By this time Mark Antony was championing Caesarion, son of Cleopatra and Caesar, as the rightful ruler of Rome. With Caesarion still too young to succeed Caesar, Antony generously offered to hold his place as the protector of Caesar's bloodline.

When Antony renounced Octavian's sister and claimed rulership of Rome on behalf of Caesarion, he closed the door to any compromise, staking everything on a decisive victory by his troops over Octavian's army. Even if this was poor judgment, Antony was certainly not, as legend would have it, throwing away his career for the sake of a woman's love. Both he and Cleopatra were using their relationship to gain a kingdom.

Octavian emerged the victor in 31 B.C., prompting Antony and Cleopatra to commit suicide rather than face being paraded through the streets of Rome as dishonored captives. Octavian promptly had Caesarion, then seventeen years old, put to death, and Egypt became a Roman province.

Back in Rome, Octavian's sister Octavia devoted her efforts to raising her family. In addition to the two daughters she had borne Mark Antony during their marriage, she had three children by her first marriage, as well as Antony and Cleopatra's two youngest sons and Antony's younger son by his first wife (her brother Octavian having had the older son put to death to eliminate a potential rival). Imagine the undercurrents in that blended family!

Cleopatra's ambitious campaign to escape Roman domination and revive the power of Egypt shows that princesses were not always helpless pawns in the marital intrigues of the ancient world. Sometimes they exerted great power in their own right, frustrating the plans of those who had arranged their marriages or hoped to profit from them. Women's power plays generally revolved around their husbands: who they might marry or scheme to discard. But the development of Christianity offered one ambitious Roman woman an alternative strategy in the politics of marriage, sexuality, and kinship.

Christianity became the official state religion of the Roman Empire in the fourth century A.D. In the fifth century the emperor's sister Pulcheria came up with a political strategy somewhat similar to that of Queen Elizabeth I in England more than a thousand years later. Pulcheria declared herself celibate, dodging an arranged marriage, and established an elaborate Christian cult to honor her virginity. Gradually she installed handpicked bishops in the churches. Upon her brother's death, she seized power and married a common soldier who, according to her official proclamations, had pledged to honor and guard her virginity, so that her spiritual authority would remain intact. While her husband directed the empire's military affairs, Pulcheria conducted most of the other government and social business through her control of the state church.[23]

In Japan in the eighth century A.D., another strong-willed princess was able to use her political skills to turn her marital and kin connections to her own ends and serve two terms as emperor of Japan. The Fujiwara clan was well known for its marriage politics. For several centuries they made sure that their sisters and daughters married the crown princes and emperors of Japan. This meant that the head of the Fujiwara family was the father-in-law or the grandfather—and often both—of the reigning emperor. As the power behind the throne, the Fujiwaras not only maneuvered the young emperors into marrying their own aunts but ensured that emperors abdicated at an early age, so that each emperor was a young man easily manipulated by the family's elders. Thus the emperor himself had little real authority. To "capture the king"—to have the emperor father a son with one's daughter—was the route to political power in the Japanese court.[24]

In the eighth century, however, before they had quite perfected their system, the Fujiwaras elevated one of their sisters, a commoner, from the position of a secondary wife to that of the Empress-Consort of Japan. Her daughter then became the crown princess, and when her father abdicated in her favor in 749, she became the Empress Koken. Nine years later her powerful kin maneuvered Koken into resigning in favor of a male with even closer links to the Fujiwara clan leaders. But Koken remained so politically effective that a few years later she was able to banish, then kill, her main opponent in the clan and depose the ruling emperor. She came back to the throne a second time, this time as the Emperor Shotoku, and ruled from 764 to 770.[25]

Marriage Among the Common Folk of Ancient Society

Marriage was a less turbulent affair among people who were not in the running for political power. But in most cases, marriage was still a matter of practical calculation rather than an arrangement entered into for individual fulfillment and the pursuit of happiness.

For people with property, marriage was an economic transaction that involved the transfer or consolidation of land and wealth as well as the development of social networks. Even small landowners manipulated kin and marriage ties to consolidate property. For families with larger amounts of wealth, marriages in the ancient world were the equivalent of today's business mergers or investment partnerships.

Parents with property to administer were no more willing than their royal and aristocratic counterparts to allow their children to choose a spouse freely, or to leave a useful marriage merely because they were personally unhappy. On the other hand, parents might force a child to abandon a partner that he or she truly cared for. In ancient Athens, if a woman became an heiress (this could happen only if her father died without leaving a son), she could be claimed as a bride by her closest male relative, even if she was already married, in order to keep the property within the family. If the kinsman who claimed the heiress was also married, he could summarily divorce his wife, though he might considerately arrange a new marriage for her.[26]

Even when individuals could make their own choices about marriage and divorce, as wealthy Romans often did, their decisions frequently had more to do with politics and finances than with feelings of love or desire. Switching marital partners sometimes took place with as little emotional turmoil as we might feel in switching phone companies. Marcus Porcius Cato (234–149 B.C.) divorced his wife Marcia and arranged for her to marry his friend Hortensius, in order to strengthen the friendship and family connections between the two men. We don't know how Marcia felt about this, but we do know that her father and Cato jointly betrothed her and that she remarried Cato after Hortensius died. Some Roman husbands were so little troubled by possessive feelings that they joined with a wife's previous husbands to build a tomb for her after she died.[27]

A husband rarely displayed such open-mindedness about a wife's sexual behavior while she was married to him, but this had as much to do with fear that she might bear another man's child as with love-based jealousy. One of the most important functions of marriage for the propertied classes was the production of legitimate children who would honor the father in his old age, show respect to the ancestors and clan gods, and perpetuate the family's property. A Greek orator in the fourth century B.C. explained: "We have hetaerae [courtesans specially trained to be pleasing companions] for pleasure, concubines for the daily care of our body, but wives to bear us legitimate children and to be the trusted guardians of our household." Under the Roman Republic, census takers determined if a Roman citizen was single by asking: "Have you married for the purpose of creating children?"[28]

When Greek husbands eulogized their departed wives, they seldom talked of their mutual love or the personal qualities they treasured in their wives. The most common words of praise for a wife were that she showed "self-control," an attribute connected in Greek thought to female chastity and to a wife's protection of her husband's property. Under Athenian law, a man's seduction of another's wife was punishable by death, but the rape of another man's wife merited only a monetary fine. The Athenians reasoned that a rapist did not pose a threat to the husband's household property because the woman could be counted on to dislike the rapist. But "he who achieves his end by persuasion," said the legislators, gained access not only to the woman's body but to her husband's storeroom.[29]

Even people with little property to protect took a calculating approach to marriage. Today we often talk about working *at* our marriages, meaning that we try to cultivate and nurture the personal relationship between husband and wife. But until two hundred years ago people who were not part of the highest elites of society worked *in* their marriages.

Marriage was one of the ways farmers and peasants organized the growing workload that accompanied the transition from hunter-gatherer and horticultural societies. Intensive agriculture or herding made a sexual division of labor within the household necessary for survival. The Greek poet Hesiod told men: "Get first a house and a wife and an ox to draw the plough."[30]

The rules that governed marriage and divorce in the upper classes were usually more relaxed for commoners. States did not generally get involved in validating marriages or regulating divorces unless substantial property or political privileges were involved. In ancient Egypt, marriage was a private matter. Propertied families usually drew up private marriage contracts, but for commoners there were no special rituals or licenses necessary to get married. A marriage came into existence when a man established a household with a woman. This loose definition of marriage also held true in ancient Rome.[31]

But formalized or not, something akin to marriage was essential for the survival of almost any commoner who was not a slave. Some historians believe that the lower classes of the ancient world were the only people who had the luxury of selecting marriage partners on the basis of love. But most commoners understood the need for a prudent approach to choosing a mate, and practicality usually trumped sentiment.

A woman needed a man to do the plowing. A man needed a woman to spin wool or flax, preserve food, weave blankets, and grind grain, a hugely labor-intensive task. A woman was also needed to bear more children to help in the fields. And households in ancient chiefdoms and kingdoms usually were required to work for their rulers as well as for themselves. Some rulers demanded that each household provide a certain amount of male services, such as plowing, and a certain amount of female ones, such as spinning or weaving. When men were called away from their farms or trades to work on state-sponsored building projects, such as irrigation systems, public storehouses, or temple complexes, someone had to take care of the house and fields in their absence.[32]

Slaves were forbidden to marry and set up their own households. But for everyone else, the intense demands on household production in ancient states practically forced people to marry or cohabit. Single-person households simply could not survive. In Rome, this became a problem during the late republic and early empire, when frequent military campaigns drained the supply of freemen living in Rome. Some freewomen reportedly sought husbands among slaves, threatening the interests of the slaveowners and causing considerable status anxiety among Roman commentators. Seneca labeled such unions "Marriage more shameful than adultery." In A.D. 52 a law was passed enslaving any freeborn woman who cohabited with a slave without the knowledge or consent of his master. In the third century A.D., the emperor Septimus Severus ruled that it was illegal for a Roman woman to free one of her slaves in order to marry him.[33]

On the other hand, the upper classes sometimes required their subjects or employees to marry. Around 160 B.C., the Roman statesman and moralist Cato the Elder wrote a book telling wealthy Roman landowners how to run their estates. He said the estate's overseer needed a wife to relieve him of all housework, "since he ought to go out with the slaves at first light, and return at twilight, exhausted by the work he has done." Assuming it was the landowner rather than the overseer who would choose the wife, Cato recommended that she should be neither ugly nor beautiful, for "ugliness will disgust her partner, while excessive beauty will make him lazy."[34]

Even when lower-class individuals got to choose their own mates, beauty and attraction were seldom the primary criteria. A strong arm was generally more important in a prospective spouse than a shapely leg. In many villages, choice of a mate was restricted by sparse population and poor transportation.

You could not get too picky when you might meet only a handful of potential marriage partners in your entire life. Few individuals of modest means had either the inclination or the opportunity to seek a soul mate. What they really needed was a work partner.

The same consideration held true somewhat higher on the economic ladder. Among landowners and craftsmen, choosing a wife was like hiring your most important employee. The Old Testament contains a detailed job description:

> Who can find a virtuous woman? For her price is far above rubies.
>
> The heart of her husband doth safely trust in her, so that he shall have no need of spoil.
>
> She will do him good and not evil all the days of her life.
>
> She seeketh wool, and flax, and worketh willingly with her hands.
>
> She is like the merchants' ships; she bringeth her food from afar.
>
> She riseth also while it is yet night, and giveth meat to her household, and a portion to her maidens.
>
> She considereth a field, and buyeth it: with the fruit of her hands she planteth a vineyard.
>
> She girdeth her loins with strength, and strenghteneth her arms.
>
> She perceiveth that her merchandise is good: her candle goeth not out by night.
>
> She layeth her hands to the spindle, and her hands hold the distaff.
>
> She stretcheth out her hand to the poor; yea, she reacheth forth her hands to the needy. . . .
>
> She maketh fine linen, and selleth it; and delivereth girdles unto the merchant.
>
> Strength and honour are her clothing; and she shall rejoice in time to come.
>
> She openeth her mouth with wisdom; and in her tongue is the law of kindness.
>
> She looketh well to the ways of her household, and eateth not the bread of idleness.
>
> Proverbs 31: 10–20, 24–27, King James Version

A husband with such a hardworking wife would be rash indeed to fire half his labor force just because someone else caught his fancy. But the continuity of the family line was also a major concern for commoners, especially farmers.

The need for children to work in the fields was so pressing that a wife who was not fertile often had to be put aside, regardless of how much affection might have developed within the couple.

The lower and middle classes made decisions about marriage and divorce according to criteria different from those used by the upper classes. But in neither case were these decisions likely to be based primarily on love and sexual attraction. For thousands of years, beginning in the earliest civilizations, the economic functions of marriage were far more important to the middle and lower classes than were its personal satisfactions, while among the upper classes, the political functions of marriage took first place.

Chapter 5

—◦◉◦—

Something Borrowed:
The Marital Legacy of the Classical
World and Early Christianity

The tremendous turmoil and frequent violence caused by shifting marital alliances, in-law intrigues, and inheritance disputes led rulers to try to restrict competing family coalitions. Groups that made their living through trade or agricultural production also had an interest in curbing the disruptive power struggles of rival dynasties. The ancient world therefore saw periodic attempts by reformers to develop less personal, more predictable forms of rule.

Ultimately, none of their efforts succeeded in displacing the marriage alliance system from its central role in politics and economics. But three attempts to curtail aristocratic family power eventually had particular significance for the development of marriage in Western Europe. The first was the establishment of democracy in Athens in the fifth century B.C. The second was the imposition of universal law and development of a professional army in the Roman Republic and early empire. A third came in the later days of the Roman Empire, when Christianity emerged as an institution that combined a universal ideal of brotherhood with many of the trappings of state power.

Ancient Athens's experiment with democracy challenged the aristocracy's monopoly over political power and justice, and also bequeathed philosophical ideals of patriotism and community that could compete with family loyalties. Rome pioneered a professional army, bureaucracy, and system of universal laws to curb the exercise of private power. And Christianity contributed spiritual beliefs that elevated loyalty to God above family and marital ties. Its changing positions on sexuality and divorce would eventually change the rules of marriage throughout the West.

The Athenian Experiment

In the eighth century B.C., Greece was a collection of regional chiefdoms ruled by warrior kings. As prosperous city-states emerged out of some of these chiefdoms, there also arose new social classes that made their living through manufacturing, trade, or administrative skills rather than relying on family ties and marriage alliances. The nobles held these groups in contempt and were especially irritated when they surpassed the old aristocracy in wealth. The merchant class in turn was infuriated that lordly families dominated political life through their kin and marriage connections and placed family advantage ahead of the broader interests of the city or state in which they lived. The fact that several equally powerful noble families, all vying for supremacy, existed in the same geographic region made Greece especially unstable and disrupted the orderly conduct of economic and political life.[1]

Loyalty to a country, institution, or abstract principle was foreign to the thinking of aristocrats and kings. Their obligations were based on family ties, marital alliances, and personal oaths of friendship. Homer's epic poem the *Iliad,* written during the eighth century B.C., reflects the intensely personal nature of obligations and loyalty in the aristocratic class. The war with Troy takes place over a case of adultery. The hero Achilles refuses to fight for Greece because Agamemnon has stolen the woman he desires. When Achilles relents, he does so only to avenge the death of his best friend.

Even the system of justice in aristocratic society was based on family ties. Traditional obligations of kinship made anyone who killed a prominent individual—even in defense of the state or at the order of a ruler—subject to vengeance and retribution from the victim's family and friends. Early laws in Greece explicitly declared that male relatives, up to and including the "sons of cousins," were responsible for avenging an individual's murder.

Sometimes families agreed that one of their own had committed a crime and needed to pay restitution. If not, the avenger was subject to revenge by the original killer's family. With everyone, including sons of cousins, obliged to seek vengeance, this system of "justice" could degenerate into feuds that triggered an ongoing cycle of killing, a situation often portrayed in Greek drama.

In the seventh and sixth centuries B.C, tyrants seized power in several Greek city-states and imposed their will on other powerful families. The word *tyrant* had a more positive meaning than it does today. Tyrants usually had the support of the impoverished peasants and the new middle classes that made their living in trade and industry and craved stability. Both groups thought that the rule of a single dictator, no matter how high-handed, was preferable to the incessant infighting of rival noble clans.

In Athens, aristocrats recognized the need for reform before a tyrant arose from their ranks, and in 594 B.C. they elected one of their number, Solon, to the office of archon. But Solon was unable to bring the feuding nobles under control. Another aristocrat then seized power and tried with only mixed success to establish a stable tyranny. Not until Cleisthenes came to power in 508 B.C., did the tyranny lay the foundation for Athenian democracy. Under Cleisthenes and his successors, the city-state of Athens was able to curb aristocratic politics and dynastic rule more drastically than any other ancient state, anticipating some of the measures adopted two thousand years later in Western Europe.

Athenian reformers promoted civil laws, abstract principles of justice, and norms of patriotism that could supplant the narrow obligations of blood ties and personal alliances. One sixth-century B.C. law enabled "anyone who wished," not just a relative, to seek redress for an injured party by initiating legal action against the culprit. The law also prohibited the culprit's kin from exacting vengeance against someone who sued for justice. Other legislation limited the inheritance rights of children born to concubines or "spear-won" women. Inheritance claims based solely on blood descent were no longer sufficient; a state-sanctioned marriage of the parents was now required. In addition, Athenian leaders tried to limit aristocratic families to a largely ceremonial role in religious cults. All these prohibitions were aimed at undermining aristocratic methods of gaining social status and attracting followers.

The most radical attack on the traditional political privileges of aristocratic families was the establishment of the Council of 500, Athens's main administrative body. By the beginning of the fifth century B.C., the Council was selected by lot, as were jurors. This prevented powerful kin groups from controlling elections and court decisions and gave every citizen the chance to play an active role in government.

In practice, Athenian democracy was very limited. There were twice as many slaves as citizens, and no woman or foreigner had citizenship rights. But for those who were included, this nascent democracy had extraordinary implications, undercutting the ability of aristocratic families to build and maintain their private power bases.

Wealth and family connections still counted. But Athenian legislators no longer allowed noble families to recruit and command their own armies on the basis of personal loyalty and family ties, instead requiring individual households to furnish soldiers directly to the city-state. On Athens's public buildings and coins, likenesses of the patron goddess Athena Nike and the owl, symbol of wisdom, replaced the crests of noble families. Athena had no conflicting family and marital allegiances. Legend said she had sprung full grown from the head of Zeus and therefore lacked any maternal in-laws to compete with her loyalty to the state.

The city-state also asserted its authority to represent the interests of orphans, minors, and even unborn children, who formerly would have been under the jurisdiction and control of the extended family. The introduction of wills, as the word implies, meant that the kin group could no longer automatically claim the properties of its deceased members. These and similar measures also made the individual nuclear family household more independent in relation to its larger kindred group.

These political changes were accompanied by vehement attacks on the privileges and customary practices of aristocratic families, especially the marital intrigues, personal power plays, and shifting alliances that characterized their struggles for power. Aristotle held that citizens owed their primary loyalties to the state, not to themselves or their families. Plato, writing about his ideal republic, suggested that families be abolished altogether.

A more common approach in Greek literature was to attack women who placed loyalty to their extended families above their wifely obligations to their husbands. A woman's continuing ties to her birth family came to symbolize the worst excesses of aristocratic rule, and Athenian playwrights developed this theme in tragedies that still capture our imagination.

Aeschylus, the first of the great Greek tragedians, leveled a powerful indictment of aristocratic governance and marriage politics in his fifth-century B.C. three-play cycle *The Oresteia*. The plays, based on a traditional Greek legend, condemn aristocratic marital intrigues and advocate a new hierarchy of obligations.

The first play of the trilogy begins as Agamemnon, king of Argos, returns home from the Trojan Wars. He does not know that his wife, Clytemnestra, has taken a lover, Aegisthus, and that together they have plotted his death.

The opening chorus explains that each of the adulterous pair has legitimate grievances against Agamemnon and his forefathers. On his way to Troy, Agamemnon had sacrificed his daughter, Iphigenia, in order to get favorable winds for his ships. Clytemnestra has brooded for years over his murder of their daughter. For his part, Aegisthus longs to avenge his brothers, whom Agamemnon's father, Atreus, had murdered and fed to Aegisthus's unsuspecting father, because the father had once slept with Atreus's wife: "Bloodshed bringing in its train/Kindred blood that flows again,/Anger still unreconciled/. . . Wreaking vengeance for a murdered child."[2]

Agamemnon, however, is oblivious to these resentments. On his return from the war, he enters the palace haughtily, giving instructions for the care of the concubine he has brought home with him. Clytemnestra then kills him offstage. She and Aegisthus proceed to banish Orestes, her son by Agamemnon, and announce they will rule together in peace. Although the play expects us to condemn the lovers' behavior, the two victors were more humane than many real-life ancient rulers, who ruthlessly killed all the descendants of their foes, even those to whom they were themselves related.

The second play in the cycle takes place seven years later. The banished son, Orestes, returns, having been ordered by the god Apollo to avenge his father's death or face the Furies, goddesses who punish those who shed the blood of kin, betray a host or guest, or blaspheme the gods. The Furies, who represent the old-fashioned principles of family vengeance, never punished Clytemnestra for killing Agamemnon, because her husband was not a blood relation. Nor did they try to get Orestes to kill her in revenge. It is only Apollo who threatens to unleash them, to prod Orestes into action. But as soon as Orestes does kill Clytemnestra, the Furies—"avenging hounds, incensed by a mother's blood"—descend upon him. Although they had done nothing to punish the murder of a husband by a wife, they are outraged by the murder of a mother by a child.

The last play addresses the dilemma the first two have posed. Which is the worse of two crimes? In one case a wife kills a husband, not a blood relation, who has shed their daughter's blood and has then insulted the wife further by bringing a concubine into their home. In the other case a son kills a mother who has committed adultery and murdered her husband. This is a tough call by aristocratic standards. The bonds between a mother and child are at least as strong as those between husband and wife, and even within the general context of male dominance, a highborn wife has a right to exact vengeance for slights against her dignity.

But in the play the answer of the state, represented by Apollo, is unequivocal: A woman's duty to her husband and ruler outweighs the claims of kinship. "He was a king/Wielding an honoured sceptre by divine command," says Apollo. Mother-child bonds are insignificant compared with the duty of wifely obedience. "The mother is not the true parent of the child/Which is called hers," Apollo declares. "She is a nurse who tends the growth/of young seed planted by its true parent, the male."

In the final moments of the play Athena, by now the patron goddess of Athens, confirms Apollo's judgment. In a conciliatory gesture, however, she offers the Furies a new role if they become the "Friendly Goddesses," blessing people's homes and gardens rather than enforcing the claims of blood. They can settle in Athens and be worshiped by a grateful citizenry if they will call an end to family feuds and blood vengeance: "Let war be with the stranger, at the stranger's gate./There let men fall in love with glory; but at home/Let no cocks fight."

In the "happy ending" to this tale of wrongs and opposing wrongs, the Furies become the defenders of a nonpolitical form of marriage and of the priority of civil law over family feuds and vendettas. They encourage people to honor such traditional aristocratic virtues as kinship ties, ancestral gods, and heroism in battle, but to do so in the service of the state rather than of family or personal interests. Marriage is to be a private affair, marked by dominance of the husband and subordination of the wife and producing orderly inheritance from father to son.

The Oresteia was not, of course, real history. But it spoke to the widespread discontent with the personal and marital intrigues of aristocratic rule. The cycle premiered in Athens just four years after a series of major reforms had expanded the authority of civic institutions and further undercut aristocratic politics based on family and marriage. These included a citizen assembly open to all male citizens over eighteen years of age; a popular court where six thousand jurors, chosen without regard to class, decided legal disputes; and an executive council chosen by lot.

The fear of powerful women expressed in *The Oresteia* and many other Greek tragedies reflected a distrust of aristocrats' extended family ties. Athenian leaders were anxious to convert marriage into an association of two individuals rather than two kin groups. While they did not prevent aristocrats or rich commoners from contracting economically and politically advantageous marriages, they did make a concerted effort to relegate women to a private, secondary sphere of life, so that women could not confer status in their own right.

One law enacted by Pericles in 451–50 B.C. declared that a man could not be a citizen of Athens unless his mother as well as his father was Athenian.

This seems to contradict the idea that women were not even the true parents of their children, merely vessels that carried men's seed. But the law aimed to reduce the number of strategic marriages in which Athenian aristocrats took foreign wives and forged connections with powerful in-laws in another city-state or empire. An Athenian who contracted such a marriage would deprive his heirs of citizenship rights.

The world's first experiment in democratic government did nothing to improve the rights and social status of wives. At every point in her life a woman in Greece was subject to the formal guardianship of a man. While she was unmarried, her father and brother controlled her behavior and were responsible for her support, including providing her with a dowry so that she could be married. Upon her marriage, the husband took control. Not even widowhood freed a woman from subordination to men because after her husband's death her sons had authority to act on her behalf.

The transfer of authority from father to husband was arranged at the betrothal, when the father declared, "I give you this woman for the procreation of legitimate children." The young man replied, "I take her," and the father announced the amount of dowry agreed upon. A husband had a unilateral right to divorce, although if he repudiated his wife without cause, he had to return the dowry with 18 percent interest.[3]

Wives in wealthy Greek families generally remained indoors or in the inner courtyards of the home, spending much of their time in upstairs rooms that could be closed off from the rest of the household. When Greeks described the activities of a virtuous woman, it was in far less active terms than those from the Old Testament. A respectable Greek wife certainly could not purchase a piece of farmland (she couldn't even go to view it), or sell her linens in public, or deliver girdles to the merchant as did the virtuous woman described in the Old Testament. One Athenian boasted: "My sisters and nieces have been so well brought up that they are embarrassed in the presence of a man who is not a member of the family." There was plenty for women to do, of course, including the spinning and weaving mentioned in the Bible and the supervision of slaves, but a respectable Greek wife did it all from inside the house.[4]

Aristotle acknowledged that it was impossible for ordinary commoners to keep their women indoors all the time, and records indicate that some women were out in public as laundresses, seamstresses, bakers, vendors, innkeepers, and the like. But Athens was one of the few societies in history prior to the nineteenth century that idealized the role of wives as dependent homemakers rather than as work mates for their husbands.

A man's responsibility for his dependent wife was seen not as part of the mutual duties of marriage but as a necessary form of social discipline, similar to the control men exercised over children and animals. Socrates made explicit the connection between women and animals, arguing that when a wife is bad, the husband is to blame for not training her properly, just as it is the rider's fault when a horse turns vicious.[5]

As in any society, there were affectionate and even passionate marriages in Greece. But the Greek model for true love was not the relationship between husband and wife. The truest love was held to exist in the association of an adult man with a much younger male.

An Athenian man, writes historian Eve Cantarella, "expressed his better side, intelligence, will for self-improvement, and a higher level of emotions" in dignified homosexual relations. Licentious sex violated the value Athenians placed on self-control, but in its proper place, homosexual sex was an accepted part of a young man's moral and political education. Interestingly, male prostitution was punished as a crime, but female prostitution was not. Cantarella believes that the rationale for this law was that the introduction of payment between men degraded a relationship that was highly valued as long as it was based on free choice.[6]

Athens's debilitating wars with Sparta from 431 to 404 B.C., the Peloponnesian Wars, brought its glory age to a close. However, Athenian philosophy, literature, and political theory survived to influence the Western civic tradition, passed down to us primarily through Rome.

Politics and Marriage in the Roman State

Rome too started as a city-state. When it became a republic at the end of the sixth century B.C., it controlled an area of just five hundred square miles. By 265 B.C. Roman rule extended to all but the northern tip of the Italian peninsula, an area of fifty thousand square miles. Two hundred years later Rome's territory included all of what is now Greece, Spain, France, and Germany, along with sizable portions of England, Asia Minor, and North Africa.

For much of their history, the Romans were able to push marital and family intrigues from the center of the political stage. Rome never curbed the political influence of aristocrats as fully as did fifth-century Athens, but the Roman state pioneered several political practices that discouraged aristocrats from destructively competing for outright rule.

For more than four hundred years, from 509 to 31 B.C., Rome was a republic. It had a powerful senate composed of aristocrats. There was also a centuriate assembly, in which successful military leaders and wealthy citizens were represented, and in 471 B.C., a council of plebs, or commoners, was established. These political institutions produced a government in which aristocratic landowners wielded immense political and economic power but seldom tried to establish themselves as rulers outside formal political channels.

Furthermore, Rome had a highly effective and disciplined army and an extensive empire that required professional administrators. These, along with such massive public works projects as road and bridge building and a systematic code of laws, gave precedence to the central government over local notables. The great landowning families could not compete for ultimate power until the second century B.C., when the destruction of small farms and the overextension of the army so destabilized the Roman state that aristocrats and military upstarts could again seize the day.

Although in Rome there was greater political inequality among free men than in Athens, Roman women had greater freedom than their Athenian counterparts. There were several reasons for this. For one thing, the continued prominence of the aristocracy fostered the comparative freedom of upper-class Roman daughters and wives. In addition, the extended absence of men in prolonged service in foreign campaigns gave Roman wives in property-holding families a chance to manage their own affairs for years at a time, amassing their own wealth and even gaining political influence.[7]

In Rome, as in all states of the ancient world, marriage and inheritance were the main methods of conveying and administering private property. As in Greece and other agricultural societies, where childlessness was reason enough for a man to divorce his wife, the Romans believed that a central purpose of marriage was to produce legitimate children. For upper-class Romans, marriage determined which children would inherit the family property and name. It also created close links between families and occasionally between men who successively married the same woman.[8]

Today too, many people believe that procreation should be the main purpose of marriage. But they would be shocked by the Roman version of this idea. Romans believed that children were brought into the world for the sake of the family and were allowed to live only with the father's permission. When the Romans talked about "raising" a child, for example, they meant something different from us. Traditionally a Roman father picked up a newborn to signal his consent that the child live as a member of the family. If he did not, the child was left to die of exposure or to be adopted by someone else.

A letter that one husband sent his pregnant wife in Roman-ruled Egypt illustrates the prevailing consensus that it was fine to let inconvenient children die. After offering his "heartiest greetings" to his family and telling his wife not to worry if he came home from Alexandria later than those he was traveling with, the husband writes: "I beg and beseech you to take care of the little child, and as soon as we receive wages I will send them to you. If—good luck to you!—you bear offspring, if it is a male, let it live; if it is a female, expose it." Right after this casual sentence of death, he adds that a mutual friend had passed on his wife's message to remember her on his journeys, and he fondly responds: "How can I forget you? I beg you not to worry."[9]

Rome was, at least in its early history, a patriarchal society in the literal sense. Power lay with the oldest male in the household. Sons as well as daughters remained under their father's power until he died. So did *their* sons and daughters. A man gained the rights of a father only after his own father died. The word *familia* encompassed everyone under the patriarch's authority or attached to his household. It even included slaves and freedmen who bore the family names of their former owner.[10]

This patriarchal definition of the family had the curious effect of excluding the head of the household, the paterfamilias, from membership in the family. Men were not *in* families; they ruled *over* them. This conception, which was adopted by the Christian families of Western Europe, helps explain why for so many centuries family advice manuals were addressed to wives rather than husbands. Husbands, it was long thought, didn't need to know how to behave in families. They simply needed to know how to make their families behave.

Despite these strict patriarchal principles, the Romans were casual about what made for a legal marriage. There were a few rules. Roman citizens had to get special permission to marry foreigners or Latins (those living in territories around Rome but not incorporated under its rule), and they could not marry slaves or prostitutes. At one point senators were prohibited from marrying women of low social origins. In addition, a union entered into without the consent of an individual's father was not valid.

Aside from these rules, the Roman state did not get involved in ratifying marriage or divorce. No special formality was needed to legalize marriage between partners who were not prohibited from marrying. There was no wedding license, and the modern distinction between cohabitation and marriage was unknown.

Rome did recognize a distinction between marriage and concubinage, in which a man kept a female slave or freed woman as a mistress. It also recognized a difference between marriage and cohabitation with a woman close in social rank. The difference, however, was entirely a question of intent. Roman jurists believed marriage was defined by a "marital attitude" on the part of the couple. The educator Quintilian (A.D. 35–95) summed up the traditional legal principle: "There is no obstacle to a marriage being valid by reason of the will of those who come together, even though a contract has not been ratified." Conversely, he noted, "it is useless to seal a contract if it turns out that the will to marriage did not exist."[11]

Divorce was also based on people's subjective intentions. A simple statement of intent to divorce was so commonly taken as immediately ending a marriage that a legal commentator from the third century A.D. warned: "It is not a true or actual divorce unless the purpose is to establish a perpetual separation. . . . [H]ence where repudiation takes place in the heat of anger and the wife returns in a short time, she is not held to have been divorced."[12] That this point had to be made explicit shows how readily the community accepted self-divorce.

There is some evidence that originally only men had the right to divorce, as was the case in many ancient states of the Middle East, but by the late republic, divorce in Rome could be initiated by either partner, who would then formally notify the other. In the reign of Augustus, the founder of the Roman Empire (27 B.C. to A.D. 14), the rules on unilateral divorce were tightened to require seven witnesses. But not until four centuries later (A.D. 449) did the law require a formal statement of repudiation beyond simple notification by the departing spouse.

We don't know how prevalent divorce was in other layers of Roman society, but in the upper levels it was common. At the end of the first century B.C., an upper-class Roman lamented in the funeral speech he composed for his wife: "Marriages as long as ours are rare, ended by death, not broken by divorce. For we were fortunate enough to be together for forty years without quarrel."[13]

The Christian emperors of the later empire attempted, without much success, to limit unilateral divorce. Even they, unlike later Christian authorities, said wife beating was a valid reason for a wife to repudiate her husband. The casual attitude toward divorce throughout most of Roman history is reflected in the story Plutarch tells about a Roman whose friend reproached him for divorcing a wife who was fertile, discreet, industrious, and faithful. The man's response, which Plutarch quoted approvingly, was that a sandal might look beautiful to an observer, but that only the wearer could tell if it pinched.[14]

If a divorce was the wife's fault, especially if she had engaged in sexual misconduct, the husband could retain part of her dowry as a penalty. Since children remained under the control of their father after a divorce, he could also keep a portion of the original dowry for child support. But the Romans also had no-fault divorce. In addition, they anticipated but rejected arrangements similar to the covenant marriages that have been adopted in several contemporary American states, in which spouses vow in advance never to exercise the no-fault divorce option. In A.D. 223, the emperor Alexander Severus decreed: "It was decided of old that marriages should be free. Hence it is settled that an agreement not to divorce is not valid and neither is a promise to pay a penalty on divorce."[15]

More than three centuries after Severus's ruling, the Christian emperor Justinian tried to make the validity of marriage dependent on state approval, requiring a special license. Justinian ruled that customary law, which said that intent was the only thing needed to make a marriage legal, should apply only to people with little wealth to pass on to their heirs. The custom was so deep-rooted, however, that Justinian later relaxed the decree. He also reinstituted the older rule that if a man had been married by intent alone and had had children and then contracted a formal marriage with another woman and produced more children, the children of the first marriage had equal inheritance rights with the children of the second.[16]

In early Rome, as in Athens, control over a woman passed from her father to her husband upon marriage. The man gained control of all possessions his wife brought with her, but she in turn gained full rights in his kin group as though she were a blood relative. Most marriages in early Rome placed a woman under the "hand"—*manus*—of her husband. But another sort of marriage—without, or *sin, manus*—wherein the woman remained under her father's control after marriage, was also possible. Marriage *sin manus* did not necessarily mean that a woman had more freedom, since her father could intervene to assert his will. But paternal supervision tended to be looser, and a father was likely to die earlier than a husband, meaning that many women gained legal autonomy in the middle years of their marriage.

The spread of marriage *sin manus* probably had more to do with family interests than with women's needs. Some scholars suggest that an offer of marriage *sin manus* allowed a father to give a smaller dowry, because the receiving family did not have to make the bride a coheir to their property. In addition, for wealthy aristocratic families, a daughter's marriage *sin manus* meant the husband's family would not get the daughter's inheritance because a woman's father or brother would inherit her property if she died intestate.[17]

As early as 230 B.C., dowries given to husbands had replaced bridewealth paid to the brides' families as the prevailing financial arrangement in Roman weddings. For the life of the marriage the husband controlled the dowry, but he had to return it in the event of divorce, unless the woman had been blatantly promiscuous. As a result, when an upper-class Roman couple separated, it was often the husband who suffered the greater financial loss.[18]

Men in the upper classes usually married in their late twenties or early thirties, while women generally married in their teens. Despite the big age difference in most married couples and the strong patriarchal bent of Roman families, Roman men tended to be more companionable with their wives and more affectionate with their daughters than Greek men were. Many loving letters between Roman husbands and wives have survived to this day, and the custom of husbands and wives socializing together was widespread. Cornelius Nepos, a historian of the first century B.C., described to his Roman audience how different the customs were in Greece: "They consider that many of the customs we think are appropriate are in bad taste. No Roman would hesitate to take his wife to a dinner party, or to allow the mother of his family to occupy the first rooms in his house and to walk about in public. The custom in Greece is completely different. A woman cannot appear at a party unless it is among her relatives; she can only sit in the interior of the house, which is called the women's quarters (*gynaeceum*); this no male can enter unless he is a close relation."[19]

Still, the emphasis on marital harmony and love in Rome was nothing like the mutuality that most modern people expect in marriage. The sexual double standard was so completely accepted by Romans that the educator Quintilian used the notion of a sexual single standard as the perfect illustration of an illogical proposition: "If a relationship between a mistress and a male slave is disgraceful, then one between a master and a female slave is disgraceful." This statement sounds reasonable to contemporary ears, along the line of what's sauce for the goose is also sauce for the gander. But to Quintilian the parallel was ridiculous, and he had no doubt his audience would agree. To suggest that men should be bound by the same moral conventions as women, he argued, was as illogical as to conclude that human morality should be the same as animal morality.[20]

The Roman Republic bequeathed to the West a system of civil laws, public works, and bureaucratic administrative principles that eventually provided an alternative to the personal rule of royal dynasties. But in its own later years the republic experienced a resurgence of personal intrigue and violent fights over political power. Four years after defeating Mark Antony and Cleopatra at the Battle of Actium in 31 B.C., Octavian transformed the republic into an empire and ruled as the Emperor Augustus, "the revered one." During the Empire, marital maneuvering and dynastic politics again dominated the process of succession to power.

Octavian's own first marriage was politically inspired and lasted just two years. He divorced his first wife, who had just given birth to their daughter, Julia, in order to marry Livia, who was married to someone else at the time and was pregnant with her husband's child. Her husband, Claudius Nero, a sophisticated and self-interested Roman, agreed to the divorce and even attended the wedding banquet.[21]

Both men gained from this marital reshuffling. Claudius Nero was a member of a powerful aristocratic family but had been a supporter of Mark Antony against Octavian/Augustus, and needed to get back into the new emperor's good graces. For Augustus, Livia's family ties were more useful than those of his first wife, and Livia brought with her the children of her previous marriage, establishing strong bonds of interest between Augustus and the kin of Claudius Nero, who were delighted that their grandchildren had become potential heirs to the throne.

When the marriage between Livia and Augustus produced no children, these hopes paid off. Augustus appointed Livia's son Tiberius as his successor, then ordered Tiberius to divorce *his* pregnant wife and marry the emperor's daughter Julia. Unlike his biological father, Tiberius complied reluctantly. The historian Suetonius reported that Tiberius pined for his former wife even after he had regretfully divorced her. "The only time he chanced to see her, he followed her with such an intent and tearful gaze that care was taken that she should never again come before his eyes."[22] Despite his heartache, Tiberius did what was required to succeed Augustus as emperor.

Having gone to great lengths to rearrange his family connections to his personal satisfaction, Augustus became a fervent public supporter of family stability and female virtue. Like many contemporary boosters of the sanctity of marriage, he did not let his own divorce and many sexual liaisons inhibit him from trying to impose marital virtue and "family values" on others. In fact, Augustus embarked upon one of the earliest promarriage campaigns in the historical record.

The family values campaign Augustus launched was in part an effort to boost the birthrate. The emperor decreed that Romans were expected to be married by a certain age, and if they were not or if they failed to remarry after divorce or bereavement, they were penalized. An unmarried person could not receive an inheritance or legacy from anyone other than a close relative. Individuals who were married but childless had to forfeit half of any such bequests. Applicants for political office received preference if they were married and a higher preference if they had children.[23]

Augustus also decreed that a freeborn woman with three children was exempted from the law that kept a woman under the lifelong guardianship of her husband or father. A freed female slave who was still under the guardianship of her former owner could escape that control once she bore four children.

Despite his pro-marriage program, Augustus did not try to restrict divorce. In fact, divorce was made compulsory if a woman committed adultery, which became a criminal offense punishable by banishment. Once adultery became an offense to be punished by the state rather than by the woman's husband and her male relatives, a husband could no longer turn a blind eye to his wife's behavior if he was so inclined. A husband who did not divorce an adulterous wife could be charged with pandering. If a husband divorced an adulterous wife but did not prosecute her within sixty days, an outsider could pursue the case. A woman convicted of adultery lost half her dowry and a third of any other property she owned and was banished to an island and forbidden to marry again.[24]

Emperor Augustus's profamily legislation was accompanied by a wave of manufactured nostalgia for the supposed virtues of earlier times, when women were not allowed to drink wine and, according to the satirist Juvenal, wives were too tired from working at their looms to engage in adultery.

The pro-family legal measures and propaganda campaigns had little impact on Roman morality and behavior. Laws promoting the birthrate did encourage young men interested in senate positions to marry and have children a bit earlier, to take advantage of the seniority this conferred. But contemporaries complained that most wives still limited the number of children they bore, whether through crude forms of birth control or by abandoning infants. The morality laws also had unintended consequences. Stiff penalties imposed on upper-class women for violating sexual edicts encouraged some of them to register as prostitutes in order to escape the punishment meted out to respectable matrons for having affairs![25]

But the rhetoric of family values remained a central theme under Augustus, and he put forward his own wife Livia and his sister Octavia (who, you will recall, had been married to Mark Antony) as paragons of female virtue. Their likenesses were placed on coins, and their statues displayed in temples and public buildings. Octavia was especially popular, pitied as a deserted wife and widely admired for her willingness to raise Antony's children by his first wife and by Cleopatra. That the family values emperor had murdered Antony's oldest son by his first wife and Caesar's son by Cleopatra went unmentioned.

Julia, the emperor's daughter by his first wife, however, posed a serious public relations problem. One reason Tiberius had been loath to leave his wife for Julia was that she already had a scandalous reputation from her previous marriage. Tradition says that when she was asked why all five of her children resembled her husband, despite her many extramarital affairs, Julia merrily replied, "I never take on a passenger until the cargo-hold is full."[26]

Julia's marriage to Tiberius did not interfere with her infidelities, which became so blatant that Augustus not only agreed to the couple's separation but disciplined his daughter publicly. Seneca reports that the emperor wrote to the senate in 2 B.C. "Adulterers were admitted to [Julia's] house in flocks; the whole state was overrun by her nocturnal debaucheries."[27]

Augustus exiled four young aristocrats who had been Julia's lovers, ordered a fifth to commit suicide, and banished Julia to an island, where she was ordered to avoid both men and wine. Six years later he exiled his granddaughter for the same offense.

The empire established by Augustus enjoyed almost two centuries of stability. But by the third century overextension of the army, agricultural problems, urban decline, barbarian invasions, and increasing social unrest had led to a collapse of orderly political succession. Military leaders usurped the throne and in turn were displaced by other leaders with stronger armies or more mercenaries. Between A.D. 235 and 284 there were twenty-six emperors, only one of whom escaped violent death.

Like Athens, however, Rome left behind a model for organizing political life, military campaigns, and the administration of justice in ways that did not allow powerful aristocrats to manipulate marriage ties and personal loyalties to gain power. It introduced mechanisms for organizing military affairs, tax collection, and legal rights that didn't depend on marital alliances, blood descent, or local allegiances. In its period of decline, the Roman state came to terms with Christianity, a synthesis that evolved into the Catholic Church, which, as both an institution and an ideology, profoundly changed the history of marital politics in the West.

The Emergence of Christianity

Christianity, which began as a movement within Judaism, was one of many popular religions and mystery cults that flourished in the waning days of the Roman Republic. What distinguished early Christianity from Judaism in its approach to marriage and family was the belief that the kingdom of God was close at hand, and people must therefore break with worldly ties to prepare for the imminent arrival of God's kingdom. In subsequent centuries this aspect was played down, but early Christianity was hostile to marital and kinship obligations to a degree unimaginable to any previous reformers aside from Plato. Jesus insisted that marriage and kin ties took second place to the urgent need to prepare people for the coming kingdom of God. "If any man come to me, and hate not his father, and mother, and wife, and children, and brethren, and sisters, yea, and his own life also, he cannot be my disciple" (Luke 14:26). When a new disciple asked if he could slip away to attend his father's funeral, Jesus told him to stay and "let the dead bury their own dead" (Matthew 8:22).

Many early Christians believed that marriage undermined the rigorous self-control needed to achieve spiritual salvation. "He that is unmarried careth for the things that belong to the Lord, how he may please the Lord: But he that is married careth for the things that are of the world, how he may please his wife. . . . The unmarried woman careth for the things of the lord, that she may be holy both in body and in spirit: but she that is married careth for the things of the world, how she may please her husband" (1 Corinthians 7:32–34).

Christian attitudes toward marriage and sexuality stood in sharp contrast with those of most ancient religions. To Hindus in India, marrying was a holy act, and a celibate or unmarried person was considered impious, or at least incomplete, and was ineligible to participate in some religious ceremonies. The Old Testament and later Jewish teachings called marriage God's commandment and celebrated sexuality within marriage. The Talmud said that scholars of the Torah should marry before embarking on their studies, "for one who is not married will be possessed the day long with sexual thoughts."[28]

The founders of Christianity agreed with Jewish scholars that it was better to marry than to be preoccupied with lust. But their acceptance of marriage was much less enthusiastic. "It is better," Paul grudgingly conceded, "to marry than to burn" (1 Corinthians 7:9). Pope Gregory the Great explained early in the sixth century that although marriage was not sinful, "conjugal union cannot take place without carnal pleasure, and such pleasure cannot under any circumstances be without blame."[29]

Although Christianity was deeply ambivalent about marriage, it also had a stringent prohibition against divorce. Jesus declared that Moses's acceptance of divorce, which was integrated into Jewish marriage laws, had been a concession to people's weakness and stubbornness. God's true intention, Jesus said, was that husband and wife should become one flesh. "What therefore God hath joined together, let not man put asunder" (Mark 10:9). Unlike most other world religions, Christianity applied this injunction against divorce equally to men and women.

Early Christianity's condemnation of divorce and polygamy was unequivocal. In practice, however, during the first thousand years of its existence the Christian church was flexible about allowing divorce. For a long time it even waffled in its support for monogamy. The conflict between theory and practice added a new wrinkle to political marriage struggles as the church's power and influence grew in the waning days of the Roman Empire.

One of the great appeals of Christianity to the polyglot population of the Roman Empire was that it was a religion that did not limit its message to one ethnic group or to the supposed descendants of a mythical common ancestor. The church offered membership and brotherhood to all, and it had special appeal to the lower classes and slaves with its insistence that humility, charity, and spirituality were superior to worldly wealth and power.

In its early years Christianity faced little official opposition and spread quickly along Rome's trade routes and military roads. But as its appeal grew, some Roman rulers worried that the Christians' refusal to participate in the worship of state gods was subversive, and in the third century several emperors tried to quash the new religion through violent persecution of its adherents. In the fourth century, however, such repression receded, and in 313 the emperor Constantine issued an edict of tolerance for Christianity. Under the reign of the emperor Theodosius, Christianity became the empire's official religion, and church officials began to act as tax collectors, record keepers, and legal representatives of the state as well as spiritual leaders of the people.

Over the next two centuries the Christian church expanded its geographical reach and took on more quasi-governmental functions. Meanwhile the bishop of Rome gained authority over his fellow bishops in the provinces and came to be known as the pope (from the Latin word *papa,* or father). When the Roman Empire fragmented and collapsed, the pope headed one of the few institutions still able to raise money, administer law, preserve records, teach literacy, conduct international diplomacy, and claim overarching moral authority.

As the empire broke up, and local aristocracies struggled to control the fledgling kingdoms that emerged in its place, the church's administrative and ideological resources grew indispensable, as did the pope's sanctification of a king's authority. Would-be rulers maneuvered relentlessly to get the pope's stamp of approval, and many popes maneuvered right back.

Early Christianity had been indifferent, even hostile, to the things of this world and had elevated celibacy over marriage. But the church's evolving political role and economic power were to embroil it deeply in the politics of marriage, divorce, and family life in the new kingdoms of Western Europe.

Chapter 6

———◦◉◦———

Playing the Bishop, Capturing the Queen: Aristocratic Marriages in Early Medieval Europe

In 1981, 750 million television viewers around the world watched the fairy-tale wedding of Prince Charles, heir to the British throne, to Lady Diana Spencer. They stayed tuned over the next eighteen years as the marriage degenerated into accusations of mutual infidelity that still fascinate the public years after Diana's death.

Prince Charles had bowed to pressure from the royal family and married a much younger woman with good bloodlines, good looks, and good health. She promptly produced what the monarchy was looking for, two sons to serve as "an heir and a spare." With the continuation of his dynastic line assured, Charles returned to the arms of his longtime lover, Camilla Parker-Bowles. Princess Diana later took lovers of her own, but her husband's earlier infidelity swayed public opinion in her favor. Diana famously complained to one television interviewer that she hadn't realized at the time of her wedding that there would be three persons involved in her marriage.

For aristocrats and monarchs in the kingdoms that emerged in Western Europe after the fall of the Roman Empire, having only three people involved in their marriages would have seemed downright lonely. In medieval

Europe, dozens of people took part in the unions of the nobility, and even more were involved in the marriages of kings and queens.

The huge cast of characters in medieval marriage dramas included all the players who had been involved in political marriages of the ancient world: parents, in-laws, rival nobles, secondary wives, concubines, siblings, uncles, and children by former wives or mistresses. But in medieval Europe, bishops, archbishops, popes, and church reformers also demanded a say. When a divorce or remarriage was at stake, the conflicts among these interested parties turned even more volatile. It was not unusual for such questions to be resolved on the battlefield.

As the Roman Empire disintegrated over the fourth and fifth centuries, it split into two very different parts. The capital of the Roman Empire was moved to Constantinople in 330, and Greek-speaking dynasties took control over the area that became the center of the Byzantine Empire. Although the Byzantine emperors continued to claim sovereignty over the whole of the old Roman Empire, their sway extended only to the eastern portions. But ruling over the large and wealthy cities of Constantinople, Nicomedia, Antioch, and Alexandria, the Byzantine rulers had the financial resources to establish a strong theocratic state with an elaborate bureaucracy. With their powerful state apparatus, supported by a centralized church, the Byzantine emperors were able to dominate the military and the aristocracy and hold their ambitions in check.

In the western part of the old Roman Empire, however, Germanic warrior tribes established a patchwork of chiefdoms and petty kingdoms during the fifth and sixth centuries. In this fragmented world, where weak new kingdoms constantly formed and fell apart, marriage and kinship politics once more rose to the fore. The Germanic conquerors used marriage to establish peace treaties, forge alliances with Roman landowners in the territories they claimed, and bolster their pretensions to aristocratic status or royal authority. Kinship and marriage politics were crucial to the struggle for power in these unstable Western kingdoms in a way that was foreign to Byzantium.

In the centralized theocratic state of the Byzantine Empire, the powerful emperor didn't need to choose a wife for her family connections. In fact, Byzantine rulers often selected their wives at a "bride show" that resembled a modern beauty pageant. Prospective brides from around the empire were paraded before the emperor, who could pick any woman, of any class, who caught his fancy. In the medieval West, few kings were secure enough in their power and status to place beauty above birth and connections.[1]

Marriages of political and economic convenience certainly took place in the upper classes of the Byzantine Empire. But noble families were rarely able to use marital alliances as a springboard to political dominance. The emperor had enough power to prevent ambitious upstarts from contracting marriages that might produce a rival dynasty or concentrate too many resources in one family. When an emperor found a marriage alliance threatening, he simply broke up the match, forcing the husband or wife—or both—to enter a religious order.

In the West, kings who interfered too much in the marriages of their noble followers were likely to be murdered or deposed. The Western church was not directly allied with any one ruler, or even united in its own views, so a Western king could not count on its support for such interference.

Because the Byzantine rulers did not have to enter political marriages to consolidate their power, they didn't need to dispense patronage to noble in-laws or risk taking secondary wives who might produce rival heirs. Instead, they minimized battles over succession to the throne by appointing eunuchs, castrated former slaves, as court officials. The eunuchs, incapable of producing children of their own and bitterly resented by the aristocrats, were far more dependent on their sovereign and thus far more loyal to him than the average royal wife and her in-laws in the West.[2]

It was almost a thousand years before any Western ruler established the kind of reliable professional army, enforceable legal code, elaborate bureaucracy, or unified church apparatus that existed in Byzantium. Until then no Western ruler had anything close to a monopoly of military force, moral authority, or legal jurisdiction.

Most significant for the politics of marriage, no Western ruler had a unique claim to either spiritual authority or noble descent. When the Germanic peoples rushed into the void left by the Roman Empire's collapse, they did not have a hereditary aristocracy, although some of their warrior kings claimed descent from the gods. But those gods meant nothing to the Romans they conquered, and many of the warrior chiefs who set themselves up as petty kings in the Early Middle Ages had only dubious claims to royal blood before they took the throne. Nor could the new rulers drape themselves in the mantle of the Roman Empire; that was the provenance of Byzantium. Questions of legitimacy, succession, and government were up for grabs.[3]

In this context, family ties and marital alliances were critical to constructing a new ruling elite and fighting for supremacy within it. With no army and no state officials to keep order and administer justice, individuals again had to rely on their broader kin group for protection and support. Just as in Homer's Greece, a crime was treated as an offense against the family rather than the state and was avenged by the victim's relatives. Members of influential families routinely flouted the king's laws, persecuted anyone who tried to enforce royal edicts with which they disagreed, and violently resisted attempts to punish any of their relatives or followers.

Early medieval kings did try to bring the great families into line. Late in the ninth century in Anglo-Saxon England, Alfred the Great decreed that if a man fought on behalf of his king, he was exempt from vendettas or blood revenge. An individual could fight on behalf of a blood relative, King Alfred conceded, "if he is attacked unjustly," but no one was allowed to defend his kindred against the king or the king's representatives.[4] The Christian Church also tried to limit the private exercise of vengeance. But it was to be many centuries before kings or popes could prevent aristocrats from placing their family loyalties above the law.

With traditional kin-based family ties so strong, and the influence of the papacy and secular institutions still weak, marriage once more became central to the conduct of politics and war. The role of wives as "peace weavers" was already crucial in containing the clan rivalries that were rampant in Germanic and Viking societies.[5] But in this new environment, wives and mothers could be kingmakers as well as peace weavers and alliance builders. Conquerors routinely married the widow of an ousted king to strengthen their claims to the crown. If a conqueror died, his son and heir would reaffirm his claim by marrying his stepmother. As historian Pauline Stafford puts it, "the master plan of a sixth- or seventh-century usurper had three stages: murder the king, get the gold-hoard, marry the widow."[6]

The complex maneuvering that might accompany such a strategy is illustrated by the history of the most powerful early Germanic kingdom in Western Europe, founded by the warlord Clovis in 481. As a young local monarch Clovis hoped to increase his power by marrying Clothild, the orphaned niece of the king of Burgundy, whose lands lay south of Clovis's realm in what is now France. But when Clovis sent envoys to propose the match, Clothild's uncle rejected his suit. She, however, secretly accepted a ring from Clovis's envoy and hid it in her uncle's treasury.

The following year Clovis pressed his claim for Clothild's hand again, pointing out that she had accepted and kept his ring. In Germanic custom, and throughout the medieval period, accepting such a token created a binding obligation. Refusal to honor it could lead to war. Mastering his fury, her uncle agreed to the match.

Clothild's acceptance of the ring was probably not girlish naiveté. If she married a man of her uncle's court or kin, her dowry would remain de facto under her uncle's control. Marriage to Clovis would make her a queen. For his part, Clovis gained Clothild's dowry and could now claim kinship with the Burgundian king. But perhaps the most important service Clothild rendered her husband was to convert him to Catholic Christianity. Other Germanic rulers embraced an interpretation of Christian doctrine that denied the authority of the papacy. The pope, eager to ally with a ruler who acknowledged his supremacy, reciprocated by giving Clovis and his descendants the official support of the Roman Catholic Church.

Clovis and Clothild had four sons, each of whom they duly baptized in the Catholic faith. Following the custom of that era, the four sons divided Clovis's kingdom among themselves after their father's death. But when Clovis's son Chlodomer died in 524, his brothers Clothar and Childebert had Chlodomer's two oldest sons murdered. Fearing for his life, Chlodomer's third son became a monk, thus eliminating all of Chlodomer's heirs as contenders for power. Clothar then married Chlodomer's widow and added his brother's kingdom to his own. Despite his profession of Christian faith, Clothar neglected to divorce his earlier wife, and she continued to share his bed until he married her sister in 537. Eventually he added a fourth wife, the daughter of the King of Thuringia, whom he had captured in war.

Clothar was not alone in practicing polygamy in the early Middle Ages. Being able to have several wives allowed kings to make wider alliances. Having multiple wives, whether at the same time or serially, also made it more likely that a king would have a male heir who survived to adulthood. The high death rates of young men forced fathers to lay in reserves of heirs. (The mortality rate from hunting accidents was remarkably high, ranking with war and murder as an occupational hazard of noble blood.) Having only "an heir and a spare" was far too risky. Lack of an heir not only meant the dynasty would end on the ruler's death but also made him an inviting target for assassination by those impatient to hasten the process of regime change. Kings needed to produce plenty of sons.

Despite the advantages of multiple marriages, they left Western European kingdoms vulnerable to the kind of instability and bloodshed we saw in the Hellenistic dynasties of Asia Minor. Wives, in-laws, and rival heirs from different mothers schemed to further their own ends. Having too many heirs to the throne could be as much of a problem as having too few. If all the heirs survived, the stage was set for struggles over how to divide the realm.[7]

Even remarriage after the death of a wife was a gamble. On the one hand, a king whose wife died after producing only one or two sons needed to produce a backup set of heirs. But if one of both sets lived, trouble often ensued. In 964, the Anglo-Saxon king Edgar lost his wife. His two sons were still young, so Edgar took a new wife and had two more sons with her. But Edgar's eldest son and heir, Edward, was still alive when the king died, and so was one of Edgar's sons with his second wife.

Upon the monarch's death, supporters of the two half brothers, both still under age, battled over the throne. Edward's faction won, and he was crowned king in 975. Four years later, when he arrived in Dorset to visit his half brother, Aethelred, his stepmother came out to greet him with a welcoming cup. As Edward drank, her servant thrust a dagger between his ribs. The young Aethelred was horrified at his half brother's murder. His unrestrained grief reportedly led his mother to beat him severely with a candleholder, a punishment that was said to have left the boy with a lifelong fear of candles. But Aethelred fulfilled his mother's ambition and succeeded his half brother on the throne.[8]

One way to reduce these bloody conflicts over succession was to make it harder for kings to take more than one wife, or to swap one wife easily for another, and to encourage kings to remain piously unmarried after they were widowed. Some rulers and reformers saw a solution in Christianity's matrimonial principles, which prohibited polygamy and sharply limited divorce and remarriage. But a king would agree to such restrictions only if everyone bowed to them at once, and it was centuries before this happened. In the meantime, however, many rulers grasped the benefit of imposing such church precepts on their rivals, giving the traditional intrigues over political marriages and divorces a distinctive shape in the West.

Charlemagne's Matrimonial and Religious Alliances

One of the earliest kings to throw his weight behind Christian principles of marriage was Charlemagne, whose family, later known as the Carolingians, had usurped the royal dynasty founded by Clovis and Clothild in the eighth century.

Charlemagne initially tried to establish his dynastic claims through traditional marriage alliances, and he certainly didn't exhibit excessive Christian piety in either his sexual or marital behavior. He already had a son by a concubine when he married a Lombard princess in 770, and he went ahead with that marriage over the strenuous objections of Pope Stephen, who feared any strengthening of Lombard power. A year later Charlemagne repudiated this princess and married the daughter of another powerful family, who provided him with allies in his brother's share of the kingdom. When this wife died in 783, Charlemagne promptly married the daughter of an ally in his wars against the Saxons. Since he had only three surviving sons from his first marriage, all still young, Charlemagne hoped for more potential heirs, but his new wife bore him only daughters. By the time of her death in 794, however, the three sons were still alive and old enough to make the succession seem secure. For the time being, Charlemagne felt no need to marry again.[9]

Meanwhile, the papacy was enmeshed in conflict with the Byzantine Empire and increasingly threatened by Lombard incursions in Italy. The pope was looking for a strong secular ally, and Charlemagne, whose marital maneuvering had already accomplished its ends, now turned his attention to establishing a religious rather than a matrimonial alliance. He offered the pope his military support and agreed to enforce Church rules on marriage. In 789 he decreed that divorced men and women could not remarry, even if one spouse had been the innocent victim of the other's adultery. Then, in 799, just before the pope arrived at his court for a state visit, he married the lover he had been living with for the past five years. In return for his military and spiritual cooperation, the pope crowned Charlemagne Holy Roman Emperor on Christmas Day 800.

For a supposedly devout Christian convert, Charlemagne showed remarkable tolerance for nonmarital sexuality. His new wife died only a year after his coronation, and Charlemagne never remarried. But he had four concubines in the ensuing fourteen years before his death and fathered several children by them. He also allowed his daughters to live unmarried at his court and conduct numerous love affairs, many of which produced illegitimate children. Was this because, as chroniclers of the day surmised, he loved his girls too much to allow them to marry and leave his side? Or was it because he didn't want to be saddled with any interfering in-laws and legitimate grandsons who might challenge his only surviving legitimate son and designated successor, Louis?

After Charlemagne, other rulers began to see the logic of allowing the Church to mediate inheritance struggles and consecrate legitimate rulers. For kings and queens, the Church's insistence on monogamy and disapproval of divorce, despite its occasional inconveniences, could have the salutary effect of imposing the matrimonial equivalent of an arms limitation agreement.[10]

But the way in which the Church developed and implemented its rules about marriage and divorce was itself a chaotic process. Aristocratic families and dynasties pressed for church endorsement of their own matrimonial arrangements and rearrangements and sought condemnation of the practices of their rivals. Feuding husbands and wives tried to enlist the church on their side in marital disputes. Competing church factions often threw their support behind different noble families and waged vicious battles within the Church over whether to validate a particular marriage or divorce.

The complicated role of the Catholic Church in mediating marriage disputes and brokering political alliances is clearly illustrated in the seven-year battle over the proposed divorce and remarriage of Lothar II. This ninth-century marriage struggle generated every bit as much prurient interest as the marriage of Prince Charles and Princess Diana in the twentieth century but had far more significant repercussions.

The Marriage Scandal of the Millennium

Today, when the marriage of a movie star or monarch unravels in public or feuding spouses detail their grievances on daytime television, people often lament the deterioration of standards of decency and hearken back to a time when couples didn't air their dirty linen in public. If such a tradition ever existed, it certainly didn't stretch back to the Middle Ages. The salacious details of marital disputes were everyday fare. And the main source of information, the medieval equivalent of today's tabloids, was the church. Like modern gossip columnists, church officials tracked down the participants in marital disputes, hounded them for details of their sex lives, and became partisan advocates for one party or another.

Nowhere was this illustrated more dramatically than in the marital crisis of King Lothar II. Lothar ruled over a fertile district encompassing much of what is now Lorraine. He had a son by his long-term consort Waldreda, a local noblewoman to whom he was very attached. But Lothar's uncles, Charles the Bald and Louis II, coveted his holdings, and he needed an ally to help him defend his southern flank if it came to war. So Lothar put Waldreda aside and married Theutberga, whose brother controlled many lands and abbeys to the south of Lothar's kingdom.[11]

After two years Theutberga was still not pregnant and her brother had yet to provide any significant aid. Fearing that if he had no legitimate heir, his uncles would attack, Lothar decided to repudiate his marriage to Theutberga, formally marry Waldreda, and make their son, Hugh, his heir.

Germanic kings had been doing this sort of thing for more than two centuries. But the Church had recently stepped up its opposition to divorce, and Lothar knew that his uncles would use Charlemagne's earlier ruling against remarriage to try to deny his son's inheritance rights. Charles the Bald was already aligning himself with Theutberga's clan; he soon married her niece. Together, these families might have the power to thwart Lothar's repudiation of Theutberga and overturn his marriage to Waldreda.

Lothar needed especially compelling grounds for the divorce if the Church was to sanction his marriage to Waldreda and legitimize his heir. Although adultery was still cause for divorce and several popes had declared that the innocent party in such cases could remarry, the current pope had more restrictive ideas. So Lothar upped the ante, accusing his wife of incestuous adultery with her brother.

Theutberga offered to prove her innocence by submitting to the ordeal of boiling water. In this method of determining guilt or innocence, boiling water was poured on the limbs of the accused—or a stand-in "champion"—and the wounds were bandaged. If the wounds were infected when they were unwrapped three days later, the accused party was judged guilty. Theutberga's champion—one has to wonder if he was a volunteer—passed the three days without infection, so she was declared innocent.

Ignoring the verdict, Lothar locked up his wife until she agreed to confess. But the bishops who heard her confession were divided about whether to allow Lothar to remarry. The opposition hardened when Archbishop Hincmar, one of the region's most respected theologians, presented a learned treatise on why Lothar's remarriage should be disallowed.

Hincmar was hardly a disinterested spectator. He was the personal chaplain of Lothar's uncle Charles the Bald. Moreover, Hincmar's marital principles were quite elastic when his patron's family interests were at stake. He didn't object when Charles the Bald's daughter married her stepson, in defiance of Church rulings on incest, and he protested only mildly when Charles forced his own son to leave a legal marriage and take a new wife. In Lothar's case, however, Hincmar wrote a forceful argument on the indissolubility of marriage, and it carried the day.

But the drama was not over. Lothar appealed to the archbishops of Cologne and Trier, who were sympathetic to him and his allies. The Archbishop of Cologne hoped his own niece might marry Lothar once he won his divorce. In 862 a synod at Aix, led by these archbishops, was convened to resolve the dispute. Lothar emotionally described the enormity of his queen's betrayal and shamefacedly confessed that he did not think he could refrain from seeking sinful sexual gratification if he were not allowed to wed again. The prelates, moved to tears by his suffering according to the chronicles, annulled the marriage and gave Lothar permission to remarry.

To the dismay of the Archbishop of Cologne, Lothar promptly married Waldreda and crowned her queen. But Theutberga's brother protested to the pope, who revoked the annulment, ordering Lothar to return Theutberga to his bed.

At first Lothar ignored the pope's orders. But in 865, when Charles and Louis threatened to enforce the pope's decision, removing him from power if necessary, Lothar took Theutberga back, nine years after he'd first married her and seven years after he had begun trying to divorce her. Still, Theutberga remained childless, and a year later Lothar bullied her into requesting a divorce. The pope ruled that she could leave her husband and become a nun, but that childlessness was not sufficient cause for divorce and Lothar could not remarry.

Lothar had gambled and lost. Without the right to remarry, his separation from Theutberga brought him no political gain. In 868, his consort, Waldreda, wrote to the pope, expressing her contrition and her desire to enter a nunnery. Lothar himself traveled to Rome the following year to receive forgiveness and died on the way home. Upon Lothar's death, his uncle Charles the Bald promptly invaded his kingdom, which he then divided up with Louis.

Lothar's struggle was an important turning point in the matrimonial politics of the Middle Ages. It demonstrated the potentially ruinous bind facing a king whose legal wife did not produce an heir and who did not have the cooperation of the church in seeking to remarry. Aristocrats and kings continued to defy the Church when they felt it necessary, but they increasingly tried to sidestep such confrontations by acquiescing to the principle of indissoluble marriage and leading their lives in a way that provided them with more acceptable excuses when they really couldn't avoid seeking a divorce. Kings who had fertile wives and good enough political alliances with their in-laws tried to avoid repudiating one wife for another. If they had heirs, they often resisted tempting offers to remarry even after a wife's death.

Monogamous marriage did not mean monogamous sexuality. One of the advantages of monogamous marriage, in fact, was that it provided a way for a royal to have his cake and eat it too. A king could continue to father sons, who could be useful to him in military campaigns and could call for assistance from their mothers' families, but who were excluded from any chance of inheriting because they were not the offspring of a legitimate marriage. If all the legitimate children died, an illegitimate son might be designated as heir. But once church and state made common ground on the principles of legitimacy, this was very rare, and the position of a bastard could never be fully secure. Legitimate brothers were all too likely to go to war over an inheritance. Bastards had to hitch their fortunes to the king and his designated heir, and many kings produced them with abandon.

Watered-down blood frequently proved thicker than full blood, and illegitimate sons were often the most loyal defenders of a regime's integrity. Henry I of England (1068–1135), himself a youngest son who had stolen the throne from his older brothers, was a king who manipulated the marital and nonmarital production of children with what one historian calls "consummate ability." He sired "twenty-one noble bastards on whom he and his successor might rely, while limiting his legitimate family to two boys and a girl."[12]

A king whose wife did not produce a legitimate heir, however, could not rely on such creative adaptations of Christian marital doctrine. He needed a way to circumvent restrictions on divorce and remarriage in order to try again with another woman. Rulers facing this dilemma often found an escape hatch in a peculiarity of medieval Church marriage doctrine, an extremely broad definition of incest.

The Peculiar History of Incest Laws

The Roman Catholic Church's definition of incest is one of the most intriguing features of medieval marriage. Neither the Old nor New Testament provided any basis for it. But in the mid-sixth century, church synods began to denounce as incestuous the Old Testament practice of marrying a brother's widow. Also, during the sixth and seventh centuries bishops began condemning marriage to first and second cousins, stepmothers or stepdaughters, and the widows of uncles. In 721, Pope Gregory II even forbade marriage with the godmother of one's child or with the mother of one's godchild.[13]

A few decades later marriage was forbidden up to the seventh degree of separation, or "as far as memory could go back." This made it illegal to marry a descendant of one's great-great-great-great-great-grandfather! By the end of the eighth century it was incestuous to marry in-laws, the kin of godparents or godchildren, or a relative of someone you had once had sexual intercourse with. It was also forbidden to marry a relative of someone you had previously promised but failed to marry. These prohibitions were so broad that almost any match could be ruled invalid. One historian notes that, at least in theory, the incest rules prohibited young village men from wedding "all the marriageable girls they could possibly know and a great many more besides."[14]

Whatever the reasons for their breadth, these incest prohibitions became very useful weapons in the power struggles of the age. If enforced consistently, these rules would have prevented kings and nobles from using marriages with kin—even very distant kin—to consolidate wealth and social status. But in the medieval period the Church still enforced most of its principles on marriage erratically and arbitrarily. It spent little time investigating the marriages of common folk, although it readily sold dispensations when a conscientious commoner asked for a formal exemption from the rules that most people simply ignored. Even in a royal or aristocratic marriage, the Church seldom inquired into the degree of familial connection unless it was engaged in a power struggle with one of the families involved or was asked to intervene.

The Church also routinely granted exemptions for the sake of political or economic advantage. In 1200, when rivals complained that the projected marriage between Otto IV of Germany and the daughter of the Duke of Brabant should be forbidden because the two were too closely related, the pope assured the duke that the Church would allow the match despite its technical violation of incest rules. "Because of the great usefulness which we hope will be procured from this marriage," the pope declared, the duke could give his daughter in marriage with his conscience "not only cleansed but cheered."[15]

Still, there was no guarantee of a dispensation if a proposed match was challenged, so aristocrats had to take the Church's definition of incest into account when planning a marriage. Although the prohibitions against incestuous marriage could usually be circumvented, a marriage that fell within the prohibited degrees of relatedness was always vulnerable to attack from enemies who hoped to illegitimize an heir or destabilize an alliance. Nobles began to avoid such marriages whenever possible and ended up creating a more far-flung set of cooperating lineages and a more inclusive noble class than in many other regions of the world.[16]

The incentive to avoid marriage within one's own family group was one of the distinctive features of the Western European upper classes. But we should not exaggerate how much influence the church's incest rules had on how aristocrats and royalty organized their marriages. Marrying a relative could be a valuable political and economic stratagem, and families often violated incest rules when it was expedient.

Allegations of incest could cut both ways for church officials and noble families. On the one hand, the oft-ignored rules could be invoked by a king or noble who enlisted a sympathetic Church official to block a rival's projected marriage. At the beginning of the twelfth century, Henry I of England, who manipulated his production of legitimate and illegitimate children so successfully, was able to torpedo an engagement between his nephew and a daughter of the House of Anjou by spreading the word that the two were cousins.

On the other hand, because the rules were so routinely ignored at the time of marriage, they could later be used to invalidate an existing marriage. A claim of incest provided an escape clause from the Church's strictures against divorce. A married couple, or one of the pair, who desired a divorce might suddenly discover that the marriage had been incestuous all along. In the late eleventh century the Count of Anjou was able to repudiate five of his own marriages by dint of diligent genealogical research. In 1152 the divorce of King Louis VII of France and Eleanor of Aquitaine was approved when the couple pointed out that they were related within four or five degrees. The excuse served, even though this had been common knowledge at the time of their wedding and Louis's next wife, Constance of Castile, was even more closely related to him than Eleanor had been. As one historian notes, the church's "abhorrence of incest provided a gap in the laws of monogamy through which a king . . . could drive a coach and horses."[17]

In 1215 the Fourth Lateran Council narrowed the definition of incest to four degrees of separation. The council's stated aim was to enforce the modified ban more stringently. But popes continued to grant dispensations for political or financial gain. Under the papacy of Boniface IV (1389–1404), marital dispensations were openly available for sale, with a sliding fee scale based on the value of the concession being sought.[18]

So for all their formal acceptance of church doctrine, kings and nobles continued to expect the Church to accommodate their marital strategies if the stakes were high enough. And one reason that the stakes were so often so high was that in the Western kingdoms, unlike Byzantium or Islam, women played an exceptionally important role in establishing claims to noble or royal blood.[19]

The Importance of a Highborn Wife

As we have seen, the insecurity of dynastic claims in early medieval Europe gave women a large role in conferring status and wealth in their own right. The ideal noble was like Sir Galahad of King Arthur's Round Table, "descended on both sides from kings and queens."[20] The commonly held belief that a couple actually mixed their blood during sexual intercourse gave women a critical role in the hereditary transmission of nobility.

A man with ambitions to rule needed a wife or mother with an exalted bloodline of her own. Even after Charlemagne's descendants had been in power for two centuries—long enough, one would think, to establish a dynastic claim through the male line—Hugh Capet refused to swear allegiance to Charles of Lorraine, the latest in the line, because he had married a wife from the lesser nobility. Hugh said he would not bend his knee to a queen who was the daughter of one of his own vassals.[21]

Marriage alliances had defensive as well as offensive purposes. Because no medieval European kingdom was powerful enough to dominate surrounding regions by force, a ruler might, if his rival married the daughter of a powerful neighbor, rush to marry her sister, in order to neutralize the benefits of the first man's marriage. In the tenth century, the rival Capetian and Carolingian dynasties engaged in just such a matrimonial arms race. When the Capetian ruler Hugh the Great married a daughter of the Anglo-Saxon king Edward the Elder, the Carolingian monarch Charles the Simple married another of Edward's daughters. Another Capetian ruler's betrothal to a woman from a powerful family in Aquitaine spurred his Carolingian rival to also marry his son off to a prominent Aquitainean.[22]

A woman in medieval Europe could inherit and transmit property as well as bloodlines, and her property could not be stripped from her and taken over by her husband or his kin. When Eleanor of Aquitaine married King Louis VII of France, her dowry doubled the size of his kingdom. When she left him, she took her territory with her. When Agnes, daughter of Count Baldwin IV of Hainault, married Raoul I of Coucy in 1160, her dowry included the right to collect the annual tax revenues from some of her father's holdings. This not only gave her leverage in her marriage but made her husband eager to defend and preserve the count's realm.[23]

A woman whose parents married her off was much more likely to have to leave her own relatives and live with her husband's family than a man in the same position. While this could put her at a disadvantage, it did not necessarily render her helpless. Many a queen or countess built up an extensive personal power base at her husband's court. With her own favored group of courtiers, attendants, and clients at hand, and jealous brothers or fathers watching from afar, her husband had to think twice about thwarting her will, so long as she produced the required heirs.

An Anglo-Saxon poem described the ideal queen as one who "shall prosper beloved among her people, shall be cheerful, shall keep a secret, shall be generous with horses and treasures." Inasmuch as these were the very traits that cemented power relations in the personalized politics of early medieval kingdoms, the royal wife was practically an officer of the state. She typically handed out the yearly gifts to knights and high officials, the closest thing to a salary they received. Frequently she also controlled the access of courtiers and favor seekers to the king. It is not surprising that courtiers wrote flattering poems to queens and countesses or that minstrels sang their praises. Most great ladies had what amounted to their own in-house public relations apparatus, producing a constant stream of songs and poetry in their honor. An intelligent and well-connected wife could be the power not only behind but alongside the throne.[24]

Queens and ladies could also use the marriages of their children, other relatives, and retainers to build far-flung networks for themselves and their families. In the thirteenth century, Beatrice of Savoy arranged the marriage of her four daughters so skillfully that the duchy of Savoy gained an alliance with the kings of England, France, and Naples. Eleanor of Castile, who married King Edward I of England in 1254, built up a personal power base in her new land by arranging nearly two dozen marriages for various godchildren, cousins, courtiers, and ladies-in-waiting. Knights who married her women were granted lands from her dower holdings and got special favors through her influence. The children of these unions were raised with Eleanor's own children, creating intergenerational networks of loyalty for the queen.[25]

A well-connected woman could also make things very sticky for her husband if she chose to leave him. In tenth-century Ireland, where Christian strictures were especially slow to take hold, one princess became the wife of four different provincial kings in succession. Each time she and her family were offered better terms, she took her wealth and her powerful kin connections to a new consort.[26]

An intractable wife might also simply abandon her husband, derailing his family's plans. In the late tenth century a Carolingian king of northern France sent his son, in his early teens, to marry the widow of a powerful count. The widow was doubly valuable because her brother was also an Angevin lord who would make a useful ally against the king's Capetian rivals. But the widow was twice the boy's age and not much inclined to play the blushing, obedient bride. After two years of mutual antipathy, she walked out on her young husband, leaving him penniless and powerless in what was essentially foreign territory. His father had to rescue him and bring him home.[27]

Other couples gritted their teeth and stuck it out. In the twelfth century Count Philip of Flanders married an heiress to extensive and valuable lands. When he caught her in adultery, he had her lover brutally murdered, but he did not divorce her. Holding on to her inheritance was more important to him than avenging the insult to his honor. The prospect of losing an heiress could make even the proudest husband put up with adultery.[28]

It became rarer for a woman to be an heiress after the eleventh and twelfth centuries, when many aristocratic families began to protect their properties from dilution by restricting inheritance to the eldest son, a practice called primogeniture. Where primogeniture took root, the right of women to inherit and dispose of property decreased, and with it, much of their centrality to marriage alliances.[29]

But restrictions on women's right to inherit property and transmit royal status developed unevenly. Male heirship may have been the ideal, but few kings were willing to pass the crown on to a nephew or cousin instead of a daughter if they didn't have a son. Even the Capetian monarchs in France, who had the demographic good luck to hand their kingdom down through consistent male descent for more than three hundred years, did not prohibit women's succession until 1328. Elsewhere, shifting political fortunes, along with high death rates for men, meant that women remained important in the politics of succession and alliance until the late Middle Ages. Primogeniture may have created fewer heiresses, but by concentrating wealth in a single heir, it created richer ones.[30]

Another long-term limitation on the independence and status of highborn women was the growing power of the Catholic Church. In the eleventh century the Church stepped up its campaign to prevent noble families from marrying their daughters to high church officials or installing them as heads of great monasteries and abbeys. Yet royal and noble women found new ways to protect themselves. Wealthy wives judiciously used religious donations to build their own networks of patronage and influence in the Church. Some even provided themselves insurance for their future retirement from marriage by founding religious houses on their ancestral lands. They would send their children to be educated there and would take up residence after their husbands died or their marriages fell apart. A wife whose religious allies allowed her to leave her marriage and become a nun could checkmate her husband if she left him without producing an heir and her church allies refused to let him remarry.

Astute queens and noblewomen were careful to cultivate ties with powerful church officials, who could aid them when they were no longer willing or able to play the high-stakes marriage game. Ecclesiastical allies could make a huge difference if a husband attempted to repudiate his wife against her will. Alternatively, a friendly monastery could provide refuge for a wife who was divorced or left her husband on her own account. Churchmen might offer women places of retreat, defend their right to remain unmarried after being widowed, or help them prevent separated husbands from remarrying.

Queens, then, were not just valuable prizes in the game of matrimonial politics. They were often accomplished players in their own right. Small wonder that when medieval Europeans adopted the game of chess from the Muslim world, the most powerful piece on the board, which the Muslims called the vizier, or adviser, was renamed "the queen."[31]

Chapter 7

———— ◆ ————

How the Other 95 Percent Wed:
Marriage Among the Common Folk
of the Middle Ages

The upper classes of medieval Europe made up only a tiny percentage of the total population, and their marital power struggles were not typical. No commoner ever received a marriage proposal delivered by hundreds of armed knights, assorted bishops, and a wagonful of treasures. When the marriage of a peasant or urban craftsman showed signs of strain, neighbors didn't write concerned letters to the papacy about whether the couple should be allowed to divorce and remarry. In fact, for the first eight centuries of its existence, the church itself showed little concern about what made for a valid marriage or divorce among the lower classes of society. Gradually, however, all social classes came to live by the rules for forming and dissolving marriages that had emerged out of the conflicts and compromises among monarchs, nobles, and various factions of the church during the early medieval period.

In the early Western kingdoms, local Church councils often accommodated both Roman traditions and Germanic custom by permitting divorce for a variety of reasons. There was even the equivalent of no-fault divorce, when a couple swore that "discord reigns between us and communal life has become impossible." One legal formula declared that because "there is no charity according to God" between a particular couple, "they have decided that each of them should be free to enter into the service of God in a monastery or to contract a new marriage."[1]

Even after the Church had begun to enforce stricter limits on divorce and remarriage toward the end of the eighth century, many peasant families still believed that childlessness was grounds to take a new mate, and local priests generally looked the other way when their parishioners acted on this assumption. Ireland, the last country in Western Europe to legalize divorce in the twentieth century, was also the last country to make it illegal in the Middle Ages. If an Irishman told secrets about his wife's sexual performance, for example, this was considered good reason for her to leave him. Long after the Church was forbidding people elsewhere in Europe from divorcing, Irish husbands and wives were still going their own way at will.[2]

Women were not necessarily impoverished by divorce in the medieval world. Because no one in the Middle Ages ever claimed that the man was the main breadwinner, a divorced wife was entitled to a percentage of the household estate in line with the labor she had contributed to it. Irish jurists ruled that divorcing women deserved a percentage of the farm's lambs and calves since wives kept the animals, made the wool into cloth, and turned the milk into cheese and butter. In tenth-century Wales the king declared that a divorced man could have the pigs because he normally kept them in the woods near home, but the wife got the sheep because she took them to the highlands during the summer. The husband got the drinking cups and the chickens; the wife got the milk and cheese-making equipment, along with the flax, linseed, wool, and butter.

Churchmen in Ireland and Wales occasionally objected to the breakup of marriages, but like their colleagues on the Continent, they had their hands full trying to get their own priests to adhere to vows of celibacy. A majority of the clergy were married in the early Middle Ages, and despite growing opposition to the practice from the fifth century, change came very slowly. In 742 Pope Zachary declared that bishops and priests who lived in adultery or had more than one wife could not perform religious rites. By the eleventh century the Gregorian reformers were spearheading an organized campaign against clerical marriage. But Church authorities who tried to force the pace sometimes ran into trouble. When the Bishop of Paris ordered his priests to give up their wives and children, they chased him out of the cathedral. In 1077, Pope Gregory VII reported that the clergy of Cambrai, Wales, had seized a supporter of priestly celibacy and burned him alive. England, Italy, and Germany also saw violent clashes over this issue. Not until 1139 did canon law completely forbid clerical marriage.[3]

The Church was also slow to insist that a priest had to officiate for marriages of the laity to be valid. In the mid-twelfth century Pope Alexander III considered issuing a ruling that a marriage was valid only if it had been solemnized in a church, but he ultimately decided the order was impractical. Marriage practices throughout Europe were still so diverse and so informal that such a declaration would, in the words of one European historian, "have rendered a massive proportion of marriages invalid."[4]

The Church was dealing with a population whose traditions considered mutual intent or the blessing of a parent sufficient to solemnize a marriage. If it had refused to accept these informal marriages as valid, how could it enforce its prohibitions against divorce and its strictures against "living in sin"? It wasn't until the sixteenth century on the Continent—and not until 1753 in England—that governments and churches could enforce a rule requiring specific legal and public formalities to validate a marriage.

Until the twelfth century the Church held that a marriage was valid if entered into by mutual consent and then sealed by sexual intercourse. This made nonconsummation grounds for annulment. Then, in the mid-twelfth century, Peter Lombard, Bishop of Paris, argued that if sex was necessary for a valid marriage, Mary and Joseph could not have been legally married. In Lombard's view, a promise to wed ("words of the future") did not create a marriage unless it was followed by sex, but he insisted that an exchange of consent in the present—"I take you as my husband" and "I take you as my wife"—made a marriage legally and sacramentally binding even if the couple did not engage in sex. Lombard's views became official church teaching.

This created a peculiar situation. If a couple claimed they were married by consent, no one could gainsay it, even if the parents could prove the two young people had never been alone long enough to have a ceremony or sleep together. But if only one of the pair claimed to have married by consent, and the Church believed it, the other was trapped for life, since nonconsummation was no longer grounds for divorce.

The Church did not like being put in the awkward position of defending young couples who, by privately exchanging their vows, married in defiance of their parents' wishes. In remedy, the Fourth Lateran Council declared in 1215 that "we absolutely prohibit clandestine marriages." For a marriage to be valid, the council stated, three things were necessary: The bride had to have a dowry, which effectively undercut the independence of a young woman from her parents; banns had to be published beforehand; and the wedding had to take place in a church.

As a result, a proper marriage became a long, drawn-out affair. It began with a formal betrothal negotiated by both sets of parents. This included a prenuptial marriage contract covering the property transactions that would occur at and after marriage, such as the amount of the dowry brought by the wife, the groom's marriage gift to her, what arrangements would be made if the bride were widowed, and how property would be dispersed to children and grandchildren. If the man was expected to take over his parents' farm or business, the marriage agreement might also stipulate the kind of support they could expect from the couple during their old age: a specific room in the house or in an adjacent home, with designated furnishings; a set amount of firewood each fall; a milk cow or a mule for personal use.

Next came the reading of the banns at church for three consecutive weeks prior to the wedding. This was a way to inform the community about the impending marriage, so anyone could come forward if he or she knew of some reason (such as a prior marriage) that the wedding should not take place.

Finally there was the formal exchange of vows at the church door, in front of witnesses and with the priest's blessing. Friars, such as the one who agreed to marry the young lovers in Shakespeare's *Romeo and Juliet,* were not under the authority of bishops and might be prevailed upon to conduct a secret or hasty wedding, but parish priests were subject to strict penalties if they married a couple in the absence of witnesses and posted banns.

These provisions should have made secret weddings rare, and people who wanted to remain in everyone's good graces took care to follow these procedures. But ultimately, the Lombard doctrine boiled down to this: A freely given consent to marry trumped all the other formalities that the Lateran Council had laid out so carefully. If a couple said, using the present tense, "I take thee as my husband" and "I take thee as my wife," they were married, with or without witnesses, banns, blessings, or anything else, whether they said the words in a chapel, a kitchen, a field, or a barn, and whether or not they had ever had sex or taken up residence together.

The Church viewed a clandestine marriage as disobedient, illicit, even reprehensible, but nonetheless valid. The basic principle of Christian marriage was that an unbreakable bond was created by the consent of the two parties. Consequently, although marriage was seldom a matter of free choice in any sense recognizable today, it was easier in medieval Western Europe to get married without the permission of parents and social superiors than it had been in the past or was in most other contemporary kingdoms or empires.

But while there were now more ways to get into a legally recognized marriage, there were fewer ways to *get out* of it. By the twelfth century, when the Gregorian reformers really began to flex their muscles on the question of no marriage for the clergy and no divorce for the laity, Church law no longer made any provision for divorce at all. A husband or wife could get a judicial separation for only three reasons: adultery; a partner's heresy, described as "spiritual fornication"; and extreme cruelty, although the cruelty had to be very extreme for a woman to initiate a separation. None of these reasons justified divorce. Even if a separation was granted, neither partner—not even the "innocent" one—could remarry.

Only an annulment freed people to marry again. And even a woman's failure to produce an heir was no longer sufficient grounds to annul a marriage. A man's *impotence* was grounds for annulment, but to prove it, he had to submit to a humiliating ordeal designed to make sure he and his wife were not colluding to end their marriage. As one church legal expert laid out the procedure, "The man and woman are to be placed together in one bed and wise women are to be summoned around the bed for many nights. And if the man's member is always found useless and as if dead, the couple are well able to be separated."[5]

In 1433, at York, England, the court recorded a case in which the "wise women" took the investigation into their own hands: "The . . . witness exposed her naked breasts and with her hands warmed at the said fire, she held and rubbed the penis and testicles of the said John. And she embraced and frequently kissed the said John, and stirred him up in so far as she could to show his virility and potency, admonishing him for shame that he should there and then prove and render himself a man. And she says, examined and diligently questioned, that the whole time aforesaid, the said penis was scarcely three inches long . . . remaining without any increase or decrease."

There were two other grounds for annulment. If the couple were too closely related, by blood or by the marriage of other relatives, their marriage could be dissolved. Annulment was also possible if one party had previously consented to marry someone else. Just as the church's incest rules provided an escape hatch for many nobles and kings, the exchange of consent rule provided a useful way for commoners to claim that a marriage was invalid.

In our day we can usually prove if a prior marriage existed by following a paper trail. But in the Middle Ages the court had only the doctrine of present consent for proof. The majority of disputes over marriage in the Middle Ages did not involve suits for divorce but were disagreements over whether a marriage had been contracted by consent. Imagine the possibilities for confusion, collusion, and outright fraud. A fortune hunter could claim that a rich woman had previously consented to a marriage and was therefore legally obliged to break off her engagement to another man. A woman in an unhappy marriage could belatedly "admit" that she had previously exchanged words of consent with another man, even though she had never lived with him, so that she now had to leave her present spouse and go live with her "real" one.

In 1337, Alice Palmer told the court that she had previously given Ralph Fouler five shillings to testify falsely that she had not agreed to marry Geoffrey Brown. Now, however, she regretted her denial and wanted the court to know that even though Geoffrey had subsequently married someone else, she had actually agreed to marry him first and was therefore his lawful wife. Was this a belated attack of conscience, or did she now believe he was a better prospect than she had first judged?[6]

In the late thirteenth century, Edmund de Nastok received a handsome dowry from Richard de Brok for marrying Brok's daughter Agnes. Then Elizabeth de Ludehale came to the court claiming a prior contract of marriage with Edmund. In this case, the court decided that Elizabeth and Edmund had cooked up the scheme beforehand, to set themselves up with the money Edmund received from Agnes's father. They had to return the dowry, along with sixteen pounds in damages.

It may surprise the modern reader to learn that until the seventeenth century the most typical prior consent suit was brought not by a deserted woman or unwed mother but by a man trying to force a woman into marriage after she had rejected him or had even married someone else. In 1470 a London court heard a case stemming from the competition of two rivals to marry a wealthy widow. One of the suitors, Robert Grene, asked a local lord of a manor to go to the home of the widow, Maude Knyff, to witness what would be said between Robert and Maude. The obliging lord testified that he looked through the window, saw the two embrace, and heard Maude pledge her troth to Robert and accept a ring from him. Maude vehemently denied this, claiming that Robert took a ring *off* her finger against her will.

She also rebutted Robert's testimony by calling a friend of hers to testify that she had seen Maude and Thomas Torald sitting together in the house and that Maude had told her, "Behold, here sits my husband," to which Thomas responded: "For the greater and more evident notice of this matter, know that this Maude is my wife."

Most marriages did not involve such complications, of course. The power plays of royalty, the schemes of fortune hunters, and the stratagems of people trying to get around the prohibitions against divorce affected only a minority of couples. Moreover, despite the Church's grudging acceptance of clandestine marriage, most people of the day did not believe marriage was meant to be a private decision. So although an enterprising young couple did have opportunities to defy their parents and neighbors, the marriage decisions of most commoners in Europe were as constrained in their own way as the marriage choices of the aristocracy.[7]

Many European peasants in the Middle Ages were legally bound to a lord and his lands. Serfs owed their master a certain number of days of labor and a certain amount of produce each year, in addition to small monetary taxes. They also had to obey the lord's will in many personal matters and submit themselves to his "justice." The feudal lord's "right of the first night," whereby a nobleman had the right to deflower a peasant's daughter upon her wedding, is a myth. But a lord typically did have a financial, if not a sexual, interest in his serfs' daughters, and the Church rarely objected to the control he exercised over their marriages.

In some regions the lord of an estate (or the abbot if a peasant worked on church lands) could prevent his serf from marrying a woman from another manor. In other regions, lords even had the right to choose husbands for their tenants' daughters. As late as 1344 the lord of a manor in the Black Forest of Germany required that each of his male householders over the age of eighteen and every female fourteen or older had to marry someone of his choosing. The regulation applied even to widows and widowers. In other cases, peasants could pay fines that freed them to choose their own partners, but they were still required to marry somebody or pay even bigger penalties. In some places lords managed to make a profit even when their tenants didn't marry. Women who were sexually active without being married had to pay *leirwite*—literally a fine for lying down, and another fine for each child born out of wedlock.[8]

Landowners had a stake in their serfs' marriages because the division of labor between husband and wife lay at the heart of rural economies. No individual, male or female, could run a farm single-handedly. The man focused on outdoor agricultural labor; indeed, a male peasant was usually called a plowman. In addition to plowing, he spread manure, dug peat for fuel, and harvested crops by hand, swinging heavy sickles or scythes. He threshed the grain, turned the hay, and sometimes hired himself out to work in the fields of larger landowners. His wife milked the cows, made butter and cheese, fed the chickens and ducks, cleaned and carded wool, prepared flax (a process that involved fifteen steps), brewed beer, and carried water. Women also took their surplus products to market, washed their clothes in the village stream, and had their grain ground at the mill. Both men and women helped with the harvest, gleaned the fields, and collected firewood. Women, like men, sometimes hired themselves out as agricultural laborers.

Only rarely could a peasant man or woman carve out an independent life as a single person. The married couple peasant household was the basic unit of production. The dues this household owed to the lord were calculated on the basis of the work done by both the man and the woman. The yearly dues of chickens and eggs on the estates in medieval Germany, for example, were so explicitly considered the wife's responsibility that a family was exempted from this payment when she was pregnant.[9]

The importance of marriage in creating a viable household economic unit meant that even free peasants, who were not bound to a lord or an abbot, were very anxious to get themselves, and later their offspring, properly married. They were equally concerned that their neighbors marry appropriate spouses, because the very geography of village life and peasant farming made marriage a public matter. A family's landholdings were often scattered into a number of separate long, narrow strips. A marriage that allowed for the amalgamation of side-by-side plots of land was considered particularly advantageous. But the regular rotation of crops and the proximity of landholdings required the whole village to decide what to plant where and when to plow and harvest. Even people with no direct economic interest in the outcome of a marriage had a stake in who married whom and whether the new husband or wife would be an asset to the neighborhood.

Family farms in the medieval European countryside could not survive without networks of mutual aid and communal accountability. Many villages had customs like those recorded in the thirteenth and fourteenth centuries for Brigstock, England. There all the men were divided up into tithing groups of ten or more who took responsibility for one another's behavior. If one committed a theft, for example, the others would have to produce him at court or be liable for punishment themselves.[10] So for social as well as economic reasons, there was pressure on villagers to choose mates and in-laws who would pull their own weight in communal enterprises.

Neighbors had many ways to prevent or punish matches they considered inappropriate. The threat of disapproval and ostracism was no small matter when you shared planting and plowing with your neighbors, did your wash together, and used a neighbor's oven to bake your bread. Villagers might also engage in ritual harassment of the offending couple. These rituals, called charivaris, or "rough music," were boisterous, obscene, humiliating, and sometimes painful ways to punish people who violated community norms. Neighbors surrounded the house, singing rude songs and burning effigies. They might even break in, pull the offenders out, and humiliate them by forcing them to ride backward on a mule or dunking them in a nearby pond.

Such community demonstrations were often directed at a couple that seemed ill matched in age or status, thereby removing an eligible single person from an already uncomfortably small pool. Marriage outside the community was also frowned upon. Sometimes the young men or women of a neighborhood would physically confront a stranger who came courting, calling out rude names and pelting him or her with rocks and vegetables.

Parents were anxious that their children marry into the "right" families. Titles and kingdoms might not be at stake in village life, but having an in-law with a cousin in the bishop's court or an uncle who was the lord's bailiff could be a big asset in mediating disputes. The wealthier peasants were usually linked through marriage alliances, although a village might split into factions along lines of kinship, patronage, and intermarriage. Here again marriage was far too central to village life to be a couple's private business.

As a result, marriages in peasant villages could involve as many interested parties as those of minor nobles. Take the case of the fourteenth-century widow Raymonde d'Argelliers, who lived in the village of Montaillou, near what is now the border of France and Spain. Her second marriage, Raymonde told a court investigating heresy in the village, was "a result of the negotiations by the brothers Guillaume, Bernard, and Jean Barbès of Niort, the brothers Bernard and Arnaud Marty of Montaillou, Pierre-Raymond Barbès, priest of Freychenet, and Bernadette Tavern and Guillemette Barbès of Niort."[11]

Although peasants zealously scrutinized who should marry whom, they tended to be cavalier about the order in which a couple engaged in childbirth and marriage. A letter written by the Bishop of Lincoln, in England, in the thirteenth century noted that the traditional custom during a wedding, if a couple had had a child born before the ceremony, was to stretch a "care-cloth" over the child as the couple knelt in front of the altar, so the child was legitimized. According to English common law, the subsequent marriage of a couple did not legitimize their previously born children, but peasants simply ignored that.

A woman who did not marry the father of her out-of-wedlock child was not necessarily considered damaged goods in peasant communities. A historian who examined the records of Halesowen Manor, in England, between 1270 and 1348 estimates that for every two women who gave birth in marriage, one woman gave birth out of wedlock. Many of these women subsequently married, some of them quite well, suggesting they did not face permanent stigmatization. Even so, richer peasants, with more to lose in inheritance disputes, tended to avoid bearing children out of wedlock.[12]

Marriage, not childbearing, marked men's and women's transition to adulthood in peasant society. In many parts of England, all unmarried men and women, regardless of age, were called lads or maids and were expected to defer to the married "masters" and "dames" of the village.[13]

The badge of adulthood meant different things for each sex. For a man, marriage was closely connected to economic independence. A man got married when he inherited land or took over his father's craft. In thirteenth-century England the word for an unmarried man—*anilepiman,* or "only man"—also meant "landless man," while the word *husbond* could mean either a married man or a man with a substantial landholding. A married man with his own land and household was the basic political figure of village life. He was responsible for his wife and children as well as for any servants or apprentices who lived in his house. He answered for their misdeeds, disciplined them when necessary, and represented them at village meetings or in the courts.[14]

For women, the relationship between marriage and authority was more ambiguous. Marriage marked a female as an adult, but it restricted rather than expanded her legal standing. A married woman lost the right to dispose of land, go to court, or handle her own affairs. Yet women in rural Europe needed marriage to achieve economic security and social status. No woman, married or not, could be part of the tithing group that kept the peace. Nor could a woman serve in any village office or act as a pledge for other people, the way peasant men frequently did. Acting as a pledge created obligations in others, and men could use the pledge system to establish dense networks of mutual aid that involved dozens of other people. Only through her husband could a woman gain this kind of influence beyond the household, even though marriage stripped her of the right to make economic contracts.[15]

Some historians argue that the mutual dependence of husband and wife in production made medieval peasant marriages economic and emotional partnerships. Certainly, the fact that peasant husbands often made wives their executors implies a good deal of mutual respect. So does the gradual adoption of jointure, in which husband and wife held their land in common so that the woman would inherit the entire property, not just the traditional widow's third, when her husband died.[16]

However, any property a woman brought to marriage came under her husband's control. He could dispose of any movable property or leases she inherited without consulting her, although he was not supposed to sell any freehold land she inherited without her consent. Court cases show that some wives successfully guarded their rights. In the countryside around Barcelona in the early eleventh century, for example, Maria, the daughter of a wealthy peasant named Vivas, agreed that her husband could sell a field she had inherited from her father in order to meet some household needs. She insisted that in return she be compensated with a piece of land from her *husband's* inheritance. He resisted, but she eventually got him in front of a scribe, where he signed over the land, according to the deed, *pro pax maritum*—for the sake of peace in the marriage.[17]

However, if a husband refused to make concessions for the sake of household peace, a wife had little recourse. By law, husbands controlled all household resources, including any earnings wives brought in, and could "discipline" their wives by force if necessary. The extent of a husband's authority in medieval thought was illustrated by the laws of England, Normandy, and Sicily defining a wife's murder of her husband as a form of treason, punishable by burning at the stake.[18]

Marriage in urban areas followed many of the same patterns. The revival of trade in Western Europe in the eleventh and twelfth centuries created densely packed towns such as Paris, London, Milan, and Florence, where artisans and merchants conducted business out of homes, shops, and taverns. These towns provided a larger pool of potential spouses than was available in agricultural villages and offered more opportunities for unsupervised courting. Nevertheless, marriage was seldom a truly private affair anywhere during the Middle Ages.

In cities, as in peasant villages, intermediaries were frequently involved in introducing a couple, testing the waters to see if a relationship might be taken to a new level, and conducting the property negotiations that accompanied marriage. Such matchmaking was not restricted to women. Indeed, according to historian Shannon McSheffrey, "it was the duty and privilege of senior men to ensure that suitable marriages were made, and unsuitable unions prevented."[19]

In cities, as in the countryside, marriage was often a business partnership, with far-reaching economic implications for friends and relations on both sides. Merchant families used marriage alliances to raise capital and build business networks, and in many areas of northwestern Europe, a merchant's wife became her husband's partner in economic activities. She might keep the books for the family business or help out in the shop, act as an agent for her husband in his absence, and carry on her husband's trade after his death.

Such working partnerships were especially common among the craftsmen and artisans of medieval towns. In Genoa, skilled workers in the same trade often married, listing in their marriage contracts the inventory and work tools that each brought to the marriage. The couple typically conducted their business out of their home or lived above their shop. If a man was a weaver, his wife might operate a loom. If he made shoes, she might sew on the uppers. Many craft guilds, taking it as a given that the wife would work alongside her husband, allowed a man to take on an apprentice only if he had no wife. In fourteenth-century London the wives of men who dyed leather were even sworn into the guild with their husbands, and many guilds required that a man marry before he advanced to the rank of master.[20]

Urban trades were often what historian Beatrice Gottlieb calls two-person careers. As with peasant marriages, this may have created mutual respect, dependence, and even love between husband and wife, but it did not leave much room for sentimentality if an untimely death cut the career in half. "When a spouse died, a job opening was created. . . . The widow or widower remarried to fill the opening, or a son or daughter took over and almost simultaneously acquired a mate."[21]

At the highest levels of the merchant elite, a wife was less likely to be an active partner in her husband's business, although she participated in a busy round of social and cultural activities that enhanced her husband's reputation. Wealthy urban merchants often married their daughters into the landed nobility. This brought nobles the ready cash of the merchant daughters' dowries, while giving the merchants access to the nobles' valuable social connections.[22]

In urban as well as rural areas, marriage expanded a man's authority while restricting a woman's. Only when a man married did he become eligible to serve as a juryman, warden, or other local official. By contrast, marriage took away a woman's freedom to enter into contracts and be held responsible for her own actions. A married woman was a *feme covert*. She was covered by her husband's identity and lacked any legal standing of her own.

In the cities, however, a married woman could petition the authorities to lift the restrictions of coverture. Such a woman, called a *feme sole* in France and England and a *Marktfrau* in Germany, was allowed to do business as if she had no husband. She was responsible for her own debts and could hire apprentices and enter into contracts without her husband's approval.

Most wives who engaged in independent businesses did so on a small scale, selling food and goods or brewing ale, tasks that could be combined with other domestic and productive activities. The frequency of such female multitasking was recognized in an English statute of 1363 that restricted male artisans to a single trade but allowed women to follow several. But men's specialization usually allowed them to command a higher price for their wares or labor.[23]

Still, some women did become prosperous merchants. Alice Chestre of Bristol, England, conducted a thriving overseas trade in cloth, wines, and iron with Flanders, Spain, and Portugal in the years after her husband's death in 1470. Another intriguing fifteenth-century woman was Margery Kempe, a successful brewer married to a debt-ridden and only intermittently employed husband. After giving birth to fourteen children, Margery became convinced that having sex with her husband was sinful. The church held that no woman was exempt from her "marriage debt," the obligation to have sex with her spouse. But Margery had the financial resources to strike a deal with her husband. In return for release from her marriage debt, she paid off all his worldly ones.[24]

Don't Be "Too Fussy": Marriage, Love, and Individual Choice

Some historians argue that the Church's doctrine of mutual consent, combined with the reemergence of commerce in the twelfth century and the loosening of serfdom after the Black Death epidemic of 1348, created an "astonishingly individualistic" marriage system in Western Europe. They say that individuals were allowed to choose their marriage partners freely and that once married, the couple was exempt from familial interference. All this, they believe, led to a unique emphasis on marital love and harmony.[25]

The doctrine of consent did provide some leverage for an individual who wished to resist the pressures of parents or social superiors. Yet parents had powerful ways of controlling their children's marital decisions. A young woman normally depended on her parents for her dowry, and often a young man could marry only if his parents agreed to set him up on the land or in the trade that he would someday inherit. The Church might feel compelled to validate the marriage of someone who married without parental consent, but in most countries secular law sided with the parents if they denied inheritance to a child who took this course of action. Parents also used such extralegal measures as intimidation, physical restraint, and even violence with impunity.[26]

Where women married very young, as in medieval Italy, it was especially easy for parents to dispose of a daughter without regard for her wishes. In 1447 in Florence, Alessandra Macinghi Strozzi, acting as head of the prominent Strozzi family after her husband's death, wrote to her son announcing that she had engaged his sixteen-year-old sister to a rich silk manufacturer and was giving her a dowry of a thousand florins: "We tried to place her in a more powerful and more distinguished family, but it would have taken 1,400 or 1,500 florins, and this would have been your undoing and mine. I do not know if the girl is pleased, for it is true that, political considerations aside this [marriage] has little to recommend it. I, having considered everything, decided to prepare the girl and not to be too fussy. I am sure that she will be as well as any girl in Florence."[27]

Even in England, where "permissive" marriage was more widespread, parents often made business and political decisions that completely disregarded their children's wishes. In 1413, two fathers from the Derbyshire gentry signed a marriage contract on which the bride's name was left blank because the bride's father hadn't yet decided which daughter to marry off. In other cases on the Continent and in England, wedding agreements explicitly provided that a younger son or daughter would take the place of their older betrothed sibling should the latter die before the marriage could take place.[28]

In the 1440s Elizabeth Paston, a daughter of the minor gentry, resisted her parents' pressure to marry a man who was thirty years her senior and disfigured by smallpox. Her mother, according to a concerned cousin, confined Elizabeth to her room, where she was beaten "sometimes twice in one day, and her head broken in two or three places." Eventually Elizabeth gave in and agreed to the marriage, provided that she was given "reasonable jointure" in the man's property. In this case, the marriage fell through, and Elizabeth was eventually married off to someone more to her liking.[29]

A truly determined pair of lovers who managed to escape being locked up by their parents and were willing to risk ostracism by friends and family could force a disapproving Church to recognize their marriage. But usually matters did not go that far. Marriage had so many economic and social ramifications for all social classes that people generally believed it would be foolish to make such a momentous decision entirely on their own. When parents and kin arranged a marriage for their child, they were investing in the child's future as surely as a modern parent who sets up a college savings fund. Individuals in the Middle Ages understood that marriage was the most important "career" decision they would ever make. Accordingly, most generally followed their parents' marital agendas. "I will do as my fader will have me," said Margery Shepherd in 1486, "I will never have none ayenst my fader's will." Young people also took their neighbors' and friends' opinions into account. As Elizabeth Fletcher of Canterbury told her suitor, "I must be ruled by my friends as well as by myself."[30]

Marriage usually grew out of a collaboration among parents, friends, and the two individuals involved, and it was often based on very practical considerations. A different member of the Paston family, acting as a marital inter-mediary for his brother, wrote to his mother that he had found a young woman in London who would have two hundred pounds cash as a dowry and a significant inheritance after her stepmother died. The stepmother, he noted pointedly, was already fifty years old. Impressed by the prospect of an imme-diate cash dowry and an early inheritance, he "spake with some of the maid's friends," he reported, "and have gotten their good wills to have her married to my brother Edmund." Edmund was consulted only after this negotiation.

Of course a marriage undertaken for mercenary reasons might develop into a relationship based on affection or even love, while a love match might deteriorate into bitter dislike. We have little access into people's internal world in this period because the habit of keeping diaries was not well established. We must rely on marital advice books, court cases, literature, and the rare memoirs that touched on married life for clues to how marriage was experi-enced. Each of these sources gives a different picture of the relations between husbands and wives.

Portraits of Medieval Marriage

Marriage advice books from the fourteenth through the sixteenth centuries are filled with monotonously detailed instructions to wives about being chaste, obedient, hardworking, and respectful, interspersed with practical tips on getting rid of fleas and an occasional sentence directing husbands to be chaste and loving too.[31] The few manuals directed at husbands invariably sound more like tips for training a horse than building a marriage. The goal was that a husband should establish such complete sway over his wife that dis-obedience was unthinkable.

Court records of the day, however, reveal that marriage was often not so orderly. Women talked back, and men violently imposed their wills. Wives could be subjected to astonishingly violent treatment without being granted relief. But most marriages never ended up in the courts, and it is risky to gen-eralize from the violent ones that did.

The published memoirs of medieval women give us a more positive view of marriage because wives almost always emphasize their reverence and fond-ness for their husbands. But a woman's letters and memoirs were not likely to be published if they were critical of her husband or father. The celebrated seventeenth-century diarist Samuel Pepys, for example, ordered his wife to de-stroy what she had written about his behavior because "it was so piquant . . .

and most of it true." When she refused, he grabbed the papers away from her and tore them up.[32]

Whatever arrangements individual couples worked out in private, married life in medieval Europe took place in a context in which the law allowed a husband to control all the income or goods his wife brought into the marriage, to detain her physically inside the house, and to beat her for disobedience, although the violence was not supposed to endanger her life. Similarly, the cultural consensus in religious manuals, advice books, and public opinion was that wives should obey their husbands in all but the most extreme circumstances.

The tale of Griselda was a staple of literature, folk stories, and marriage manuals in the thirteenth and fourteenth centuries. Griselda, a beautiful peasant, married a marquis who put her through a series of extraordinary tests. First he took away her infant daughter, telling her he had decided to have the baby killed. Griselda responded meekly that she deferred to her lord's judgment. Four years later she bore a handsome son. As soon as he was weaned, however, the marquis told her that his subjects did not want their future ruler to come from a peasant woman, so he was taking the son away to be killed too. Griselda replied that her love for her husband prevented her from wanting anything that did not please him.

Twelve years later the marquis announced he was casting Griselda aside for a young maiden of more noble birth, and he wanted her to prepare the wedding celebration. She readily agreed, exclaiming with pleasure when she saw how beautiful the young lady was. Just before the wedding was to take place, the marquis revealed that the radiant young "bride" was really her own dear daughter, who had been raised all these years, along with her brother, by their aunt. Once Griselda revived from a joyous faint, she and the marquis "lived together in great love and peace and concord" for the rest of their lives.[33]

Griselda was the "surrendered wife," fourteenth-century style. But most fourteenth-century commentators who repeated the tale conceded that the marquis had gone a bit too far. In the version repeated in a marital advice book written by "The Goodman of Paris," the author explains that he does not expect such complete obedience from his bride, "for I am not worthy thereof, and also I am no marquis nor have I taken in you a shepherdess." Yet he immediately calls her attention to the most important moral of the tale: "that by good obedience a wise woman gains her husband's love and at the end hath what she would of him." It is not always wise, the Goodman admonishes his wife, "to say to one's ruler: 'I will do naught, it is not reasonable'; greater good cometh by obeying."[34]

Marriage, a History

In *The Canterbury Tales,* written in the last two decades of the fourteenth century, Geoffrey Chaucer purports to record the stories told by a cross section of English people from all walks of life who come together on a pilgrimage to Canterbury. His collection paints some of the most vivid and engaging portraits of marriages in all medieval literature. Chaucer had his own version of the Griselda story, but his version ends wryly "one word more, my lords, before I go. It isn't very easy nowadays to find Griseldas round the town you know."[35]

The Wife of Bath, another Chaucer character, is the opposite of Griselda. A lusty, brash, and wealthy clothmaker who has been married five times, the Wife of Bath prefaces her tale with a vigorous attack on the Church's idealization of virginity, then proceeds to tell the company her marital history. She married her first four husbands for money, she explains, and gleefully describes how she twisted them around her finger. Her fifth—"the one I took for love and not for wealth"—posed more of a problem, because she rashly handed her money and lands over to him, forgoing her chance to continue as a *feme sole.* She soon repented of this act because he began haranguing her about the proper duties of a wife and often beat her.

Finally, she got fed up with his reading her endless tales from a book about "wicked wives." She tore the book from his hand and slapped him so hard that he fell into the fire. In a rage, he hit her back even harder, and she fell down senseless. Playing on his fear that he might be charged with murder, she managed to get him to swear he would never hit her again. Finally, the Wife of Bath reports, "we made it up together. He gave the bridle over to my hand, gave me the government of house and land . . . I made him burn that book upon the spot. . . . From that day forward there was no debate. So help me God I was as kind to him as any wife from Denmark to the rim of India, and as true. And he to me."[36]

The coexistence of these contradictory and exaggerated stories illustrates the problem of describing *the* medieval marriage. Things get even more confusing when we look at the messages from the Catholic Church. Some churchmen insisted that although celibacy was the ideal, marriage was also a positive good. A thirteenth-century French handbook for priests states that a married couple "are all one body and one soul . . . and therefore should be of one heart by true love."[37]

But there were many more religious books about "wicked wives" than about married couples with "one body and one soul." In the Middle Ages women were thought to be the lustier sex, and in their campaign against clerical marriage, the Gregorian reformers were vitriolic in their denunciations of how women entangled men in "the slimy glue" of their sexuality. In the mid-eleventh century a prominent reformer wrote that women were "bitches, sows, screech-owls, night-owls, she-wolves, blood-suckers" who seduced clerical men with the "appetizing flesh of the devil." He thundered: "Hear me, harlots, with your lascivious kisses, your wallowing places for fat pigs." Leave your clerical husbands and lovers or face enslavement.[38]

In some cases, the Church attacked marriage from the woman's point of view. One such treatise, titled "Holy Maidenhood," tried to convince young women to become nuns. The picture it paints of marriage makes the complaints of twentieth-century feminists sound tame: "Now thou art wedded, and from so high estate alighted so low: . . . into the filth of the flesh, into the manner of a beast, into the thraldom of a man, and into the sorrows of the world. . . . When he is out, thou shalt await his homecoming with all sorrow, care, and dread. While he is at home, all thy wide dwellings seem too narrow for thee; his looking on thee makes thee aghast; his loathsome mirth and his rude behaviour fill thee with horror. He chideth and jaweth thee, as a lecher does his whore; he beateth thee and mauleth thee as his bought thrall and patrimonial slave."[39]

By the sixteenth century there was a lively ongoing debate about the relative merits of women and men. But aside from humorous characters in bawdy popular literature, almost no one disputed the principle that a wife must be subordinate to her husband. Marriage was still an authority relationship as much as a personal one. Advice books warned wives not to be too familiar in the way they addressed their husbands, telling them to avoid nicknames and endearments that undermined the dignity of a man's position. Even women in loving marriages wrote to their husbands as "sir" and signed with protestations of obedience.[40]

When wives failed to submit of their own free will, popular culture and actual law allowed husbands to extort obedience by force. While the charivaris of rural villages sometimes taunted men who inflicted severe injuries on their wives, they were more often directed at men who *failed* to discipline their wives. A "henpecked" man might be strapped to a cart or ridden around backward on a mule, to be booed and ridiculed for his inversion of the accepted marital hierarchy. One sixteenth-century rhyming proverb opined: "A spaniel, a woman, and a walnut tree, the more they're beaten the better they be." In the same century a London law forbade wife beating after 9:00 P.M., but only because the noise disturbed people's sleep.[41]

As we shall see, the pace of change in marital relationships was glacially slow. There were many differences between the role of marriage in the petty kingdoms of the early Middle Ages and its place in the powerful nation-states that began to emerge in sixteenth-century Europe. But there was surprisingly little change in the basic power relations between husbands and wives right up to the early modern era. It was not until the last two hundred years that wives began to gain any real protection from abuse or that love began to be valued over obedience. Nevertheless, by the fifteenth century Western Europe had developed distinctive patterns in marriage norms and gender roles that eventually left the landscape of marriage, so unchanging for thousands of years, irrevocably transformed.

Chapter 8

═══◄◉►═══

Something Old, Something New: Western European Marriage at the Dawn of the Modern Age

Historians are usually skeptical about the saying "The more things change, the more they remain the same." We are more interested in transformations beneath the surface of daily life than in things that seem to persist throughout the ages. It's as if we're all sitting in the backseat of history's car saying, "Are we there yet?"

Over the years this impatience has pushed back the dating of the origins of the love match. When I studied history as an undergraduate in the 1960s, I was taught that people didn't begin marrying for love until the nineteenth century. In the 1970s many historians began dating the love match from the eighteenth or even the seventeenth century. Today many scholars trace the celebration of married love and companionship to the Protestant Reformation in the sixteenth century. A few even believe the basic contours of modern marriage took shape as far back as the thirteenth century.[1]

I believe that the older system of marrying for political and economic advantage remained the norm until the eighteenth century, five thousand years after we first encountered it in the early kingdoms and empires of the Middle East. But between the fourteenth and seventeenth centuries, northwestern Europe developed a unique mix of marriage behaviors and values that paved the way for the rapid changes of the 1700s.[2]

One distinctive feature of Western European marriage was that as early as the twelfth century, polygamy was prohibited. Many men kept mistresses, and wives were expected to ignore such behavior. But mistresses had no legal rights or social standing. By the fifteenth century the children of mistresses had lost the inheritance rights they had had in the early medieval period. A man's heir had to be born in marriage. For a long time the Church even prohibited adoption.

The decisive victory for the Church in the battles over divorce from the ninth to the thirteenth century reinforced the importance of getting a fertile wife the first time around. Men rarely got a second chance to produce a male heir. Aristocrats could often win an exemption from prohibitions against divorce, and the lower classes frequently evaded the rules. But laws against divorce were far stricter than almost anywhere else. Even Eastern Europe was more lenient. Under Russian law, for example, a wife could divorce her husband if he raped her, went heavily into debt, or became a drunkard. In northwestern Europe, a wife had no such recourse. In most cases, marriages were truly "for better or for worse."

At the same time, though, the principle that men and women should be able to choose or refuse a partner was more widely accepted in northwestern Europe than in most other areas of the world. There were substantial limits on people's free choice, and during the sixteenth and seventeenth centuries, many countries passed laws that made it harder for individuals to marry as they pleased. But the traditional doctrine of consent, for all its limitations, had created fertile soil for tolerance of consensual unions and individual choice. Even as the rules for what constituted a valid marriage became stricter after the sixteenth century, the long tradition of informal marriage encouraged evasion and resistance.

Another distinctive feature of northwestern Europe was that upon marriage a couple usually established their own household. Marriage marked a sharper transition for men as well as women than in societies where the extended family or its patriarch determined the couple's residence and work roles. Upon marriage, a husband gained authority over his wife, but she gained authority over their servants, apprentices, unwed relations, and even the older unmarried women in her neighborhood. A seventeenth-century theologian explained that marriage was "the ordinary means" to turn men and women "into masters and mistresses." This was quite different from

China, India, Japan, and much of Southern and Eastern Europe, where sons as well as daughters-in-law usually remained under the thumbs of parents or grandparents.[3]

In societies where a couple is incorporated into a larger family compound or productive unit, marriage and childbearing generally take place at a young age because a couple doesn't need to be economically self-sufficient to wed. But in northwestern Europe, when a man and woman married, they were expected to work their own land or establish their own trade, rather than live as part of a larger family collective.[4] Because a couple was expected to support the partners and their children, marriage had to wait until they had accumulated or inherited enough to sustain a separate household. Many guilds required journeymen and apprentices to remain single until they had passed the examination to become a master and could be assured of a steady livelihood.

As a result, people in northwestern Europe generally married later than elsewhere in the world. In England between 1500 and 1700 the median age of first marriage for women was twenty-six, which is higher than the median age of marriage for American women at any point during the twentieth century. The age of marriage was sometimes much lower for the very wealthy, especially for aristocrats, but they were a small minority of the population.[5]

A woman's lack of a dowry was not always an impediment to marriage in rural areas. Neighbors often pitched in to help a couple furnish their house or acquire enough seed and animals to get started. In rural Yorkshire, England, a bride was traditionally paraded through the village in a wagon, while neighbors loaded the cart with old pots and pans and furniture or tossed in some coins. In many German villages, unmarried women would get together to sew the linens the betrothed couple needed for their new home. But often men and women left home to find work and accumulate some resources before embarking on marriage. Marriage started on a stronger financial footing when the woman as well as the man had worked for several years to accumulate some capital.

The most common way to save up for marriage was to work as a servant in someone else's home for several years. Working as a servant was as much a rite of passage for young people in the late Middle Ages and early modern era as going off to college is today. In contrast with other societies around the world, where servants were usually a class of people doomed to servitude for their entire lives, in northwestern Europe large numbers of young people passed through a phase of service before forming their own households and working their own lands or trades. In northern Europe, anywhere between one-third and one-half of all young people put in time as servants in the sixteenth and seventeenth centuries. In the early 1700s, according to one study, 60 percent of all English youths aged fifteen to twenty-four worked as servants at some point in their lives.

Girls were as likely as boys to work as servants, away from their own families, another distinctive feature of Western Europe. The expectation that young women would be servants for a period between adolescence and marriage was so widespread that the German word *Magd,* like the English word *maid,* meant both a servant and a never-married female.

In England, a servant couple had typically saved between fifty and sixty pounds by the time they married. After several years in the city an industrious French silk worker might have three or four hundred livres to help her husband set up shop. A servant girl who had saved a hundred livres could pool her resources with an apprentice butcher, baker, cook, or wine seller to set up a small business that they could run together. Or a young woman who had worked for a while in the city might simply return to her village with enough cash to buy some animals or perhaps a little land, making her an attractive catch.[6]

Rural women who became servants in the city tended to marry especially late. For one thing, these women were less likely to have living fathers by the time of their marriages, so they had to amass their own dowries. In addition, household employers typically didn't allow a girl to marry until a given term of service was completed. Once these women were free to marry, they usually had more choice about their partners than women who remained in rural villages. But because the craft guilds often forbade apprentices and journeymen from marrying, a woman might also have to wait until her intended had completed his apprenticeship.

In the 1950s, if a woman in Western Europe or the United States delayed marriage past her early twenties, she often never married at all. But many European townswomen in the sixteenth and seventeenth centuries married for the first time in their thirties and forties. Because marriage in Western Europe established a productive partnership, rather than simply adding another female to an existing family enterprise, the main reason for marriage was not necessarily, as it had been in Roman times, "for the procreation of legitimate children." In London, when Dorothy Ireland, a thirty-six-year-old servant, married her forty-year-old stable "boy" fiancé in 1610, they had already been going together for eight years. Their priority had been to save up enough to start an independent business, not to hurry up and start a family.[7]

The relationship between marriage and starting a household enterprise affected marriage rates and timing. In Marseilles, France, for instance, there was a dramatic increase in the marriage rate after an outbreak of plague in

1720. Researchers assumed that people had married to replenish the population after all the plague deaths. But looking more closely, they discovered that many of these people were past childbearing age. The marriage boom occurred because the plague deaths had opened new inheritance prospects in business or land, and shopkeepers and farmers needed new partners in their businesses. As Historian Beatrice Gottlieb writes, "empty slots had been created in the social structure that only marriage could fill."[8]

Northwestern Europe also had many more unmarried adults in the population than other regions of the world. In the 1500s, one-third to one-half of all European adults were single. Part of this was due to the prevalence of late marriage for both sexes. Still, many people never married at all. In the thirteenth and fourteenth centuries some cities in northern Germany, Holland, and Belgium had thousands of single women living communally in convents that ranged in size from a handful to a hundred women. In mid-thirteenth-century Cologne, there were two thousand single women in 163 convents, supporting themselves as brewers, bakers, weavers, spinners, and laundresses.[9]

Between the fourteenth and the seventeenth centuries, depending on the region and the century, anywhere between 10 and 20 percent of women in northwestern Europe remained single their whole lives. In southern Europe, by contrast, only 2 to 5 percent of women were lifelong singles.

The convents of the Catholic Church had long offered women a respectable alternative to marriage. But after the fifteenth century, growing numbers of laywomen remained single as well. A survey of wills in fifteenth-century York, England, found that 17 percent of all laywomen who left wills, admittedly not a cross section of all women, had never been married.

Many factors contributed to these high rates of nonmarriage. In the lower classes, some people never accumulated enough to set up independent households or be considered attractive marriage partners. In the upper classes, early marriage for a family's heir often meant late marriage or lifelong singlehood for the remaining children because parents were reluctant to deplete the heir's inheritance by providing marriage portions for the rest of the children. Aristocrats often used convents and monasteries as dumping grounds for their non-inheriting children. Yet singlehood was sometimes a voluntary alternative to marriage, and some European women remained single even though they had enough land and resources to find mates.[10]

It may seem paradoxical, but although Europeans were more likely to postpone marriage or even skip it altogether than people in other parts of the world, when they did wed they placed a stronger emphasis on the couple bond. By the fifteenth century marriage was no longer, as in so many other societies, a universal and automatic experience. However, when people did marry, they tended to form working partnerships that could be ended only by death. They therefore had to think about how to create harmonious, or at least bearable, conjugal unions.

In old-fashioned aristocratic political marriages, husband and wife did not need to cooperate in daily activities. Each could go his or her own way. And in many peasant villages, the feudal lord or the community, not the household, made decisions about planting, plowing, and harvesting. Good communication between husband and wife was not always essential.

But the weakening of serfdom after the Black Death epidemic of the mid-fourteenth century and the development of new, urban occupations in the fifteenth eroded the power of feudal lords and village institutions to dictate individual behavior. More people became involved in trades or jobs that could be conducted independently of neighbors or social superiors. For the growing numbers of artisans, craftsmen, merchants, and small urban manufacturers, as well as prosperous country yeomen, the everyday work unit became the married couple household, working alone or with servants or apprentices. A harmonious, well-functioning marriage was a business necessity as well as a personal pleasure. The married couple was thus more prominent in Western Europe than in societies where each partner's first allegiance remained to his or her own kinship group and extended family.

The greater prominence of the married couple household in northwestern Europe should not be confused with nuclear family self-sufficiency. The poor lived in truncated families, with their teenagers and sometimes even their young children sent to work in others' homes. The rich, along with the lower-class youths who worked as their servants, lived in large households that gave a married couple very little privacy. Even among the middle classes, households typically included servants or lodgers. Few couples could carve out private spaces where they might take their meals, or even conduct their sex lives, discrete from other household members.

The comparative independence of Western European nuclear families was also limited by a continuing dependence on neighbors and mutual aid networks. A striking feature of village life in northern Europe from the Middle Ages to the early modern period was the frequency with which people shared labor and exchanged services with neighbors rather than relatives. Several households in a community would get together to build a water mill, put up a fence, buy a breeding bull, share a plow, or set up a blacksmith forge. In towns, too, people relied on neighbors for aid. To a greater extent than in most of the world, day-to-day interactions were likely to be with neighbors, servants, or community institutions rather than with kin. Demographer Ron Lesthaeghe argues that long before the development of the welfare state, families in northwestern Europe relied more on local poor relief committees and fraternal organizations such as guilds or corporations than on extended kin groups. Friends, servants, neighbors, and patrons were expected to offer one another the kind of support that in other times and places has been limited to blood relatives.[11]

The Church's incest rules, which made marriages between cousins less frequent than in Africa, the Middle East, and Mediterranean countries, reinforced the tendency to form mutual aid groups beyond close kin. Because it was required to marry outside the close family, the Western European nobility gradually became a more open social group than the aristocracy in other societies. Intermarriage among different noble families and even between aristocrats and government officials or wealthy merchants became common. Within the lower classes as well, there was a higher level of exogamous marriage than in many other parts of the world.[12]

The prevalence of delayed marriage, combined with the niches for unmarried individuals and the existence of nonfamily institutions for cooperation and mutual aid, had important economic and cultural consequences. Because marriage required more significant resources than elsewhere, savings and capital formation occurred more widely, even at lower socioeconomic levels. Furthermore, the fact that women married in the prime of life, rather than in their dependent years, made marriage a more productive partnership right from its beginning. Women came into marriage with skills and experience. Also, because they were older when they first gave birth, they were less likely to be worn out by nonstop childbearing. Moreover, because men tended to be closer in age to their wives, husbands were less likely to die while their children were very young, forcing wives to return to their parents' homes or immediately to remarry.[13]

There were of course many variations in the age of marriage, depending on the region, time, and social class. Demographer E. A. Wrigley suggests that the Western European marriage system "is better described as a repertoire of adaptable systems than as a pattern." But this adaptability was precisely what distinguished this marriage system from so many others. Because people's marriage decisions had to be based on the availability of jobs and decent wages, this meant that even before effective birth control was available, fertility rose and fell depending on the demand for labor and the productivity of land. When people postponed marriage in hard times, they ended up restricting population before starvation accomplished the same end. Historian

Wally Seccombe argues that this is why famines were not as deep or prolonged in Western Europe as in other preindustrial societies. And when economic conditions improved, the large pool of single adults of prime childbearing age could produce a wave of new marriages, followed quickly by new births.[14]

The northwestern European marriage pattern also provided a larger pool of adolescent labor, especially female, than was available elsewhere. The availability of so many single women for the workforce gave Western Europe a comparative economic advantage over regions where women were restricted to childbearing and unpaid household tasks from an early age. Western European employers had unique access to a flexible supply of inexpensive labor. This flexibility is one reason the Industrial Revolution came early to England. English entrepreneurs built cotton mills and hired young women to work in them full-time, paying them only a little more than they would have earned as servants. Using cheap female labor, these mills could outproduce the spinning and weaving that took place in private households, where wives performed these tasks as part of the family economy. In places like China, where there was no pool of single women to employ, entrepreneurs would have had to hire men, whose higher pay rates would have made their products uncompetitive with the goods made at home by daughters and wives.[15]

The greater tendency of Western European women to live apart from parents and kin before marriage gave women more independence once they embarked on marriage. A woman who married as an adult, often having earned her own dowry, had greater bargaining power with her parents over whom she married and was better able to hold her own within marriage than one who married very young or, as in Asia, entered a multigenerational household in which the husband's parents joined with their son to keep his wife in line.[16]

Let me be clear. In Western Europe and the colonial outposts it established in the Americas, women were still subordinate to men. The married couple's comparative independence from the extended family and the importance of the productive partnership between husband and wife did not create equality for wives. In fact, the household pooling of resources usually meant that a woman's property and earnings were controlled by her husband, in contrast with many African societies where women controlled their own separate property. But a wife in northwestern Europe could exert more pressure on her husband than in an extended family system, where the husband's authority was reinforced by all his kin. She also had more incentive to exert that pressure.

In the areas of classic patriarchy, such as the Middle East, North Africa, India, and China, where girls are married at very young ages and placed in households headed by their husbands' fathers, a woman can gain leverage in the family only by producing male heirs. The best strategy for a woman to ease her subordination to husband, father-in-law, and mother-in-law is to raise many boys and establish a strong relationship with them so that when they bring their brides home, she can exercise authority over her daughters-in-law.[17]

Even in the late twentieth century, a study of upper-class Hindu men and women found that most men were loath to develop close ties with their wives because time spent together as a couple undermined the intense bonds between men as fathers and sons and brothers. The women maximized their limited influence in the family not by seeking to deepen their relation with their husbands but by trying to maintain the allegiance of their sons; this they did by undercutting each son's attachment to his wife.[18]

A woman in a classical patriarchal society can wield formidable power within the family, even over her own husband, but only by maneuvering within the family's reproductive system. In doing that, rather than by resisting male dominance within marriage or seeking closer ties with her husband, she ends up strengthening the patriarchal family. In such societies, women are likely to fear ideologies and movements that undermine family hierarchies, even if they elevate women's individual autonomy. Any such disruption would be a threat to the protections they need when young and the power they gain when old.

The Western European marriage system, by contrast, offered women more opportunities to affect the terms on which they entered marriage and more incentive to challenge patriarchal authority instead of bending it to their own ends. Furthermore, wives and daughters in Western Europe had more inheritance rights than in many other systems around the world. With divorce illegal and the sons of a mistress ineligible to be heirs, a man had little choice but to pass his estate to his female heirs if his wife was barren or bore only daughters, as happened in about 20 percent of marriages. Widows in particular often controlled substantial property.

Except for *femes soles,* wives remained without significant legal rights in Western Europe. But even as early as the fifteenth century, the growing importance of the married couple household as an economic unit made marital harmony a desirable goal. In the 1430s the Renaissance humanist Leon Battista Alberti, advising men on family life, wrote: "There is no one to whom you have more opportunity to communicate fully and reveal your mind than to your own wife." The fifteenth-century Catholic canon Albrecht von Eyb asked, "What could be happier and sweeter, than . . . where husband and wife are so drawn to one another by love and choice, and experience such friendship between themselves, that what one wants, the other also chooses, and what one says, the other maintains in silence as if he had said it himself?"[19]

The Protestant Reformation accelerated this trend toward idealizing marriage. When Martin Luther attacked the Church's practice of selling indulgences in 1517, he ignited a firestorm. Within a few years, many German princes converted to Lutheranism. It rapidly became the state religion of Denmark, Norway, and Sweden. Between 1520 and the 1550s, different varieties of Protestantism were adopted by various Swiss cities. The papacy's thousand-year monopoly over Christian doctrine was destroyed. And one of the central disputes between Catholics and Protestants was over the role of marriage.[20]

The Protestant Reformation

Protestants bitterly opposed the papacy's policies and pronouncements on marriage. They argued that clergy should be allowed to marry, because clerical celibacy only encouraged priests to keep concubines and seduce their parishioners. Catholics were wrong, they said, to call marriage a necessary evil or a second-best existence to celibacy. Rather, marriage was "a glorious estate." They also believed there was no biblical foundation for monasteries and convents. Wherever they gained power, Protestants closed those institutions down. Even before they took power, they supported escapes and "rescues" of cloistered nuns.[21]

There were plenty of nuns dissatisfied with their enforced commitment to celibacy. Katharina von Bora, later to become Luther's wife, managed to get herself and eight other nuns smuggled out of their convent in a delivery wagon. She moved to Wittenberg, where she hoped to marry, but the marriage fell through because the man's parents opposed his wedding an ex-nun with no dowry. Martin Luther, an acquaintance, offered to arrange her marriage to a local parson. Katharina replied that she was not interested in the parson but would marry another of Luther's friends or Luther himself. Luther, no advocate of youthful freedom of choice, first got permission from his father, then married her. Luther's political patron gave them a former monastery as a wedding present, and Katharina soon presided over a house that included five children, several orphaned nephews and nieces, four children of a widowed friend, and several servants, tutors, boarders, and refugees, quite a change from her former cloistered life.[22]

Some rulers converted to Protestantism for political reasons, to free themselves from the long-distance interference of the pope and to gain control over economic and political resources held by the church, including the regulation of marriage. This was dramatically illustrated in England. In 1501, King Henry VII had married his fifteen-year-old son Arthur to eighteen-year-old Catherine of Aragon, daughter of the King of Spain. When Arthur died just five months later, Catherine, perhaps hoping to be sent home, claimed that their marriage had never been consummated. If Henry had sent Catherine back to her father, he would have lost his alliance with Spain and her dowry of two hundred thousand ducats. So he decided to marry her to his second son, twelve-year-old Henry. Although this violated the Church's rules on incest, the pope granted a dispensation.

The young Henry succeeded to the throne in 1509, ruling as Henry VIII. But Catherine experienced several stillbirths, and their only surviving child was a daughter. When Henry became infatuated with his wife's maid of honor, Anne Boleyn, and she refused to become his mistress, he resolved to marry Anne and produce a male heir. To do this, he needed the pope to annul his marriage to Catherine.

Henry's timing was terrible. Charles, the Holy Roman Emperor, who was also Catherine's nephew, had recently captured Rome and made the pope his virtual prisoner. So the pope, perhaps under duress, rejected Henry's request. A century earlier we might have seen a reprise of the international struggle over Lothar's attempt to divorce Theutberga. But by this time rulers in Germany and Scandinavia had already broken with Rome and established alternative church hierarchies of their own, and Henry decided to follow suit. He declared himself the new "protector" of the English clergy and replaced the pope's archbishop with his own man, who obligingly annulled the marriage to Catherine. Henry married Anne, already pregnant with the future Queen Elizabeth. In 1534 Henry seized all the Catholic Church's property and set up the Church of England.

When Henry's marriage did not produce the desired male heir and his sexual attentions began to wander again, he had Anne jailed on trumped-up charges of adultery, then had her executed. Eleven days later he married her successor.

Henry eventually went through six different wives and still ended up with only two daughters and one very sickly son as potential heirs. A memory aid helps British schoolchildren keep track of the fate of Henry's successive wives: "Divorced, beheaded, died, divorced, beheaded, survived." The surviving wife, Catherine Parr, was fortunate that Henry died only four years after their marriage or the chant might have ended differently.[23]

Not all nuns and monks welcomed the dissolution of the convents and monasteries. But Protestant governments ignored their protests in the rush to get their hands on the vast lands and wealth of the Catholic Church. In England and parts of Germany, many nuns and monks were simply dumped back into lay society, completely unprepared for the secular life.

Faced with these attacks, the Catholic Church stiffened its position on the spiritual superiority of celibacy. In 1563 the Council of Trent declared: "If anyone says that the married state excels the state of virginity or celibacy, and that it is better and happier to be united in matrimony than to remain in virginity or celibacy, let him be anathema."[24]

Protestants, in turn, insisted that marriage was the fundamental building block of society. Luther argued that "all creatures are divided into male and female; even trees marry; likewise budding plants; there is also marriage between rocks and stones."[25]

But these differences meant less in practice than in theory. The growing economic importance and political independence of the nuclear family led writers of all religious persuasions to direct more attention to relations between husband and wife. Because marriage was so important, sixteenth- and seventeenth-century commentators agreed, people ought to think carefully about the character, as well as the wealth, of their partners. The best mate was someone whose social station, temperament, values, and work ethic were similar to one's own. There should also be enough love, or least mutual respect, between prospective partners to prevent quarrels that might disrupt the orderly functioning of the household.[26]

These notions seem to have spread rapidly during this period. Some parents even expressed sentiments like those of the Duchess of Suffolk, who wanted her son to marry the daughter of the Duke of Somerset but wrote to a friend in 1550 that she hoped the young couple would "begin their love of themselves, without forcing."[27]

More and more, the words *love* and *marriage* were used in the same sentence, and the outright idealization of adultery that had marked the courtly love poetry and popular literature of the Middle Ages became rarer. Whereas medieval religious writers had used the word *love* to describe the relationship between man and Jesus or the feelings that neighbors should have toward one another, in the sixteenth century sermons began to emphasize love between husband and wife. By the seventeenth century preachers were condemning husbands who governed by fear alone, without an equal measure of love. The English Puritan Robert Cleaver said that a husband should not command his wife like a servant but exert his authority in a way that would "rejoice and content her." Catholic writers expressed similar sentiments. And the growing number of middle-class households in the expanding commercial economy created a large pool of families that were especially receptive to these ideas.[28]

A new emphasis on the married couple's right to privacy also emerged in the sixteenth century, as Protestants and Catholics alike began to condemn the noisy public rituals that had marked a community's acceptance or rejection of a marriage. We have already seen what a fracas could break out when a community in the late Middle Ages disapproved of a particular marriage. But neighbors were traditionally just as boisterous in celebrating a wedding. They escorted the newlyweds to bed, playing loud music and making sexual jokes. In England, wedding guests played games such as throwing the stocking, in which the male bachelors in the crowd threw the couple's stockings at the bride while she sat in bed with her new husband. The first man to hit her on the nose with a stocking was said to be the next to marry. Although the revelers eventually retired so that the couple could consummate their vows, they returned the next morning to wake the couple with more music and merriment.

By the seventeenth century religious reformers were unanimously condemning these customs as insults to the dignity of marriage, but many individuals clung to the old ways. In 1667, Samuel Pepys wrote that he had attended a wedding at which the neighbors were not invited, as was customary, to wake the couple with music in the morning, "which is very mean methinks, and is as if they had married like dog and bitch."[29]

Are We There Yet?

Despite the growing emphasis on the special relationship between a husband and wife, Western Europeans were still far from accepting the idea that marriage should be based on love and intimacy. Even as reformers rejected neighbors' right to regulate and supervise marriage, they encouraged the state to tighten the definition of a legal marriage and shore up the right of parents to veto a proposed match. Luther argued that parents did not have the right to force a child into a loveless match but that they were totally justified in forbidding a match, even if the couple loved each other. In the sixteenth century Catholic theologians also backed away from their earlier commitment to the validity of a marriage based on consent.

During this period the same social changes that were creating more family partnerships and increasing the independence of the nuclear family were eroding the constraints that had led youths to defer willingly to parents and neighbors on matters of marriage and sex. More and more individuals were making their living by doing day labor for wages, rather than by farming, entering long-term apprenticeships, or being live-in servants.[30]

Authorities became alarmed by the new breed of "masterless" men and women: beggars, migrant workers, mercenary soldiers, servants who claimed the right to change employers, and "idle persons" who tried to gather food in what used to be the "commons" instead of just accepting whatever work they were offered. The number of such rootless people grew as real wages for farm workers and landless laborers dropped sharply between 1500 and 1620. Officials saw the young men wandering from town to town as a threat to public order. Established journeymen and apprentices feared having to compete with them for work. Unmarried women were considered worrisome on moral as well as economic grounds.

In Germany and France, cities passed laws forbidding unmarried women from establishing residence unless they were employed as a servant in a household and requiring them to leave town if they gave up such a position. In many regions, city and parish officials, fearing that impoverished individuals who married would be unable to maintain independent households, started to forbid such people from marrying at all. A typical concern was expressed in 1628 by an English minister who wrote of a young woman in his parish that "she hath no house nor home of her own." He noted that she would likely be a "charge on the parish, and therefore will hardly be suffered to marry."[31]

But what about those who ignored such rules and married "by consent"? In theory Protestants may have held marriage in higher esteem than Catholics, but in practice they were far less willing to accept the validity of an informally contracted marriage. In Zurich, a 1525 ordinance decreed that a marriage was not valid unless attended by "two pious, honorable, and incontestable witnesses." In Zurich and Geneva, a marriage contracted by young people without parental consent could be rescinded by the courts, even if the couple had been living together for some time. In 1534, Nuremberg officials ruled that parental consent, up to the age of twenty-five for men and twenty-two for women, was needed for a legal marriage. In the 1520s and 1530s, Strasbourg raised the legal age of marriage for men to twenty-five and for women to twenty, and then changed it again, to twenty-five for both sexes, in 1565. Protestant courts were quick to invalidate clandestine marriages, even if based on "words of the present" and consummated by sexual intercourse or long-term cohabitation.[32]

Catholics also narrowed their criteria for a valid marriage. In France a 1556 edict required parental consent for men up to the age of thirty and for women until age twenty-five. A later law in France provided that a couple of any age who married without parental consent could be banished or imprisoned.[33]

These rulings could be catastrophic for women and children. Elizabeth Pallier and Pierre Houlbronne, for example, had lived together for eight years, had children together, and eventually, though belatedly, were married in church. According to traditional canon law, this was a perfectly valid marriage. But when Pierre got a job at the Palais de Justice, a post that suddenly made him a very desirable marriage partner, his parents petitioned to have the marriage declared invalid because he had not received their consent. In 1587 the court upheld the parents. After eight years with Pierre, Elizabeth instantly became an unwed mother. Her children were suddenly illegitimate, with no claim on their father's property. Pierre, on the other hand, was free to contract a more advantageous marital alliance.[34]

Penalties for sex outside marriage also increased in this period. Protestant cities in Germany and Switzerland imposed new sanctions on couples who consummated their marriage before the public ceremony, in hopes of ending the long-standing acceptance of a pregnancy that occurred between betrothal and marriage. In England, in the 1620s, parish officers began sending women who were pregnant at the altar to church courts for punishment. Some Protestant jurisdictions encouraged neighbors to spy on one another to ferret out illicit sex. Meanwhile the practice of annulling clandestine marriages increased the number of illegitimate children.[35]

Catholics also stepped up the effort to penalize women for sexual activity outside marriage. In 1556 in France, Henri II issued an edict requiring single or widowed women who were pregnant to register at local government offices and submit to interrogation.

So even as the abstract celebration of married love increased, the enhanced right of parents and authorities to veto or invalidate marriages set limits on the number of love matches. In many cases, courts upheld the parents' control from beyond the grave. In sixteenth-century England, a father's will often made his child's inheritance conditional on whether a future marriage was approved by "overseers" he had designated before his death. A poignant case from Holland involved Agatha Welhoeck, who fell in love with an older widower in 1653. After trying for nine years to win her father's consent to the match, Agatha appealed to the court in The Hague. The judges, unmoved by her declaration that she and her intended were as well matched "as I believe two true souls have ever lived," declared her a fugitive and returned her to her parents' home. In his will, Agatha's father instructed his widow to continue refusing permission for the match. It took until 1670, seventeen years after they had fallen in love and five years after her father had died, for Agatha and her soul mate finally to marry. Their efforts to gain permission to marry lasted almost twice as long as the marriage itself, which was cut short by the husband's death nine years later.[36]

The American colonies were not much more permissive than the Old World, although unsettled conditions allowed for more evasion of the rules. Eight of the thirteen colonies had laws requiring parental approval for at least some categories of young people. In New England a man could be whipped or imprisoned if he "inveigled" or "insinuated" himself into a woman's affections without her parents' or guardian's consent to the courtship.[37]

Even where individuals were free to make their own marriage choices, children generally continued to accept their parents' right to supervise their courting. If the parents actively opposed a match, the children usually backed down. The consequences of defying a parent could be very severe, financially and personally. A woman might disobey her parents to become engaged to a man of her choice, only to be left estranged from her kin and compromised in her community if the man succumbed to pressure and backed out of the marriage. Many men *did* back out of a match if the bride's parents disapproved, worrying that their prospective wife would be disinherited or that there was no advantage in having hostile in-laws. Few people in the sixteenth and seventeenth centuries believed that "love conquers all."[38]

The prudent woman obliged her kin unless she had taken a violent dislike to a prospective suitor or developed an unusually intense attachment to another. In 1651, when Alice Wandesford of Yorkshire was twenty-five, her family urged her to marry and identified several prospective suitors. In her autobiography, Alice recorded that after a second visit, her mother told one gentleman "that she was willing he should proceed with his suit, if I should see cause to accept." Alice had no particular desire to give up her "happy and free condition." But she decided that getting married would please God, her family, and her friends. This particular suitor, she reflected, "seemed to be a very godly, sober, and discreet person, free from all manner of vice, and of a good conversation"—as well as possessed of "a handsome competency."[39] Alice's acceptance of his proposal was a free choice, based in part on her feeling that she would get along with him once they were married. But her decision-making process was hardly starry-eyed.

Men too made their choices with an eye toward financial advantage, convenience, and desire to please parents and friends. In sixteenth-century Cologne, Hermann von Weinsburg's parents suggested he marry an older widowed neighbor who owned a nearby wool and yarn shop. Weinsburg told his parents that he would be happy to take their advice, noting "the wisdom of the proverb: 'one should marry the experienced in the neighborhood.' "[40]

In seventeenth-century England, Samuel Pepys's cousin was exceptionally blunt about his motives for marriage. He asked Pepys to help him find a wife to replace his sister, who had kept house for him until her death, specifying that he wanted a widow without children but with a good income. She should be sober and industrious and not someone who would make great demands upon his time.[41]

Marriages based too much on love were cause for comment. In the late seventeenth century the nephew of a Yorkshire businessman remarked disapprovingly that his uncle was "the strangliest inchanted and infatuated in his first marriage that I think ever any wise man was." In the colony of Virginia, London Carter noted that one woman of his acquaintance "was more fond of her husband perhaps than the Politeness of the day allows."[42]

For most men, marriage was part of the "credentialing" required for adulthood, or even a necessary career move. Historian Rosemary O'Day points out that young men frequently "decided to marry without reference to any specific individual," either because they needed the financial stake of a dowry or had reached the stage in their profession or self-employment where respectable society would expect them to begin a family. In seventeenth-century New England, Thomas Walley wrote in his diary that just when he had made up his mind to go to Boston to seek a wife, God "sent me a wife home to me and saved me the labor of a tediouse [sic] journey." These sound like the words of someone who has been spared an irritating shopping expedition, not a man who has found the love of his life just down the road.[43]

People valued love in its proper place. But it is remarkable how many people still considered it a dreadful inconvenience. In the 1690s Elizabeth Freke, wife of the sheriff of Cork, Ireland, thought her husband's plan to marry their son to the daughter of an earl was too ambitious, but she went ahead and arranged the meeting. To her great annoyance, her son not only was smitten with the girl but had the poor judgment to show it, thus weakening his family's bargaining position in negotiations over the financial settlement. The girl's parents, Freke wrote crossly, "found my son so taken with the young lady that they would have made us . . . paymasters to the young company." But Elizabeth was not intimidated. "I cared not to be frightened out of my money, nor my son either," she recorded, and the match fell through, "though my son was bitterly angry with me for it."[44]

Some seventeenth-century parents were more indulgent toward their children's personal preferences than Lady Freke. But when they weren't, they rarely felt a need to justify their intransigence or cloak it in concern for their children's long-term happiness. And even individuals who believed that love was a vital part of marriage defined love in ways that were very different from the mutual esteem and reciprocal obligations that most modern couples wish for. Wives, for example, were expected to ignore their husbands' extramarital adventures. In the early sixteenth century Elizabeth Stafford, wife of the Duke of Norfolk, became so angry about her husband's affairs that it caused a family scandal. Her brother wrote to the duke commiserating with him about the couple's deteriorating marriage, which he blamed not on his brother-in-law's infidelity but on his sister's "wild language" and "wilful mind."[45]

Few men prior to the eighteenth century seem to have questioned the sexual double standard, even if they were in affectionate marriages. In Miriam Slater's study of the seventeenth-century marriage of Sir Ralph and Mary Verney, there is a frankness about male sexual privilege that later generations of men were more likely to conceal. The couple was clearly devoted to each other. Yet on the eve of Lady Verney's departure for an extended trip, Sir Ralph's uncle, who was close to both, wrote cheerfully to his nephew: "I presume that once within these 3 or 4 months you will have as fair an old time of whoring as . . . you are like to have." After Lady Verney's return home, she became ill, and Sir Ralph asked his uncle to find them a maidservant. His uncle replied that he found just the woman. "Because you writ me word that you were in love with Dirty Sluts, I took great care to fit you with a Joan that may be as good as my Lady in the dark." He noted that a former maidservant of the Verneys "is very confident she will match your cock, and she should know for they lived half a year together in one house."[46]

Here we have Sir Ralph's sexual infidelity being lightly discussed, not only by a relative of the couple but by a former servant—and a female one to boot. In the eighteenth and nineteenth centuries, such carrying-on became more discreet. At the very least it was cloaked in more hypocrisy, indicating the existence of a social standard that people did not care to challenge openly. Such a standard for mutual sexual fidelity was comparatively rare outside the ranks of religious reformers before the eighteenth century.

The definition of marital companionship also remained very limited throughout this period. The fifteenth-century humanist Leon Battista Alberti told men they had "the opportunity to communicate fully" with their wives. But he advised a husband to hide his personal papers from his spouse and "never to speak with her of anything but household matters or questions of conduct, or of the children."[47]

Two centuries later the Puritan moralist William Gourge assured his audience that "man and wife are *after a sort* even fellows and partners." But he insisted that a wife should always address her spouse with reverence, avoiding such overly familiar endearments as "sweetheart," "love," "dear," "duck," and "chick." Governor John Winthrop of Massachusetts wrote in the seventeenth century: "A true wife accounts her subjection her honor and freedom." Another New England Puritan urged wives to repeat a catechism that ended: "Mine husband is my superiour, my better." In England in 1663, Lord Chief Baron Matthew Hale declared flatly that "by the law of God, of nature, or reason and by the Common Law, the will of the wife is subject to the will of the husband."[48]

Secular authorities and religious moralists continued to accept a husband's use of force against his wife. He was usually urged to see violence as a last resort and not to make it too severe, but his right to "chastise" his wife was rarely challenged. Throughout Europe, community shaming rituals were typically aimed at "scolds"—wives who disobeyed, talked back, or actually fought with their husbands—rather than at husbands who battered their wives.[49]

In colonial America too, authorities and neighbors alike remained more concerned with wives who challenged patriarchal power than with husbands who abused it. Men were so sensitive on this question that they sometimes sued for slander when neighbors gossiped, as they frequently did, that a husband was allowing his wife to usurp his authority. A husband could be fined or ducked in the village pond for not controlling his wife. Even the governor of New Haven colony was once prosecuted and found guilty of "not pressing ye rule upon his wife."[50]

The new respect for the institution of marriage that had developed in Western Europe by the sixteenth century is beautifully expressed in the words for the solemnization of matrimony that were adopted by the Church of England in the mid-sixteenth century and are still used today. "Dearly beloved," the ceremony opened, "we are gathered together here in the sight of God . . . to joyne together this man and this woman in holy matrimony, which is an honorable state, instytuted of God in Paradise." At the end of the ceremony the man was instructed to say to his wife: "With this ring I thee wed: with my body I thee worship; and with all my worldly goodes, I thee endow."[51]

A moving promise, but one that illustrated the gap between ideal and reality in early modern Europe. Those words should really have been spoken by the bride. The wife was legally required to worship her husband with her body. He could force sex upon her, beat her, and imprison her in the family home, while it was she who endowed him with all her wordly goods. The minute he placed that ring upon her finger he controlled any land she brought to the marriage and he owned outright all her movable property as well as any income she later earned. Prior to the late eighteenth century, few voices challenged these inequities.

Part Three

---●◆●---

The Love Revolution

Chapter 9

––––⊷•‹◉›•⊶––––

From Yoke Mates to Soul Mates:
Emergence of the Love Match and the
Male Provider Marriage

I f you've ever tried to alter your own marital patterns you know that change doesn't happen overnight. In history, as in personal life, there are very few moments or events that mark a complete turning point. It takes a long time for ideas to filter through different social groups. Typically, individuals adopt only a few new behaviors at any one time, and old habits hang on long after most people have agreed they should be dropped.

But by the beginning of the seventeenth century a distinctive marriage system had taken root in Western Europe, with a combination of features that together not only made it different from marriage anywhere else in the world but also made it capable of very rapid transformation. Strict divorce laws made it difficult to end a marriage, but this was coupled with more individual freedom to choose or refuse a partner. Concubinage had no legal status. Couples tended to marry later and to be closer to each other in age. And upon marriage a couple typically established an independent household.

During the eighteenth century the spread of the market economy and the advent of the Enlightenment wrought profound changes in record time. By the end of the 1700s personal choice of partners had replaced arranged marriage as a social ideal, and individuals were encouraged to marry for love. For the first time in five thousand years, marriage came to be seen as a private relationship between two individuals rather than one link in a larger system of political and economic alliances. The measure of a successful marriage was no longer how big a financial settlement was involved, how many useful in-laws were acquired, or how many children were produced, but how well a family met the emotional needs of its individual members. Where once marriage had been seen as the fundamental unit of work and politics, it was now viewed as a place of refuge from work, politics, and community obligations.

The image of husbands and wives was also transformed during the eighteenth century. The husband, once the supervisor of the family labor force, came to be seen as the person who, by himself, provided for the family. The wife's role was redefined to focus on her emotional and moral contributions to family life rather than her economic inputs. The husband was the family's economic motor, and the wife its sentimental core.

Two seismic social changes spurred these changes in marriage norms. First, the spread of wage labor made young people less dependent on their parents for a start in life. A man didn't have to delay marriage until he inherited land or took over a business from his father. A woman could more readily earn her own dowry. As day labor replaced apprenticeships and provided alternatives to domestic service, young workers were no longer obliged to live in a master's home for several years. They could marry as soon as they were able to earn sufficient wages.

Second, the freedoms afforded by the market economy had their parallel in new political and philosophical ideas. Starting in the mid-seventeenth century, some political theorists began to challenge the ideas of absolutism. Such ideas gained more adherents during the eighteenth-century Enlightenment, when influential thinkers across Europe championed individual rights and insisted that social relationships, including those between men and women, be organized on the basis of reason and justice rather than force. Believing the pursuit of happiness to be a legitimate goal, they advocated marrying for love rather than wealth or status. Historian Jeffrey Watts writes that although the sixteenth-century Reformation had already "enhanced the dignity of married life by denying the superiority of celibacy," the eighteenth-century Enlightenment "exalted marriage even further by making love the most important criterion in choosing a spouse."[1]

The Enlightenment also fostered a more secular view of social institutions than had prevailed in the sixteenth and seventeenth centuries. Marriage came to be seen as a private contract that ought not be too closely regulated by church or state. After the late eighteenth century, according to one U.S. legal historian, marriage was increasingly defined as a private agreement with public consequences, rather than as a public institution whose roles and duties were rigidly determined by the family's place in the social hierarchy.[2]

The new norms of the love-based, intimate marriage did not fall into place all at once but were adopted at different rates in various regions and social groups. In England, the celebration of the love match reached a fever pitch as early as the 1760s and 1770s, while the French were still commenting on the novelty of "marriage by fascination" in the mid-1800s. Many working-class families did not adopt the new norms of marital intimacy until the twentieth century.[3]

But there was a clear tipping point during the eighteenth century. In England, a new sentimentalization of wives and mothers pushed older anti-female diatribes to the margins of polite society. Idealization of marriage reached such heights that the meaning of the word *spinster* began to change. Originally an honorable term reserved for a woman who spun yarn, by the 1600s it had come to mean any woman who was not married. In the 1700s the word took on a negative connotation for the first time, the flip side of the new reverence accorded to wives.[4]

In France, the propertied classes might still view marriage as "a kind of joint-stock affair," in the words of one disapproving Englishwoman, but the common people more and more frequently talked about marriage as the route to "happiness" and "peace." One study found that before the 1760s fewer than 10 percent of French couples seeking annulments argued that a marriage should be based on emotional attachment to be fully valid, but by the 1770s more than 40 percent thought so.[5]

Romantic ideals spread in America too. In the two decades after the American Revolution, New Englanders began to change their description of an ideal mate, adding companionship and cooperation to their traditional expectations of thrift and industriousness.[6]

These innovations spread even to Russia, where Tsar Peter the Great undertook westernizing the country's army, navy, bureaucracy, and marriage customs all at once. In 1724 he outlawed forced marriages, requiring bride and groom to swear that each had consented freely to the match. Russian authors extolled "the bewitchment and sweet tyranny of love."[7]

The court records of Neuchâtel, in what is now Switzerland, reveal the sea change that occurred in the legal norms of marriage. In the sixteenth and seventeenth centuries, judges had followed medieval custom in forcing individuals to honor betrothals and marriage contracts that had been properly made, even if one or both parties no longer wanted the match. In the eighteenth century, by contrast, judges routinely released people from unwanted marriage contracts and engagements, so long as the couple had no children. It was no longer possible for a man to force a woman to keep a marriage promise.[8]

In contrast to the stories of knightly chivalry that had dominated secular literature in the Middle Ages, late eighteenth-century and early nineteenth-century novels depicted ordinary lives. Authors and audiences alike were fascinated by domestic scenes and family relations that had held no interest for medieval writers. Many popular works about love and marriage were syrupy love stories or melodramatic tales of betrayals. But in the hands of more sophisticated writers, such as Jane Austen, clever satires of arranged marriages and the financial aspects of courtship were transformed into great literature.[9]

One result of these changes was a growing rejection of the legitimacy of domestic violence. By the nineteenth century, male wife-beaters rather than female "scolds" had become the main target of village shaming rituals in much of Europe. Meanwhile, middle- and upper-class writers condemned wife beating as a "lower-class" vice in which no "respectable" man would indulge.[10]

Especially momentous for relations between husband and wife was the weakening of the political model upon which marriage had long been based. Until the late seventeenth century the family was thought of as a miniature monarchy, with the husband king over his dependents. As long as political absolutism remained unchallenged in society as a whole, so did the hierarchy of traditional marriage. But the new political ideals fostered by the Glorious Revolution in England in 1688 and the even more far-reaching revolutions in America and France in the last quarter of the eighteenth century dealt a series of cataclysmic blows to the traditional justification of patriarchal authority.[11]

In the late seventeenth century John Locke argued that governmental authority was simply a contract between ruler and ruled and that if a ruler exceeded the authority his subjects granted him, he could be replaced. In 1698 he suggested that marriage too could be seen as a contract between equals. Locke still believed that men would normally rule their families because of their greater strength and ability, but another English writer, Mary Astell, pushed Locke's theories to what she thought was their logical conclusion. "If Absolute Sovereignty be not necessary in a State," Astell asked, "how comes it to be so in a Family?" She answered that not only was absolutism unnecessary within marriage, but it was actually "more mischievous in Families than in kingdomes," by exactly the same amount as "100,000 tyrants are worse then one."[12]

During the eighteenth century people began to focus more on the mutual obligations required in marriage. Rejecting analogies between the absolute rights of a husband and the absolute rights of a king, they argued that marital order should be based on love and reason, not on a husband's arbitrary will. The French writer the Marquis de Condorcet and the British author Mary Wollstonecraft went so far as to call for complete equality within marriage.

Only a small minority of thinkers, even in "enlightened" circles, endorsed equality between the sexes. Jean Jacques Rousseau, one of the most enthusiastic proponents of romantic love and harmonious marriage, also wrote that a woman should be trained to "docility . . . for she will always be in subjection to a man, or to man's judgment, and she will never be free to set her own opinion above his." The German philosopher J. G. Fichte argued in 1795 that a woman could be "free and independent only as long as she had no husband." Perhaps, he opined, a woman might be eligible to run for office if she promised not to marry. "But no rational woman can give such a promise, nor can the state rationally accept it. For woman is destined to love, and . . . when she loves, it is her duty to marry."[13]

In the heady atmosphere of the American and French revolutions of 1776 and 1789, however, many individuals dared draw conclusions that anticipated feminist demands for marital reform and women's rights of the early twentieth century. And even before that, skeptics warned that making love and companionship the core of marriage would open a Pandora's box.

The Revolutionary Implications of the Love Match

The people who pioneered the new ideas about love and marriage were not, by and large, trying to create anything like the egalitarian partnerships that modern Westerners associate with companionship, intimacy, and "true love." Their aim was to make marriage more secure by getting rid of the cynicism that accompanied mercenary marriage and encouraging couples to place each other first in their affections and loyalties.

But basing marriage on love and companionship represented a break with thousands of years of tradition. Many contemporaries immediately recognized the dangers this entailed. They worried that the unprecedented idea of basing marriage on love would produce rampant individualism.

Critics of the love match argued—prematurely, as it turns out, but correctly—that the values of free choice and egalitarianism could easily spin out of control. If the choice of a marriage partner was a personal decision, conservatives asked, what would prevent young people, especially women, from choosing unwisely? If people were encouraged to expect marriage to be the best and happiest experience of their lives, what would hold a marriage together if things went "for worse" rather than "for better"?

If wives and husbands were intimates, wouldn't women demand to share decisions equally? If women possessed the same faculties of reason as men, why would they confine themselves to domesticity? Would men still financially support women and children if they lost control over their wives' and children's labor and could not even discipline them properly? If parents, church, and state no longer dictated people's private lives, how could society make sure the right people married and had children or stop the wrong ones from doing so?

Conservatives warned that "the pursuit of happiness," claimed as a right in the American Declaration of Independence, would undermine the social and moral order. Preachers declared that parishioners who placed their husbands or wives before God in their hierarchy of loyalty and emotion were running the risk of becoming "idolaters." In 1774 a writer in England's *Lady Magazine* commented tartly that "the idea of matrimony" was not "for men and women to be always taken up with each other" or to seek personal self-fulfillment in their love. The purpose of marriage was to get people "to discharge the duties of civil society, to govern their families with prudence and to educate their children with discretion."[14]

There was a widespread fear that the pursuit of personal happiness could undermine self-discipline. One scholar argues that this fear explains the extraordinary panic about masturbation that swept the United States and Europe at the end of the eighteenth century and produced thousands of tracts against "the solitary vice" in the nineteenth. The threat of female masturbation particularly repelled and fascinated eighteenth-century social critics. To some it seemed a short step from two people neglecting their social duties because they were "taken up with each other" to one person pleasuring herself without fulfilling a duty to anyone else at all.[15]

As it turned out, it took another hundred years for the contradictions that gave rise to these fears to pose a serious threat to the stability of the new system of marriage. But in the late eighteenth century many people already recognized what Anthony Giddens has called "the intrinsically subversive character of the romantic love complex."[16]

Evidence of a slippery slope leading directly from the celebration of free choice to the destruction of family life was provided by the mounting demands to liberalize divorce laws. In the mid-seventeenth century, the poet John Milton had already argued that incompatibility should be reason enough to declare a marriage contract broken. His view found little support in the seventeenth century but gained much broader backing in the eighteenth. By the end of the eighteenth century Sweden, Prussia, France, and Denmark had legalized divorce on the grounds of incompatibility. Moreover, people who were the most ardent proponents of the love match also tended to favor divorce reform.[17]

The revolutions in America and France inspired calls to reorganize marriage itself. On March 31, 1776, Abigail Adams wrote to her husband, John, who became the second president of the United States, that she longed to hear that American independence had been proclaimed. She urged him, "in the new Code of Laws which I suppose it will be necessary for you to make," to "Remember the Ladies, and be more generous and favourable to them than your ancestors." She pleaded, "Do not put such unlimited power into the hands of the Husbands. Remember all Men would be tyrants if they could." She then warned that "if particular care and attention is not paid to the Ladies, we are determined to foment a Rebellion, and will not hold ourselves bound by any Laws in which we have no voice, or Representation."[18]

Abigail complained to a friend that John's response to her proposals was "very saucy." In fact he wrote her that he had to laugh at her "extraordinary code of laws." But other men were more receptive to the idea that women should have a place in public life independent of their husbands. At Yale a frequent topic of debate in that period was "Whether Women ought to be admitted to partake in civil Government, Dominion & Sovereignty." Many men vigorously argued yes. New Jersey granted women the right to vote two days after the Declaration of Independence.[19]

America's first novelist, Charles Brockden Brown, argued in 1796 that the reason few women were philosophers or lawgivers was that they had been forced to remain seamstresses and cooks. "Such is the unalterable constitution of human nature. They cannot read who never saw an alphabet. They who know no tool but the needle, cannot be skillful at the pen." Brown advocated a world in which men and women shared work equally and faced no sex-linked restrictions in education, occupation, dress, or conversation. In the same decade Judith Sargent Murray, author of a history of the American Revolution, declared that since men benefited as much as women from a well-set table and a delicious meal, they should share those labors with their wives.[20]

The French Revolution of 1789 produced even more radical challenges to traditional marriage. In 1791, Olympe de Gouges published a feminist manifesto calling for universal suffrage, women's access to public office, and equal property rights and decision-making powers for husbands and wives. The same year Etta Palm d'Aelders argued that "the powers of husband and wife must be equal and separate."[21]

The revolutionary government in France made divorce the most accessible it would be until 1975 and also abolished the legal penalties for homosexual acts. Such penalties ran contrary to the Enlightenment principle that the state should remain aloof from people's private lives. "Sodomy violates the right of no man," said Condorcet. Although Napoleon repealed France's liberal divorce law in the early 1800s, he reaffirmed the decriminalization of homosexuality, and in 1811 and 1813 the Dutch and Bavarian legal codes followed suit.[22]

During the 1790s the French revolutionaries redefined marriage as a freely chosen civil contract, abolished the right of fathers to imprison children to compel obedience, mandated equal inheritance for daughters and sons, and even challenged the practice of denying inheritance rights to illegitimate children, the cornerstone of property rights for thousands of years. "Let the name 'illegitimate child' disappear," urged one legislator in 1793. "Nature . . . has not made it a crime to be born," declared another. A revolutionary slogan proclaimed proudly: "There are no bastards in France."[23]

The international debate over marriage and family life in the 1790s was not confined to the centers of political revolution. Germany and Italy heard new calls for women's rights. In England, Jeremy Bentham wrote critically that sodomy laws put the legislator in the bedroom between two consenting adults.[24]

Traditionalists of all political stripes were horrified by the ferment. "The social order is entirely overturned," wrote two defenders of the right of wealthy families to disregard their daughters and leave their property to whichever of their children they pleased. Another family's lawyer argued that forcing families to recognize the rights of "natural" children "seems to chase man out of civil society and push him back into a state of savagery." Another French lawyer declared: "All families are trembling."[25]

In 1799 the British conservative Hannah More predicted that the agitation for "rights" would undermine all family ties. First there was "the rights of man," she said. Then came the "rights of women." Next, she warned, we will be bombarded by "grave descants on the *rights of youth,* the *rights of children,* and the *rights of babies.*"[26]

But hierarchy and paternalism were not yet vanquished. In a conservative reaction to the revolutions, American and French legislators rolled back the political freedoms that women and children had gained at the height of revolutionary activity and backed away from far-reaching interpretations of individual rights. The Napoleonic Code of 1804 prohibited wives in France from signing contracts, trading property, or opening bank accounts in their own names. In America, no state followed New Jersey's lead and gave women the vote. Indeed, during the postrevolutionary period most states passed their first explicit prohibitions on women's political rights, and New Jersey soon followed suit.[27]

Even ardent republicans were eager to reestablish order and hierarchy in the family. Many men who supported the revolutionary slogan of "Liberty, equality, and fraternity" interpreted it literally, believing that the rule of all men, bound together as brothers, should replace the rule of despots. For their part, many women worried that in the context of their economic dependence on men, full legal and sexual equality would expose them to new risks rather than expand their opportunities. As the nineteenth century dawned, the control of husbands over their wives was reaffirmed, although it was now usually described as protection. Women as a gender were excluded from the new rights that were being extended to men, and the goal of guaranteeing all children equal claims on their parents was abandoned. As Napoleon put it, "Society has no interest in recognizing bastards."[28]

But this is not to say that gender relations remained unchanged. It was harder to dismiss calls to extend equal rights to women when people no longer believed that every relationship had to have a ruler and a subject. Only a few radicals insisted that the logic of Enlightenment thought meant women should have the same rights as men. But only a few of their opponents still insisted that marriage turned every man into a monarch within his home.

People thrashed about in search of a new understanding of the relationship between men and women, one that did not unleash the "chaos" of equality but did not insist too harshly on women's subordination. What emerged was a peculiar compromise between egalitarian and patriarchal views of marriage. People began to view each sex as having a distinctive character. Women and men were said to be so completely different in their natures that they could not be compared as superior or inferior. They had to be appreciated on their own, completely dissimilar terms. In this view, women were no longer seen as inferior to men. Indeed, they were now assigned a unique moral worth that had to be protected from contamination by involvement in men's mundane spheres of activity. Therefore, the exclusion of women from politics was not an assertion of male privilege but a mark of respect and deference to women's special talents.[29]

In the early nineteenth century, many writers took up a related theme, which had first been articulated by the Dutch journalist and preacher Cornelius van Engelen in 1767: the idea that sustaining married love depended upon emphasizing and maintaining the mental, emotional, and practical differences between the sexes. "Were a Woman to have the same authority as a

Man, or a Man the same kind-heartedness as a Woman," van Engelen warned, "the former possessing a man's courage and resolve, the latter women's tenderness and charm, *they would be independent of one another.*" Such independence was incompatible with marital stability. The different nature of men and women was precisely what made them dependent upon each other for "Marital bliss."[30]

Granting women equal rights, in this view, would actually work to their disadvantage. Arguing for rescinding women's right to vote, a New Jersey man wrote in 1802:

> *Let not our fair sex conclude that I wish to see them deprived of their rights. Let them rather consider that female reserve and delicacy are incompatible with the duties of a free elector, that a female politician is often subject to ridicule, and they will recognize in this writer a sincere Friend to the Ladies*[31]

Today it is easy to dismiss such reasoning as hypocritical, and in some cases it was. But in fact, most women *were* dependent on marriage and had recently become even more dependent. The new ideas about the inherent differences between men and women were not just a way of resolving the contradictions in Enlightenment thought. They also reflected real changes in the kind of work that husbands and wives did in the family. The same processes that had eroded parental and community controls over young people's marriage choices in the seventeenth century—the expansion of wage labor, the triumph of a cash economy, and the reorientation of production from local to regional or national markets—were also transforming the division of labor between husband and wife and the very structure of marriage.

Inventing the Male Breadwinner Marriage

In earlier periods, the household had been the center of production, both for its own consumption and for local barter. Storekeepers, merchants, and laborers received much of their pay in produce or services. But as wage labor and a market economy spread, people demanded money in payment for goods or services. Diaries and letters of the time reflected the growing realization that household production and informal barter could no longer meet a family's needs. "There is no way of living in this town without cash," Abigail Lyman complained of Boston in 1797.[32]

But there was as yet no way of living on cash alone. Household production was still essential for survival because few commodities could be bought ready to use. Even store-bought chickens needed to be plucked. Factory-made fabrics had to be cut and sewn. Most families had to make their own bread, and the flour they bought came with bugs, small stones, and other impurities that had to be picked out by hand. As a result, in the early stages of the cash economy most families still needed someone to specialize in household production while other family members devoted more hours to wage earning. Typically, that someone was the wife.

Traditionally, middle- and lower-class wives had combined their productive tasks with child rearing and cooking. But as wage-earning work and commerce moved out of the home into separate work sites, this became more difficult. Many women worked for wages prior to marriage, but it was very hard to combine all the heavy work involved in running a household with the hours required to hold a job outside the home. For some families it became a mark of economic success and social status to have the wife concentrate on homemaking. But even for low-income families, who typically needed more than one wage earner, it made economic sense for the wife to stay home once the children were old enough to take jobs. A full-time housewife's work at home could usually save a family more than she could earn in wages.[33]

As the division between a husband's wage-earning activities and a wife's household activities grew, so too did the sense that men and women lived in different spheres, with the man's sphere divorced from domesticity and the woman's divorced from the "economy." A historian of the German Enlightenment writes that in earlier centuries, when economic production was still centered in the household, "domesticity was a virtue shared by males and females, a shorthand term for thrift, hard work, and order." Advice books in the late seventeenth century still urged husbands as well as wives to practice domesticity. But "a century later, domesticity had tumbled out of the constellation of masculine virtues."[34]

At the same time, women's traditional tasks—growing food for the family table, tending animals, dairying, cooking, repairing household implements, and making clothes—though no less burdensome, were no longer viewed as economic activities. In the older definition of housekeeping, women's labor was recognized as a vital contribution to the family's economic survival. Wives were regularly referred to as "helps-meet" and "yoke mates." But as housekeeping became "homemaking," it came to be seen as an act of love rather than a contribution to survival.[35]

"For all its value within households, . . ." writes American historian

Catherine Kelley, "women's labor was radically undervalued in the world of cash transactions." Homemakers, now cut off from the sphere of the cash economy, became more dependent on their husbands financially. Women's diaries in the early nineteenth century reflect a new self-doubt about the worth of their contributions to the household economy, even while recording their huge amounts of unpaid work tending livestock, carding wool, sewing clothes, churning butter, hauling wood, cooking, and putting up preserves.[36]

While the new division of labor stripped many women of their identities as economic producers and family coproviders, it also freed them from the strict hierarchy that had governed the old household workplace, where the husband had been the "boss" of his family's economic activities. These economic changes, interacting with Enlightenment ideology, shifted the basis of marriage from sharing tasks to sharing feelings. The older view that wives and husbands were work mates gave way to idea that they were soul mates.

No longer was the exclusion of women from political and economic power explained in terms of male power or privilege, as had been frankly admitted in the past. Many men and women came to believe that wives should remain at home, not because men had the right to dominate them, but because home was a sanctuary in which women could be sheltered from the turmoil of economic and political life. Conversely, the domestic sphere became a place where husbands could escape the materialistic preoccupations of the workaday world of wages.

The new theory of gender difference divided humanity into two distinct sets of traits. The male sphere encompassed the rational and active ideal, while females represented the humanitarian and compassionate aspects of life. When these two spheres were brought together in marriage, they produced a perfect, well-rounded whole.

This ideal was a creation of the middle and upper classes, but it was reinforced by what they saw in the lower classes. As educated elites were reworking their ideas about the nature of marriage and the proper roles of husbands and wives, men and women of the lower classes were going through their own tumultuous rearrangements of personal life.

The same economic and political changes that made it harder for parents to control marriage and gave young men and women more freedom to pursue their desires also reduced the possibility of forcing a man into marriage if he got a young woman pregnant. For the working classes of Western Europe, especially landless laborers, the spread of wage labor and the breakdown of older community constraints on courting led to a sharp increase in out-of-wedlock births. The percentage of out-of-wedlock births doubled in England during the eighteenth century and quadrupled in France and Germany between the 1740s and the 1820s.[37]

The Eighteenth-Century Sexual Crisis

The elimination of older social controls on youthful courting had an enormous impact on childbearing patterns. By the early nineteenth century some regions in Europe had higher rates of out-of-wedlock childbearing than the United States and Western Europe were to have at the end of the twentieth. But because unwed mothers and their children in this earlier era had few of the legal protections in place by the end of the twentieth century, there was a surge in the number of women who turned to prostitution to support themselves and their children or abandoned their babies entirely. In Paris between 1760 and 1789, some five thousand children were abandoned each year, a threefold increase over the first two decades of the 1700s.[38]

This explosion of out-of-wedlock childbearing in the poorer classes confirmed the worst fears of the middle and upper classes that personal freedom and romantic love could easily run amok. Middle-class families, trying to prosper in a new social and economic environment, were especially worried that their sons and daughters would succumb to these temptations. That anxiety was expressed in hundreds of novels and short stories published in Europe and North America in the late 1700s, poignantly describing the plight of innocent young women led astray by male rakes and libertines.

Samuel Richardson's wildly popular novel *Clarissa* (1748) spoke directly to middle-class parents' concerns. The tragedy has two villains, one representing all that was wrong with the marriage system of the past, the other representing all that might go wrong with the new one. The first villain is Clarissa's family, who try to force her into a loveless marriage with a wealthy suitor and lock her up when she defies them. The second is the charming gentleman who helps Clarissa escape but then lodges her in a brothel and tries to seduce her. Clarissa virtuously rejects the gentleman's sexual demands, but he drugs and rapes her. Her rescue by a virtuous man worthy of her love comes too late to save her from decline and death.

In real life, a young woman's resistance could often be undermined without recourse to imprisonment and drugs. *Charlotte Temple,* published in 1791 and the most widely read novel in the United States until the publication of

Uncle Tom's Cabin in 1852, was based on the true story of a fifteen-year-old girl seduced by a British army officer who brought her to America and then abandoned her once she was pregnant.[39]

Premarital sex seems to have soared in the new United States in the two decades after the American Revolution. Most of the resulting pregnancies were legitimized by subsequent marriage, but the geographic and occupational mobility of the day meant that a man might not necessarily stick around. "Every town and village" in America, declared a writer in the *Massachusetts Magazine* in 1791, "affords some instance of a ruined female who has fallen from the heights of purity to the lowest grade of humanity."[40]

A shotgun wedding was not a huge problem for people in rural occupations if the young couple had access to the resources needed to set up a new household. As for unskilled and semiskilled laborers, whose earning power had often peaked by the end of their teens, it could be an advantage to marry and have children early, because after only a short period of dependence, the children could enter the labor force and increase total household income.[41]

But for middle-class parents, an unexpected marriage was a bigger problem. To achieve success in the expanding category of middle-class occupations, a man had to have an education or serve a long period of training in his craft or profession. A young man in the middle class usually had to postpone marriage until this phase was complete and he had established himself in his chosen field. Even after marriage it was prudent to restrict childbearing, because middle-class children stayed at home longer and were more of an economic burden on parents. This made deferred gratification a cherished principle of middle-class family strategy.[42]

In earlier centuries the transition to adulthood was regulated by the need to wait for land or to finish a period of apprenticeship. But in the late eighteenth century it was becoming harder to enforce a delay in youthful courting. While middle-class children were in school or establishing themselves on the lowest rungs of the clerical job ladder in hopes of achieving middle-class security, working-class teenagers were already out earning their own money and participating freely in youthful peer group activities. Middle-class parents had to figure out how to convince their children to accept more restraints in the interest of long-term security.

As the social regulation that had once been imposed by the church, state, and community eroded, middle- and upper-class individuals in the eighteenth and early nineteenth centuries looked instead to personal morality to take the place of those external constraints. The propertied classes concerned themselves less with controlling the sexual and marital behaviors of the poor and focused more on regulating their own behavior and that of their children.

Central to this internal moral order was an unprecedented emphasis on female purity and chastity. Individuals whose parents and grandparents had blithely participated in such customs as bundling, kissing games, or nighttime courting visits now denounced these practices as scandalous. They also condemned the traditional rural practice of a couple marrying only after a woman got pregnant. In fact, the middle classes and the respectable gentry began to define themselves in terms of sexual self-control and abhorrence of premarital or extramarital sex. They blamed the large numbers of "fallen women" on the weak family morals of the poor and the self-indulgent sexuality of male aristocrats, staking out a unique middle-class identity based partly on male self-control but especially on female virtue.

Throughout the Middle Ages women had been considered the lusty sex, more prey to their passions than men. Even when idealization of female chastity began to mount in the eighteenth century, two recent historians of sexuality say, few of its popularizers assumed that women totally lacked sexual desire. Virtue was thought to "be attained through self-control; it was not necessarily innate or biologically determined."[43]

The beginning of the nineteenth century, however, saw a new emphasis on women's innate sexual purity. The older view that women had to be controlled because they were inherently more passionate and prone to moral and sexual error was replaced by the idea that women were asexual beings, who would not respond to sexual overtures unless they had been drugged or depraved from an early age. This cult of female purity encouraged women to internalize limits on their sexual behavior that sixteenth and seventeenth authorities had imposed by force.

The emphasis on women's intrinsic purity was unique to the nineteenth century. Its result was an extraordinary desexualization of women—or at least of *good* women, the kind of woman a man would want to marry and the kind of woman a good girl would wish to be. Given the deeply rooted Christian suspicion of sexuality, however, the new view of women as intrinsically asexual improved their reputation. Whereas women had once been considered snares of the devil, they were now viewed as sexual innocents whose purity should inspire all decent men to control their own sexual impulses and baser appetites.

The cult of female purity offered a temporary reconciliation between the egalitarian aspirations raised by the Enlightenment and the fears that equality would overturn the social order. The doctrine of men's and women's separate spheres encouraged men to take a more enlightened attitude toward their wives than in the past without giving women the right to rebel. The cult of purity suggested that parental power could be loosened without fear of sexual anarchy, because a "true" woman would never choose the dangerous route of sexual independence. Putting women on a pedestal was a way of forestalling a resurgence of 1790s feminism without returning to traditional patriarchy.

But the critical word here is *temporary*. Even as the cult of the pure woman and her male protector seemed to sweep all other values aside during the first half of the nineteenth century, the new concept that marriage should be based on love and deep intimacy was working beneath the surface to subvert the family hierarchy and destabilize the relations between men and women.

Chapter 10

"Two Birds Within One Nest": Sentimental Marriage in Nineteenth-Century Europe and North America

At the beginning of the twenty-first century a rash of media stories trumpeted the rise of "postfeminist" women—young women who had backed away from the career ambitions of their mothers or grandmothers to focus instead on marriage and motherhood. The postfeminist label greatly oversimplifies the complexity of women's beliefs and behaviors in the early twenty-first century. But it accurately describes a generation of women in Europe and America in the early nineteenth century. Women whose mothers had eagerly embraced the feminist demands of the 1790s turned their backs on earlier calls for equality and wholeheartedly embraced the doctrine of separate spheres for men and women.

Sophia Peabody, who married the American novelist Nathaniel Hawthorne in 1842, is a good example of the nineteenth-century postfeminist. Sophia's mother had been influenced by the feminist unrest of the late eighteenth century and admired the nineteenth-century women, like Margaret Fuller, who continued to advocate equal rights for women. But Sophia herself believed that a good marriage was enough to satisfy all of a woman's needs and ambitions. Any woman who was "truly" married, she wrote to her mother, "would no longer be puzzled about the rights of woman." If there had "never been false and profane marriages," she claimed, "there would not only be no commotion about woman's rights, but it would be Heaven here at once."[1]

Sophia Peabody Hawthorne was not alone in her beliefs. By the middle of the nineteenth century there was near unanimity in the middle and upper classes throughout Western Europe and North America that the love-based marriage, in which the wife stayed at home protected and supported by her husband, was a recipe for heaven on earth.

And what a sugar-drenched recipe it was. From a modern perspective, it is tempting to see the syrupy paeans to women's purity, domesticity, and righteousness that emerged in the early nineteenth century as a sop thrown to women to compensate for their exclusion from the expanding political, legal, and economic opportunities of the day. But many women of that era jumped at the chance to sequester themselves from men's "silly struggle for honor and preferment" in the larger world and to claim the moral high ground for their lives at home.[2]

The English author Sarah Lewis wrote in 1840: "Let men enjoy in peace and triumph the intellectual kingdom which is theirs, and which, doubtless, was intended for them; let us participate in its privileges without desiring to share its domination. The moral world is ours—ours by position, ours by qualification, ours by the very indication of God himself." As Sophia explained to her skeptical mother, wives "can wield a power which no king or conqueror can cope with."[3]

The postfeminist generation quickly internalized the idea of women's innate purity. Early in the century there was a sharp fall in out-of-wedlock conceptions and births among native-born white women in the United States and Canada. In Britain, rates of premarital pregnancy fell by approximately 50 percent in the second half of the nineteenth century. These declining numbers were as much the result of the new middle- and upper-class ideals as they were of improvements in birth control.[4]

In several European countries, out-of-wedlock births continued to climb among the poorer classes during the first half of the nineteenth century. In some parts of Central Europe, out-of-wedlock birthrates did not begin to fall until the 1870s. But by the early decades of the nineteenth century, middle-class men and women in Europe and North America had become markedly more constrained in their premarital sexual and socializing behavior. Advice books for "young ladies" told them to avoid being alone with gentlemen callers and to make sure they never walked too close, allowed their hands to touch, or accidentally revealed their legs. Women encased themselves in a protective barrier of clothing: By the late nineteenth century the average weight of a woman's fashionable outfit totaled thirty-seven pounds.[5]

It became accepted wisdom in the nineteenth century, at least among middle-class advice writers and physicians, that the "normal" woman lacked any sexual drives at all. The influential British physician William Acton wrote in 1857 that "the majority of women (happily for society) are not very much troubled with sexual feelings of any kind. . . . love of home, of children, and of domestic duties are the only passions they feel." Dr. Acton's advice manuals were among the most widely read books of their kind in Britain, Canada, and the United States, and they found a wide audience in France as well. American and British writers labeled female "frigidity" a "virtue" rather than, as in the twentieth century, a sexual disorder.[6]

In place of the debates over the character of women that had marked the Late Middle Ages and the vigorous disputes about woman's rights in the eighteenth century, the early nineteenth century was characterized by seeming consensus about women's innate domesticity and purity. Homages to love, marriage, home and hearth were the subject of thousands of short stories, poems, and sermons, all of which vastly outsold what we now think of as the great works of nineteenth-century European and American literature. The 1863 poem "Home," by Dora Greenwell, captures the sentiments and literary style of the day:

> *Two birds within one nest;*
> *Two hearts within one breast;*
> *Two souls within one fair*
> *Firm league of love and prayer. . . .*
>
> *An ear that waits to catch*
> *A hand upon the latch;*
> *A step that hastens its sweet rest to win;*
> *A world of care without*
> *A world of strife shut out,*
> *A world of love shut in.*[7]

This poem was just an abbreviated version of the Victorian veneration for home. In 1886 Walter T. Griffin published an extremely popular celebration of family life that expounded on the same theme for six hundred pages. Griffin, not given to understatement, asserted that if you collected "all tender memories, all lights and shadows of the heart, all banquetings and reunions, all filial, fraternal, paternal, conjugal affections, and had just four letters with which to spell out that height and depth and length and breadth and magnitude and eternity of meaning, you would write it out with these four capital letters: H-O-M-E." Four capital letters summed up all the longings of the human heart, Griffin claimed. But Griffin was unable to achieve similar brevity even in the title of his tome: *The Homes of Our Country: Or the Centers of Moral and Religious Influence; the Crystals of Society; the Nuclei of National Character.*[8]

For hundreds of years, the word *house* had carried more emotional weight than the word *home.* Today we tend to think of a house simply as a physical structure. But in earlier centuries it meant the family's lineage and social networks beyond the nuclear family. The emotions associated with the house, writes historian Beatrice Gottlieb, involved "antiquity, honor, and dignity" rather than intimacy, privacy, and affection. One's responsibility to the house was very different from responsibility to a spouse and child, and often greater. As the sixteenth-century French philosopher Montaigne remarked, "We do not marry for ourselves, whatever we say. We marry just as much for our posterity, for our family."[9] For Montaigne, the word *family* meant the lineage or house, not the couple and their home life.

During the nineteenth century, however, people transferred their loyalties from house to home. The home was a "sanctuary of domestic love," an "oasis," a "hallowed place," a "quiet refuge from the storms of life." When "we go forth into the world," a nineteenth-century American magazine article explained, "we behold every principle of justice and honor disregarded, and good sacrificed to the advancement of personal interest." Only in "the *sanctuary* of *home*" do we find "disinterested love . . . ready to sacrifice everything at the altar of affection."[10]

The *Magazine of Domestic Economy,* which began publishing in London in 1835, proudly displayed its motto on every issue: "The comfort and economy of home are of more deep, heartfelt, and personal interest to us, than the public affairs of all the nations in the world." The French observer Hippolyte Taine looked down his nose at English sentimentality about marriage and sniffed that every Englishman "imagines a 'home,' with the woman of his choice, the pair of them alone with their children. That is his own little universe, closed to the world."[11]

But many of Taine's French compatriots waxed equally lyrical about the *foyer,* the hearth, and the sanctity of the *maîtresse de maison,* the mistress of the home. The German author C. F. Pockels expounded on the same theme: "When it storms in the world outside . . . what more remains to the best of men than confident association with his household happiness, intimate contact with his noble wife, with her kindness and quiet goodness?"[12]

In her best-selling advice manual *Women of England: Their Social Duties and Domestic Habits* (1839), Sarah Stickney Ellis conjured up an awesome picture of a wife's moral dominion. Everywhere, she wrote, the voices of the marketplace appeal to a man's "inborn selfishness, or his worldly pride," tempting him into ignoble behavior. But whenever his resolution starts to give way "beneath the pressure of apparent necessity, or the insidious pretences of expedience," he thinks of "the humble monitress" guarding the fireside of his home. Then "the remembrance of her character, clothed in moral beauty, has scattered the clouds before his mental vision, and sent him back to the beloved home a wiser and better man."[13]

Writers on domesticity across Europe and the United States held that women could exert a unique and sorely needed role in the public world through their influence at home. Only a wife could combat the businessman's tendency to close his ears to "the voices of conscience" as he competed in the struggle for "worldly aggrandizement." But a wife could do this only if she herself stood apart from the pressures of competitive capitalism. Keeping women in the home guaranteed that someone in the family would uphold the "higher" ideals of life.[14]

Most women who boasted of their moral "empire" implicitly admitted the limits of that power, warning that women must ask for improvement in their menfolk or in society "as a favor," rather than try to "exact it as a right."[15] Even some of the most sincere admirers of women, including many women themselves, believed that although they were exceptionally virtuous in personal matters, they did not have sufficient reasoning powers to deal with issues of *public* morality, such as political and economic reform.

Still, for most women, the concrete gains of what historian Daniel Scott Smith calls domestic feminism were preferable to the abstract promises of political equality. And many men truly believed that women, especially their own wives, had a stronger sense of right and wrong and a more accurate moral compass than they themselves. "The habits of men," wrote Sylvester Judd in 1839, "are too commercial and restrained, too bustling and noisy, too ambitious and repellent." One Baptist minister urged his son to marry, so that each evening his wife could "whisper in [his] ear thoughts of holier and better things, to encourage [him] in domestic devotions."[16]

Women were the majority of early converts in the nineteenth-century religious revival movements that swept across England and America. It was usually wives who brought their husbands and other male relatives to the revival meetings and cajoled, pleaded with, or even nagged their menfolk into converting or making public confessions.[17]

Men acknowledged their reliance on women for moral guidance in more secular settings as well. While still a young officer, the future U.S. Civil War general and president Ulysses S. Grant wrote to his fiancée: "You can have but little idea of the influence you have over me, even while so far away. If I feel tempted to anything that I now think is not so right I am shure [sic] to think, 'Well, now if Julia saw me would I do so' and thus it is, absent or present, I am more or less governed by what I think is your will."[18]

For centuries, a man had been the head of his family rather than part of it. His social status rested on his right and ability to represent his family in the outside world. Now men came to view the lives they led outside the home as morally ambiguous. Their greatest satisfactions and highest moral strivings were transferred to the sanctuary of home. Historian John Tosh argues that the cult of domesticity transformed men's roles even more than it changed women's. "By elevating the claims of wife and mother far above other ties," says Tosh, the ideology of home and domesticity "imposed new constraints on men's participation in the public sphere" and curtailed many of men's traditional associations with other men.[19]

Middle- and upper-class men in Europe and North America had already begun to turn their backs on older obligations beyond the family, such as dining out with business associates several evenings a week, hosting meals for neighbors and dependents, or "treating" social inferiors to drinks in public festivities. Now their activities, apart from work and formal political occasions, began to center on their homes and the company of their wives and children. Everyday meals were taken *en famille,* with the husband, wife, and children eating alone instead of with servants or boarders.

In the early nineteenth century, one English laborer looked back nostalgically to the days of his youth, when the married couple did not retreat to a private space away from their employees and servants. "When I was a boy," he recalled, "the Farmer sat in a room with a Door opening to the Servants' Hall, and everything was carried from one Table to the other." But now, he complained, "they will rarely permit a Man to live in their Houses." As a result, the relationship between employers and employees had become "a total Bargain and Sale for Money, and all Idea of Affection is destroyed."[20]

The narrowing of affections to the immediate family accelerated as the nineteenth century progressed. In the late eighteenth and early nineteenth centuries, newlyweds who could afford to do so took "bridal tours" to visit kin who had been unable to attend the wedding. Even when honeymoons to romantic locales such as Niagara Falls came into vogue, couples often took friends or relatives along for company. After 1850, however, the honeymoon increasingly became a time for couples to get away from others. By the 1870s wedding planning books were advising couples to skip the "harassing bridal tour" and enjoy a "honeymoon of repose, exempted from the claims of society."[21]

After the couple settled into marriage, nuclear family privacy became even more prized. The Sunday dinner, once a haphazard affair, became a cherished family ritual. The nineteenth century also saw a shift from public, community-wide celebrations toward what historian Peter Stearns calls domestic occasions, smaller gatherings in private homes, centered on such family celebrations as birthdays, christenings, and anniversaries. Prior to the mid-nineteenth century, families rarely gathered together at holidays such as Christmas. That day had been a time to visit friends and neighbors and to greet a constant round of mummers, who came to the door dressed in costumes and expected to be offered food and alcohol.[22]

But in most urban areas of England and the United States, mummers were being turned away from the doors of "respectable" houses by the 1850s. One London observer commented with a twinge of regret that Christmas gatherings "are now chiefly confined to family parties, which may be characterized as *happy,* though not *jovial,* as they were wont to be." Only in rural areas, he continued, "and among the working classes" could "the older merriment" still be witnessed. In the United States, Thanksgiving too was originally celebrated in a carnival mode. Middle-class advocates of more private family observances were not able to undermine this tradition among the working classes until very late in the nineteenth century, but in "respectable" circles the tradition was almost gone by the 1850s.[23]

The one family occasion that became more public in the nineteenth century was the wedding, although it was limited to invited guests. When Queen Victoria broke with convention and walked down the aisle to musical accompaniment, wearing pure white instead of the traditional silver and white gown and colored cape, she created an overnight "tradition." Thousands of middle-class women imitated her example, turning their weddings into the most glamorous event of their lives, an elaborate celebration of their entry into respectable domesticity.[24]

Men as well as women were redefining domestic obligations as the most significant activities of their lives. Indeed, if women's moral responsibilities expanded in the nineteenth century, a good case can be made that men's contracted. In the early American Republic, men had been divided into four distinct categories. The bachelor was considered the lowest of the four. But the married man who focused on home life and domestic happiness was only one step higher on the ladder of virtue. The greatest respect had gone to those who moved beyond narrow family obligations and domestic concerns to become active in civic affairs ("the better sort of man") or a "hero," the highest pinnacle of manhood. In the eighteenth century the term *virtue* had referred to a man's political commitment to his community, not to a woman's sexual commitment to her husband. John Adams argued that the basis of a virtuous republic must be "a positive Passion for the public good." For him, this commitment was "Superior to all private Passions."[25]

During the nineteenth century, by contrast, manly virtue came to be identified with such "private passions" as supporting one's own family and showing devotion toward one's wife and children. Religious as well as secular moralists came to view doing well for one's family as more important than doing good for society. In 1870 an American minister, Russell Conwell, wrote the first version of a lecture titled "Acres of Diamonds." He delivered it more than six thousand times during the next twenty-five years, and in print form it reached an audience of millions. "I say that you ought to get rich," Conwell told his followers, "and it is your duty to get rich." Traditional religious injunctions to divest oneself of unnecessary luxuries or to distribute charity were, in his view, wasteful. When one man at a Philadelphia prayer meeting described himself as "one of God's poor," Conwell asked the audience disapprovingly, "I wonder what his wife thinks about that?"[26]

In the 1870s the popular American preacher Henry Ward Beecher embarked on a similar campaign to reorient men's moral priorities. Beecher assured his parishioners that they should have no "scruples" about focusing their resources and energies on their own immediate families. The family, he said, "is the digesting organ of the body politic." Feeding your family was the best way to feed society as a whole. Home "is the point of contact for each man with the society in which he lives. Through the family chiefly we are to act upon society."[27]

But while the Reverend Beecher urged his prosperous parishioners to spend their money to "uplift" their own homes and make an "altar" of their living rooms, millions of working-class people in Europe and North America could not hope to achieve family privacy or shield their women and children from the outside world. The idealized family life portrayed in Victorian writings about the joys of home was out of reach for most of the population.

In the southern United States, slaveowners had no respect for the "sanctity" of marriage when it came to their slaves, and even after emancipation, most African Americans had neither the time nor the resources to make sanctuaries of their homes. In nineteenth-century urban tenements of the North, 6 to 10 people often occupied a single room. Not until the twentieth century did most working-class city dwellers get private bathrooms or parlors. When reformer Lawrence Veiller surveyed thirty-nine tenement buildings on the Lower East Side of New York in 1900, he counted 2,781 residents with 264 toilets among them, and not a single bathtub. Living conditions in Glasgow, London, Liverpool, Vienna, and Paris were no better. A physician in Paris reported visiting a patient in a room where twenty-two other adults and children lived, sharing five beds among them.[28]

By limiting their moral concerns to domestic and sexual behavior, many members of the middle class were able to ignore the harsh realities of life for the lower classes or even to blame working people's problems on their not being sufficiently committed to domesticity and female purity. Yet the establishment of a male breadwinner/female homemaker family in the middle and upper classes often required large sections of the lower class to be *unable* to do so. Women who could not survive on their husbands' wages worked as domestic servants in other people's homes and provided cheap factory labor for the production of new consumer goods. Without their work, middle-class homemakers would have had scant time to "uplift" their homes and minister to the emotional needs of their husbands and children. In mid-nineteenth-century cities, just providing enough water to maintain what advice writers called "a fairly clean" home required a servant to lug almost a hundred liters of water from a public pipe every day.[29]

The new reverence for female domesticity had a flip side for women who were unable to live up—or down—to its expectations of sheltered purity. Women who were unable to be full-time wives and mothers were often labeled moral degenerates. In the mid-nineteenth century the French radical anarchist Pierre-Joseph Proudhon sounded just like the most hidebound British conservative when he declared that there was no middle ground between housewife and harlot. A woman who slipped briefly off the pedestal got no second chances. One American novelist wrote that "even as woman is supremely virtuous," she becomes, "when once fallen, the vilest of her sex."[30]

The sharp distinction between the virtuous woman and her fallen sister left little room for the traditional tolerance toward sexual relations during a couple's engagement. A middle-class woman's marriageability could be compromised forever by an indiscreet act. In the late nineteenth century, according to historian Josef Ehmer, it became acceptable among the German middle classes "for a man to refuse to marry a girlfriend or fiancée if she had permitted him to have sexual contact with her prior to marriage." In America the slightest hint of sexual expressiveness raised fears of deviance. One Boston physician even referred to the case of a "virgin nymphomaniac."[31]

The doctrine that men and women had fundamentally different natures, then, was a mixed blessing even for middle-class women ensconced in male provider households. It could lead, as we have seen, to idealization of women's special aptitudes. But the doctrine of difference could be used to vilify as well as to venerate women. Dr. Charles Meigs explained to his all-male gynecology class in 1847 that a female had "a head almost too small for intellect and just big enough for love." Women who attempted to use their heads for more than love were "only semi-women, mental hermaphrodites," declared Henry Harrington in the *Ladies' Companion*. They ran the risk, he warned, of driving themselves mad by diverting blood and energy from their true center, the womb.[32]

The concept that men and women were suited to entirely separate spheres of activity closed off avenues to women who in an earlier time might have had independent roles as *femes soles,* "deputy husbands," or dispensers of family patronage. Women were no longer thought of as "lesser" men. But they were no longer allowed to act "like men" at all. Some historians even argue that the new romantic ideals were simply a way to justify male dominance at a time when overt patriarchy and absolutism were no longer defensible.[33]

Still, the new ideals of marriage and womanhood were more than simply a face-lift for patriarchy. Women derived many advantages from the new theories about female nature. The insistence on purity and female "passionlessness" sounds repressive to modern ears, but it gave women a culturally approved way to say no to a husband's sexual demands. In twelfth-century France the abbot of Perseigne was expressing conventional wisdom when he told the unhappily married Comtesse du Perche that she had to submit sexually to her husband. While only God could possess her soul, the abbot explained, God had granted her husband a leasehold over her body, and she could not refuse him its use. As late as the 1880s English law allowed a man to hold a wife prisoner in her home if she refused him his "conjugal rights."[34]

Once the concept of female purity was established, however, and vouched for by the medical profession, women gained the moral right to say no to sex even though husbands continued to have legal control over their bodies. Furthermore, the cult of female purity was not, as a modern cynic might initially assume, a one-way street. Men were called upon to emulate this purity themselves. Although they were thought to have strong sexual urges, these were seen as unfortunate impulses that had to be controlled and repressed. Advice writers insisted that even within marriage, men must not give way to "the unbridled exercise" of their animal passions.[35]

Many nineteenth-century medical and religious authorities warned that having sex as often as once a week could make a man "slave" to his sexual passions. The best-selling author Sylvester Graham cautioned his readers in 1833 that "the mere fact that a man is married to one woman, and is perfectly continent to her, will by no means prevent the evils which flow from sexual excess, if his commerce with her exceeds the bounds of . . . connubial chastity." Sylvester calculated that "as a general rule, it may be said, to the healthy and robust: it were better for you, not to exceed in the frequency of your indulgences, the number of months in the year."[36]

Nineteenth-century letters and diaries testify that many men were extremely uncomfortable with their sexual urges and struggled mightily to control them. Although many turned to prostitutes for the sexual relief they could not ask of their sweethearts, it was often with intense guilt. Others begged their loved ones for help in resisting temptation. "Help me fight myself—my worst self that has so long had the mastery," wrote one man to his betrothed. Another declared to his beloved, "[y]ou are the very incarnation of purity to me . . . and you shall help to cleanse me."[37]

A wife's new prerogative to say no to sex was especially important in a world where birth control was still unreliable. And many men, now more interested in their marriages than in the future of the lineage, worried about the dangers their wives faced while giving birth. Letters from nineteenth-century husbands display a strong current of anxiety on their wives' behalf and even a sense of guilt about exposing them to the risks of childbirth. Samuel Cormany, an American of the Civil War era, wrote of his wife's impending labor: "O that I could take upon myself every pang she has to feel and could suffer for her . . . because in a sense I am the cause or occasion of much of her pain and miseries."[38]

Husbands often agreed to use birth control practices, such as withdrawal, that limited their own sexual pleasure. Many also acquiesced in a wife's decision to have an abortion, a very common practice among respectable married women by the middle of the nineteenth century.[39]

In the United States, birthrates for married white couples fell sharply during the nineteenth century, from an average of more than seven children per couple in 1800 to fewer than four in 1900. By then, women with husbands in business or the professions had even fewer children. The reduction in marital births in the early nineteenth century was seen first in Catholic

France and the mainly Protestant United States, but other countries followed their lead as the century progressed. In Canada and Britain, women who bore children in the early 1900s typically cared for only half as many offspring as their grandmothers. In Belgium and Germany too, marital fertility was falling by the early 1880s.[40]

This significant reduction in fertility, largely concentrated in the middle and business classes, relieved women of the nonstop round of bearing and nursing children and gave couples more time for domesticity. Yet in combination with women's much-lauded purity and virtue, it also gave them the opportunity to express themselves on moral and ethical issues outside the home. Middle-class women played a large role in the campaigns to abolish slavery as well as in movements to get rid of child labor and reduce the widespread abuse of alcohol. They also fought to raise the age at which a girl could be deemed to consent to sex. Through much of the nineteenth century, most U.S. states set the age of consent for girls at ten, eleven, or twelve. In Delaware, it was seven![41] By the end of the nineteenth century reformers in the United States and Europe had established sixteen to eighteen as the legal age of consent.

Although the social purity movement had a repressive edge toward women and men who did not share the world view of its Protestant evangelical leaders, it was part of a larger humanitarian campaign against sexual violence and the exploitation of children. And in the process of working against these evils, many middle-class reformers gradually adopted a less punitive and judgmental attitude toward "fallen women," including prostitutes, arguing that since women were naturally pure, only the deprivation of poverty and abuse could drive them into a way of life so contrary to their deepest instincts.

The new respect for women's morality and purity had a particular impact on family law. In North America and Britain, and increasingly across the rest of Europe, courts and legislatures rejected the long-standing assumption that if a husband and wife separated, the husband should get the children. In England, an 1839 law gave the wife automatic custody of any children under the age of seven if she was the innocent partner in a separation or divorce. Later acts got rid of that age limit. By the end of the nineteenth century most Western European countries, along with Canada and the United States, also gave a wife rights to the property she brought to the marriage and to at least some of the income she might earn or inherit during the course of her marriage.

A wife's right to inherit from her husband was also enhanced by the new primacy given to the husband-wife relationship. Legal scholar Mary Ann Glendon notes that after the late 1700s in Western Europe and the United

States there was a gradual decline in the legal rights of "family members out-side the conjugal unit of husband, wife, and children." In inheritance laws, the rights of the surviving spouse "steadily improved everywhere at the expense of the decedent's blood relatives." During the nineteenth century it became harder for a man to disinherit his wife or slight her in his will in favor of other kin.[42]

The sentimentalization of marriage made domestic violence much less acceptable as well. Across Europe and the United States, judges began to characterize serious abusers as "disgraceful" and "shameful," displaying an indignation about spousal brutality that had been largely absent in court proceedings before the late eighteenth century. In 1871 the Massachusetts Supreme Court explicitly rejected the traditional view that a husband had the right to "chastise" his wife physically. "Beating or striking a wife violently with the open hand is not one of the rights conferred on a husband by marriage," ruled the court, "even if the wife be drunk or insolent."[43]

In addition, the unique moral influence accorded to mothers contributed to an expansion of educational opportunities for women. In most of Western Europe and North America, women's literacy had lagged far behind men's in the early eighteenth century. But literacy rates for men and women converged during the first half of the nineteenth century, as women's education was linked to a wife's role in teaching morality and good citizenship to her children. By the second half of the century women were even gaining access to colleges and universities.

Changes in material life also encouraged more affectionate relationships within the nuclear family. As the nineteenth century progressed, more middle-income people could afford houses that included a living room or parlor and separate bedrooms for parents and children. These architectural changes provided more space for joint family activities as well as greater privacy for the married couple.[44]

Advances in medicine and nutrition likewise boosted the centrality of marriage in people's lives. In England in 1711 the median age at death for men was thirty-two. By 1831 it had risen to forty-four. By 1861 it had reached forty-nine, and by the end of the century the median age of death was in the high fifties. "The average duration of marriage," estimates historian Roderick Phillips, "increased from about fifteen to twenty years in preindustrial Europe to about thirty-five years in 1900."[45]

By the end of the century many of these improvements in medicine and nutrition had begun to trickle down to the lower classes as well, as did some middle-class family values. While most farm families and industrial workers retained older patterns of socializing beyond the family unit until the twentieth century and were slow to adopt high expectations of married intimacy, they did begin to appropriate middle-class values about womanly domesticity. For many workers, having a wife stay home came to represent the highest level of prosperity they could ever hope to achieve. But in many cases it also made good economic sense.

Given that a woman generally earned only one-third the wages of a man, a wife who stayed home and made the family's clothes, prepared its food, grew some vegetables, kept a few chickens, and possibly took in boarders generally contributed more to its subsistence than a wife who worked for wages. Working-class wives of the period were most likely to work when their children were very young and then withdraw from the labor force once the children were old enough to get jobs. Wives might bring in extra income after they "withdrew" from the labor force, by taking seasonal jobs or doing sewing at home. But unless the man's wages were far below the subsistence level, as was the case for many African Americans and immigrants in the United States and for Irish laborers in Britain, a family usually ended up better off economically if the wife could stay home for most of the year. Year-round employment was generally the domain of men, teenagers, and single women.[46]

Until the end of the nineteenth century, trying to "make do" on the small wage a laborer brought home was a full-time job in its own right. It is hard for us today to grasp the slim margin that made the difference between survival and destitution for so many people in the past. Today it is generally not worth the time or car fuel for a wife to go to different stores to get the best price on every single item on her shopping list. But a hundred years ago this time-consuming activity was often the only way a family could get by. A man who grew up in Yorkshire, England, during the 1860s, for example, recalled that a woman of that day might visit four different shops and buy a pound of apples or vegetables at each, rather than buy four pounds from one merchant. This strategy gained her the benefit of the "draw" of the scales. Because each shopkeeper would weigh out slightly more than one pound, the woman might get the equivalent of an extra apple or a couple of potatoes at no extra charge from four smaller transactions.

Considering the time and effort it took for a housewife to stretch her family's wages and the wretched working conditions and low wages available to women who did go out to work, it is no wonder that so many low-income women aspired to be "ladylike" homemakers. Even though many working-class women had to work outside the home for large parts of their lives, the ideology of male breadwinning and female homemaking became entrenched in working-class aspirations. By the end of the nineteenth century women often refused to label themselves as workers even when they earned wages. When an interviewer asked a ribbon-maker in France if her mother had ever worked, the ribbonmaker replied, "No never." Her mother, she explained "stayed at home, but she did mending for other people. She was never without some work in her hands." An older married Welsh woman interviewed in the 1920s reported that she had "never worked" after marriage. "Oh—I went out working in *houses* to earn a few shillings, yes, I worked with a family . . . and took in washing . . . I'd do *anything* to earn money."[47] Anything, it seems, but work.

The ideal of the male provider/female homemaker marriage was also attractive to working-class families because it provided an argument for improving welfare provisions and raising wages. In England, writes historian Anna Clark, Poor Law officials "began to believe that a breadwinner wage was a reward ordinary working men should be able to earn by proving their respectability." Instead of forcing women to go to work when their husbands were ill or unemployed, charities and welfare institutions provided them some aid to allow them to stay home—as long as they met the middle-class reformers' criteria of respectability.[48]

By the last third of the nineteenth century labor organizers were using the male provider ideal to demand that all workingmen should be able to earn a breadwinner wage. Growing numbers of middle-class observers, even those not normally sympathetic to unionism, agreed. Advocates of the "protected domestic circle" were shocked to find that many working-class families depended on their children's wages for more than half their yearly income. Boston minister Joseph Cook declared in 1878 that "if our institutions are to endure," the price of labor "ought to include the expense of keeping wives at home to take care of little children."[49] But the struggles of working people for higher wages and better working conditions were to teach some of their middle-class allies, especially women, the power—and the thrill—of leaving the home to work for social change.

———·———

In the late eighteenth century, conservatives had warned that unions based on love and the desire for personal happiness were inherently unstable. If love was the most important reason to marry, how could society condemn people who stayed single rather than enter a loveless marriage? If love disappeared from a marriage, why shouldn't a couple be allowed to go their separate ways?

If men and women were true soul mates, why should they not be equal partners in society?

At the beginning of the nineteenth century, the doctrine that men and women had innately different natures and occupied separate spheres of life seemed to answer these questions without unleashing the radical demands that had rocked society in the 1790s.

The doctrine of separate spheres held back the inherently individualistic nature of the "pursuit of happiness" by making men and women dependent upon each other and insisting that each gender was incomplete without marriage. It justified women's confinement to the home without having to rely on patriarchal assertions about men's right to rule. Women would not aspire to public roles beyond the home because they could exercise their moral sway over their husbands and through them over society at large. Men were protecting women, not dominating them, by reserving political and economic roles for themselves.

But the tenets of separate spheres and female purity posed their own dilemmas. Even in the best of matches, how could two people with such different natures and disparate experiences really understand each other? And what about a match that went wrong? Should a "fallen woman" really have to marry the very man who had seduced and betrayed her? Did a man have to live thirty-five years with a wife who was less high-minded than she had led him to believe during courtship? Did a woman have to stay with a husband who did not respect her innate purity? These questions became more pressing as the aspirations for intimacy raised by the cult of married love came up against the rigid barriers of gender segregation. They were to become more urgent still when the struggles of working-class men and women and of middle-class dissidents showed people alternative ways of organizing personal life.

Chapter 11

⸺ ⸢◉⸣ ⸺

"A Heaving Volcano":
Beneath the Surface of
Victorian Marriage

I t's ironic that the staid Victorians—the same people who wrote glowing odes to married life and were so frightened of sexual impropriety that they said "white meat" and "dark meat" to avoid mentioning a chicken's breast or thigh—opened the door to the most radical critique of marriage and most far-reaching sexual revolution that the West had yet seen. Who would have thought that behind their formal dress and sober portraits, underneath their preoccupation with chastity, their reticence about sex (even after marriage), and their syrupy sentiments about wives as "the angel in the home," they were revolutionizing marital ideals and behaviors?

But in fact the new sentimentalization of married love in the Victorian period was a radical social experiment. The Victorians were the first people in history to try to make marriage the pivotal experience in people's lives and married love the principal focus of their emotions, obligations, and satisfactions. Despite the stilted language of the era, Victorian marriage harbored all the hopes for romantic love, intimacy, personal fulfillment, and mutual happiness that were to be expressed more openly and urgently during the early

177

twentieth century. But these hopes for love and intimacy were continually frustrated by the rigidity of nineteenth-century gender roles.

The people who took idealization of love and intimacy to new heights during the nineteenth century did not intend to shake up marriage or unleash a new preoccupation with sexual gratification. They meant to strengthen marriage by encouraging husbands and wives to weave new emotional bonds. In the long run, however, they weakened it. The focus on romantic love eventually undercut the doctrine of separate spheres for men and women and the ideal of female purity, putting new strains on the institution of marriage.

In the seventeenth and eighteenth centuries even the most enthusiastic advocates of love matches had believed that love developed after one had selected a suitable prospective mate. People didn't *fall* in love. They *tiptoed* into it. Love, wrote Benjamin Franklin, "is changeable, transient, and accidental. But Friendship and Esteem are derived from Principles of Reason and Thought."[1]

During the nineteenth century, however, young people started to believe that love was far more sublime and far less reasoned than mutual esteem. In 1819, Catharine Sedgwick, later one of the most successful nineteenth-century American champions of domesticity, wrote to her brother announcing she had just broken off her engagement because her esteem for her fiancé had not blossomed into love. "I am degraded in my own opinion," Sedgwick wrote, "but I cannot help it. It is strange but it is impossible for me to create a sentiment of tenderness by any process of reasoning, or any effort of gratitude."

Over the next several years fewer and fewer people were to see anything "strange" in the idea that falling in love, or failing to do so, was something that you "cannot help." Just six years later Sedgwick noted in her diary that she had been naive about the mystery of love. "Not knowing quite as much . . . as I [now] do, I fancied that liking might ripen into something warmer." People were starting to believe that the heart had a mind of its own.[2]

And as the century wore on, lovers became ever more eager to obey its will, embracing the romantic excesses that earlier generations had warned against. In 1840 the novelist Nathaniel Hawthorne wrote to his fiancée, Sophia Peabody, "[W]here thou are not, there it is a sort of death." Albert Janin wrote to his girlfriend in 1871: "I kissed your letter over and over again, regardless of the smallpox epidemic at New York, and gave myself up to a carnival of bliss before breaking the envelope." A few months later Janin declared: "I cannot have a separate existence from you. I breathe by you; I live by you."[3]

Surprisingly, women's letters were usually less effusive than men's, perhaps because a woman's reputation suffered more if she expressed her love to a man she ended up not marrying. Gradually, however, women stopped fearing romantic love as "a dangerous amusement" and instead found in falling in love the kind of self-fulfillment that the previous generation had sought in religious revivals.[4]

Just as conservatives of the late eighteenth century had warned, this intensification of romantic love encouraged couples to be so "taken up with each other" that the lover or spouse rivaled God in people's affections. In 1863, Annie Fields wrote to her husband: "Thou art my church and thou my book of psalms." Charles Strong actually called his fiancée "the Idol of my heart" and described sitting in church feeling like "a new being just made," not because he had been reborn in Christ but because he had fallen in love. In colonial days such "idolatry" might have gotten him expelled from the church.[5]

Yet the exaltation of romantic love also made some people, especially women, more hesitant to marry. Many nineteenth-century women went through a "marriage trauma," worrying about what would happen if a spouse did not live up to their high ideals. Such disparate characters as Catharine Sedgwick, the great defender of domesticity, and Susan B. Anthony, the future leader of the woman suffrage movement, had recurrent nightmares about marrying unworthy men. In the end neither ever married. Rates of lifelong singlehood, which had fallen in the eighteenth century, rose again in America and Britain as the century wore on. "Better single than miserably married" was a popular catchphrase in that era, and women repeated it to one another when they became discouraged in their search for romance.[6]

The insistence that marriage must be based on true love also implied that it was immoral to marry for any other reason. In the 1790s, ladies' debating societies in England had posed the question: Which was worse, love without money in a marriage or money without love? Novelists such as Jane Austen usually skirted the issue by arranging for their female characters to find love and financial security in the same man. But for nonfiction writers, the contradictions between the goal of marrying for love and the practical need to find a male provider could lead to some surprisingly radical critiques of marriage. The British social commentator Harriet Martineau wrote that although marriage was an institution "designed to protect the sanctity of love," it had become the means of destroying love, because so many women were forced into marriage merely to survive.[7]

In 1850 the French journalist Jeanne Deroin was put on trial in France for her "inflamed opinions" about love, and marriage. According to the court transcript, Deroin declared: "It has been said that I was dreaming of promiscuity. Heavens, nothing has ever been further from my thought. On the contrary, what I dream of . . . [is] a social state in which marriage will be purified, made moral and egalitarian, according to the precepts laid down by God himself. What I want is to transform the institution of marriage which is so full of imperfections—" At this point the judge interrupted, saying, "I cannot let you go on. You are attacking one of the most respectable of all institutions."[8]

But, many people wondered, what was so respectable about entering a loveless marriage? Conversely, how could an economically dependent woman truly choose a love match? In England the radical journalist W. R. Greg shocked respectable society by arguing in an 1850 article in the *Westminster Review* that antiprostitution campaigners were only chipping away at the tip of an iceberg. For every woman who sold herself to a client, Greg asserted, ten sold themselves to a husband. "The barter is as naked and as cold in the one case as the other; the thing bartered is the same; the difference between the two transactions lies in the price that is paid down."[9]

Even moderate reformers began to reject the idea that a "fallen" woman should redeem herself by getting her seducer to "make an honest woman of her." Wrote James Beard Talbot: "What a withering sarcasm upon our ethical notions is contained in that coarse expression. If the poor girl can induce or compel the man who has betrayed her to swear a lie of fidelity to her at the altar," he complained, "then, on that hard condition, and on that only, can her character be whitewashed. The pardon of society is granted or withheld, according as she can or cannot obtain a legal hold on her betrayer!"[10]

As had been foreshadowed in the late eighteenth century, the insistence that marriage be based on true love and companionship spurred some to call for further liberalization of divorce laws. The strongest proponents of the love match in Europe, Canada, and the United States were also the greatest champions of loosening restrictions on divorce. To them, a loveless union was immoral and ought to be dissolved without dishonor. The strongest opponents of divorce in the nineteenth century were traditionalists who disliked the exaltation of married love. They feared that making married love the center of people's emotional lives would raise divorce rates, and they turned out to be right.[11]

As the ideal of marital intimacy spread, judges became more sympathetic on a case-by-case basis to couples who sought divorce, and many countries liberalized their legal codes. In America, fewer than half the states had accepted cruelty as a reason for divorce before 1840, and the cruelty had to be extreme. But after 1840 cruelty began to be defined more loosely, and by 1860 a majority of states also allowed divorce in case of habitual drunkenness. Divorce also became significantly easier in Canada and most countries of Western Europe. The French Revolution's legalization of divorce, which Napoleon had revoked in 1816, was reinstituted in 1884.[12]

The United States was simultaneously a world leader in embracing the ideals of married romance and a world leader in divorce rates. Between 1880 and 1890 it experienced a 70 percent increase in divorce. In 1891 a Cornell University professor made the preposterous prediction that if trends in the second half of the nineteenth century continued, by 1980 more marriages would end by divorce than by death. As it turned out, he was off by only ten years![13]

The Victorian elevation of the love match had yet another destabilizing effect on traditional marriage. Intense emotional bonds between husband and wife undermined the gender hierarchy of the home. Although most men still believed they were the rightful heads of their households, they became more likely to exert their control through love and consent than by coercion. Hawthorne expected his "dove" Sophia "to follow my guidance and do my bidding." But, he added, "I possess this power only so far as I love you," and his goal was simply "to toil for thee, and to make thee a happy wife." Lincoln Clark assured his wife that he wished to command her heart, not her will.[14]

Some husbands went so far as to renounce their legal rights formally. One such pioneer was the philosopher John Stuart Mill, who married Harriet Taylor in 1851. Many antislavery activists in the United States thought long and hard about how to establish egalitarian marriages that were untainted by any resemblance between the "master" of the family and the master of the plantation. Women's rights activist Lucy Stone and her husband, Henry Blackwell, wrote their own marriage vows, declaring that in entering "the sacred relationship of husband and wife," they intended to disobey all laws that "refuse to recognize the wife as an independent rational being [and] confer upon the husband an injurious and unnatural superiority." The 1850s saw a revival of a women's rights movement in North America and much of Western Europe, with reform of marriage laws at the top of its agenda.[15]

Many nineteenth-century women felt that their own marriages were based on mutual consideration, despite their husbands' legal authority over them. Elizabeth Elmy, an English critic of Victorian gender roles, led an unsuccessful fight to make marital rape a crime and to win wives' right to control their own property. Despite her failures in the legal and political realm, she believed that in individual homes across the land, love was already breaking down the barriers to equality that lawyers and politicians still defended. "In every happy home the change is complete. There no husband claims supremacy, and no wife surrenders her conscience and her will. There the true unity, that of deep and lasting affection . . . reigns alone."[16]

Elmy's enthusiasm was premature. In most households husbands still wielded ultimate supremacy and wives usually surrendered their will. But optimists like Elmy had good reason to believe that further change was in the air. And conservatives had good reason to fear it.

Even the accepted wisdom that females were more pure and moral than men could subvert male domination, giving women an entrée into the political sphere through a different route from that proposed by feminists in the 1790s. Ascribing morality almost exclusively to women had been used to justify their confinement to domesticity as a way of protecting them from the wickedness of the world. But it inspired some women to demand access to political rights, not because they were men's equals but because they were in fact their moral *betters*.

Women who accepted the ideals of separate spheres for males and females could be remarkably scathing in condemning the moral failures of the "so-called braver sex." In the 1830s, the New York Female Moral Reform Society, arguing "that the licentious male is no less guilty than his victims," started publishing the names of men whom they deemed guilty of sexual immorality. "We think it proper even to expose names, for the same reason that the names of thieves and robbers are published, that the public may know them and govern themselves accordingly."[17]

Even the temperance movement, which began as an attempt to pull men out of taverns and send them home to their wives, became political. Within a few decades many of its leaders began to argue that because women were more refined and civilized than men, they needed to extend the values of the home beyond the parlor and into the streets. By the late nineteenth century, women reformers were asserting that females should apply their housekeeping skills to society and sweep away the evils of the world.[18]

Beneath the middle-class celebration of the sanctity of marriage and female purity, then, there were potent forces for change in Victorian marriage and gender roles. Thoughtful observers of the day worried that the seeming stability of marriage and male-female relations was a facade. Lydia Maria Child, a courageous antislavery activist and radical proponent of racial integration, declined to join any movement to reform marriage, fearing that such changes might shake the very foundations of civilization. As she declared in 1856, "I am so well aware that society stands over a heaving volcano, from which it is separated by the thinnest possible crust of appearances, that I am afraid to speak or even think on the subject."[19]

The volcano heaved, but it did not yet erupt. Most women, including feminists, married. Women who remained single did not try to exercise the same prerogatives as men. Indeed, many of them, like Catharine Sedgwick, made their livings writing about the joys of domesticity. The idea of complete equality between men and women, either in marriage or in public life, garnered little support. And the divorce rates that so shocked contemporaries seem ludicrously small by today's standards: In 1900 there were just 0.7 divorces per thousand people in the United States, while in Europe, most countries had fewer than 0.2 divorces per thousand.[20]

One reason that rising expectations about love and marriage did not pierce through the thin crust of surface stability was that these ideals were still confined to a relatively small segment of the population, the most well-published group, to be sure, but not the most representative. Even those who most enthusiastically embraced the goal of achieving happiness through marriage had not yet discarded many of the older values and social constraints that were hostile to the full pursuit of marital happiness. The Victorians did not have some secret formula, since lost, about how to expect the best of marriage and still put up with the worst. Rather, they were much more accepting than we are today of a huge gap between rhetoric and reality, expectation and actual experience. In large part, this was because they had no other choice.

Despite society's abstract glorification of romance and married love, the day-to-day experience of marital intimacy was still quite circumscribed compared to the standards that would prevail in the twentieth century. These limits kept the institution of marriage and the relations between the sexes stable in the nineteenth century. Only when those limits were overcome did people discover just how thin a crust separated Victorian marital ideals from an explosion of new expectations about love, gender roles, and marriage.

Although the relationship between husband and wife was romanticized in the nineteenth century in ways that would have horrified seventeenth-century Protestants and Catholics alike, ongoing commitments to parents and siblings prevented the nuclear family from becoming completely private. Obligations to distant kin had weakened dramatically since the Middle Ages, but husbands and wives felt stronger ties to their birth families than they would in the twentieth century. Nineteenth-century advice books waxed as lyrical about the sentimental bonds between brothers and sisters as those between husbands and wives. The unmarried sister or widowed mother who lived contentedly with a married couple was a standard figure in Victorian novels.

In actual life, moreover, the percentage of households containing parents or unmarried siblings *increased* during the nineteenth century before declining again in the twentieth. Historian Steven Ruggles points out that this increase was most notable among families where economic necessity was not at work, suggesting that including members of one partner's birth family in the married couple's home remained a cultural ideal.[21]

Another limit on intimate marriage in the nineteenth century was that many people still held the Enlightenment view that love developed slowly out of admiration, respect, and appreciation of someone's good character. Coupled with the taboos on expressions of sexual desire, these values meant that the love one felt for a sweetheart often was not seen as qualitatively different from the feeling one might have for a sister, a friend, or even an idea. The 1828 edition of Webster's dictionary defined love as an "affection of the mind" that is "excited by beauty or worth . . . [or] by pleasing qualities of any kind, as by kindness, benevolence, charity." The first definition of *love* as a verb was "to be pleased with, to regard with affection. We love a man who has done us a favor."[22]

As the century wore on, such sedate definitions of *love* lost favor. But the conviction that men and women had inherently different natures remained an impediment to the intensification of romantic love and intimacy. While the doctrine of difference made men and women complementary figures who could be completed only by marriage, it also drove a wedge between them. Many people felt much closer to their own sex than to what was seen as the literally "opposite"—and alien—sex.

In letters and diaries, women often referred to men as "the grosser sex." In 1863, Lucy Gilmer Breckinridge confided to her diary her fear that she could "never learn to love any man" and lamented, "Oh what I would not give for a *wife!*" Some men "are *right* good," she conceded, but on the whole, "women are so lovely, so angelic, what a pity they have to unite their fates with such coarse brutal creatures as men."[23] Men repeatedly noted how much easier it was to talk to other males than to women, and their journals often expressed the worry that being married to an angel might not be as easy as it sounded.

Because the sexual aspect of a person's identity was so much more muted than it later became, intense friendships with a person of the same sex were common and raised no eyebrows. People did not pick up the sexual connotations that often make even the most innocent expression of affection seem sexual to our sensibilities today. Perfectly respectable nineteenth-century women wrote to each other in terms like these: "[T]he expectation once more to see your face again, makes me feel hot and feverish." They carved their initials into trees, set flowers in front of one another's portraits, danced together, kissed, held hands, and endured intense jealousies over rivals or small slights.[24]

Quasi-romantic friendships also existed among men, although unlike women's friendships, they generally ended at marriage. While they lasted, male friendships included much more physical contact and emotional intensity than most heterosexual men are comfortable with today. James Blake, for example, noted from time to time in his diary that he and his friend, while roommates, shared a bed. "We retired early," he recorded one day in 1851, "and in each other's arms did friendship sink peacefully to sleep." Such behavior did not bother the fiancée of Blake's roommate a bit.[25]

In Herman Melville's novel *Moby-Dick,* Ishmael first meets the harpooner Queequeg when they have to share a bed at an inn. Ishmael awakens in the morning to find "Queequeg's arm thrown over me in the most loving and affectionate manner. You had almost thought I had been his wife." Only at the end of the nineteenth century did physical expressions of affection between men begin to be interpreted as "homosexual," and only in the early 1900s did ardent woman-to-woman bonds start to seem deviant.[26]

Nineteenth-century Victorians knew that active sexual relations between two people of the same sex did occur. In 1846, a New York policeman, Edward McCosker, was accused of lewdly touching a man's private parts. But a colleague came to his defense, saying that he had "been in the habit of sleeping with said McCosker for the last three months," and that McCosker had never "acted indecent or indelicate." So despite general condemnation of outright homosexual acts, the acceptance of same-sex affection as normal allowed a more diffuse intimacy for heterosexual men and women than became possible in the twentieth century.[27]

But the biggest single obstacle to making personal happiness the foremost goal of marriage was that women needed to marry in order to survive. Jane Austen wrote to her niece that "anything is to be preferred or endured rather than marrying without affection." But, she added, "single women have a dreadful propensity for being poor—which is one very strong argument in favor of Matrimony."[28]

Single women could rarely support themselves living on their own for more than a few years at a time, much less save for their old age. Many women saw marriage as the only alternative to destitution or prostitution or, even in the best case, genteel dependence on relatives. In the absence of job security and pensions, a woman who was not married by her thirties generally had to move in with relatives. Sentimental novels aside, this was not always an idyllic life.

The need for economic security and the desire for a home of her own tempered many a Victorian woman's romantic dreams and led her to settle for a marriage that promised less intimacy and mutual respect than she might have hoped for. Not until the late twentieth century did a majority of women tell pollsters that love outweighed all other considerations in choosing a partner. For men too, romantic love had to be moderated by practical calculations so long as their careers and credit depended upon how neighbors, kin, banks, employers, and the community at large assessed their respectability.

Once a Victorian woman entered marriage, she was still legally subordinate to her husband, and this too acted to keep individualistic aspirations in check. There was a remarkable continuity in the legal subjugation of women from the Middle Ages until the end of the nineteenth century. In the thirteenth century the English jurist Henry de Bracton declared that a married couple is one person, and that person is the husband. When Lord William Blackstone codified English common law in 1765, he reaffirmed this principle. Upon marriage, he explained, "the very being or legal existence of the woman is suspended." Blackstone noted that "a man cannot grant anything to his wife, or enter into covenant with her, for the grant would be to suppose her separate existence." This doctrine of coverture, in which the legal identity of a wife was subsumed ("covered") by that of her husband, was passed on to the colonies and became the basis of American law for the next 150 years.[29]

Despite the tendency of the new marital ideals to mitigate male dominance in practice, the Victorians stoutly resisted the expansion of women's rights, fearing that giving women "a fancied equality with men" would threaten marriage. In 1857 an English publication, the *Saturday Review,* declared: "Men do not like, and would not seek, to mate with an independent factor, who at any time could quit . . . the tedious duties of training and bringing up children, and keeping the tradesmen's bills, and mending the linen, for the more lucrative returns of the desk or counter." The editors concluded that society should discourage the development of any type of woman who was not "*entirely dependent on man* as well for subsistence as for protection and love."[30]

Women might ask their protectors for favors, polite society believed, and decent husbands would oblige them. But demanding rights was quite another matter. Women had no choice but to wheedle for the concessions they were granted in family life. For example, the new nineteenth-century preference for granting maternal custody of children in a divorce, says legal scholar Michael Grossberg, "remained a discretionary policy . . . [that] could be easily revoked any time a mother did not meet the standards of maternal conduct decreed by judicial patriarchs."[31]

Even the liberalized divorce laws of the nineteenth century retained a powerful double standard. The 1857 Matrimonial Causes Act in Britain allowed any husband to get a divorce on grounds of a wife's adultery. But for a woman to get a divorce, she had to prove not just adultery but an additional "matri-monial offense," such as desertion or cruelty.[32]

The preservation of male dominance even undercut the doctrine that it was a man's duty to protect and revere his wife. Though marital coercion and violence were increasingly condemned in the nineteenth century, progress in actually protecting wives from battering was extremely limited. Indeed, the sanctity of the home protected the batterer. In 1874 the North Carolina Supreme Court rejected the traditional view that a wife's "provocation" was an acceptable defense against assault charges. But, said the court, punishing the wife beater was not an appropriate response to the crime. It was "better to draw the curtain, shut out the public gaze, and leave the parties to forgive and forget."[33]

Many Victorian women were sincerely cherished by their husbands. But their ultimate well-being depended on his goodwill. Women had to adjust their expectations and desires to the reality that they had few rights in mar-riage and few options outside it. The main reason nineteenth-century mar-riages seem so much less conflicted than modern ones is that women kept their aspirations in check and swallowed their disappointments. The English domestic advice writer Sarah Ellis put the issue bluntly. A wife, she said, "should place herself, instead of running the risk of *being placed,* in a second-ary position."[34]

Such ideas still have their proponents. In 1999 the neoconservative William Kristol, who has made a lucrative career out of rehashing nineteenth-century ideas, argued that modern women must move "beyond women's liberation to grasp the following three points: the necessity of marriage, the importance of good morals, and the necessity of inequality within marriage."[35] Most nineteenth-century men and women would have agreed, though they might have more delicately substituted the word *difference* for *inequality.*

The "good morals" of Victorian women and the inequality of Victorian gender roles did indeed make most marriages in that era stable, although de-sertion, unofficial divorce, and therefore technical bigamy were not uncom-mon in some social groups. But the economic, legal, and ideological forces that limited people's individualist aspirations and maintained the stability of most marriages also had some very problematic consequences for people's personal lives and created a great deal of discontent under the surface. The principle that each sex supplies what the other lacks, for example, could turn courtship and marriage into a meeting of two gender stereotypes rather than two individuals. A prospective partner was judged against a gender yardstick that left little room for individual deviation from "manly" or "womanly" conventions. It was the idea of Woman, not actual women in their variety and individuality, that was cherished. Writing in 1839, Francis J. Grund, a German immigrant to America, commented that the sanctification of womanhood in the United States was very shallow. "Whenever an American gentleman meets a lady, he looks upon her as a representative of her sex; and it is to her sex, not to her peculiar amiable qualities, that she is indebted for his attentions."[36]

A woman who didn't conform to the conventions of femininity was ineligible for its privileges and was often considered fair game for abuse. A man who couldn't conform to the middle-class ideal of the male provider also lost his standing. In earlier generations a man whose wife worked for pay could call on positive images of marriage as a union of yoke mates, or proudly see himself as the head of the family workforce. But a Victorian middle-class man in that situation was likely to believe that he had lost his manhood. Unemployment or business failure was a direct threat to his personal identity as well as to his family's subsistence. "I may be a man one day and a mouse the next," complained a British seed merchant who had experienced economic reverses.[37]

To "be a man," a husband had to rule his household. Victorians might laud the wife's role as "moral monitress," but it was a withering insult to describe a household as being under "petticoat government." Now, however, unlike the past, men were expected to *inspire* rather than to extort submission. In the absence of women's voluntary deference, husbands could still resort to force, and often did, but the exercise of physical force no longer had the social support and respectability that it once had had. Male identity was precariously poised between not being able to assert supremacy at all and being too inclined to assert it by force.

The rigid separation between men's and women's spheres made it hard for couples to share their innermost dreams, no matter how much in love they were. The ideal of intimacy was continually undermined in practice by the reality of the different constraints on men and women, leading to a "sense of estrangement" between many husbands and wives. Often the odes to family and domesticity in people's diaries and letters were totally abstract, without any reference to the distinctive characteristics of one's own particular family. One man reared in a Victorian family later complained that home and family were more a "*feeling* of togetherness" than a place "of actual interaction."[38]

The definition of men as providers and women as dependents also laid the groundwork for outright resentment on both sides. Women wrote of weeping with loneliness after yet another day alone in the house. For their part, men could be excused for thinking that wives acted almost like the agents of employers, making sure their husbands kept their shoulders to the grindstone. "If all is well at home we need not watch him at the market," a nineteenth-century writer opined. "One will work cheerfully for small profit if he be rich in the love and society of the home." Henry Ward Beecher believed that female dependence, along with debt, was a useful form of social discipline: "[I]f a young man will only get in debt for some land, and then get married, these two things will keep him straight, or nothing will."[39]

An 1834 essay explicitly described how marriage was a bulwark against labor unrest: "When his proud heart would resent the language of petty tyrants . . . from whom he receives the scanty remuneration for his daily labors, the thought that she perhaps may suffer thereby, will calm the tumult of his passions, and bid him struggle on, and find his reward in her sweet tones . . ."[40]

A man with any tendency to chafe against the burdens of marriage could have found ample justification in one domestic advice author's surprisingly *un*self-sacrificing exhortation to wives: "[E]njoy the luxuries of wealth, without enduring the labors to acquire it; and the honors of office, without feeling its cares; and the glory of victory, without suffering the dangers of battle."[41]

By the last decades of the nineteenth century there was considerable resentment among some men about the obligations of marriage. Why, demanded one British writer, should a man take on "the fetters of a wife, the burden and responsibility of children" and be tied down to "the decent monotony of the domestic hearth"? In this period, a "bachelor" subculture emerged in Western Europe and North America as some men rebelled against these constraints.[42]

While the doctrine of difference inhibited emotional intimacy, the cult of female purity in particular made physical intimacy even more problematic. Some Victorian husbands and wives developed satisfactory, even joyful sex lives. But in many cases couples could not escape the ideal of passionlessness. According to the cult of true womanhood, only men had sexual desires, but they were supposed to combat their "carnal" urges. Most men took this injunction seriously, and diaries of the day record their prodigious struggles to control their impulses. Many men patronized prostitutes (often seeing this as a lesser evil than masturbation), but they rarely did so without guilt. As one middle-class man recalled, he "learned to associate amorous ardors with the vulgar . . . and to dissociate them sharply from romance."[43]

The cult of female purity created a huge distinction in men's minds between good sex and "good" women. Many men could not even think about a woman they respected in sexual terms. One man wrote to his fiancée, "When I tried to tell you how I love you, I thought I was a kind of criminal and felt just a little as though I were confessing some wrong I had done you." The doctrine of domesticity also blurred the distinction between wife and mother, adding to a man's ambivalence about "subjecting" his wife to sex.[44]

For many women brought up with the idea that normal females should lack sexual passion, the wedding night was a source of anxiety or even disgust. In the 1920s, Katharine Davis interviewed twenty-two hundred American women, most of them born before 1890. Fully a quarter said they had initially been "repelled" by the experience of sex. Even women who did enjoy sex with their husbands reported feeling guilt or shame about their pleasure, believing that "immoderate" passion during the sex act was degrading.[45]

Many men also found it unnatural if a woman enjoyed sex "too much." Frederick Ryman, who in the 1880s wrote frankly and joyfully about his sexual encounters with prostitutes, was taken aback when any woman took the initiative during sex. He described one young prostitute as a "little charmer" but commented, "I usually prefer to have a woman lie perfectly quiet when I am enjoying a vigil. This 'playing up' is not agreeable to me but she was truly one of the finest little armfulls of feminine voluptuousness I ever yet laid on the top of."[46]

Of course many women *did* have sexual urges, and the struggle to repress them led to other problems. Victorian women suffered from an epidemic of ailments that were almost certainly associated with sexual frustration. They flocked to hydrotherapy centers, where strong volleys of water sometimes relieved their symptoms. Physicians regularly massaged women's pelvic areas to alleviate "hysteria," a word derived from the Greek word for womb. Medical textbooks of the day make it clear that these doctors brought their patients to orgasm. In fact, the mechanical vibrator was invented at the end of the nineteenth century to relieve physicians of this tedious and time-consuming chore![47]

The more sexuality was repressed, and the more emphasis was placed on its forbidden qualities, the more preoccupied with it some people became. Victorian society saw an explosion of pornography and prostitution that could not be concealed by restricting whorehouses and pornographic bookstores to the most unsavory sections of town. By the end of the nineteenth century venereal disease was a serious problem for many middle-class men and their unsuspecting wives.[48]

The marriage of Mary and Edward Benson illustrates the sexual tensions that could fester below the surface of an outwardly conventional Victorian marriage. From their wedding night in 1859, their sexual relationship was a disaster, and it never improved over the course of the marriage. Describing her honeymoon in Paris, Mary later wrote, "How I cried . . . The nights! I can't think how I lived." For the next ten years she blamed herself for not being able to match her husband's "strong human passion."[49]

When Mary finally did discover her own passion, it was in a lesbian relationship that involved full sexual consummation. Yet she and Edward stayed married. As far as we know, he followed his religious principles and refused to seek any other outlet for his sexual energies, including masturbation. He fell into moods of deep depression, and Mary grappled with her guilt about not being able to comfort him. "I never feel my own want of womanliness so much as when he is in trouble or ill," she wrote in her diary.

Mary and Edward Benson's incompatibilities and disappointments were, if not typical, far from rare. By the end of the century some reformers had begun to promote sex as a desirable part of marriage that ought to give pleasure to both parties. In the early twentieth century a whole new genre of sex education and advice manuals appeared. The immediate, heartfelt response to these books speaks to the pent-up frustrations of people who had been reared on Victorian ideas about sexuality and marriage.

When Marie Stopes published *Married Love: A New Contribution to the Solution of Sex Difficulties* in England in 1918, a middle-aged husband with considerable premarital experience wrote to thank her for teaching him that a "good" woman, like a "bad" one, might have sexual needs of her own: "But for your advice I should not have hazarded preliminaries for fear of shocking my wife and giving her the feeling that I was treating her as a mistress." Another man asked whether fondling was "too indecent to the nicely minded woman." An older man thanked Stopes on behalf of the new generation of men, reporting that when he married, he had been so ignorant about female sexuality that when his wife had an orgasm, he "was frightened and thought it was some sort of fit."[50]

But even before these new manuals brought comfort and release to so many individuals, other changes in economic and political life were pushing the boundaries of Victorian norms. The rapid progress of industrialization, urbanization, and political reform in the late nineteenth century only exacerbated the strains on the system of gender segregation and the cult of female purity.

Challenges to Victorian Marriage

Since early in the nineteenth century young men who got jobs in the cities had been establishing a social life that was not controlled by parents, kin, church, community leaders, or employers. Until the last decades of the century, however, young women who joined the labor force generally lived in more closely supervised settings, such as boardinghouses, or as servants in their employers' homes. Men who wanted premarital sex or even unsupervised evenings with young women in this period had to consort with prostitutes in the red-light districts that existed in virtually every city in Europe and America.

But gradually young working-class women also began to gain more freedom from adult supervision. Throughout Western Europe and America, clerical and service jobs proliferated, giving lower-class women alternatives to domestic service and middle-class women more respectable places to work or shop outside the home. The percentage of working women employed as domestic servants fell sharply in the last two decades of the nineteenth century. By 1900 one-fifth of urban working women were living on their own, and these young women could socialize with men in lunchrooms, dance halls, cabarets, or the new amusement parks that were springing up near urban areas.

By the late nineteenth century many working-class youths were rejecting the segregation of the sexes and the ideal of female modesty. Some working girls found a middle ground between prostitution and seclusion. Contemporary reformers labeled them "charity girls"—girls who gave away sexual favors for treats, gifts, or an evening's entertainment. But to the surprise of reformers, these young women were not interested in the "rescue" missions that they organized. Within their own circles their behavior did not hurt their marriageability.[51]

Behavior patterns in the middle class were also changing. In the late nineteenth century middle-class girls began to attend high school in growing numbers. These young women developed habits and skills that made it hard for them to adjust to their mothers' circumscribed domestic lives when school was over. Many of them aspired to work outside the home before marriage or to pursue higher education. In the United States, there were forty thousand women in college in 1880, representing a third of all students. The number of women attending college tripled between 1890 and 1910.[52]

As more young middle-class women became department store clerks, typists, or government employees, some reformers complained that even these "respectable" young women socialized with men at work, allowed men to "treat" them at public establishments, and went unchaperoned with male companions to amusement parks or cabarets. But as other reformers got to understand the lives of working girls better, many broke the conventions of ladylike behavior themselves, joining the picket lines when working women demanded safer work conditions or higher pay. It was getting hard to tell the "good" woman from the "bad," at least by the standards that had been in place just fifty years earlier.

The increasing freedom of commercial life also undermined sexual reticence in the late nineteenth century. By the 1880s rubbers, "womb veils" (diaphragms), chemical suppositories, douches, and vaginal sponges were widely available in Europe and North America, and abortionists openly advertised their services. One doctor complained that enterprising entrepreneurs scoured the papers for wedding announcements and sent birth control advertisements to the new brides. Scandalized conservatives tried to roll back the availability of birth control. In America, the Comstock Law of 1873 outlawed any medicine or article used for contraception or abortion and made it a crime to advertise such devices. In the long run, however, these campaigns could not reverse women's expanding access to birth control. In fact, the controversy over these issues helped break the silence that had until then surrounded sexuality.[53]

The growing women's rights movement weighed in with its critique of male-female relations. Although the movement was primarily focused on winning women the right to vote, by the 1880s a radical wing was insisting that thousands of women were trapped in repressive marriages. In England, Mona Caird shocked readers of the *Daily Telegraph* in 1888, when she claimed that the institution of marriage was an invasion of women's personal liberty. In two months the paper received twenty-seven thousand letters, pro and con, leading the editor to cut off all further discussion. Henrik Ibsen's play *A Doll's House* made another radical critique of marriage. First performed in Copenhagen in 1879, the play's ending, in which Nora leaves her family to find the self-fulfillment denied her as a wife, outraged most critics. Yet it played to packed audiences all across Europe during the 1890s (although Ibsen bowed to pressure and changed the ending for the German production).[54]

In England, the case of Emily Hall and Edward Jackson spurred a radical transformation in traditional marriage law. Hall and Jackson had married in 1887 but lived together for only a few days before she returned to her family. In 1889 Jackson got a court order against Hall for "restitution of conjugal rights." Emily simply ignored the order because five years earlier Parliament had abolished penalties for spouses who refused to grant conjugal rights. In 1891 the frustrated Jackson kidnapped his erstwhile wife on her way home from church. Emily's family immediately took Edward to court to win her freedom. A lower court ruled in Jackson's favor, on the traditional grounds that a husband was entitled to custody over his wife. The Court of Appeal, however, reversed the decision, holding that no English subject could be imprisoned by another, even if he was her husband.[55]

Responding to the ruling, feminist Elizabeth Elmy wrote ecstatically to a friend, "Let us rejoice together . . . coverture is dead and buried." Writing from an opposing viewpoint, antiwoman's rights journalist Eliza Lynn Fulton complained that the Court of Appeal had "suddenly abolished [marriage] one fine morning!"[56]

As it turned out, Elmy's hopes and Fulton's fears were premature. Most governments in Europe and most states and provinces in North America retained "head and master" laws that allowed husbands to make family decisions without consulting their wives right up until the 1970s. Still, improvements in women's legal status continued to accumulate in the 1880s and 1890s, and the women's rights movement gained converts as the century drew to an end.[57]

Even women who had spent most of their lives celebrating woman's special sphere began to endorse the demand for political rights and personal freedoms. Frances Willard had become a leader of the temperance movement because of her commitment to domesticity: She hated alcohol because it pulled men away from their duties to wives, children, and home. In time, however, she came to believe that women needed the vote. At age fifty-three she published a book describing the joys of learning how to ride a bicycle, even though, she told her readers, just ten years earlier she would have found the idea of engaging in such unladylike activity horrifying.[58]

"We have got the new woman in everything except the counting of her vote at the ballot box," commented suffragist Susan B. Anthony in 1895. "And that's coming."

The "protectors" of women's special sphere reacted to these changes with near hysteria. Physicians claimed that bicycle riding was a woman's first step down the road to sexual abandon. In 1890 the British anthropologist James Allen predicted that granting married women the vote would lead to "social revolution, disruption of domestic ties, desecration of marriage, destruction of the household gods, dissolution of the family." In 1895, James Weir warned readers of the *American Naturalist* that establishment of equal rights would lead directly to "that abyss of immoral horrors so repugnant to our cultivated ethical tastes—the matriarchate."[59]

When women finally got the vote in England after World War I, the editor of the *Saturday Review* called it a form of treason. "While the men of England were abroad dying by the hundreds of thousands for the preservation of

England," he charged, Parliament "handed over the government of England to the women . . . who were living at home in ease. Surely valour and suffering and death never had a poorer reward."

But by that time traditional patriarchal powers had been under siege for two decades, and the system of gender segregation was already crumbling. A new woman was indeed entering the scene. Whether she was marching in a suffrage demonstration, shedding her corset to pedal her bicycle down a country lane, working or shopping at the huge new department stores in the cities, or decorously demanding sex education for her daughter, the New Woman was stepping off the pedestal of homebound domesticity and female purity. Many observers believed that the thin crust separating society from "the heaving volcano" of marriage and gender tensions was on the verge of collapse. And they were right.

Chapter 12

—————⇒«◎»⇐—————

"The Time When Mountains Move Has Come": From Sentimental to Sexual Marriage

In 1911 the Japanese poet Yosano Akiko captured the tectonic shift in male-female relations that was shaking up the industrializing world:

The time when mountains move has come.
People may not believe my words
But mountains have only slept for a while.
In the ancient days
All mountains moved,
Dancing with fire,
Though you may not believe it.
But oh, believe this.
All women, who have slept,
Wake now and move.[1]

A similar revolution was transforming the role of youth in society. In both cases, it was the middle class—bulwark of female purity and domesticity in the nineteenth century—that overturned the Victorian system of gender seg-regation and sexual reticence.

In the first two decades of the new century, men and women began to socialize on more equal terms, throwing off the conventions that had made nineteenth-century male-female interactions so stilted. People gained un-precedented access to information about birth control and sexuality, relieving many of the sexual tensions and fears that had plagued Victorian marriage. The old veneration of same-sex friendships and holy motherhood, which had competed with the couple bond in many people's emotional loyalties, was tossed aside as people redoubled their search for heterosexual romance. Yet just as the Victorians' efforts to sanctify marriage had created unanticipated tensions and contradictions, so the innovations of the 1920s resolved old frus-trations only to create a whole new threat to the stability of the love-based male breadwinner marriage.

The idea that men and women should move in separate spheres swiftly collapsed. Between 1900 and the late 1920s the struggle for suffrage became a powerful international movement. The largest women's movements were in Western Europe and North America, but in the early 1900s the International Woman Suffrage Alliance and the International Council of Women gained affiliates in Latin America, Central and Eastern Europe, South Africa, China, India, and Palestine. New Zealand women won the vote as early as 1900.[2]

In the first twenty years of the century, the late-nineteenth-century cru-sade against birth control was turned back. In America the *Ladies' Home Jour-nal* championed sex education, and in 1916 Margaret Sanger opened the first public birth control clinic in the country. By the 1920s H. L. Mencken could claim that "the veriest schoolgirl today knows as much [about birth control] as the midwife of 1885."[3]

Perhaps most shocking was the emergence of a new generation of women more interested in pursuing their personal liberation than expanding the polit-ical goals of their suffragist predecessors or quietly incorporating birth control into their married lives, as their mothers had done. America had the flapper. France had *La Garçonne,* the French word for boy with a feminine ending. Brazil had its Carioca girl. In Germany she was called the *Bubikopf,* the woman with bobbed hair. In Japan she was the *moga* or *modan gaaru* (modern girl). In Italy, even Mussolini's Fascists couldn't get rid of *la maschietta,* who, like her counterparts in the rest of Europe and in the United States, bobbed her hair, smoked cigarettes, favored short dresses, and went out on the town without any chaperone.[4]

Unlike the female social reformers of the 1890s, the New Woman of the 1900s embraced the idea that women had sexual passions. The designation *La Garçonne* came from Victor Margueritte's controversial 1921 novel of the same title, which got the author expelled from the French Legion of Honor. Margueritte's heroine walked away from marriage to a man who was more interested in her family's money than in her love. She became a career woman and chose to have sexual relationships outside marriage. The novel caused a sensation. A million copies of the book had been sold by 1929, and it was translated into thirteen languages.[5]

Suddenly sex was the number one topic of conversation. From Vienna, Sigmund Freud circulated his theories about the power of the sexual instinct. In Sweden, feminist Ellen Key developed an international reputation for her work on "the new erotic ethics." In England, the renowned "sexologist" Havelock Ellis declared that sex was one of "the great driving forces of human life." Sex, he maintained, was "an ever-living fire that nothing will extinguish." In Germany, Helene Stocker's magazine *Die Neue Generation* ("The New Generation") set out to discredit a hundred years of middle-class theorizing about women's passive sexuality.[6]

Poets and novelists joined sociologists and psychologists in the celebration of sex. Odes to mother, home, and "the angel in the house" continued to appear. But alongside these, poems and novels with dramatically different themes and imagery sprang up. The very title of one poem, "Climax," published in 1925 by the American Gladys Oaks, would have horrified most Victorians.[7]

The growing openness about sex spread beyond intellectuals and bohemians. Memoirs of the time show that even people who had never read Freud or Ellis had seen or heard simplified versions of their theories in popular magazines and at cocktail parties. A decade later a French social critic remarked that the popularization of Freud was "one of the greatest moral revolutions that ever happened in America." Americans, he claimed, had greeted Freud's theories about sexuality "as the one missing link in the general program of universal improvement."[8]

Popular culture became saturated with sex. The new advertising industry quickly discovered the appeal of a provocatively posed woman. Silent movies in the United States contained so much sexual innuendo that the government instituted film censorship in 1910. Even after censorship, movies could get pretty steamy. Young people in the 1920s went to see films like *Flaming Youth,* advertised as an exposé of "neckers, petters, white kisses, red kisses, pleasure-mad daughters, sensation-craving mothers, by an author who didn't dare sign his name." One seventeen-year-old commented: "No wonder girls of the older days, before movies, were so modest and bashful. They never saw Clara Bow and William Haines . . . If we did not see such examples . . . where would we get the idea of being 'hot'?" Dance halls and cabarets proliferated across Europe and the Americas, and people flocked to classes to learn the sexually suggestive moves of such dance rages as the tango.[9]

The rejection of Victorian gender segregation and sexual reticence was most visible among young people. Indeed, the growth of an independent youth culture was one of the most dramatic features of the early 1900s. Young people had gained the right to select their own marriage partners more than a century before. Now they were starting to sample the merchandise before making their final selection. The youth culture burst upon the scene across Europe and North America during the 1920s, and the American version was especially well publicized by the new mass media.

As early as the 1880s young working-class men and women were already socializing in ways that blurred the Victorian distinction between "reputable" and "disreputable" youth. But in that same period, middle-class parents had shored up their defenses against "contamination" of their children by such lower-class "vices." By the end of the nineteenth century the middle class had developed an elaborate courtship ritual whereby a young man would be invited to "call" at a woman's home and the two would develop their romantic relationship in the parlor or on the front porch, closely supervised by the girl's family.[10]

"Calling" gave a girl's parents extensive control over whom she saw and how she behaved. It took place at the girl's home, with hospitality provided by her family. For that reason, it was considered unseemly for a man to take the initiative in calling. As late as 1909 one young man asked the advice columnist at the *Ladies' Home Journal* if it would be all right "to call upon a young woman whom I greatly admire, although she had not given me the permission." He wondered if she would be "flattered at my eagerness . . . or would she think me impertinent?" The columnist warned that such a presumptuous act would certainly incur the girl's "just displeasure." It was the "girl's privilege" to ask a man to call, although "nothing forbids a man to show by his manner that her acquaintance is pleasing to him and thus perhaps suggest that the invitation would be welcome."[11] This was the same advice later doled out to girls once the dating system replaced calling.

The word *date* was not used in its modern sense until the 1890s, and even then it was only used in working-class slang. By 1914, however, the respectable middle-class *Ladies' Home Journal* had begun to use the word, putting it in quotation marks to indicate its novelty.[12]

A date took place in the public sphere, away from home. It involved money, because when you moved from drinking mother's lemonade on the front porch to buying Cokes at a restaurant, someone had to pay. And because in the context of women's second-class economic status, the boy would have to pay, a girl could not ask a boy to take her out. The initiative thus shifted from the girl and her family to the boy.

The new custom of dating spread rapidly, and it was sped along by the automobile. In 1924 a journalist in the *Literary Digest* wrote that in earlier days, when a boy "took the girl 'buggy-riding,' . . . the return was usually long before the stars had begun to fade . . . but nowadays the gay young gallant steps on the gas, and the pair are soon beyond any sort of parental or other surveillance." The car, noted one anxious observer of new trends fretfully, was "a house of prostitution on wheels."[13]

In 1994, several students and I interviewed a ninety-five-year-old woman for an oral history project. She told us that as a teenager she went to the movies to learn the right way to kiss, and after the movie she and her boyfriend would drive to the local lovers' lane to try out the new techniques. Overhearing, the woman sitting next to her in the nursing home lounge exclaimed: "Oh, my goodness, I always thought I was so bad for doing that!"

Not every young woman of the 1920s felt guilty about such behavior. Dorothy Dix, the best-known advice columnist of that era, commented acerbically that "modern" young women think nothing "of kissing every Tom, Dick and Harry who comes along and in indulging in petting parties and 'necking.'" One fourteen-year-old wrote in her diary, "I want to be modern and whicked [*sic*] and sophisticated." A few years later, after a weekend without a date, the same girl complained: "I want to be necked! I do! It gives me a sensation I love."[14]

Ninety-two percent of American college girls surveyed in the 1920s reported engaging in petting—fondling body parts below the neck. Historians estimate that at least a third, and probably closer to half, of women who came of age in the 1920s had had sex before marriage, twice the rate of premarital intercourse reported by the generation immediately preceding them. By this time young middle-class men were more likely to lose their virginity with women of their own class than with prostitutes.[15]

Alcohol and drugs stimulated youthful experimentation. Drinking was fashionable among the "modern" set in the 1920s, and cocaine was easily available, often in over-the-counter "medicines." Coca-Cola, as its name suggests, contained small amounts of cocaine in its early years, and Gray's Catarrh Powder, a cough remedy, contained as much pure cocaine as the street cocaine of the 1980s. Most of the youths who used compounds such as Gray's lived in "tough" urban neighborhoods. But cocaine use was also common among affluent urban sophisticates. The Cole Porter verse we now hear as "I get no kick from champagne" was written as "I get no kick from cocaine."[16]

Not surprisingly, contemporaries reported a huge "generation gap" between young and old. A 1917 article in *Good Housekeeping* commented that mothers of modern girls feel "very much like hens that have hatched out ducks." Some blamed youths for "going wild"; others blamed their parents. A letter to the *Ladies' Home Journal* complained of "immodest dress, profanity . . . the disease of materialism, the lost sense of duty," and the "disregard of marriage vows," all of which were due to the "criminal negligence" of modern parents and "the excess of liberty they permit."[17]

Once again observers worried about the future of marriage, and with some reason. The boundaries between men's and women's spheres of activity had been blurred. The doctrine of sexual purity had fallen by the wayside. The combined assaults of sexual freedom and women's political emancipation seemed likely to topple marriage from its recently installed place as the center of people's emotional commitments. One observer complained that modern teachings were leading to "the wreck of love," as sex and love became "so accessible, so un-mysterious, and so free" that they were trivialized.[18]

Women's rejection of domestic self-sacrifice got much of the blame. In 1907, Anna Rogers complained in the *Atlantic Monthly* that women's traditional commitment to family had given way to "the worship of the brazen calf of Self." The man who wrote *Flaming Youth* acerbically dedicated his book to the woman of the 1920s: "restless, seductive, greedy, discontented, craving sensation, unrestrained, a little morbid, more than a little selfish, . . . slack of mind as she is trim of body, . . . fit mate for the hurried, reckless and cynical man of the age."[19]

Fears about women's political and personal emancipation were compounded by the surge in women's employment between 1900 and 1920. William Sumner wrote in the 1924 *Yale Review* that this had produced "the greatest revolution" in the history of marriage since the invention of the father-headed family many millennia earlier. It gave women "careers and ambitions which have dislodged marriage from its supreme place in their interest and life plan."[20]

At the same time, the new focus on sexual pleasure upped the ante for a successful marriage. Nineteenth-century writers had already declared that a loveless marriage was a tragedy. In the 1920s some began to say the same thing about marriages in which the sex was unsatisfactory. New Zealand reformer Ettie Rout claimed that a marriage lacking in "joy" was "easily the most dangerous of all our social institutions." In 1928, in a book titled *The Marriage Crisis,* sociologist Ernest Groves worried that pursuit of "the pleasure principle" was creating unrealistic expectations that marriage could "furnish individual satisfaction" that outweighed all its traditional burdens.[21]

There was, in fact, good reason to worry about the future of marriage. In a 1928 survey, one-quarter of married American men and women admitted to having had at least one affair. The surge in divorce across Europe and North America during and after World War I was another troublesome sign. In the United States a marriage that began in 1880 had one chance in twelve of ending in divorce. By the late 1920s the chance was about one in six.[22]

Conservatives had long claimed that rising expectations about finding happiness in marriage would lead to an increase in divorce. They were now proved right. Increasingly, people filed for divorce because their marriages did not provide love, companionship, and emotional intimacy, rather than because their partners were cruel or had failed to perform their marital roles as housekeeper or provider. President Theodore Roosevelt was horrified by the idea that lack of love could "excuse the breaking up of a home." But many ordinary Europeans and Americans chuckled approvingly when they read George Bernard Shaw's argument for no-fault divorce: "Send the husband and wife to penal servitude if you disapprove of their conduct and want to punish them; but don't send them back to perpetual wedlock."[23]

The stigma attached to sex outside marriage was fading in many circles. Calls were heard for the legalization of trial marriages. Progressive-era businessman and political activist William Carson thought it unfair "that any woman whose maternal instinct was strong, but was unable to marry, should be deprived of the opportunity to satisfy that instinct."[24]

Some public figures even argued that the pleasures of sexuality and love should not be denied to individuals who sought them with their own sex. Havelock Ellis, for example, whose work was widely read in the United States, believed that "sexual inversion," his term for homosexuality, was inborn. Therefore, he argued, it was wrong to deny the rights of intimacy to gays and lesbians. Others went even further. In 1915, Margaret Anderson claimed that mere "tolerance" of homosexual love was patronizing, for there was "no difference between the normal and the inverted type." A 1918 book, *Despised and Rejected,* praised homosexual men for evolving "a new humanity . . . not limited by the psychological bounds of one sex."[25]

Homosexual subcultures existed in large cities and small, at steam baths and gay bars, and often around YMCAs. In mass culture, the attitude toward gays and lesbians was hardly approving, but there was a surprising level of tolerance for everything from discreet clubs in small communities to openly gay dances and parades in larger cities. Historian Sharon Ullman notes that "intense curiosity" about shifting gender and sex norms made female impersonators "among the most successful and highly paid stars" during the first two decades of the twentieth century.[26]

Socialists and feminists such as Henrietta Rodman called for radical changes to the nuclear family, with communal kitchens and housing arrangements freeing women from household drudgery. Charlotte Perkins Gilman paved the way for almost a hundred years of nail biting about what women's rights activists *really* want with her 1915 novel *Herland,* where women live and raise children entirely without men's assistance.[27]

Some observers despaired of the future. "Is Marriage Bankrupt?" asked a newspaper article. Columnist Walter Lippmann warned that the spread of birth control had made regulation of women's chastity impossible. In 1928, John Watson, a widely read child psychologist in the United States, predicted that fifty years hence there would be "no such thing as marriage."[28]

Once more, these fears were premature. There was no widespread rejection of marriage in the 1920s; indeed, rates of lifelong singlehood fell. Most people who supported women's emancipation and the new openness about sexuality thought these changes would improve marriage by making it more intimate. And during the course of the decade, radicals who had argued for overturning marriage either changed their views or were marginalized.

It is very common for people who are advocating a new set of ideas to exaggerate their attack on the status quo in order to shake things up and then to back off in favor of more modest goals. This happened in the 1920s, just as it would in the late 1960s and early 1970s. One activist of the 1920s explained that the sexual radicalism just before and after World War I was an "ideological overcompensation" against the sexual repressiveness of nineteenth-century marriage, an overcompensation that most right-thinking people, including himself, had corrected by the end of the decade.[29]

The revolutionary innovations of the early twentieth century were meant to strengthen, not weaken, marriage's hold on people's emotions and loyalties. Deep marital intimacy had been difficult to achieve in the nineteenth century, in the face of separate spheres for men and women, sexual repressiveness, and the strong cultural, practical, and moral limits on a couple's autonomy. Now it seemed attainable. And because the progress of industrialization and democratization had weakened the political and economic constraints forcing people to get and stay married, such deep intimacy was now seen as the best hope for stability in marriage.

Floyd Dell is a good example of the essentially conservative aims of many "overcompensators." He had initially expressed his criticism of Victorian marriage by advocating free love but later became a proponent of the sanctity of "modern" marriage. In his major sociological work on marriage and family, published in 1930, Dell explained that the "destruction of the patriarchal family and its accompanying social sexual institutions" was a good thing, not because it was a revolution against the love-based, male provider marriage ideal that had emerged in the nineteenth century but rather because that destruction was needed to *complete* the love revolution. In the "patriarchal" and "repressive" era, Dell argued, love often had been forced to exist outside marriage. The rejection of "old-fashioned" values was necessary so that young people could live "happily ever after in heterosexual matehood."[30]

But living "happily ever after" without outside constraints meant that people had to reach greater depths of emotional and physical intimacy than had been possible (or necessary) in the past. This focused even more attention on sexuality. Experts of the day believed that the success or failure of marriage was largely determined by the couple's sexual adjustment. Many even believed, as marital advice expert William Robinson claimed in 1912, that "every case of divorce had for its basis lack of sexual satisfaction." Good sex, the experts argued, was the glue needed to hold marriages together now that patriarchy had lost its force.[31]

And good sex didn't just fall from the trees. "Sex-love and happiness in marriage . . . do not just happen," wrote Margaret Sanger. "Eternal vigilance is the price of marital happiness." The logic led directly to supporting the sexual revolution as a route to improving marriage. If sexual magnetism was important to keeping a marriage alive, then young people needed opportunities to interact with a number of possible mates and explore the depth of their mutual attraction. Women had to discard the doctrines of sexual purity that so often led to frigidity in marriage. Entrepreneurs were glad to help. For just ten cents a woman could buy a discreetly wrapped book titled *How I Kept My Husband,* which instructed her in how to give oral sex.[32]

Traditionalists worried that these changes in sexual expectations might lead women to put their own happiness above that of their husbands. Instead, historian Nancy Cott suggests, "sex appeal" replaced "submission" as a wife's first responsibility to her husband, and women learned the new rules on the big screen at their local theater. In movie after movie, foolish women nearly lost their husbands by spending too much time on housework or on intellectual self-improvement. In Cecil B. DeMille's 1920 film *Why Change Your*

Wife?, the usually glamorous Gloria Swanson played a wife who wore glasses, listened to classical music, and read such books as *How to Improve Your Mind*. It was obvious to the audience why her husband left her for a perfumed, short-skirted man chaser. But a happy ending was achieved when Swanson's character ordered some sleeveless, backless dresses and devoted herself to improving her dance steps instead of her mind.[33]

The New Woman of the 1920s did not reject marriage, although she rejected her elders' advice about how to find and keep a husband. She did not want to spend her time hanging out with other girls and waiting to get flowery love letters. She wanted to mix it up with the guys, to be a girl "with sport in her blood," someone who "kisses the boys" and wins their admiration by keeping up with them.[34] And after marriage she expected to hold her husband not by her "quiet goodness" but by her active sexuality.

Thus the two twentieth-century innovations that most shocked traditional Victorians—the sexual revolution and the attack on separate spheres—did not reflect any widespread rejection of marriage or of women's duty to please men. Indeed, the pressure for couples to put marriage first and foremost in their lives led many women to become *more* dependent on their relationships with men. Proponents of "modern" sexuality and marriage were deeply suspicious of close ties between women. By the 1920s the profound female friendships that had been such an important part of nineteenth-century female culture were under attack.

As late as the first decade of the twentieth century, children's books commonly contained love poems from one teenage girl to another. *The Story of Mary MacLane by Herself,* published in 1902, detailed her love for a former teacher. She described feeling "a convulsion and a melting within" in her loved one's presence and wished she could go off with her friend to "some little out-of-the-world place . . . for the rest of my life." The book gives no hint that these feelings should be interpreted as sexually deviant or a sign of lesbianism.[35]

By the 1920s, however, few self-respecting "modern" women would have admitted to such feelings. By that time intense relationships between women were usually considered childish "crushes" that girls were encouraged to outgrow. At worst, they raised the specter of "abnormal" sexual or emotional development that could make heterosexuality unsatisfactory and marriage unstable.[36]

By the end of the 1920s American psychoanalysts were warning that one of the most common "perversions of the libido" was the tendency of teenage girls to fix their "affections on members of the same sex." Such perversions, they claimed, were a serious threat to normal development and to marriage. The best way to avoid them was to allow teenage girls to engage in some degree of sexual experimentation with boys.[37]

"The idealization of married love and the collapse of women's female networks left women more isolated and emotionally dependent than in the past," argue historians John Spurlock and Cynthia Magistro. "Married women had the home and children, as they had in the nineteenth century, but they lacked the cultural support and the network of contacts that formed the separate sphere of nineteenth century women."[38] When marriage worked, it probably worked better than in the past, but when a husband was not emotionally engaged, a wife had fewer opportunities to cultivate intimate relationships, even asexual ones, outside marriage.

By the 1920s men too faced the stigma of being labeled "homosexual" if they expressed affection for someone of the same sex or did not display an aggressive "masculinity" toward women that would formerly have been frowned upon as ungentlemanly. By the early 1930s tolerance of open homosexual subcultures and interest in female-impersonating entertainers had pretty much disappeared.[39]

The new emphasis on heterosexual bonding also called into question the veneration of mothers and the close sibling ties that had made it hard for nineteenth-century married couples to retreat into their own private world. Traditional Victorians were shocked by the contempt that modern young people often expressed toward the older generation. But this was another way those of the new generation turned their backs on whatever stood in the way of achieving marital intimacy. In Floyd Dell's words, "emancipation" from parents' claims was necessary to reach "full capacity for love of the other sex." Many experts believed that Victorian mothers were a special threat to their children's marriages because their own unsatisfactory sex lives made them cling too tightly to their children's affections.[40]

The new "antimother" but promarriage psychology was exemplified in a popular Broadway play, *The Silver Cord,* which opened in 1927. The play takes place in the home of Mrs. Phelps, who has two grown sons. One son has brought his fiancée to meet his mother. The older son has brought home his new wife, Christina. Mrs. Phelps sets out to prevent the one marriage and break up the other. She succeeds with the unmarried son but is thwarted when the other's wife exposes Mrs. Phelps's ploys.

The play's climactic moment comes when Christina puts into words what many advocates of modern marriage considered the most serious threat to marital unity: "You belong to a type that's very common in these days, Mrs.

Phelps—a type of self-centered, self-pitying, son-devouring tigress." Ignoring the shocked protests of the family, Christina continues: "You and your kind beat any cannibals I've ever heard of! And what makes you doubly deadly and dangerous is that people admire you and your kind. They actually admire you! You professional mothers!" Christina's final, devastating "insight" for her husband is that his mother cannot "bear the thought of our loving one another as we do . . . because down, down in the depths of her, grown man that you are, she still wants to suckle you at her breast!"[41] Such rhetoric was just extreme enough to shock audiences of the 1920s and 1930s and just enough in tune with popular sensibilities to be greeted as a harsh but needed truth.

The rejection of close same-sex friendships and extended family ties reflected the growing primacy of the couple in people's range of commitments. During the first three decades of the twentieth century, the age of marriage fell for both men and women, and the proportion of men and women who remained single declined. Marriage rates increased among all social classes and racial-ethnic groups, but the biggest changes were seen in the two groups that had been least likely to marry in the late nineteenth century.

One group consisted of urban native-born white men. In the nineteenth century such men tended to postpone marriage while they pursued education or established careers. As late as 1910 fewer than one in four white urban native-born men were married by the time they were twenty-four. By 1930 almost one in three had married by that age. The other group was educated women. Almost half of all college-educated women had remained unmarried in the late nineteenth century, largely because of the difficulty in reconciling domesticity with educational aspirations. But between 1913 and 1923, 80 to 90 percent of female college graduates married.[42]

Even before marriage, people were more likely to pair off. Pioneering sociologists Helen and Robert Lynd observed a "growing tendency to engage in leisure-time pursuits by couples rather than in crowds" in their study of Muncie, Indiana, during the 1920s. As a result, the Lynds argued, "the unattached man or woman" was "more 'out of it' in the highly organized paired social life of today than a generation ago when informal 'dropping in' was the rule." The Lynds also reported that the growing tendency to have sex before marriage was generally confined to already committed couples.[43]

By the end of the 1920s the idea that marital privacy was more important than adults' ties with their parents was firmly established. Psychiatrists began to insist that misplaced loyalties to parents were a sign of serious maladjustment. In 1946, psychiatrist Edward Strecker offered women a questionnaire designed to sort out the old-style Victorian mom from the successful "modern mother." If you thought you should bring an aging parent into your own home, he informed his readers, "rather than put that parent in a good institution . . . where they [sic] will receive adequate care and comfort," you were an old-fashioned mom who was probably neglecting your husband and children. In fact, the percentage of couples who shared homes with their parents did fall markedly between 1900 and 1950.[44]

The twentieth-century revolution in gender roles and sexuality, then, contrary to fears at the time, actually increased the primacy of marriage in people's lives. It also did not seriously threaten the traditional gender order. As in the previous century, the new intimacy between men and women stopped considerably short of establishing equality between them.

Most women who adopted the styles, language, and behavior associated with "modern" womanhood were not career-minded feminists. They were usually more eager to marry than the proponents of domesticity and "true womanhood" in the nineteenth century, and many explicitly rejected the women's rights movement that had paved the way for their new freedoms. By the 1920s popular magazines were trumpeting stories like that of Dorothy Dunbar Bromley's 1927 "Feminist—New Style," who "is not inclined to air her knowledge and argue about woman's right to a place in the sun," or of the "ex-feminist" who told the world about "The Harm My Education Did Me." Zelda Fitzgerald, wife of the novelist F. Scott Fitzgerald, wrote that she wanted her daughter to be a flapper rather than a feminist, or a career woman, or an intellectual, "because flappers are brave and gay and beautiful."[45]

Brave and gay and beautiful perhaps, but certainly not autonomous. The sexual liberation of women in the 1920s did not translate into female independence. Dating gave young women more freedom from parental control and more options to explore their own sexuality. For many women, this was an exhilarating change. But the shift from the girl inviting a boy to "call" to the boy inviting a girl to go out meant that she lost the protection as well as the inconvenience of having her parents nearby. She became more dependent on the man taking the initiative to ask her out as well as on his *not* taking the initiative to push sexual freedoms too far.

The twentieth-century redefinition of *masculinity* made women more responsible for applying the brakes on sex than their nineteenth-century predecessors. Women had long been urged to hold men's "baser instincts" in check. But respectable nineteenth-century middle-class men had also been expected to curb their sexual passions. By the 1920s, though, men were told it was positively unhealthy to repress their masculine desires. Women, on the other hand, had to walk a narrow line between having sexual desires and act-

ing on them. As a sociologist at Vassar College put it, a "woman may consci-
entiously allow herself to feel passion to the same extent as the man, if she
controls its expression."[46]

The idea that a certain amount of sexual exploration was okay for both
sexes forced women to take more responsibility than in the past for enforcing
the sexual limits that respectable couples were still expected to honor. In the
1920s, people increasingly remarked that "if a man goes too far, it is [the
woman's] fault." An American advice book of the 1940s summed up two
decades of dating advice to women by asserting that the average man "will go
as far as you will let him go."[47]

Once married, the woman was supposed to let down her sexual barriers,
but this put new pressures on wives. The nineteenth-century focus on female
purity had inhibited sexual openness between husband and wife, but it had
also accorded women a high moral stature that made it difficult for a man to
insist on sex if his wife was unwilling. The twentieth-century preoccupation
with the orgasm, by contrast, entitled a woman to more sexual consideration
in lovemaking but increased the pressure on her to have sex whenever it was
suggested.

A wife must "cease to take pride" in "outgrown maidenly reserve," scolded
sociologist Ernest Groves. She should accept her husband's sexual initiative
and follow his lead, because "his attitude toward sex is less likely to be warped"
than hers. Physicians and marriage counselors came to believe, in the words
of one contemporary, that women "have to be bluntly reminded that one main
source of prostitution and unfaithfulness is the selfish and unsurrendered wife."
Women who failed to find physical satisfaction in such surrender were told
that they were not "fully adult" in their sexuality.[48]

Nor, contrary to the fears of William Sumner, did the greater acceptance
of women's work and social activities outside the home after World War I dis-
lodge marriage "from its supreme place" in women's lives. Most people still
believed that women should retire from work after a few years. And such a
course of action became possible for wider segments of the population as
men's wages rose in the unprecedented prosperity of the 1920s. It was during
this period that for the very first time in U.S. history, a majority of American
children lived in families in which the man was the primary wage earner, the
wife was not involved in full-time labor outside the home or alongside her
husband, and the children were in school instead of in the labor force.[49]

It was not just antifeminism but practicality that made women continue
to think that retiring from the workplace upon marriage was the best course.
African American wives usually had to work outside the home, because their

husbands were seldom paid enough to support a family. But there were few inducements for wives and mothers to take paid work if they didn't absolutely have to. During the 1920s at least half of all working women labored in menial, tedious jobs characterized by long hours, low pay, and unpleasant, dangerous, or unhealthy working conditions. Manufacturing jobs paid higher wages than domestic work and service occupations, but women still earned, on average, only half as much as men.[50]

Job segregation and pay discrimination against women actually increased during the first forty years of the twentieth century. In the 1920s women were excluded from many better-paid jobs by "protective" legislation, which limited the hours and improved the working conditions of many employed women but also kept them out of higher-paid jobs that might involve nonstandard hours or working conditions. There were fewer female physicians in 1930 than at the start of the 1920s, and women were a smaller proportion of the college population.[51]

Some companies, notably the Ford Motor Company, experimented with paying men a family wage. But as with Victorian charity, this was contingent on the character and family situation of the worker, and the flip side was that company policy forbade the hiring of married women whose husbands were able to work.[52]

One acceptable career for middle-class women, just as in the previous century, was dispensing domestic advice. The new breed of "scientific" home economists raised the standards for what constituted adequate homemaking, encouraging women to spend more time shopping and doing laundry than in the past. A 1920s study found that 90 percent of urban housewives in the United States spent thirty-five hours a week or more on household tasks, and rural housewives spent even longer.[53]

The home economics experts believed that modern household tools made this investment of time an element of woman's self-fulfillment rather than, as formerly, an act of self-sacrifice. Any woman who was dissatisfied with her domestic role now that she had such helpful appliances, they argued, suffered from "personal maladjustment." Popular magazines in the 1920s trumpeted stories like "You May Have My Job, a Feminist Discovers Her Home" or "I Gave Up My Law Books for a Cook Book."[54]

Some people continued to worry that instability was built into the new marriage patterns. Again, however, most of those who condemned the sexualization of marriage and the doctrine that happiness was the main purpose of marriage had never bought into the romantic ideal of intimacy in the first place. The well-known ethicist Felix Adler, for example, blamed the "evil of divorce" on the primacy of personal choice and love in marriage decisions. Individual choice, he wrote, may have overcome some of the tragedies caused by arranged marriages, but it produced a new set of tragedies because of its "pretension that nothing is now to be considered except the happiness of madame and monsieur." Echoing the complaints of conservatives back in the late eighteenth century, Adler argued that the doctrine of love and marital fulfillment led people to "forget that they are servants, that there are great social ends to which they must bow."[55]

Adler lambasted the "pernicious" idea that husbands and wives should be friends and comrades. "Comradeship," he warned, "is obnoxious and antagonistic to the idea of marriage." It "depends on free choice and free choice can be annulled. There is nothing permanent in the idea of comradeship." Happiness, explained Adler, "is an incident, a concomitant [of marriage], and you cannot make it the highest end, without coming to the intolerable position that marriage should cease when happiness ceases."

Supporters of modernity, by contrast, believed that the new emphasis on individual fulfillment, sexual satisfaction, and close comradeship in marriage would encourage individuals to cherish marriages even *more* than in the past. Putting marital commitments above ties to friends, parents, and community, they held, built deeper relationships between husband and wife. Still, they were uneasily aware that, as Adler charged, love marriages were prone to divorce if those ideals were not fulfilled.

Divorce rates did increase during the 1920s. Also, after a brief upswing in births right after World War I, fertility resumed its fifty-year decline, leading some to worry that women were engaging in a "birth strike." The only thing that kept birthrates from dropping more sharply was the unreliability of birth control. A study of Indianapolis couples marrying in the late 1920s found that only half of those who tried to postpone their first birth succeeded in doing so.[56]

So even the most enthusiastic proponents of "modern" marriage had to acknowledge that there were risks associated with the new sexual and marital values. But since the Victorian marriage model had created so many problems of its own, they believed it was neither possible nor desirable to eliminate these features of modern marriage. Instead they sought to make them less disruptive.

Historian Elaine Tyler May has said of the 1950s that when the expansion of sexuality and consumerism in post–World War II America began to threaten the preservation of family life and marriage, Americans adopted a domestic version of diplomat George Kennan's 1950s containment policy toward the Soviet Union, which involved forgoing any direct attempts to topple the USSR but aggressively combating any efforts to spread communist institutions or ideas. In family life, says May, domestic containment meant tolerance of sexual expression and the pursuit of individual happiness, before as well as during marriage, but aggressive efforts to channel those energies into marriage and to punish or quarantine personal behaviors that might serve as an *alternative* to marriage.[57]

May's analogy is extremely useful, but I think domestic containment began in the 1920s. Floyd Dell explained the rationale for it at the time, arguing that while the "excesses" of the early twentieth century had been necessary to tear down gender segregation and false modesty, the task now was to return people to a more moderate course, rejecting extreme ideas such as the right to engage in sex for pure "amusement." In the same vein, encouraging women to work had "served an excellent social purpose in getting girls out of the dying patriarchal home," wrote Dell. "But now that they are out of the old patriarchal home, the problem is for them to get back into the home on modern and self-respecting terms; and it does not help them to pretend otherwise."[58]

Sexuality was one arena where reformers consciously applied a policy of containment during the 1920s. While they encouraged "healthy" sexuality, they developed new ways of penalizing "unhealthy," "precocious," or "promiscuous" sexual behavior. Girls or young women who engaged in activities that reformers considered unhealthy were labeled "delinquent" and charged with "sex offenses" in the newly expanded juvenile court system.[59]

Anxiety about sexual promiscuity converged with the emergence of the pseudoscience eugenics to fan fears that the lower and "unfit" classes were reproducing like rabbits while middle- and upper-class women were restricting their fertility. The eugenics movement, warning that this disparity would debase society's gene pool, provided another tool for containment.[60]

The virulently racist eugenics program of the Nazis during the 1930s is well known, but few people realize how popular the ideas of eugenics were in Western Europe and North America during the 1920s. Paul Popenoe, one of the movement's leading advocates in the United States, estimated that on the basis of their IQ results, ten million Americans ought to be sterilized. In the late 1920s, before the Nazis came to power, California had the most extensive eugenics program in the world, performing more sterilizations than all other countries combined. Most of the men were sterilized because they were unable to perform the breadwinner role. Three-fourths of the sterilized women were "sex delinquents."[61]

Many American states tried to contain the "excesses" of personal marital freedom by enacting statutes prohibiting interracial marriage. In 1912, Representative Seaborn Roddenberry of Georgia proposed a constitutional amendment forbidding "intermarriage between Negroes or persons of color and Caucasians . . . forever." The antimiscegenation amendment never went anywhere, but by 1913 forty-two of the forty-eight states had enacted such laws, and several states had narrowed their definition of whiteness. Virginia, for example, had traditionally defined a person with one-fourth African blood as black. In 1916 the legislature dropped the fraction defining blackness to one-sixteenth, and in 1924 it declared that "one drop" of African ancestry made a person black.[62]

Other forms of containment were less repressive. Sociologist Ernest Groves was a modernizer, but he shared the fears of many traditionalists about the future of marriage. He worried that the decline in marriage's economic and political functions, the rise of the "pleasure principle" in personal life, and the liberating impact of birth control were making marriage unstable. Unlike Adler, however, Groves believed that there was "no hope of improving or reforming marriage by any scheme that hampers affection or pushes it into a subordinate position." He thought that with a little adjustment, the "more just and more flexible" controls of love could be made as effective in stabilizing marriage as the repressive controls of the past. His solution was to replace the sentimental and religious approach to marriage with a new therapeutic approach that would be spread to the masses by "family-service providers" and marriage counselors. "It is folly," Groves wrote, to expect people to establish stable marriages if they hadn't been educated about the requirements for a good relationship. But with such education, marriage could thrive.[63]

Eugenics proponents also had high hopes for marriage counseling. Popenoe became one of the most influential marriage counselors in America during the 1930s, 1940s, and 1950s after deciding "that if we were going to promote a sound population, we would not only have to get the right kind of people married, but we would have to keep them married." Another eugenics advocate turned marriage counselor was Robert Dickinson, who believed that sexual maladjustment was the main reason for the rising divorce rate. For marriage to take its rightful place as "the ultimate in human relationships," he argued, couples needed to be trained in "sexual adjustment."[64]

Given their interest in eugenics, Germany and the United States became the world's leaders in the marriage counseling business. By the early 1930s marriage counseling was also thriving in Canada and most of Western Europe. Courses in marriage and family life, covering everything from dating to marital sex to birth control, proliferated. As Groves had hoped, marriage counselors and psychoanalysts were gradually replacing preachers as the pre-eminent advisers on marriage and family life.

Despite these efforts, divorce rates reached new highs in many countries during the 1920s, and they would have been even higher had it not been for the persistence of restrictive fault-based divorce codes. On a case-by-case basis, judges and juries in America often treated divorce petitions, especially by women, more sympathetically than required by law. But because no one could count on such magnanimity, the law served as another form of containment. Historian Norma Basch argues that the combination of "a strict official code" and "a lax unofficial one" regarding divorce allowed many individuals to escape particularly onerous situations without establishing any widespread *right* to divorce.[65]

Right up through the 1950s, judges routinely ruled that individuals seeking to end a marriage could get a divorce only if they were free from any "suspicion" that they had "contributed" to the problems they were complaining about. In 1935, for instance, the Supreme Court of Oregon reviewed the divorce suit of Louise and Louis Maurer. The judge acknowledged that the husband was "domineering and overbearing" and given to sudden bursts of temper that "caused his wife and children to fear him." But he noted that the wife had also engaged in behavior that "can not be condoned" and therefore denied the divorce. Because neither party came to court "with clean hands," the court found, neither of them deserved relief from the marriage, even though their quarreling "would drive happiness out of any home."[66]

By the end of the 1920s advocates of "modern" marriage had reason for cautious optimism. Early twentieth-century transformations in sexuality, gender relations, and youth culture had updated Victorian marriage, making it possible for more people to place marriage at the center of their emotional lives. Love and marriage had become vital to most people's sense of personal identity, with attachments to parents, siblings, and friends paling by comparison. Marriage rates had risen, and unwed childbearing had dropped. In most countries, people married earlier and died later, so more people spent more of their lives married than ever before, despite the rise in divorce rates. The separation of spheres between men and women had eroded without unleashing the "excesses" of feminism. And although women were joining the workforce in increasing numbers, more wives and mothers devoted themselves to full-time homemaking than ever before.

Still, as the 1920s came to a close, many observers worried that the contradictions and tensions of the love-based marriage could not be contained indefinitely. In 1929, Samuel Schmalhausen, an ardent supporter of modernity and one of the few unrepentant advocates of the right to engage in sex outside marriage, wrote: "The old values are gone. Irrevocably. The new values are feverishly in the making. We live in a state of molten confusion. Instability rides modernity like a crazy sportsman. Civilization is caught in a cluster of contradictions that threaten to strangle it."[67]

What, people wondered, would the next decade bring? Would the precarious balance between personal freedom and social stability hold?

Chapter 13

—⟫⟨⟪—

Making Do, Then Making Babies:
Marriage in the Great Depression
and World War II

In September 1929, twenty-year-old Cora Winslow was not worrying about the future of marriage. Newly engaged, she looked forward to quitting work and giving dance lessons on the side until she had the first of the three children she wanted. "Which just shows you shouldn't count your chickens before they hatch," then eighty-two-year-old Cora told me wryly when I interviewed her in her retirement apartment in Lacey, Washington.[1]

Cora was a teenager in Seattle during the Roaring Twenties and loved every minute of it. When she was sixteen, she started teaching the new jazz dances after school, and soon she was giving exhibitions of the tango and Charleston at local grange and community halls. At eighteen she took a secretarial job near the waterfront. There were lots of men to date in those days, she told me, and she played the field for more than a year before accepting a marriage proposal from a man who worked in the same firm. He popped the question on September 15, and they decided to marry after he got the promotion he'd been promised in the spring of 1930.

But the month after they got engaged, the Jazz Age ended abruptly with the stock market crash and the ensuing worldwide economic collapse. By

November, both Cora and her beau had lost their jobs. She was forced to move back in with her parents, while he headed for California to follow up on a job lead. He'd send for her when he got settled, he said, and they'd get married in the Golden State. She never heard from him again.

Over the next few years Cora held several jobs, none of which paid enough to let her move back out on her own. In 1934, at the age of twenty-five, she got engaged again, after a five-year period when "dates were a lot harder to come by than before the crash." But before she and her fiancé, Paul Archer, had saved enough to marry, Cora got pregnant. Her family doctor directed her to an abortionist.

Shortly after the abortion, Cora and Paul did get married. The following year she got pregnant again and had another abortion because Paul had been laid off from his job at a sawmill and "we couldn't afford another mouth to feed." In those days, Cora told me, "you just asked your doctor if he could do something. Doctors understood how hard things were. When my daughter got in trouble in the mid-1950s, I couldn't believe it when she said her doctor wouldn't help."

Cora's daughter was born in 1938. By then Cora and her husband had moved in with her brother on his dairy farm in eastern Washington. "Those were tough years," she told me, filled with family tensions. Her sister-in-law looked down on Cora's husband for not having a found a new job, and Cora worried constantly that he would get so discouraged with his inability to find work that like her earlier fiancé, he would run off.

When the United States entered World War II in December 1941, Cora's husband, who was rejected by the army, found work in Seattle and moved the family there. In 1942, as labor shortages led to new job opportunities for women, Cora got a job in the shipyards, relying on a neighbor for child care. She enjoyed the work, she told me, but when the war ended and the servicemen began coming home, she and the other women were laid off.

By then Paul was making enough money managing a furniture store to take out a mortgage on a house, and Cora became a full-time housewife. "Sometimes I missed the girls at work," she said. "But it was better this way because he felt like more of a man when he was supporting the family on his own."

By 1953 Cora and her husband were the proud owners of a two-bedroom house on the outskirts of Seattle, and their teenage daughter was going steady with the boy she eventually married—a little sooner than planned, after the doctor refused to "do something" about her pregnancy. "He was a nice boy," said Cora, "and he turned out to be a good husband." But, she added, "I always thought it was a shame she didn't get the chance to date the way I did. Boy, those memories got me through some hard times. I still have my dance cards and movie stubs."

Like Cora, millions of people around the world had their lives dramatically changed by the Great Depression. The economic consequences of the 1929 stock market collapse were swift and staggering. Within three years, unemployment had tripled across Europe and North America and industrial production had fallen by almost 50 percent. By 1935 world trade had collapsed to just one-third of its 1929 level. In the United States, nine million families lost their savings in bank failures.[2] Everywhere the Depression shifted attention away from social and sexual issues to questions of survival. The once red-hot concerns about the future of marriage were put on the back burner.

As it had done to Cora, the Depression scuttled tens of thousands of marriages. On the other hand, the divorce rate also fell in the 1930s. Some traditionalists, still reeling from the family turmoil of the 1920s, saw this as a silver lining in the clouds of the Depression. "Many a family that has lost its car," intoned one newspaper editorial, "has found its soul." But adversity had not made families more stable. Many people who hoped to divorce simply couldn't afford to set up separate households. Cora knew a couple in this situation who just hung a blanket across the living room to mark off their individual territory. More often, people split up without going through the expense of getting a legal divorce. By 1940 more than 1.5 million wives in the United States were living apart from their husbands.[3]

Certainly, many couples weathered the difficult decade with their love intact or even strengthened by the hardships. One woman reflected that "marriage was much less difficult then for one reason. You really didn't have choices. You accepted what you had and made the most of it rather than to think, 'if I had something better, I'd such and so.' Because you knew you couldn't have it anyway." But other couples saw the chronic economic stress eat away at their marriage. "All that worrying [about money] made him spiteful," recalled another woman. "But I'd always give in. It seems I had to give in to keep peace. There weren't any divorces in my day."[4]

The Depression accelerated the influx of married women into the workforce. In 1900 less than 6 percent of married women in the United States worked outside the home. By the mid-1930s more than 15 percent of wives were recorded as employed, and many thousands held jobs off the books.[5]

But unlike the 1920s, almost no one saw women's work in the 1930s as liberating. Few women held prestigious or well-paid jobs. In fact, women increasingly lost ground in such high-status occupations as medicine and teaching, and wage discrimination actually grew. Many women took jobs as poorly paid store clerks; others worked as laundresses or in low-skill assembly jobs, frequently supervised by sexually predatory male foremen.[6]

Even as more wives took paying jobs during the Depression, their unpaid workload increased. Less able to afford the conveniences that had begun to lighten the homemaker's load in the 1920s, women had to sew more of their own clothes, can more of their own preserves, do more of their cooking from scratch. "Use it up, wear it out, make it do, or do without" was a popular saying of the day. One woman recollected that she and her neighbor made sure to shop together. "You could get two pounds of hamburger for a quarter, so we'd buy two pounds and split it," she explained. "One week she'd pay the extra penny and the next week I'd pay."[7]

When a woman had to seek work because her husband lost his job, this threatened the "modern" ideas of masculinity and marriage that most men had come to embrace over the previous two decades. Unemployed men often lost their sense of identity and became demoralized. Many turned to drink. Tempers flared at home. It is not surprising, then, that the experience of the Depression undercut the societal support for working women that had emerged in the early years of the twentieth century. Children raised in Depression-era families associated a working mother with high levels of family tension, with their father's failure rather than their mother's success.[8]

Hostility toward working women was especially sharp if a woman's husband also had a job. Many people believed such families were double-dipping into an already shallow pool of work. The U.S. Economy Act of 1932 prohibited the federal government from employing two people from the same family. Despite the act's gender-neutral language, nearly all the fifteen hundred people fired in its first year were women. Twenty-six American states passed laws explicitly prohibiting or limiting the employment of married women in various fields. By 1940 more than three-quarters of the school systems in the United States refused to hire married women as teachers.[9]

Governments also used positive measures to shore up male breadwinner marriages. In the United States women as well as men benefited from New Deal programs such as the Social Security Act of 1935. But Social Security's safety net had a large hole: Agricultural and seasonal workers, who were disproportionately African American and Latino, were exempted. New Deal policies also codified a two-tier form of social welfare assistance: Government aid to working men and their families was an "entitlement," while aid to unmarried women and widows was available only through means-tested "charity" programs, which offered lower levels of assistance.[10]

In 1939 the Social Security Act was amended to provide survivors' benefits for the wives and minor children of men who died before age sixty-five, though these benefits were forfeited if wives remarried. The 1939 reforms also increased a married man's retirement benefit by 50 percent once his wife reached age sixty-five, even if she had never held a paid job. Policy makers recognized that single male workers and all female workers were being over-taxed to support married couples. But this was seen as a good thing because it increased a man's incentive to marry and decreased his wife's incentive to take paid work.[11]

European governments also experimented with social programs to encourage male breadwinner families but reacted in more diverse ways to the 1930s plunge in birthrates. In Germany, the Nazis launched a two-prong approach. They went on an aggressive campaign to sterilize the "unfit"—drunkards, deaf-mutes, epileptics, mentally ill individuals, and the like. Historian Gisela Bock estimates that four hundred thousand individuals were sterilized in the course of this campaign. But the Nazis also banned the birth control groups that had emerged during the 1920s, in order to ensure that "Aryan" women produced as many children as possible for the "master race."[12]

In the United States, by contrast, legislators were as eager as most individual families to avoid having "too many mouths to feed." The federal government relaxed prohibitions on birth control and even funded contraceptive programs. Southern states, hoping to limit the growth of their already substantial African American populations, were pioneers in providing birth control services. But most states soon joined the trend, and many also promoted forced sterilization, although on a much smaller scale than in Germany. In this way, birth control lost its earlier association with women's autonomy and became centered on population control.[13]

"You Are Now the Husband of a Career Woman"

The onset of World War II reversed many of the Depression-era trends in marriage. A "marriage fever" swept most countries in the early years of the conflict. In Europe the coming of the war turned attention away from the marriage counseling programs of the 1920s. In the United States, however, marriage counselors and educators argued that the war made it all the more imperative to educate young people about the value of marriage.

One teacher of a course on marriage and family life reported to the National Council on Family Relations how she had buoyed up her female students after the announcement that war had been declared. Many of the girls, she reported, put their heads down on their desks in fear and despair. But she sternly instructed them to get hold of themselves. If you react this way "when dangers are yet at a distance," she quoted herself as saying, "what will you do in the face of emergencies in marriage—when John may say that he does not like your cooking and is going home to Mother?" This challenge to their womanly resolve, she said, did the trick. "Heads lifted and faces became set with determination."[14]

When John actually went off to war, however, many wives decided that improving their cooking was less urgent than contributing something more tangible to the war effort. Married women poured into the workforce during World War II, on a much more financially rewarding and culturally approved basis than in the past. The female labor force increased by almost 60 percent in the United States between 1940 and 1945, and three-fourths of the new women workers were married. More than 350,000 women enlisted in the Woman's Army Corps and the nursing units of the army and navy, although the U.S. military set a 2 percent cap on the proportion of women in the armed forces.[15]

As part of the war effort, women worked in jobs that had previously been unthinkable for their sex. They became pipe fitters, mechanics, welders, carpenters, and shipfitters. They not only did "men's jobs" but earned "men's wages." The feeling of empowerment this generated radiates from the excited letter one American woman wrote to her soldier husband on June 12, 1944: "Darlin': You are now the husband of a career woman—just call me your Little Ship Yard Babe. . . . Opening my little checking account too and it's a grand and a glorious feeling to write a check all your own and not have to ask for one."[16]

The war opened unprecedented opportunities for African American women. Most had already worked all their adult lives, but unlike white women, they had remained pigeonholed in menial and domestic work during the economic expansion of the 1920s. Suddenly, many were able to get higher-paid manufacturing or white-collar jobs. Decades later a black woman commented that it was really Hitler, not Lincoln, who had freed the slaves![17]

In contrast with the Depression years, the government encouraged paid work for women, married as well as single, during the war years. Public service ads warned that soldiers would die unless women took over the production lines that the men had left behind. The lovely face and well-muscled arms of the fictional "Rosie the Riveter" graced the cover of the *Saturday Evening Post* and thousands of posters. A song about Rosie came out in 1942.

"She's making history,/Working for victory," went the lyrics. "Keeps a sharp lookout for sabotage,/Sitting up there on the fuselage. That little girl will do more than a male will do." The songwriters were careful to note that Rosie had a boyfriend: "Charlie, he's a Marine./Rosie is protecting Charlie,/ Working overtime on the riveting machine."

Initially, women saw their work as "just for the duration," an emergency measure undertaken for patriotism, not personal fulfillment. Most expected to leave the workforce when the war ended. A June 1944 *Ladies' Home Journal* article on women workers assured readers that women would happily give up their jobs after the war. "If the American woman can find a man she wants to marry, who can support her, a job fades into insignificance beside the vital business of staying at home and raising a family," the author wrote.[18]

But many women came to enjoy the work they did during the wartime emergency, as well as its economic benefits, and wanted to remain at their jobs after the war. As production was scaled back in late 1945, women in many cities protested the layoffs they faced, and a few unions went to bat for them. The protests had little effect. Women, especially those in well-paid, unionized jobs, were ushered out of the labor force in droves between 1944 and 1947.

Most women agreed the veterans should get their old jobs back, but many felt a searing sense of loss. A former servicewoman wrote in the April 1945 issue of the *Canadian Home Journal* that sending women back to the home was "like putting a chick back in the shell—it cannot be done without destroying spirit, heart or mind."[19]

By associating women's work with men's economic failure, the Depression had reinforced the appeal of the male breadwinner family. World War II, by contrast, left a much more positive image of working women. For years afterward women spoke nostalgically about their wartime work experiences, and many sought to rejoin the workforce in the 1950s. But the end of the war also brought a renewed enthusiasm for marriage, female homemaking, and the male breadwinner family.

In part this was a reaction to the deprivation of the war years. The United States and Canada did not suffer the same privations and physical destruction as Europe, the Soviet Union, and Japan during the war, but even in North America, the years of separation, worry, and material shortages had taken their toll. Consumer goods and housing had become scarce as the economy concentrated on war production. Couples who married during the war often had to live with one set of parents. Canadian historian Doug Owram argues that a "romanticized and idealized vision of family was a natural reaction to years of disruption."[20]

Making Do, Then Making Babies

Marriage experts of the day worried, however, that while the men were off at war, women had gotten too used to being in charge of the house and the checkbook. "He's head man again," the American magazine *House Beautiful* reminded its female readers. "Your part . . . is to fit his home to him, understanding why he wants it this way, forgetting your own preferences." In 1945, James Bossard, a leading family sociologist in the United States, declared that women's hearts had to be stoked to "a white glow of appreciation" for their role as homemakers. To prepare female students for their future as wives and mothers, the head of marriage and family life courses at the University of Illinois in 1947 exempted them from doing a term paper if they did six hours of babysitting during the term.[21]

Postwar social welfare states in Europe and North America provided more substantive incentives for men and women to embrace the male breadwinner/female homemaker model of marriage. In America, the GI Bill paid full tuition and a living stipend for veterans who enrolled in college. Veterans with families got extra money, and none of the money had to be repaid.[22]

The GI Bill was, hands down, *the* most successful affirmative action program in American history. By the end of the 1940s returning veterans made up nearly half the student bodies of most colleges and universities. The government also made very cheap mortgages available to veterans. These federal subsidies moved millions of working-class Americans into middle-class occupations and lifestyles in the 1950s. People who had never even expected to finish high school became engineers, accountants, teachers, physicians, dentists, and bank officers.

However, this affirmative action policy primarily benefited white men. African American veterans faced such widespread discrimination in housing and education that their ability to reap the full benefits of the GI Bill was limited, while women, only 2 percent of all veterans to begin with, got fewer benefits than their male counterparts. A female veteran who attended college got a smaller allowance for her spouse than a male veteran. Sometimes female veterans had to prove that they were not being supported by a male wage earner. There was no such requirement for male veterans, many of whose wives were working to supplement the GI Bill's living stipends.[23]

In 1948 even the U.S. federal income tax was changed to favor married couples who had one primary earner. Married couples could now file jointly and split their income. Joint filing allowed the high earner in the family to attribute half his income to his wife even if she earned little or nothing, which moved the family into a lower tax bracket. A man who supported a nonemployed wife often paid only half the taxes of a single man making the same

223

amount of money.[24] (This tax provision still gives a bonus to male breadwinner families, but it has become known as the marriage tax because in two-earner couples, now the majority of marriages, each has to pay the higher rate.)

Yet it was not clear that even the combined strength of all these marriage-friendly measures could counteract the social disruption and family instability that had marked the war years. The United States saw a sharp rise in unwed births during the war, and the end of the conflict brought a huge jump in divorce. By 1946 more than one in every three marriages was ending in divorce. Even when couples stayed together, tensions often simmered beneath the surface. A study of young families after the war found that four times as many veterans reported painful, even traumatic reunions as remembered joyful ones.[25]

Once again the "crisis" of marriage and gender roles became a huge public concern. In their best-selling 1947 book *The Modern Woman: The Lost Sex,* American authors Marynia Farnham and Ferdinand Lundberg accused career women of symbolically castrating their husbands. The only thing worse than a married career woman, in their view, was an unmarried one. They argued that "all spinsters be barred by law from having anything to do with the teaching of children on the ground of . . . emotional incompetence." Feminism, they said, was a "deep illness," caused by modern women's neurotic desire to be like men, and it posed a massive threat to the family.[26]

A more optimistic school of thought held that male-female roles had stabilized since the war and marriage was regaining its appeal. In 1948 sociologist John Sirjamaki claimed that modern Americans were well-nigh unanimous in their values about marriage and family life. His description of these values included many of the very same features that had worried observers in the 1920s. But Sirjamaki, unlike his predecessors, did not perceive them as a serious threat.[27]

Sirjamaki declared that marriage was now universally seen as "the normal and desirable" condition for all adults. People chose their mates on the basis of affection, and all agreed that the mark of a successful marriage was "the personal happiness of husband and wife." Americans now embraced "individual, not familial, values," so that in a reversal of the past, "the family exists for its members rather than the members [existing] for the family." He also pointed to two other features of "modern" marriage: the crucial importance of a satisfying sexual relationship and women's tremendous advance toward legal equality.

But Sirjamaki did not believe these elements were a threat to the establishment of lasting marriages. He expressed no worry that the pursuit of personal happiness might collide with the preservation of marital stability. Although sex "exploded" in importance once a couple married, the new emphasis on sexuality would not create alternatives to marriage, he contended, because most people frowned on sex outside wedlock. And even though women had attained "near equality" with men in public life, this did not threaten the male provider family, because Americans still thought that marital roles "should be based on a sexual division of labor, . . . with the male status being superior."

So as the 1940s came to an end, popular opinion and scholarly thought were divided about what the 1950s would bring. One school of thought held that the modern values of individualism, the "pleasure principle," sexual expressiveness, and women's rights would destabilize marriage. The other school believed that the male breadwinner marriage would remain the cultural norm, with sex safely contained inside it.

The Dawn of Marriage's Golden Age

The early 1950s seemed to confirm the optimistic view about the stability of postwar marriage and gender roles. Women around the world seemed happy to leave their wartime experiences behind and embrace their role as homemakers and mothers. No 1950s version of the New Woman arose to flout convention or celebrate the single life. Nor was there any sign of a resurrected feminist movement. It's true that in France, Simone de Beauvoir's 1949 book *The Second Sex,* which criticized marriage and domesticity, sold twenty-two thousand copies in its first week. But response from critics and most of the reading public was hostile.[28]

Despite wartime sexual experimentation at home and on the front, with the end of the war most men and women rushed to marry and start families. In most of Europe and all across North America, the age of marriage fell and the rates of marriage rose. By 1950 American women were marrying at a younger age than any time in the past half century, and later in the decade the age of marriage reached an all-time low. By 1959 almost half of all women were married by age nineteen, and 70 percent were married by twenty-four. Men were also marrying younger and in greater numbers. In 1900, only 22 percent of American males between twenty and twenty-four were married, but in 1950 more than 40 percent of that age-group had tied the knot. Meanwhile, divorce rates were dropping from their postwar peak. By 1958 the divorce rate was less than half as high as it had been in 1947.[29]

The postwar enthusiasm for marriage was not unique to the United States. Across Europe and Scandinavia, and in Australia and New Zealand too, the age of marriage fell, the rate of marriage rose, and the divorce rate dipped.

In France and Australia the percentage of twenty-four-year-old men who were married in the early 1950s was twice as high as fifty years earlier.

The unprecedented surge in marriage was not just a temporary readjustment to the backlog of postponed marriages that had built up during the Depression and the war. The marriage bandwagon rolled along in North America and Western Europe for fifteen amazing years, producing what some historians call the long decade of the 1950s. In the United States the long decade began in 1947 and lasted until the early 1960s. In Europe, it took longer to overcome the severe disruptions of the war, so European marriage patterns didn't stabilize until the early to mid-1950s. But once they did, the newly established norms of early marriage and male breadwinner families also lasted longer. I would date the European long decade from 1952, the year wartime rationing finally ended in Britain, until the late 1960s.[30]

This long decade was, without question, the golden age of marriage in the West. By the 1960s marriage had become nearly universal in North America and Western Europe, with 95 percent of all persons marrying. In addition, as people married younger, life spans lengthened, and divorce rates fell or held steady, individuals were spending much more of their lives in marriage than ever before or since. In England the marriage of a woman born in 1850 lasted, on average, twenty-nine years before the death of her husband. The marriage of a woman born in 1950 was likely to last forty-five years. The same pattern was seen in France, where the average marriage lasted twenty-eight years in the 1860s and forty-two years in the 1960s.[31]

In this unique period in Western history, marriage provided the context for just about every piece of most people's lives. Marriage was how practically everyone embarked on his or her "real" life. It was the institution that moved you through life's stages. And it was where you expected to be when your life ended.

No longer did people postpone marriage until they could establish their economic independence, as had been the case for the middle classes in Western Europe and North America up to the late nineteenth century. Nor was marriage, as had been the case in so many peasant villages, something you entered only after a woman had gotten pregnant and showed that she could produce children to work on the family farm. Certainly it was not something you entered to set up a joint business enterprise, as had been the case for many craftsmen and artisans in the past. Nor was it an informal arrangement scarcely distinguishable from just living together, as it had been among many lower-class individuals of earlier days, of whom their neighbors often said they were "married, but not churched."

Marriage in the long decade of the 1950s was simply the be-all and end-all of life. In a remarkable reversal of the past, it even became the stepping-off point for adulthood rather than a sign that adulthood had already been established. Advice columnists at the *Ladies' Home Journal* encouraged parents to help finance early marriages, even for teens, if their children seemed mature enough. A common saying in Germany prior to World War II had been *Ein Student verlocht sich nicht*—"A student does not get engaged." But across Europe and North America, marriages between college students became much more common during the 1950s, and universities built married students' housing to accommodate them.[32]

The norm of youthful marriage was so predominant during the 1950s that an unmarried woman as young as twenty-one might worry that she would end up an "old maid." American psychiatrist Sidonie Gruenberg was probably exaggerating when she wrote in 1953 that "a girl who hasn't a man in sight by the time she is 20 is not altogether wrong in fearing that she may never get married." But, says historian John Modell, in the 1950s "the 'sorting' of women into the marriageable and the future spinsters occurred early and vigorously." The small, and suspect, minority of women who did not marry at the same age as their peers had less chance of *ever* getting married than their counterparts a hundred years earlier. They were what the Japanese called Christmas cake, likely to stay on the shelf after the twenty-fifth.[33]

Young couples also had babies at much higher rates than their parents and grandparents. After falling for most of the previous hundred years, the birthrate of married couples soared during the 1950s. By 1957, the peak of the U.S. baby boom, the fertility rate in the United States was 123 births per thousand women, compared with only 79.5 per thousand in 1940. The baby boom peaked later in Western Europe, but was just as dramatic. The birthrate for twenty-one-year-old West German women rose from 92.2 per thousand in 1950, to 120 per thousand in 1961, and then to 133.8 per thousand in 1969.[34]

But even as women, on average, were having more babies, there was a continuing decline in the number of *very* large families in the 1950s. The postwar baby boom was produced by a decrease in childless or one-child families and an uptick in the number of three-child families, so the ideal of the small, couple-oriented family continued to spread. Moreover, because women had their children younger and completed their child rearing at an earlier age, the proportion of a couple's marriage that was devoted to childbearing and child rearing kept dropping.[35]

Remarkably, the golden age of marriage crossed socioeconomic and ethnic lines. In earlier centuries there had been huge class differences in the timing and organization of marriage and childbearing. Not so in the postwar era. People from all walks of life were moving, almost in lockstep, through a rapid sequence of transitions in the space of just a few years: Leave the parental home for work or school, get married in a more elaborate ceremony than ever, move into a home of one's own, and have a baby.[36]

The ideal of the male breadwinner marriage had already spread beyond the middle classes by the 1920s. But that ideal was still unattainable for many families involved in farming or running family businesses and for the majority of workers whose wages were too low to support a family: As late as 1929, after more than a decade of unprecedented economic growth, more than half of American families lived at or below the minimum standard of subsistence. But from the 1940s through the 1960s, real wages rose rapidly across the population, fastest of all in the bottom half. More families than ever before could achieve a decent, if modest, standard of living on the wages of a single male breadwinner. In 1950 only 16 percent of children in the United States had mothers who earned income outside the home, and because child labor had been abolished in the 1930s, a higher percentage of children were growing up in one-earner families during the long decade of the 1950s than ever before or since.[37]

This unprecedented marriage system was the climax of almost two hundred years of continuous tinkering with the male protector love-based marital model invented in the late eighteenth century. That process culminated in the 1950s in the short-lived pattern that people have since come to think of as traditional marriage. So in the 1970s, when the inherent instability of the love-based marriage reasserted itself, millions of people were taken completely by surprise. Having lost any collective memory of the convulsions that occurred when the love match was first introduced and the crisis that followed its modernization in the 1920s, they could not understand why this kind of marriage, which they thought had prevailed for thousands of years, was being abandoned by the younger generation.

Chapter 14

⊸═◈═⊷

The Era of Ozzie and Harriet:
The Long Decade of
"Traditional" Marriage

The long decade of the 1950s, stretching from 1947 to the early 1960s in the United States and from 1952 to the late 1960s in Western Europe, was a unique moment in the history of marriage. Never before had so many people shared the experience of courting their own mates, getting married at will, and setting up their own households. Never had married couples been so independent of extended family ties and community groups. And never before had so many people agreed that only one kind of family was "normal."

The cultural consensus that everyone should marry and form a male breadwinner family was like a steamroller that crushed every alternative view. By the end of the 1950s even people who had grown up in completely different family systems had come to believe that universal marriage at a young age into a male breadwinner family was the traditional and permanent form of marriage.

In Canada, says historian Doug Owram, "every magazine, every marriage manual, every advertisement . . . assumed the family was based on the . . . male wage-earner and the child-rearing, home-managing housewife." In the United

States, marriage was seen as the only culturally acceptable route to adulthood and independence. Men who chose to remain bachelors were branded "narcissistic," "deviant," "infantile," or "pathological." Family advice expert Paul Landes argued that practically everyone, "except for the sick, the badly crippled, the deformed, the emotionally warped and the mentally defective," ought to marry. French anthropologist Martine Segalen writes that in Europe the postwar period was characterized by the overwhelming "weight of a single family model." Any departure from this model—whether it was late marriage, nonmarriage, divorce, single motherhood, or even delayed childbearing—was considered deviant. Everywhere psychiatrists agreed and the mass media affirmed that if a woman did not find her ultimate fulfillment in homemaking, it was a sign of serious psychological problems.[1]

A 1957 survey in the United States reported that four out of five people believed that anyone who preferred to remain single was "sick," "neurotic," or "immoral." Even larger majorities agreed that once married, the husband should be the breadwinner and the wife should stay home. As late as 1961, one survey of young women found that almost all expected to be married by age twenty-two, most hoped to have four children, and all expected to quit work permanently when the first child was born.[2]

During the 1950s even women who had once been political activists, labor radicals, or feminists—people like my own mother, still proud of her work to free the Scottsboro Boys from legal lynching in the 1930s and her job in the shipyards during the 1940s—threw themselves into homemaking. It's hard for anyone under the age of sixty to realize how profoundly people's hunger for marriage and domesticity during the 1950s was shaped by their huge relief that two decades of depression and war were finally over and by their amazed delight at the benefits of the first real mass consumer economy in history. "It was like a miracle," my mother once told me, to see so many improvements, so quickly, in the quality of everyday life.

Up until 1950 most families' discretionary income did not cover much more than an occasional meal away from home; a beer or two after work; a weekly trip to the movies, amusement park, or beach; and perhaps a yearly vacation, usually spent at the home of relatives. Few households had washing machines and dryers. Refrigerators had only tiny spaces for freezing ice and had to be defrosted at least once a week. Few houses had separate bedrooms for all the children.

But starting in the late 1940s, millions of new houses were built and furnished with conveniences and comforts that would have been unimaginable ten years earlier. Separate bedrooms suddenly became the norm. The number of Americans with discretionary income, money left over after the basic bills were paid, doubled during the 1950s. By the mid-1950s nearly 60 percent of the population had "middle-class" income levels, compared with only 31 percent in the "prosperous twenties." By 1960 nearly two-thirds of all American families owned their own homes, 87 percent had televisions, and 75 percent owned cars.[3] Progress was slower in war-ravaged Europe, but there too each year brought measurable gains in families' living standards and conveniences.

This was the first chance many people had to try to live out the romanticized dream of a private family, happily ensconced in its own nest. They studied how the cheery husbands and wives on their favorite television programs organized their families (and where the crabby ones went wrong). They devoured articles and books on how to get the most out of marriage and their sex lives. They were even interested in advertisements that showed them how to use home appliances to make their family lives better.

I like to show my students an hourlong film put out by General Electric in 1956. In this long advertisement for electricity, mom discovers that her new clothes dryer gives her the chance to bond with her daughter and pick up some of the "groovy" slang of the expanding teen pop culture. Mom then shows her daughter how to use the family's new freezer and self-timing oven to make a meal that will impress the cute roommate her older son has brought home from college. The visitor likes his oven-baked ham, frozen orange juice, and electrically whipped dessert so much that he skips the dreary lecture he'd planned to attend and takes the ecstatic daughter dancing. All this was achieved by living better electrically.

My students are incredulous that people would actually sit and watch this corny stuff for a whole hour. But one day the grandmother of one student was visiting class when we watched the GE film, and she mentioned having seen it in the 1950s. To her, it had been not a cliché but a revelation.

An editor of a 1950s women's magazine in Britain commented later that nowadays "you cannot imagine people buying a magazine to learn how to use a fridge." But "that was the excitement of the 1950s. What is a washing machine? What is a steam iron? And how soon can I try one in my own home?"[4] American women's magazines too taught their readers how to use new home appliances and what the latest household gadgets did, how to decorate a home more tastefully, and what to do with the exotic new foods, such as artichokes and onion soup mixes, that could now be found in supermarkets.

As for women whose husbands couldn't afford such wonders, there was always the dream of being chosen "Queen for a Day." Premiering in 1955, this TV show was watched by thirteen million Americans each day, more than tuned in to the now-iconic *Ozzie and Harriet* or *Leave It to Beaver.* Each day five women, usually women whose husbands were dead, disabled, or unemployed, but occasionally single mothers, told their sad tales on the air. The one whose story elicited the strongest audience response, as measured on the "applause-o-meter," received a cornucopia of new products for the home: furniture, silverware, household appliances, wardrobes. Losers took home a consolation prize, such as a new toaster.[5]

Today strong materialist aspirations often corrode family bonds. But in the 1950s, consumer aspirations were an integral part of constructing the postwar family. In its April 1954 issue, *McCall's* magazine heralded the era of "togetherness," in which men and women were constructing a "new and warmer way of life . . . as a family sharing a common experience." In women's magazines, that togetherness was always pictured in a setting filled with modern appliances and other new consumer products. The essence of modern life, their women readers learned, was "abundance, emancipation, social progress, airy houses, healthy children, the refrigerator, pasteurised milk, the washing-machine, comfort, quality and accessibility."[6] And of course marriage.

Television also equated consumer goods with family happiness. Ozzie and Harriet hugged each other in front of their Hotpoint appliances. A man who had been a young father in the 1950s told a student of mine that he had had no clue how to cultivate the family "togetherness" that his wife kept talking about until he saw an episode of the sitcom *Leave It to Beaver,* which gave him the idea of washing the car with his son to get in some "father-son" time.

When people could not make their lives conform to those of the "normal" families they saw on TV, they blamed themselves—or their parents. Assata Shakur, a young black girl growing up in this period, remembered how angry she was that her mother didn't act more like Donna Reed: "Why didn't my mother have freshly baked cookies ready when I came home from school? Why didn't we live in a house with a back yard and a front yard instead of an ole apartment? I remember looking at my mother as she cleaned the house in her raggedy housecoat with her hair in curlers. 'How disgusting,' I would think. Why didn't she clean the house in high heels and shirtwaist dresses like they did on television?"[7]

At this early stage of the consumer revolution, people saw marriage as the gateway to the good life. Americans married with the idea of quickly buying their first home, with the wife working for a few years to help accumulate the down payment or furnish it with the conveniences she would use once she became a full-time housewife. People's newfound spending money went to outfit their homes and families. In the five years after World War II, spending on food in the United States rose by a modest 33 percent and clothing expenditures by only 20 percent, but purchases of household furnishings and appliances jumped by 240 percent. In 1961, Phyllis Rosenteur, the author of an American advice book for single women, proclaimed: "Merchandise plus Marriage equals our economy."[8]

In retrospect, it's astonishing how confident most marriage and family experts of the 1950s were that they were witnessing a new stabilization of family life and marriage. The idea that marriage should provide both partners with sexual gratification, personal intimacy, and self-fulfillment was taken to new heights in that decade. Marriage was the place not only where people expected to find the deepest meaning in their lives but also where they would have the most fun. Sociologists noted that a new "fun morality," very different "from the older 'goodness morality,'" pervaded society. "Instead of feeling guilty for having too much fun, one is inclined to feel ashamed if one does not have enough." A leading motivational researcher of the day argued that the challenge for a consumer society was "to demonstrate that the hedonistic approach to life is a moral, not an immoral, one."[9]

But these trends did not cause social commentators the same worries about the neglect of societal duties that milder ideas about the pleasure principle had triggered in the 1920s. Most 1950s sociologists weren't even troubled by the fact that divorce rates were *higher* than they had been in the 1920s, when such rates had been said to threaten the very existence of marriage. The influential sociologists Ernest Burgess and Harvey Locke wrote matter-of-factly that "the companionship family relies upon divorce as a means of rectifying a mistake in mate selection." They expressed none of the panic that earlier social scientists had felt when they first realized divorce was a permanent feature of the love-based marital landscape. Burgess and Locke saw a small amount of divorce as a safety valve for the "companionate" marriage and expected divorce rates to stabilize or decrease in the coming decades as "the services of family-life education and marriage counseling" became more widely available.[10]

The marriage counseling industry was happy to step up to the plate. By the 1950s Paul Popenoe's American Institute of Family Relations employed thirty-seven counselors and claimed to have helped twenty thousand people become "happily adjusted" in their marriages. "It doesn't require supermen or superwomen to succeed in marriage," wrote Popenoe in a 1960 book on saving marriages. "Success can be attained by almost anyone."[11]

There were a few dissenting voices. American sociologist Robert Nisbet warned in 1953 that people were loading too many "psychological and symbolic functions" on the nuclear family, an institution too fragile to bear such weight. In the same year, Mirra Komarovsky decried the overspecialization of gender roles in American marriage and its corrosive effects on women's self-confidence.[12]

But even when marriage and family experts acknowledged that the male breadwinner family created stresses for women, they seldom supported any change in its division of labor. The world-renowned American sociologist Talcott Parsons recognized that because most women were not able to forge careers, they might feel a need to attain status in other ways. He suggested that they had two alternatives. The first was to be a "glamour girl" and exert sexual sway over men. The second was to develop special expertise in "humanistic" fields, such as the arts or community volunteer work. The latter, Parsons thought, was socially preferable, posing less of a threat to society's moral standards and to a woman's own self-image as she aged. He never considered a third alternative: that women might actually win access to careers. Even Komarovsky advocated nothing more radical than expanding part-time occupations to give women work that didn't interfere with their primary role as wives and mothers.[13]

Marriage counselors took a different tack in dealing with housewives' unhappiness. Popenoe wrote dozens of marital advice books, pamphlets, and syndicated newspaper columns, and he pioneered the *Ladies' Home Journal* feature "Can This Marriage Be Saved?," which was based on case histories from his Institute of Family Relations. The answer was almost always yes, so long as the natural division of labor between husbands and wives was maintained or restored.

In one case history, "Marilyn" saved her marriage by giving up her "glamour girl" fantasies about becoming a movie star to do volunteer work with her local church. In another, Ava learned to control her bossiness. After therapy, she allowed "Chad to feel, as she now feels, that he is the head of the family." In a third case, a couple had been unhappily married for six years. Diana complained that her husband constantly criticized her, while he resented his wife's friendship with her boss. In this case, both partners were judged to be selfish and immature. The counselor had the husband read about women's sexual needs and the wife focus on finding satisfaction at home, rather than at work. At the end of their counseling, Diana had given up her job and was pregnant with her second child, and the couple had found a shared interest in gardening at their new home.[14]

In retrospect, the confidence these experts expressed in the stability of 1950s marriage and gender roles seems hopelessly myopic. Not only did divorce rates during the 1950s never drop below the highs reached in 1929, but as early as 1947 the number of women entering the labor force in the United States had begun to surpass the number of women leaving it.[15] Why were the experts so optimistic about the future of marriage and the demise of feminism?

Some were probably unconsciously soothed into complacency by the mass media, especially the new television shows that delivered nightly images of happy female homemakers in stable male breadwinner families. Some may have had their critical judgment impaired by the rigid Cold War atmosphere that associated questioning marriage or gender roles with support for communism. But on the whole, it was not unreasonable of social scientists and trend watchers to think that marriage and family life had stabilized in the 1950s and early 1960s. People tend to judge the seriousness of social trends by the direction in which things seem headed rather than by an absolute standard. By that criterion the problems that had plagued the sexualized, companionate marriage system during the first fifty years of the century seemed to be subsiding.

Although divorce rates were higher in 1950 than they had been in 1929, they were falling each year, and at their low point in the 1950s they were 50 percent lower than they had been in 1946. Similar declines in divorce were seen in Canada, Britain, West Germany, and France. An eighty-year upward trend seemed to be coming to an end.[16]

When divorce did occur, it was seen as a failure of individuals rather than of marriage. One reason people didn't find fault with the 1950s model of marriage and gender roles was that it was still so new that they weren't sure they were doing it right. Millions of people in Europe and America were looking for a crash course on how to attain the modern marriage. Confident that "science" could solve their problems, couples turned not just to popular culture and the mass media but also to marriage experts and advice columnists for help. If the advice didn't work, they blamed their own inadequacy.[17]

More puzzling was the complacency about the growing labor force participation rates of wives and mothers. By 1952 there were two million more working wives than there had been at the height of World War II. Married women accounted for the majority of the growth in the female labor force throughout the 1950s, and there was a 400 percent increase in the number of mothers in the workforce over the course of the decade.[18] Yet the image of the "emancipated woman" of the 1950s was not the working girl but the full-time housewife, armed with time-saving appliances that freed her from the drudgery of "old-fashioned" housework.

This image too had a basis in reality. True, more wives were entering the workforce early in their marriages or after their children had grown up. But they were in fact devoting longer stretches of their lives to full-time child rearing and homemaking. Most of the wives and mothers who joined the workforce in the 1950s were older than forty-five. Their mothering duties were largely done. At the same time postwar prosperity allowed more younger mothers to stay home while their children were small. While they were home, they could devote more time to child rearing and their families' comfort or recreation, because new appliances and convenience products had substantially lightened the chores involved in housekeeping.

When wives and mothers did take paid employment, they tended to hold part-time or seasonal jobs that were unlikely to make paid work a central part of their identities. Furthermore, the huge boost that the GI Bill and similar policies gave young male workers meant that gender inequality in pay and jobs grew substantially during the 1950s and early 1960s.[19] So even wives who worked were likely to feel they were doing so to bring in a few "extras" rather than helping to support the family.

The focus of college women, who had led the feminist movement in the early years of the twentieth century, also turned toward marriage. This was the era when people first began to joke about women attending college to earn an MRS degree. Two-thirds of women who started college in the 1950s dropped out, usually to get married. In 1952 an advertisement for Gimbel's department store wryly defined college as the place "where girls who are above cooking and sewing go to meet a man so they can spend their lives cooking and sewing."[20]

African American wives and mothers were much more likely than whites to work outside the home, even while their children were young. And although they were less likely to go to college than white women, they were less likely to drop out once they got there. But black families were still below the radar screen for the mass media, whose picture of family life was one in which dads went off to work and moms took care of the home.[21]

At every turn, popular culture and intellectual elites alike discouraged women from seeing themselves as productive members of society. In 1956 a *Life* magazine article commented that women "have minds and should use them . . . so long as their primary interest is in the home." The author believed that it was good for women to have some work experience and for men to know how to dry dishes, so that they could understand and help each other. But they had to avoid "trading primary responsibilities or trying to compete with each other." Adlai Stevenson, the two-time Democratic Party candidate for president of the United States, told the all-female graduating class of Smith College that "most of you" are going to assume "the humble role of housewife," and "whether you like the idea or not just now," later on "you'll like it."[22]

Under these circumstances, women tried their best to "like it." By the mid-1950s American advertisers reported that wives were using housework as a way to express their individuality. It appeared that Talcott Parsons was right: Women were compensating for their lack of occupational status by expanding their role as consumer experts and arbiters of taste and style. First Lady Jackie Kennedy was the supreme exemplar of this role in the early 1960s.[23]

Youth in the 1950s saw nothing to rebel against in the dismissal of female aspirations for independence. The number of American high school students agreeing that it would be good "if girls could be as free as boys in asking for dates" fell from 37 percent in 1950 to 26 percent in 1961, while the percentage of those who thought it would be good for girls to share the expenses of dates declined from 25 percent to 18 percent. The popular image was that only hopeless losers would engage in such egalitarian behavior. A 1954 Philip Morris ad in the *Massachusetts Collegian* made fun of poor Finster, a boy who finally found a girl who shared his belief in "the equity of Dutch treat." As a result, the punch line ran, "today Finster goes everywhere and shares expenses fifty-fifty with Mary Alice Hematoma, a lovely three-legged girl with side-burns."[24]

No wonder so many social scientists and marriage counselors in the 1950s thought that the instabilities associated with the love-based "near-equality" revolution in gender roles and marriage had been successfully contained. Married women were working outside the home more often than in the past, but they still identified themselves primarily as housewives. Men seemed willing to support women financially even in the absence of their older patriarchal rights, as long as their meals were on the table and their wives kept themselves attractive. Moreover, although men and women aspired to personal fulfillment in marriage, most were willing to stay together even if they did not get it. Sociologist Mirra Komarovsky interviewed working-class couples at the end of the 1950s and found that "slightly less than one-third [were] happily or very happily married." In 1957, a study of a cross section of all social classes found that only 47 percent of U.S. married couples described themselves as "very happy." Although the proportion of "very happy" marriages was lower in 1957 than it was to be in 1976, the divorce rate was also lower.[25]

What the experts failed to notice was that this stability was the result of a unique moment of equilibrium in the expansion of economic, political, and personal options. Ironically, this one twenty-year period in the history of the love-based "near-equality" marriage when people stopped predicting disaster turned out to be the final lull before the long-predicted storm.

The seeming stability of marriage in the 1950s was due in part to the thrill of exploring the new possibilities of married life and the size of the rewards that men and women received for playing by the rules of the postwar economic boom. But it was also due to the incomplete development of the "fun morality" and the consumer revolution. There were still many ways of penalizing nonconformity, tamping down aspirations, and containing discontent in the 1950s.

One source of containment was the economic and legal dependence of women. Postwar societies continued the century-long trend toward increasing women's legal and political rights outside the home and restraining husbands from exercising heavy-handed patriarchal power, but they stopped short of giving wives equal authority with their husbands. Legal scholar Mary Ann Glendon points out that right up until the 1960s, "nearly every legislative attempt to regulate the family decision-making process gave the husband and father the dominant role."[26]

Most American states retained their "head and master" laws, giving husbands the final say over questions like whether or not the family should move. Married women couldn't take out loans or credit cards in their own names. Everywhere in Europe and North America it was perfectly legal to pay women less than men for the same work. Nowhere was it illegal for a man to force his wife to have sex. One legal scholar argues that marriage law in the 1950s had more in common with the legal codes of the 1890s than the 1990s.[27]

Writers in the 1950s generally believed that the old-style husband and father was disappearing and that this was a good thing. The new-style husband, said one American commentator, was now "partner in the family firm, part-time man, part-time mother and part-time maid." Family experts and marital advice columnists advocated a "fifty-fifty design for living," emphasizing that a husband should "help out" with child rearing and make sure that sex with his wife was "mutually satisfying."[28]

But the 1950s definition of fifty-fifty would satisfy few modern couples. Dr. Benjamin Spock, the famous parenting advice expert, called for men to get more involved in parenting but added that he wasn't suggesting equal involvement. "Of course I don't mean that the father has to give just as many bottles, or change just as many diapers as the mother," he explained in a 1950s edition of his perennial bestseller *Baby and Child Care*. "But it's fine for him to do these things occasionally. He might make the formula on Sunday."[29]

The family therapist Paul Popenoe was equally cautious in his definition of what modern marriage required from the wife. A wife should be "sympathetic with her husband's work and a good listener," he wrote. But she must never consider herself "enough of an expert to criticize him."[30]

Many people recoiled from even the rhetorical assertion of equality. *McCall's* magazine campaigned for "togetherness" and partnership in marriage but repeatedly warned its readers not to go too far. Throughout the decade, calls for partnership and mutuality in marriage alternated with public hand-wringing about whether people were taking these ideas to extremes. "No one wants fathers to go back to acting like tyrants," asserted one writer. "But they should wield more authority in their families than they are currently doing. The family needs a head." Sociologist Ralph LaRossa examined magazine articles, TV shows, and child-rearing manuals of the 1950s and found that as the decade progressed, there was a reassertion of more traditional male dominance, perhaps reflecting a sense that even "near equality" must not be allowed to get out of hand.[31]

The sexualization of mass culture continued in the 1950s. *Playboy* magazine was a huge commercial success from its first appearance in 1953. *The Bob Cummings Show* (1955–59) depicted the life of a swinging photographer who couldn't keep his hands off the gorgeous models he photographed. Barbie, the first children's doll to have breasts, came on the market in 1959. But girls who "gave in" to sexual temptation in real life were almost universally condemned. As one woman later recalled, there were "Stop-Go lights flashing everywhere we looked. Sex, its magic spell everywhere, was accompanied by the stern warning: Don't do it."[32]

Plenty of women did "do it." But the extent of the sexual revolution that had already resumed its 1920s progress was obscured by the falling age of marriage and the willingness of most young men and women to marry if the girl got pregnant. A 1950s woman who married at age seventeen told a student interviewer many years later, "I sometimes wish I hadn't had to marry the first man I slept with, but that's just what you did in those days." Women who got pregnant out of wedlock and couldn't get the father to marry them were encouraged—at least, if they were white—to give their children up for adoption and start over, pretending it had never happened.[33] The penalties for defying these sexual norms were severe. This was a period when children born out of wedlock had "illegitimate" stamped on their birth certificates and school records.[34]

Most women did not need the threat of external sanctions to get them to enter male breadwinner marriages and make homes of their own. A Canadian woman recollected that moving to the suburbs in the 1950s was not as stifling as some women later complained. Those were "good years," she said. "My husband was getting ahead and I saw myself as a helpmate." Suburbia "tended to narrow our vision of the outside world," she admitted, but it "really worked" for children. "We thought we had the ideal life. . . . We knew little about the outside world of poverty, culture, crime and ethnic variety. We were like a brand new primer, 'Dick and Jane.'"[35]

These were the feelings of thousands of women in the United States as well. American historians are fortunate to have an exceptionally long-term study of families begun in the 1930s by the Institute for Human Development at the University of California, Berkeley. The researchers followed the same group of individuals throughout their lives and continued by interviewing their children and grandchildren. Their interviews reveal that men did indeed become more domestic during the 1950s. Husbands and wives relaxed gender stereotypes in their division of grocery shopping, garden work, and household repairs. The majority of couples aspired to mutual decision making in the home, and nearly a third of the couples claimed that they regularly met that ideal.[36]

Many 1950s men did not view male breadwinning as a source of power but as a burdensome responsibility made worthwhile by their love for their families. A man who worked three jobs to support his family told interviewers, "Although I am somewhat tired at the moment, I get pleasure out of thinking the family is dependent on me for their income." Another described how anxious he had been to finish college and "get to . . . acting as a husband and father should, namely, supporting my family." Men also remarked on how wonderful it felt to be able to give their children things their families had been unable to afford when they were young.[37]

A constant theme of men and women looking back on the 1950s was how much better their family lives were in that decade than during the Depression and World War II. But in assessing their situation against a backdrop of such turmoil and privation, they had modest expectations of comfort and happiness, so they were more inclined to count their blessings than to measure the distance between their dreams and their real lives.

Modest expectations are not necessarily a bad thing. Anyone who expects that marriage will always be joyous, that the division of labor will always be fair, and that the earth will move whenever you have sex is going to be often disappointed. Yet it is clear that in many 1950s marriages, low expectations could lead people to put up with truly terrible family lives.

Historian Elaine Tyler May comments that in the 1950s "the idea of a 'working marriage' was one that often included constant day-to-day misery for one or both partners." Jessica Weiss recounts interviews conducted over many years in the Berkeley study with a woman whose husband beat her and their children. The wife often threw her body between her husband and the young ones, taking the brunt of the violence on herself because "I can take it much easier than the kids can." Her assessment of the marriage strikes the modern observer as a masterpiece of understatement: "We're really not as happy as we should be." She was not even indignant that her neighbors rebuffed her children when they fled the house to summon help. "I can't say I blame the neighbors," she commented. "They didn't want to get involved." Despite two decades of such violence, this woman did not divorce until the late 1960s.[38]

A 1950s family that looked well functioning to the outside world could hide terrible secrets. Both movie star Sandra Dee and Miss America of 1958, Marilyn Van Derbur, kept silent about their fathers' incestuous abuse until many years had passed. If they had gone public in the 1950s or early 1960s, they might not even have been believed. Family "experts" of the day described incest as a "one-in-a-million occurrence," and many psychiatrists claimed that women who reported incest were simply expressing their own oedipal fantasies.[39]

In many states and countries a nonvirgin could not bring a charge of rape, and everywhere the idea that a man could rape his own wife was still considered absurd. Wife beating was hardly ever treated seriously. The trivialization of family violence was epitomized in a 1954 report of a Scotland Yard commander that "there are only about twenty murders a year in London and not all are serious—some are just husbands killing their wives."[40]

Even very accomplished, prominent women could not escape these inequities. Take Coya Knutson, an immigrant's daughter who grew up in the 1930s on a farm in North Dakota and went on to study music at the Juilliard School in New York City before returning to the Midwest to teach school. Coya married in 1940 but could not be a full-time homemaker because her husband made no effort to support his family.

In 1950, Coya ran for the Minnesota State House of Representatives and won. In 1954 she was elected to the U.S. House of Representatives, where she championed family farms, medical research, and campaign finance reform. She also originated the federal student loan program. But according to her son, when she was in Congress, her husband regularly beat her so badly that she had to wear dark glasses when she returned to Washington, D.C., from her visits home.

In 1958, her husband, collaborating with her political opponents to get her out of Congress, wrote an open letter urging his wife to come back to the "happy home we once enjoyed." The press jumped on the bandwagon. The words *Coya, Come Home* screamed out of headlines all across the country. Knutson won the primary but lost the election to an opponent who campaigned on the slogan "A Big Man for a Man-Sized Job."[41]

Even in less extreme situations there was plenty of unhappiness to go around. When *McCall's* ran an article in 1956 titled "The Mother Who Ran Away," it set a new record for readership. An editor later said, "We suddenly realized that all those women at home with their three and a half children were miserably unhappy." This may have been hyperbole, but when *Redbook's* editors asked readers to explain "Why Young Mothers Feel Trapped," they got twenty-four thousand replies.[42]

Still, these signs of unhappiness did not ripple the placid waters of 1950s complacency. The male breadwinner marriage seemed so pervasive and so popular that social scientists decided it was a necessary and inevitable result of modernization. Industrial societies, they argued, needed the division of labor embodied in the male breadwinner nuclear family to compensate for the impersonal demands of the modern workplace. The ideal family—or what Talcott Parsons called "the normal" family—consisted of a man who specialized in the practical, individualistic activities needed for subsistence and a woman who took care of the emotional needs of her husband and children.[43]

The close fit that most social scientists saw between the love-based male breadwinner family and the needs of industrial society led them to anticipate that this form of marriage would accompany the spread of industrialization across the globe and replace the wide array of other marriage and family systems in traditional societies. This view was articulated in a vastly influential 1963 book titled *World Revolution and Family Patterns,* by American sociologist William F. Goode. Goode's work became the basis for almost all high school and college classes on family life in the 1960s, and his ideas were popularized by journalists throughout the industrial world.[44]

Goode surveyed the most up-to-date family data in Europe and the United States, the Middle East, sub-Saharan Africa, India, China, and Japan and concluded that countries everywhere were evolving toward a conjugal family system characterized by the "love pattern" in mate selection. The new international marriage system, he said, focused people's material and psychic investments on the nuclear family and increased the "emotional demands which each spouse can legitimately make upon each other," elevating loyalty to spouse above obligations to parents. Goode argued that such ideals would inevitably eclipse other forms of marriage, such as polygamy. Monogamous marriage would become the norm all around the world.

The ideology of the love-based marriage, according to Goode, "is a radical one, destructive of the older traditions in almost every society." It "proclaims the right of the individual to choose his or her own spouse. . . . It asserts the worth of the *individual* as against the inherited elements of wealth or ethnic group." As such, it especially appealed "to intellectuals, young people, women, and the disadvantaged."

Goode marshaled an impressive array of figures and surveys to make his case that the modern love-based marriage was gaining ground around the world.[45] The one major region he neglected was Latin America, where marital record keeping was especially spotty and inconsistent. This was a significant omission because the widespread prevalence of cohabitation in Latin America would have been hard to fit into his schema of linear evolution toward universal monogamous marriage.[46]

But on the basis of data they had available, Goode and other sociologists of the 1950s and early 1960s saw no challenge to the primacy of marriage or the permanence of the male breadwinner family. Goode recognized that the modern economy gave women unprecedented bargaining power because for the first time they could hold jobs independent of their families and were legally entitled to keep the money they earned. But this would not undercut the male breadwinner family, he predicted, because society clearly needed women in the home to raise the children and because "families continue to rear their daughters to take only a modest degree of interest in full-time careers."[47]

Despite women's legal gains and the "radical" appeal of the love ideology to women and youth, Goode concluded that a destabilizing "full equality" was not in the cards. Women had not become more "career-minded" between 1900 and the early 1960s, he said. In his 380-page survey of world trends, Goode did not record even one piece of evidence to suggest that women might become more career-minded in the future.

Most social scientists agreed with Goode that the 1950s family represented the wave of the future. They thought that the history of marriage had in effect reached its culmination in Europe and North America and that the rest of the world would soon catch up. As late as 1963 nothing seemed more obvious to most family experts and to the general public than the preeminence of marriage in people's lives and the permanence of the male breadwinner family.

But clouds were already gathering on the horizon.

When sustained prosperity turned people's attention from gratitude for survival to a desire for greater personal satisfaction . . .

When the expanding economy of the 1960s needed women enough to offer them a living wage . . .

When the prepared foods and drip-dry shirts that had eased the work of homemakers also made it possible for men to live comfortable, if sloppy, bachelor lives . . .

When the invention of the birth control pill allowed the sexualization of love to spill over the walls of marriage . . .

When the inflation of the 1970s made it harder for a man to be the sole breadwinner for a family . . .

When all these currents converged, the love-based male-provider marriage would find itself buffeted from all sides.

Part Four

———◦《》◦———

Courting Disaster?
The Collapse of Universal
and Lifelong Marriage

Chapter 15

━━◦《◦》◦━━

Winds of Change:
Marriage in the 1960s and 1970s

I t took more than 150 years to establish the love-based, male breadwinner marriage as the dominant model in North America and Western Europe. It took less than 25 years to dismantle it. No sooner had family experts concluded that the perfect balance had been reached between the personal freedoms promised by the love match and the constraints required for social stability, than people began to behave in ways that fulfilled conservatives' direst predictions.

In barely two decades marriage lost its role as the "master event" that governed young people's sexual lives, their assumption of adult roles, their job choices, and their transition into parenthood. People began marrying later. Divorce rates soared. Premarital sex became the norm. And the division of labor between husband as breadwinner and wife as homemaker, which sociologists in the 1950s had believed was vital for industrial society, fell apart.[1]

To many at the time, it seemed as if change had just come out of the blue. "It was the 1960s—all that turmoil, all that disillusion with authority and tradition," said Gary, a World War II veteran I interviewed in the early 1990s. Gary had married his girlfriend in 1942 when she got pregnant. But "aside from that," he recalled, he had "a Norman Rockwell family" through the 1950s.

Then his three children got involved in civil rights and protests against the war in Vietnam and began to argue with their parents about women's liberation.

"Some of it was the fault of the establishment," Gary said, looking back, "like my kids always claimed. Some of it was wild-eyed radicals. Some of it was just sort of a fun liberation from the conformity of the 1950s. But it tore our family apart for a while."

When pressed for specifics, Gary realized that it started earlier than the 1960s. Back in 1958, his sixteen-year-old daughter Florence was already arguing with him about everything from the Cold War to racial integration to rock and roll and, above all, to her curfew. Several times during the 1950s he came home from work to find his wife crying in the bedroom, the breakfast dishes still undone. This was not the family he'd pictured when he'd married his high school sweetheart, bought a house in the suburbs after the war, and raised his three children, each two years apart, "in a nice environment—a lot better than where I grew up."

"Florence was right about the integration thing," he said in retrospect. "There were kids down South being beaten up, even killed, just for trying to go to school. And we grownups were sitting around worrying about the immorality of rock and roll. The kids did something about it. But man, they could get self-righteous."

On reflection Gary thought that perhaps 1950s parents had gotten what they'd wished for, and it had come back to bite them. "We raised our kids to think they were a new generation that was going to make everything better than we'd been able to do. But we didn't expect them to try to remake us as well. Things just got out of control in the 1960s—not just the kids, but all sorts of things." Including, as it turned out, his own marriage. Despite his wife's crying jags, Gary was taken completely by surprise when she said she wanted a divorce after thirty-one years of marriage.

As happened in Gary's family, the political movements against segregation and the war in Vietnam in the 1960s were followed by a struggle that took place much closer to home, an attack on the whole 1950s package of beliefs about women's roles, courtship, and marriage. In 1968, supporters of women's liberation garnered headlines around the country by tossing girdles, bras, and pictures that "degraded" women as "sex objects" into a trash can outside the Miss America contest. The following year the Redstockings, a small radical feminist group in New York, issued a manifesto declaring that marriage turned women into "breeders" and "domestic servants." That was also the year a routine police raid on the Stonewall Inn, a gay bar in New York, sparked a full-scale riot, leading within weeks to the formation of the Gay Liberation Front.

All the old mores seemed up for grabs. In 1972, Nena and George Mc-
Neil's bestseller *Open Marriage* suggested that some couples might choose to
tolerate extramarital affairs as part of a frank and open relationship. Popular
women's magazines discussed the pros and cons of introducing "swinging"
and spouse swapping into a marriage. Some radical feminists claimed that
childbearing itself was inherently oppressive and that women could be liberated only by the development of artificial wombs.[2]

The idea that "traditional" marriage was overturned by 1960s revolutionaries makes a dramatic story. But many of the forces that transformed marriage
in the 1970s and 1980s were already at work under the surface in the 1950s,
and other changes were spurred in later decades by people who had no intention of challenging traditional marital norms.

The depth and influence of the radicalism of the late 1960s and early
1970s are often exaggerated. The most extreme attacks on monogamy and
marriage were generally another instance of what 1920s sexual reformer
Floyd Dell called ideological overcompensation, an attempt to break with the
past by pushing as far as possible in the opposite direction. Within just a few
years, many advocates of the more extreme positions were backpedaling. Nena
McNeil wrote in 1977 that some of the ideas in *Open Marriage* had been unrealistic and extremist. "In our haste to correct the obvious inadequacies of
the old order in marriage," she wrote, "the baby has been thrown out with
the bathwater."[3]

By the end of the 1960s most women still did not support even the more
moderate ideas of women's liberation. As late as 1968 two-thirds of women
aged fifteen to nineteen, and almost as many aged twenty to twenty-four, still
expected to become full-time homemakers. A 1970 poll reported that more
than three-quarters of married women under age forty-five said the best marriage was one in which the wife stayed home and only the husband was employed.[4]

By the mid-1970s an organized campaign against the changes that had
been effected in gender roles and sexual norms was in full swing. Right-wing
activist Phyllis Schlafly led a successful fight against ratification of the Equal
Rights Amendment. When Dade County, Florida, passed an ordinance that
prohibited discrimination on the basis of sexual orientation, former Miss
America Anita Bryant and the Reverend Jerry Falwell, soon-to-be founder of
the self-styled Moral Majority movement, campaigned to repeal all laws man-
dating equal treatment for what Bryant called "this human garbage." Falwell
warned that "so-called gay folks would just as soon kill you as look at you."[5]
New groups were founded to bolster "traditional" marriage, and at that time

any article by a reformed or repentant feminist was virtually guaranteed publication.

Nevertheless, the pace of change in marriage behavior accelerated after the mid-1970s, though the majority of the people who adopted "radical" new behaviors had either never heard of or disagreed with the radical critics of marriage and gender roles. Most women changed their attitudes toward work, marriage, and divorce only after they themselves had already gone to work or experienced divorce. In 1980 even Anita Bryant, by then divorced herself, told the *Ladies' Home Journal,* "I guess I can better understand the gays' and the feminists' anger and frustration."[6]

It is impossible to sort out neatly in order of importance all the factors that rearranged social and political life between the 1960s and the 1990s and in the process transformed marriage as well. Sometimes it is even hard to say which changes caused the transformation and which were consequences. But the changes were not effected by a single generation or a particular political ideology.[7]

Such a simplistic view ignores the fact that even as early as the end of the eighteenth century there were people warning that making personal happiness the goal of marriage could end up destroying the stability of the institution. And in the 1920s the subversive potential of making intimacy and sexual fulfillment the criteria for a successful marriage became crystal clear. The crisis of the 1920s was relegated to the back burner by the Depression of the 1930s and the turmoil of World War II. But when peace and prosperity returned in the 1950s, aspirations for personal fulfillment and sexual satisfaction returned to center stage and were adopted by larger sectors of the population than had ever dared harbor such hopes before. As psychologist Abraham Maslow predicted in 1954, once people's basic needs for survival and physical security were met, "higher order needs," such as self-expression and high-quality relationships, began to take priority over material needs.[8]

Men and women initially tried to find fulfillment at home. But when marriage did not meet their heightened expectations, their discontent grew proportionately. The more people hoped to achieve personal happiness within marriage, the more critical they became of "empty" or unsatisfying relationships.[9]

Looking back on their lives a few decades later, men and women who had been in male breadwinner marriages in the 1950s and 1960s told interviewers that the division of labor in which they'd hoped to find fulfillment had so divided their lives that intimacy had become difficult, if not impossible. Wives were especially likely to regret their choices. Of women interviewed during the late 1950s and 1960s, even those who were content with their marriages almost always wanted a different life for their daughters. When it came to her daughter, one woman told interviewers in 1957, "I sure don't want her to turn out to be just a housewife like myself." Another explained to the researchers in 1958 that she hoped her daughters would "be more independent than I was." A third, interviewed in 1959, said nearly the same thing: "I want them to have some goal in life besides being a housewife. I'd like to see them make a living so the house isn't the end of all things."[10]

What an interesting pattern, with what interesting implications for the future! A 1962 Gallup poll reported that American married women were very satisfied with their lives. But only 10 percent of the women in the same poll wanted their daughters to have the same lives that they had. Instead they wanted their daughters to postpone marriage and get more education.

These sentiments were not conscious endorsements of feminism. The 1950s housewives who wanted something different for their girls did not expect them to choose lifelong careers. But they wanted their children to have more options for self-expression than their own lives had afforded. So they encouraged behavior in their daughters that, in combination with economic and political changes in the 1960s and 1970s, ended up overturning 1950s gender roles and marriage patterns.

Men had their own complaints about the typical family arrangement of the 1950s. In fact, Barbara Ehrenreich argues that it was men, not women, who first revolted against the male breadwinner marriage. Even before Betty Friedan voiced the discontents of the trapped housewife in her 1963 book *The Feminine Mystique,* men were detailing the discontents of the trapped breadwinner. In 1963, Friedan described the loneliness and alienation of housewives as "the problem that has no name." But men had named the problem of the alienated *breadwinner* a decade earlier. They called it conformity. In his 1955 best seller *Must You Conform?,* Robert Lindner wrote that when a man tried to live up to all of society's expectations at work and at home, he became "a slave in mind and body . . . a lost creature without a separate identity." In his 1957 book *The Crack in the Picture Window,* John Keats described the suburbs as "jails of the soul."[11]

In 1953 Hugh Hefner founded *Playboy* magazine as a voice of revolt against male family responsibilities. Hefner urged men to "enjoy the pleasures the female has to offer without becoming emotionally involved"—or, worse yet, financially responsible. In *Playboy's* first issue, an article titled "Miss Gold-Digger of 1953" assailed women who expected men to support them. Another article the same year lamented the number of "sorry, regimented husbands trudging down every woman-dominated street in this woman-dominated land." By 1956 the magazine was selling more than one million copies a month.[12]

Dissatisfaction was as high among the many people who subscribed to 1950s ideals of marital intimacy as among those who dissented from them. Historian Eva Moskowitz argues that the very advice columnists who were trying to help women save their marriages were also teaching wives to articulate their grievances. Alongside lessons in femininity and homemaking, the women's magazines of the 1950s and 1960s nourished a "discourse of discontent" by promoting intimacy and self-fulfillment as the purpose of marriage. It was by reading about what marriage *ought* to be that many women saw what their own marriages weren't.[13]

As early as 1957 divorce rates started rising again in the United States and several other countries. In fact, one of every three American couples who married in the 1950s eventually divorced.[14]

This acceleration of divorce rates began well before no-fault divorce was legalized in the 1970s. By the end of the 1950s grounds for "fault" divorce had become so routine in many jurisdictions as to be laughable. Nearly every plaintiff testified in almost exactly the same words, describing behavior that included the exact minimum requirements and even the precise legal phrases needed for a fault-based divorce. "The number of cruel spouses in Chicago, both male and female, who strike their marriage partners in the face exactly twice, without provocation, leaving visible marks, is remarkable," noted the author of one 1950s divorce study.[15]

By the 1960s divorce by mutual consent, "disguised as fault divorce," had already become "routine legal procedure" in many countries. And when women's heightened expectations of personal fulfillment interacted with their growing economic independence, divorce accelerated further. The spread of no-fault divorce in the 1970s and 1980s was more a result of the rising discontent with marriage than a cause.[16]

The movement of married women into the workforce was another trend that had its roots in the 1950s. Every single decade of the twentieth century had seen an increase in the proportion of women in the workforce, and the trend accelerated in the postwar economy, which had growing numbers of low-paid clerical, sales, and service jobs to fill. Women were considered ideal workers because they were not entrenched in the then heavily unionized industrial jobs and could be paid less than men with families to support.[17]

But because women were marrying so young in the 1950s, there simply were not enough unmarried women available to fill all the open jobs. In response, businesses reorganized their hiring policies to recruit married women, and the government relaxed legal barriers to women's participation in the economy. As more wives entered the workforce, a new market opened up for such household conveniences as wash-and-wear clothes and prepared foods, which in turn made it easier for wives and mothers to participate and remain in the workforce.

As long as women were concentrated in low-paid jobs, they typically saw their work as just a supplement to their husbands' income and they adjusted their time in the labor force to the schedules of their husbands and the rhythms of motherhood. Women got jobs in the early years of adulthood, quit their jobs during the child-rearing years, then went back to work again after the children had grown up.

But as women saw more opportunities in the workplace before and after marriage, their aspirations grew. More women postponed marriage to complete college. Many women who had no college plans followed their mothers' advice and spent a few years enjoying the life of a single working girl before settling down to marriage. The year before Betty Friedan put a feminist spin on the boredom of housewives, Helen Gurley Brown, influential editor of *Cosmopolitan* magazine, told women that marriage was "insurance for the *worst* years of your life. During your best years you don't need a husband," she asserted. "You do need a man of course every step of the way, and they are often cheaper emotionally and a lot more fun by the bunch."[18]

As women stayed single longer, gaining experience at work and school, their personal aspirations and self-confidence grew. But so did their frustration at the remaining limits on their progress. This altered perspective paved the way for a broad-based women's rights movement that would further accelerate women's entry into the workforce and higher education, on better terms.[19]

The expansion of married women's employment in the 1950s had been spearheaded by women with a high-school education or less. But the improvement of work opportunities and the declining challenge of full-time homemaking made work more attractive to educated middle-class wives. By the end of the 1960s college-educated wives were more likely to be employed than wives with only a high-school degree. The very women with husbands who earned enough to support a family were the ones most likely to reject full-time homemaking.[20]

Until women had access to safe and effective contraception that let them control when to bear children and how many to have, there was only so far they could go in reorganizing their lives and their marriages. That too was on the horizon by the 1950s, as Margaret Sanger and other birth control advocates worked tirelessly to find a way for women to avoid conception without having to depend on their partners' cooperation. Sanger helped fund the invention of the first oral contraceptive in 1951. But only in 1960 did a birth control pill, Enovid, become commercially available. The impact was instantaneous, forever altering the relationship between sex and reproduction.

The contraceptive revolution of the 1960s was a much more dramatic break with tradition than the so-called sexual revolution, which had actually been in the making for eighty years. Premarital sex increased gradually but steadily from the 1880s through the 1940s. During the 1950s there was an ideological backlash to the sexual permissiveness of the wartime era, but over the course of the fifties many women came to accept what some researchers have called a transitional sexual standard. Premarital sex came to be viewed as acceptable for men under most conditions and for women if they were in love.

Women in that decade clung to the notion that sex was acceptable only with someone they loved because they still had to worry about pregnancy. A woman had to be prepared to marry her sexual partner if she became pregnant, and she had to make sure that her partner knew this was her expectation. So women continued to be the ones who set the boundaries of sexual behavior in the 1950s, as they had in the 1920s. By the end of the 1950s, however, claimed American sociologist Ira Reiss in 1961, the typical teenage girl had become only a "half-willing guardian" of such boundaries.[21] Even this hesitation disappeared after the invention of the pill.

"All these years I've stayed at home while you had all your fun," sang the legendary country singer Loretta Lynn. "And every year that's gone by another baby's come. There's gonna be some changes made right here on Nursery Hill. You've set this chicken your last time, 'cause now I've got the Pill."[22]

For the first time in history any woman with a modicum of educational and economic resources could, if she wanted to, separate sex from childbirth, lifting the specter of unwanted pregnancy that had structured women's lives for thousands of years. Within five years of FDA approval, more than six million American women were taking the pill. By 1970, 60 percent of all adult women, unmarried as well as married, were using the birth control pill or an intrauterine device or had been sterilized. Birthrates fell even lower than they had been during the Depression.[23]

The pill gave unmarried women a degree of sexual freedom that the sex radicals of the 1920s could only have dreamed of. But when a large number of married couples stopped having children, it also radically changed marriage itself. Not only did effective contraception allow wives to commit more of their lives to work, but it altered the relationship between husbands and wives. Without a constant round of small children competing for their attention, many couples were forced to reexamine their own relationships more carefully. In addition, the growing number of childless marriages weakened the connection between marriage and parenthood, eroding some of the traditional justifications for elevating marriage over all other relationships and limiting it to heterosexual couples.

The social movements of the 1960s and early 1970s, in concert with these fundamental changes in women's work roles and reproductive rights, brought on a series of far-reaching transformations in the 1970s. After 150 years of only incremental progress, women's legal status and access to civil rights underwent a true revolution. On paper, workplace discrimination in the United States had been outlawed by the Civil Rights Act of 1963, but the law was not extensively enforced until the 1970s, and then mainly as a result of pressure from women themselves. That pressure became strong enough in the 1970s to push down other legal barriers that had persisted for hundreds of years. In 1972, Title IX of the Education Act prohibited discrimination by sex in any program receiving federal aid, forcing schools to start funding women's athletics and other programs. In 1973, in *Roe v. Wade,* the U.S. Supreme Court ruled that women had the right to choose abortion. In 1975 it became illegal to require a married woman to have her husband's written permission to get a loan or a credit card.

In rapid order, legislators across North America and Western Europe repealed all remaining "head and master" laws and redefined marriage as an association of two equal individuals rather than as the union of two distinct and specialized roles. A husband could no longer forbid his wife from taking a job because it interfered with his right to her homemaking or child-rearing duties. A wife could no longer assert an absolute right to be supported by her husband if she was capable of holding down a job.[24]

In homes throughout America, couples were rethinking how their marriages should function. In 1972, feminist Alix Kates Shulman went so far as to write up a marriage contract with her husband. It stipulated that each had "an equal right to his/her own time, work, values, and choices." It also stated that "the ability to earn more money is already a privilege which must not be compounded by enabling the larger earner to buy out of his/her duties and put the burden on the one who earns less, or on someone hired from outside." Few couples actually signed formal agreements, but the underlying principles were widely discussed and debated. In 1972, *Life* magazine devoted a cover story to Shulman's marriage agreement, and *Redbook* reprinted it under the title "A Challenge to Every Marriage." By 1978 even *Glamour* magazine was explaining how to write your own marriage contract.[25]

The 1960s and 1970s generated many radical critiques of marriage. But the civil rights climate of the time also encouraged people to think of marriage as a basic human right. This took the principle of free choice of partners farther than ever before. For hundreds of years the state had upheld parents in disputes over whether young people had a right to choose their own mates. Even after this choice had been ceded to young people, most governments retained some control over who could marry whom or permitted local authorities and employers to exercise such control.

In 1923 the U.S. Supreme Court had broken new ground when it listed marriage as one of "the privileges . . . essential to the orderly pursuit of happiness," but it stopped short of declaring marriage a fundamental right. At the end of the 1920s, forty-two states still banned marriage between whites and blacks, Mongolians, Hindus, Indians, Japanese, or Chinese. In the 1930s several states had added "Malays" to the list, a prohibition usually aimed at Filipinos. And until the 1960s, employers still had the right to require female employees to stay single as a condition of employment.

During the 1950s, however, state legislatures started to repeal their antimiscegenation laws. By 1965 laws prohibiting interracial marriage were found only in the South. When Richard and Mildred Loving appealed their arrest for miscegenation, a Virginia judge declared: "Almighty God created the races white, black, yellow, malay and red, and he placed them on separate continents. . . . The fact that he separated the races shows that he did not intend for the races to mix."[26]

But by the late 1960s there was a widespread sense that marriage was too basic a human right to be left to the whim of state governments. In 1967 the U.S. Supreme Court overturned the Lovings' conviction for violating Virginia's antimiscegenation law, claiming that marriage was "one of the 'basic civil rights of man,' fundamental to our very existence and survival." Courts in Europe and North America invoked the same principle to uphold prisoners' right to marry and to prohibit airline companies from firing flight attendants who got married.[27]

Almost immediately, several gay and lesbian partners argued that they too should have a fundamental right to marry. In 1970, President Richard Nixon commented that he could understand allowing the intermarriage of blacks and whites, but as for same-sex marriage, "I can't go that far—That's the year 2000."[28] Little did he realize just how close his estimate would turn out to be.

Another momentous outcome of the civil rights climate of the 1960s and 1970s was the erosion of the traditional role of marriage in defining legitimacy. Distinguishing between "legitimate" and "illegitimate" offspring had been critical to economic, political, and social order in most societies throughout history. "Illegitimacy" was how families protected themselves from having to share their power or property too widely. Politically, as long as claims to power descended through kinship, the very existence of the state depended on the principle of legitimacy.[29]

However, on the personal level, these distinctions had severe consequences. Obviously a child born out of wedlock had little claim upon its father. But few people today realize that even the relationship between an unwed mother and her child was not protected by law. An illegitimate child could be taken away from its mother and given up for adoption. If the mother kept her child, their relationship did not have the same legal rights as her relationship with a child she bore while married. Children born out of wedlock could not recover debts owed to their mother and could not bring a wrongful death suit if their mother was killed by negligence. Nor could a mother sue for the wrongful death of her nonmarital child. This was the case in the United States until 1968, when the Supreme Court ruled in *Levy v. Louisiana* that the Fourteenth Amendment's equal protection guarantee extended to the children of unwed parents.

As early as the eighteenth century, humanitarians began complaining that the principle of legitimacy allowed a man to seduce and abandon a woman without taking any responsibility for the child he might have fathered. There was a growing sense that it was wrong to penalize children for the sins or mistakes of their parents, but few countries took any action before the 1960s. Then, in the late 1960s and early 1970s, there was an avalanche of reform in North America and Western Europe. A series of Supreme Court rulings in the United States between 1968 and 1978 expanded the rights of nonmarital children and unwed mothers. In 1969, West Germany, Sweden, and the United Kingdom gave inheritance rights to out-of-wedlock children. France gave all children the same legal rights in 1973, finally fulfilling the slogan of the 1790 revolutionaries that "there are no bastards in France." In 1975, the European Convention on the Legal Status of Children Born out of Wedlock recommended that all countries abolish discrimination between children born in and out of marriage.[30]

Breaking down the distinction between legitimacy and illegitimacy was a humane response to an ancient inequity. But it stripped marriage of a role it had played for thousands of years and weakened its hold on people's political and economic rights and obligations.

The Gathering Storm

By the late 1970s all these trends had merged to produce an enormous change in people's attitudes toward personal relationships. Surveys from the late 1950s to the end of the 1970s found a huge drop in support for conformity to social roles and a much greater focus on self-fulfillment, intimacy, fairness, and emotional gratification. More people believed that autonomy and voluntary cooperation were higher values than was obedience to authority. Acceptance of singlehood, unmarried cohabitation, childlessness, divorce, and out-of-wedlock childbearing increased everywhere in North America and Western Europe.[31]

By 1978 only 25 percent of Americans still believed that people who remained single by choice were "sick," "neurotic," or "immoral," as most had thought in the 1950s. By 1979, 75 percent of the population thought that it was morally okay to be single and have children.[32]

Some of these changes in attitude and behavior resulted from the increased prosperity of the postwar world and the shift "from survival to self-expression" in people's values.[33] But other challenges to conventional gender roles and marital norms were driven by a countervailing trend, the increasing economic pressure on families in the wake of the international recession of 1973.

The surge of women taking jobs in the fifties and sixties was fueled by the new opportunities created by an expanding economy. But in the 1970s many women were pushed into the workforce by a combination of recession and inflation that kicked off a two-decade-long decline in real wages and job security. Men working in traditional manufacturing jobs were hit especially hard by the downturn, requiring their wives to pick up the slack. In the quarter century between 1947 and 1973, purchasing power of the average American more than doubled. And the poorer sectors of the population made the greatest gains, giving many working-class families their first experience with a male breadwinner/female homemaker marriage. But between 1973 and the late 1980s average real wages for the majority of workers fell, with the bottom 20 percent of the population experiencing the biggest loss. Young people just starting their families were particularly hard hit: Between 1973 and 1986 the median income of families headed by men under age thirty fell by 27 percent. That's almost exactly the same percentage as per capita income fell during the Great Depression.[34]

While men faced job and income insecurity during the 1970s and 1980s, employment expanded steadily in female-dominated service jobs. Women, starting from a lower earnings base than men, actually saw their real wages rise during this period. In this context, a wife's job was the best hedge most families had against inflation and the increasing insecurity of traditional "male" jobs. Women's earnings became crucial to the economic security of many families.

The surge in housing prices in the 1970s also pushed women into the workforce. As the largest generation in U.S. history began to set up its own households, it faced rampant housing inflation. Between 1972 and 1987 the average price of a new house rose by 294 percent. No longer could the "average Joe" with a pretty good job buy a house. Many families needed two earners to carry the mortgage on a home in a middle-class neighborhood.

This was not just an American phenomenon. A survey of twenty-one industrial countries reported that in the 1970s and 1980s female employment rose twice or even three times as fast as the growth in total employment. In almost every case, *married* women accounted for the majority of the increase in women's workforce participation.[35]

By the 1980s women's workforce participation was beginning to look much more like men's. Women still spent fewer total years at work, and they were more likely to drop out in the prime child-rearing years. But their dips in labor force participation had become shorter and less pronounced, and women were much less likely to quit work after giving birth.[36]

Here's something else interesting. As women spent more of their lives working, men were starting work later and retiring earlier, creating even more convergence. By 1970, women worked about 60 percent as long as men did over the course of their lives. Just a decade later, their lifetime employment was more than 75 percent that of men's.[37]

As women spent more of their lives at work, they became more likely to define having a job as an important part of their identity. In 1957, fewer than 60 percent of women who worked outside the home said they would keep their jobs if they didn't have to work, while 85 percent of men said they would stay on the job. By 1976, more than three-quarters of employed women said they would keep working even if they didn't need the money.[38] Many wives who had only gone to work to help out their husbands in the economic downturn now reported that their jobs gave them a sense of importance they had never gotten from full-time homemaking.

In the 1930s increased economic insecurity had reversed both the rise in divorce and the acceptance of unconventional lifestyles or gender roles. That did not happen in the downturn of the late 1970s and 1980s. For one thing, there was a social safety net that had not existed in the 1930s. For another, the end of the 1970s saw the dawn of a different kind of insecurity. A churning global economy wiped out old jobs and entire industries, but opened up tempting new opportunities in different arenas, then shifted again suddenly. This constantly changing economic and technological environment forced people to move away from conventional scripts for behavior.[39] In this context, German researchers Ulrich Beck and Elizabeth Beck-Gernsheim argue, men and women had to maximize their individual freedom of action and keep their options open. As people became more likely to change jobs and even neighborhoods frequently, they became more tolerant of the unconventional marital or familial choices that accompanied this upheaval.

All these changes led to new tensions between men and women. Single women complained that modern men were afraid to commit to relationships. Men muttered that modern women demanded the same respect as men at work but still expected a man to pay for dinner. Male breadwinners had to work longer hours to get by. Full-time housewives anxiously looked over their shoulders at the increased possibility of divorce. When husbands and wives both worked, they often argued over how to rearrange the division of housework. Working women scrambled to find trustworthy child care and re-sented husbands who didn't feel equally responsible for doing so. More couples described themselves as "very happy" in 1976 than in 1957, but they were much more likely to say there were problems in their marriage than they had been in 1950's polls.[40]

Anyone who thinks that male-female hostility was invented in the 1970s never spent time in a beauty parlor in the 1950s. When I was a teenager hang-ing out while my mother had her hair done, I got to listen in as "happily mar-ried" women routinely expressed contempt toward their husbands and toward men in general. And I knew from my father and his male friends that hostility toward women ran rampant in all-male settings. But I remember be-ing amazed at the end of the 1970s and in the early 1980s by how much anger I heard in the discussion periods after lectures I gave on family issues. What startled me wasn't the *amount* of mistrust and tension between men and women but the fact that it was being discussed so openly in mixed company.

One meeting in Dallas in 1981 actually broke down into a shouting match. Men complained that their wives or girlfriends asked them to help with house-work and then criticized them for doing everything wrong. Women coun-tered that their partners volunteered to help but then bothered them with so many questions about what to do next that it was easier to do it themselves.

One man said that everyone at work thought his wife was Superwoman. But when she got home, she took out her stress on him. "I'm thinking every-thing is going fine," he said, "and then she flips out over a sock on the floor or because I didn't put the kids' shoes where she always does." A woman, not his wife, shot back: "There's no time to hunt for things when we're all trying to get out the door at once. How come you don't know where things go? Were we invisible all those years when we had to do everything around the house? Not only couldn't you help, you couldn't even see what we were doing?"

If they had thought about the broader picture, these men and women would probably have agreed that the real problem was the lack of work policies amenable to family life. But in practice their daily tensions turned them on each other rather than on their employers. "My wife says, 'Tell the boss you *have* to leave at five tonight because it's your turn to pick up the kids,'" said one man angrily. "She doesn't realize how that gets held against you." Another woman said, "My husband says I should be the one to adjust," mimicking him sarcastically, " 'because supervisors are more understanding when a woman needs to ask for family time.' Yeah, they're understanding, and that's why they never give you a raise. If a woman wants to prove herself on the job, she has to put in *more* hours than the men."

Women who worked for pay weren't the only ones with resentments. At a women's book club in Arizona some homemakers in the group confided their fear that accessible divorce and society's new approval of working women gave men handy excuses to abandon them. Full-time housewives complained that their husbands and employed female friends did not understand how hard they worked, not only in their own homes but in the neighborhood. "I have to let repairmen into my employed friends' houses when they can't get home from work," said one woman. "I pick up their cleaning for them when they can't get off before the cleaner's closes. The neighborhood kids come to me for after-school snacks because their own parents won't be home until six. I actually subsidize their two-income families, and then they look down on me because I don't earn money."

People were not just letting off steam. The divorce rate more than doubled between 1966 and 1979. There were also glimpses of a new trend that was to explode in the 1980s. As the age of marriage rose, many women actually postponed marriage longer than they postponed motherhood. Rates of childbearing by unmarried women began to climb, and the number of children born out of wedlock was all the more noticeable because the birthrate of married couples continued to fall.

In less than twenty years, the whole legal, political, and economic context of marriage was transformed. By the end of the 1970s women had access to legal rights, education, birth control, and decent jobs. Suddenly divorce was easy to get. At the same time, traditional family arrangements became more difficult to sustain in the new economy. And new sexual mores, growing tolerance for out-of-wedlock births, and rising aspirations for self-fulfillment changed the cultural milieu in which people made decisions about their personal relationships. During the 1980s and 1990s, all these changes came together to irrevocably transform the role of marriage in society at large and in people's personal lives.

It is natural to speculate about what would have happened if one or another of these trends had been sidestepped or reversed. What if youthful civil rights activists had been less influential in challenging traditional authority? What if "hippie" values had not spread to such large numbers of middle-class kids? What if courts and governments had not erased the distinction between illegitimate and legitimate children? What if more wives and mothers had stuck to part-time work? What if most men had continued to earn wages high enough to buy a good house and send their kids to college without their wives needing to go to work? What if technology hadn't separated sex from reproduction so rapidly? What if no-fault divorce hadn't been passed? What if?

But removing one or two of these factors would not have made an appreciable difference. Most of these changes were inextricably intertwined, and in the few countries that avoided one or two of these trends, the other shifts in women's work patterns, the timing of marriage, and fertility control happened anyway.

The erosion of the male breadwinner family is a classic example of what some historians call an overdetermined event. In the 1960s and 1970s, wives increased their workforce participation for many reasons. When real wages for women rose, wives joined the workforce. When real wages for men fell, wives joined the workforce. When families suffered economic losses, wives joined the workforce. When families anticipated significant economic progress, wives joined the workforce. When a wife was happy in her marriage but bored at home, she joined the workforce. When she was unhappy in her marriage and stressed at home, she joined the workforce.

The male breadwinner marriage began to decline all across North America and Western Europe during the last third of the twentieth century, even in regions least affected by changes in individual values, marriage laws, and legal codes. Everywhere too marriage began to lose its power to organize sexual behavior, living arrangements, and child rearing. All these economic, cultural, demographic, and legal changes converged in the 1980s and 1990s to create "the perfect storm" in family life and marriage formation. And nothing in its path escaped unscathed.

Chapter 16

——◉——

The Perfect Storm:
The Transformation of Marriage at the
End of the Twentieth Century

In 1977, sociologist Amitai Etzioni warned that if present trends in divorce continued, "not one American family" would be left intact by the 1990s. By 1980 the divorce rate stood at 50 percent. Half of all people who married could be expected to divorce.[1]

The divorce revolution, as some people have called it, transformed the lives of millions of people. But the surge in divorce was only an early precursor of the bigger storm that swept across marriage and family life between the late 1970s and the end of the century.

As long as rates of marriage and remarriage remained high, the increase in divorce did not threaten the universality of marriage, however disruptive and painful those divorces and remarriages were to the particular families involved. But at the end of the 1970s the impact of high divorce rates was accelerated by a plunge in the number of remarriages and a whole flood of new alternatives to marriage.

After 1981, divorce rates leveled off and began a slow decline, despite the fact that by then no-fault divorce was ubiquitous. But fewer people remarried after divorce. A generation earlier, in the 1950s, two-thirds of divorced women in the United States married again within five years. By the end of the century only half of divorced women were married or even living with partners five years later.[2]

Equally dramatic was the number of people who waited past their mid-twenties to marry for the first time. In 1960 only one in ten American women aged twenty-five to twenty-nine was single. In 1998, nearly 40 percent of women in that age group were unmarried.

An even more momentous change was the number of couples who lived together without marrying. Between 1970 and 1999 the number of unmarried couples living together in the United States increased sevenfold. When this trend began, most couples married if the woman got pregnant. But by the 1990s, marriage was no longer regarded as the obvious response to pregnancy or childbirth.[3]

The repercussions were staggering. In 1960, one American child in twenty was born to an unmarried woman. By the end of the century it was one child in three. In 2003, the U.S. census reported that almost 40 percent of cohabiting couples had children under eighteen living with them, a figure nearly as high as the 45 percent of married couples with children under eighteen.[4]

In the late 1990s the pace of change began to slow, leading some observers to hope that the storm had passed and marriage would soon return to "normal." By 1998 the divorce rate was 26 percent lower than in 1979. Birthrates for unmarried white women stabilized in the 1990s, and those of black and Hispanic women actually declined. Also, more out-of-wedlock babies were now born to cohabiting couples than to women living alone, the earlier pattern. In popular culture, marriage and family life seemed to be regaining some of their luster. Attitudes toward promiscuity and adultery turned significantly more disapproving, and women's magazines began to run articles with titles like "Why Marriage Is Hot Again."[5]

One particular statistic from the 2000 U.S. census inspired several years of news stories announcing a revival of the male breadwinner family. For the first time in a quarter century, the labor force participation of women with infants under age one had gone down instead of up—from 59 percent in 1988 to 55 percent in 2000.[6]

That percentage stayed steady through 2002, encouraging some people to conclude that the forty-year erosion of the male-breadwinner marriage had come to an end. An article in *The New York Times Magazine* in 2003 combined Census Bureau statistics with a few anecdotes about high-achieving women who quit their jobs to announce the arrival of "The Opt-Out Revolution" among working mothers. Five months later *Time* magazine proclaimed that "More Women Are Sticking with the Kids."[7]

It is not surprising that the pace of change in gender roles, marriage behaviors, and sexual values slowed during the 1990s. In many arenas these changes were already nearing saturation point. And as people became more comfortable with new gender roles and social mores, the more extreme responses to the first traumatic years of change subsided.[8]

Such stabilization may have signified a normalization of new family patterns, but it was a far cry from any return to the past. The number of children being raised by unmarried parents did not decrease in the 1990s. Nor did the number of two-earner families, which rose from 39 percent of all married couples in 1970 to 62 percent in 1998. Rates of cohabitation increased among heterosexual and same-sex couples alike. More elders joined the trend toward "shacking up." As sperm banks opened their doors to unmarried women in the 1980s, increasing numbers of older single heterosexual women and lesbians took advantage of the chance to form unconventional families.[9]

Despite the much-ballyhooed dip in the number of working mothers with children under the age of one, more than 50 percent of such mothers were still in the workforce in 2003, compared with just 30 percent at the beginning of the 1980s. And women with children aged one and over now have the same labor force participation rates as childless women.[10]

Despite some reports by "trend spotters," highly educated professional mothers have not been turning their backs on career aspirations. Such women are actually less likely to "opt out" of paid employment while their children are young than lower-paid or lower-skilled ones. Among all mothers with children under six in 2002, more than two-thirds of women with college degrees and three-quarters of mothers holding graduate or professional degrees were in the labor force.[11]

Nor—again contrary to many media reports—have children of working mothers resolved to do things differently because of their "bad experiences" growing up. At the end of the 1990s sociologist Kathleen Gerson conducted life history interviews with a cross section of young men and women between eighteen and thirty-two. Four out of five of those who grew up with working mothers were glad their mothers had worked. Young women were especially likely to say that they appreciated having a working mother as a role model.[12]

Sons and daughters who grew up in families where only fathers worked were more evenly divided about whether that family arrangement had been a good thing. Only half said they were glad they had a mother who devoted herself exclusively to their care. The other half thought their mothers would have been happier working outside the home.

Parents and children may feel real ambivalence about how mothers combine work and family life. But working wives and mothers are here to stay, in large part because of structural changes in the demand for labor and the rewards of work. Demographer Donald Hernandez points out that from the mid-nineteenth to the mid-twentieth century, there were three routes to family economic advancement: The first was to send the children to work, allowing the parents to accumulate enough to buy a house and possibly send a later generation to school; the second was to move from farm to city, to take advantage of higher wage rates in urban areas; and the third was to invest in increased training and education for male members of the family.[13]

But child labor was abolished in the early twentieth century, and by the end of the 1950s the move out of agricultural work was largely completed. By the mid-1960s families were also getting diminishing returns from higher education or training for men. As these older strategies for achieving upward mobility faded, women's employment became central to family economic advancement and could not as easily be postponed or interrupted for full-time child raising.

Despite the economic recovery of the 1990s, most men's wages still lagged behind even the low rate of inflation in the first few years of the twenty-first century, while women's wages continued to grow from their lower starting point. The result was that in most American families, even if the wife's wages were lower than her husband's, her wages accounted for any income *growth* the family achieved.[14]

But in another major shift, most women, regardless of class, no longer worked solely for the needs of their families. By the turn of the century a wife's decision either to take a job or to remain at home depended less on her husband's wage and more on her own earnings capacity. Even when they continue to pool resources within marriage, women increasingly make cost-benefit decisions about working or staying home on the basis of their own employment opportunities rather than moving in and out of the labor market in response to changes in their husbands' jobs and earnings.[15]

This doesn't necessarily mean that working mothers are happy with their schedules. In many occupations, particularly in the United States, the demands and hours of work have risen over the past two decades. Today the United States surpasses even Japan in the amount of time workers spend on the job. No wonder workers with families—both men and women—report higher levels of stress balancing work and family life than they did twenty-five years ago. Many mothers would certainly like to cut back on their hours. So would many fathers.[16]

For almost thirty years I have asked my students how they expect to balance work and family in their own lives. Until recently most expected both partners to work but said the wife would try to take time off after the birth of a child. In the past five years, however, students have stopped assuming the woman will be the one to stay home. They tend to think it makes sense for the higher earner to keep working, and most are open to having the husband quit work if both partners earn the same wages.

That kind of financial equality is increasingly common in dual-earner households. In fact, in 2001, the working wife earned more than her husband in more than 30 percent of all households. The percentage of stay-at-home dads is still small, but social acceptance of that arrangement has skyrocketed. And as of 2002, more than two million working fathers were providing the primary child care in their families while their wives were at work.[17]

Of course, most wives and mothers who work outside the home now do so for psychological and social as well as financial reasons. Working wives consistently tell interviewers they like the respect, self-esteem, and friendships they get from a job, even though they find it stressful to arrange acceptable child care and negotiate household chores with their husbands. One of my older female students told me she went back to work for financial reasons when her child was nine months old. "I almost cried every time I left him at the babysitter," she said, "and I couldn't wait to see him again when I came home. But the truth is that once I was a couple of blocks from the babysitter's house I'd turn up the radio and sing along all the way to work. I was so excited to be able to talk to adults and to know that I was needed for my mind as well as my mothering."

In a 1995 survey by Louis Harris & Associates, fewer than one-third of working women said they would prefer to stay home if money were no object, although many women are reluctant to admit that to their husbands. Psychologist Francine Deutsch found when she interviewed working-class dual-earner couples together that the official family line was usually that the wife worked only for financial reasons. But when she spoke separately with the men and women, they often told different stories. "She would have loved to be home," said one husband. "I wanted to get out of the house," his wife said.[18]

Women consistently say they get more respect when they are employed, not only from society but from their own husbands. Women who earn incomes have much more decision-making power in their marriages than those who are full-time housewives. Moreover, the higher the proportion of the couple's joint income a wife earns, the more help she gets from her husband in housework and child care.[19]

Male breadwinner families are still a significant form of marriage, especially among couples with young children. Certainly many American women would stay home longer if they had the subsidized family leaves available to workers in much of Europe. But today approval of dual-earner marriages is as widespread as approval of male breadwinner marriages was in the 1950s, and this approval is highest among young women, who will be making decisions about work and marriage in the coming decades.[20]

Nor do falling divorce rates, however welcome they may be, herald a return to 1950s norms. As alternatives to marriage have multiplied, fewer people get married, and that means fewer people will get divorced. There does seem to have been a statistically significant increase in a couple's chance of staying togther during the 1990s, but those who do get married still face daunting odds: Forty-three percent of all first marriages in America end in divorce within fifteen years.[21]

We can't expect divorce rates to drop back to the rates of the 1950s, far less to those of earlier decades. In the century between the 1880s and the 1980s divorce rates rose steadily. If we set aside the short-term spikes in divorce right after World War II and at the end of the 1970s, America's divorce rate today is right where you would predict from its rate of increase during the last decade of the nineteenth century and the first fifty years of the twentieth.

For better or worse, people decide what they will and won't put up with in a relationship today on a totally different basis from before. Now that most husbands and wives earn their livings separately, rather than from a jointly run farm or business, it is much easier, though not less painful, for couples to go their separate ways and to survive economically if the union dissolves. Women still generally face a drop in their standard of living after divorce. But never before in history have so many women been capable of supporting themselves and their children without a husband.

The dramatic extension of adults' life expectancy since 1970 has also changed the terms of marriage. An American who reaches age sixty today can expect to live another twenty-five years. The average married couple will live for more than three decades after their kids have left home.[22]

This extension of life expectancy makes staying together "till death do us part" a much bigger challenge than ever before. What might seem an acceptable relationship when you expect to spend most of your married life raising kids together may seem unbearable when you realize that you will still have thirty years of one-on-one time once the kids are gone. No previous generation has ever been asked to make such a long-term commitment.

Many dissatisfied couples grit their teeth and try to tough it out until the children leave home. But the stress of raising children puts a strain on even the happiest of marriages and can wreak havoc on an unstable union. An older divorced student of mine wrote in her autobiographical essay: "I really tried to make it last for the sake of the kids. But then I started thinking, 'What if I come down with cancer right after they leave? Would it be worth it to be so unhappy for so long and then never even get the pay-off? Or what if I hit fifty and it was too late to find a decent relationship or build a rewarding life for my next thirty years?' After a while I was so miserable that I wasn't even a good parent anymore, which sort of spoiled the point of trying to stick it out."

Making divorce laws stricter would have little effect on the number of marriages that break down, and it might actually discourage some people from getting married in the first place. The adoption of no-fault divorce laws in the 1970s certainly made it easier to dissolve marriages that were already in trouble, and everywhere they were enacted, these laws were followed by a brief spike in divorce. But there was a similar long-term rise in divorce rates in the 1970s in states with and without no-fault divorce. Moreover, by 1985, when every state offered some form of no-fault divorce, divorce rates in America had already been falling for five years.[23] Yet even as divorce declined, more people were living together outside marriage. Stricter laws would not prevent those households—40 percent of which have children present—from dissolving.

Divorce and its nonlegal equivalent—the breakup of cohabiting couples—are here to stay. That means that single-parent households and stepfamilies are not going to disappear. Unwed parenting is also here to stay, partly because of the dramatic rise in women's age at first marriage. Women who marry at an older age are less likely to divorce than women who marry early, and they are more likely to have accumulated economic, emotional, and educational advantages that benefit their children. But because they remain unmarried for more years, they also face a longer period when they are "at risk" for—or might choose—an unmarried birth.

Ironically, some of the increase in unwed motherhood in the 1980s and 1990s may have been a reaction *against* the rise in divorce in the 1960s and 1970s. For more than thirty years sociologist Frank Furstenberg has been following a group of economically disadvantaged women in Baltimore, mostly African American, who became pregnant as unwed teenagers in the 1960s. Most of these women married the fathers of their children. But 80 percent of those marriages broke down before the children reached age eighteen.

One-third of the daughters also became pregnant and gave birth as teenagers. But in the 1980s few of that generation of young women married the fathers. One reason they did not marry, they told Furstenberg, was that they thought that their boyfriends would not be able to support a family in the tough economic times of the 1980s. Many also said their mothers' experiences had convinced them that being a single mother was preferable to entering a bad or unstable marriage.[24]

In the 1970s and 1980s most babies born out of wedlock were unplanned. But a 1997 study found that more than 40 percent of births to unmarried American women in recent years were intentional pregnancies. We may be able to continue bringing down the rates of childbirth for teenage girls, whose decision to have a baby often reflects their *lack* of choice over other aspects of their lives. But the choices made by economically independent women over the age of twenty-five are a different matter, and these women account for a growing percentage of nonmarital births.[25]

When you combine the fact that married women are having fewer children with the fact that the proportion of unmarried women in the population is rising, simple arithmetic predicts that a large percentage of children will be born out of wedlock, even if rates of childbearing by unmarried women stabilize or fall.[26] And in today's climate of choice, it is hard to imagine that single women will completely forgo having children.

When I speak on family issues to audiences across the country, single women generally tell me that they plan to marry and then have kids. But they often add that if at a certain point they haven't found a partner they trust to stay with them for life and share the child rearing, they would consider having a child on their own. "My mom was married, but she was the single mother of two children—me *and* my dad," said a twenty-four-year-old I spoke with at a college in Ohio. "I guess she was pretty happy. But I want more than a paper partnership, and if I can't get that, I'd be willing to go it alone."

One-third of the fifty thousand children adopted in the United States in 2001 went to single women. These women are not being irresponsible. Indeed, the Adoption Information Clearinghouse believes that single-parent homes may be especially well suited for "special needs" children who require close, intense relationships. Single women—most of them African American—accounted for 30 percent of adoptions of hard-to-place foster children.[27] Yet this trend too contributes to the multiplying ways that people organize their lives—and their children's lives—outside marriage.

Population experts predict that 50 percent of children in the United States will spend part of their lives in a household that does not contain both their married, biological parents. Perhaps we can reduce that number. But we cannot return to a world where almost all child rearing and care giving take place in and through marriage.[28]

As the age of marriage rises, people are also less and less likely to wait for a wedding to initiate them into sex. Some people see hope for a revival of traditional sexual mores in the declining support for promiscuous sexual behavior and the new popularity of virginity pledges among teenagers in the opening years of the twenty-first century. Certainly, the spread of sexually transmitted diseases, especially AIDS, and the emotional turmoil that comes with casual sexual relationships have made promiscuous sex less attractive. With divorce readily available, there are also fewer excuses not to honor existing marital commitments. So more people now expect fidelity within committed relationships than in the 1970s, even as acceptance of premarital sex, cohabitation, and divorce has continued to grow.

Still, this does not mark a return to conservative sexual mores, especially among young people. There has been a decline in early sexual initiation, but it has been more marked for boys than for girls and more likely reflects the continuing decline of the double standard than a return to "traditional morality." As was foreshadowed in the racy 1920s, when "respectable" young women began engaging in premarital sex on a larger scale, boys today are more likely to begin their sexual lives in romantic relationships than in exploitative encounters with so-called bad girls. A girlfriend has more influence than a casual partner over the timing of sexual initiation and the use of contraception when sex occurs.[29]

Seen in this light, maintaining virginity longer does not necessarily signal a return to traditional sexual mores but may reflect young women's growing sexual independence and control over their sexual relationships. Moreover, many teenagers who delay the onset of genital intercourse are substituting other behaviors, such as oral sex, which increased significantly among teens in the 1990s.[30] I was completely flummoxed a couple of years ago in Minnesota when a group of teenage girls told me that several of them were having oral sex with their boyfriends so they could still be virgins when they graduated from high school.

Many people who are turned off by casual sex but not yet ready to marry have resorted to cohabitation, which is a more stable and committed relationship than dating but less likely to last than marriage. Even as divorce and unwed pregnancy slowed, cohabitation rates have continued to increase in the new century. For many, living together has become a normal stage in courtship—the majority of marriages now begin as cohabitation—but for others, living together has become an alternative to marriage.

British demographer Kathleen Kiernan suggests that in Europe and North America, a four-stage process has made cohabitation almost equal in status to marriage. In the first stage, most people marry without having lived together first. Only a small bohemian minority and some of the very poor live together outside marriage. In the second stage, more people from more walks of life live together for a time but usually move on to marriage and almost invariably marry if they become parents.[31]

The third stage is achieved when cohabitation becomes a socially acceptable alternative to marriage. A woman is comfortable taking her unmarried partner to a party at work or a family gathering. A man can tell his boss about his live-in lover. In this stage, says Kiernan, couples living together no longer feel compelled to marry if the woman becomes pregnant, even if they decide to have the child. Far from hiding their unmarried state, as couples used to do, they proudly send out birth announcements with both parents' names. However, most couples who have a child and stay together eventually do marry at some point, especially if they plan to have a second child.

In the fourth stage, however, cohabitation and marriage become virtually indistinguishable legally and socially. Couples may have several children without ever marrying. The number of married couples and cohabiting couples is about the same, and children living with both parents are almost equally distributed between the two categories.

The United States, it appears, was transitioning from stage two to stage three at the end of the twentieth century. Sweden, however, had by then reached stage four. In fact, more children are now born each year to cohabiting couples in Sweden than to married ones, and the tendency for couples to marry after the second birth has faded. Some observers believe that America is headed in this direction. Personally, I am skeptical. Sweden's family patterns have very distinctive cultural roots and are supported by an equally distinctive political and economic system. People in the United States still place much more importance on getting married than Swedes do, and demographers calculate that 90 percent of Americans will eventually marry.

However, there is no question that marriage had lost its privileged legal and cultural position in the United States by the end of the twentieth century. And anyone dreaming of a return to traditional marriage at the beginning of the twenty-first century was in for a shock.

When President Nixon remarked in 1970 that the issue of gay marriage would have to wait until 2000, he picked that year to symbolize the inconceivable future. In fact, though, his prediction turned out to be remarkably accurate. In July 2000, Vermont made same-sex civil unions legally equivalent to marriage. In 2003, Canada legalized gay and lesbian marriage in two of its most populous provinces. On November 18, 2003, the Massachusetts Supreme Court ruled that its state constitution guaranteed equal marriage rights for same-sex couples.

Then things really heated up. President Bush declared in his January 20, 2004, State of the Union address that the nation must "defend the sanctity of marriage." The newly elected mayor of San Francisco, Gavin Newsome, indignant at the thunderous applause that followed the president's announcement, directed city hall to start issuing marriage licenses to gay and lesbian couples on February 12. The first two people he invited to get their licenses were Del Martin and Phyllis Lyon, lesbian activists who had been a committed couple for fifty-one years. "Why should my wife and I, who have been married for only two years, be entitled to more rights than they are after half a century?" Newsome asked assembled reporters.[32]

Newsome's directive provoked a storm of activity on both sides of the issue. More than thirty-two hundred gay and lesbian couples, many from out of state, flocked to San Francisco to get married. President Bush called for an amendment to the U.S. Constitution prohibiting same-sex marriage. This spurred defiant local officials in New Mexico, New York, and Oregon to issue same-sex wedding licenses. Commissioners in one Oregon county decided they didn't feel comfortable defying their state's ban on same-sex marriage but didn't feel ethical not doing so. Their solution was to stop issuing wedding licenses to anyone, same or opposite sex!

Commentators who had been predicting a return to traditional marriage immediately changed their tune. Phyllis Schlafly claimed that "the gays have moved in to deliver the knockout punch" to marriage. The fundamentalist Protestant minister James Dobson, founder of Focus on the Family, put it even more starkly. "The institution of marriage is on the ropes," he wrote in September 2003, following the U.S. Supreme Court's rejection of antisodomy laws and Canada's acceptance of same-sex marriage. "Barring a miracle," Dobson warned in his April 2004 newsletter, "the family as it has been known for more than five millennia will crumble, presaging the fall of Western civilization itself."[33]

Opposition to same-sex marriage comes from a number of directions. For some Americans, denying gays and lesbians the right to marry is a matter of deep religious conviction. Others believe that legalizing gay and lesbian marriage would send the message to heterosexuals that it's okay to raise a child without both a mother and a father in the home. Still others see gay marriage as the final nail in the coffin of traditional marriage and family life. Stanley Kurtz, writing in the August 4–11, 2003, *Weekly Standard,* an influential conservative magazine, predicted that gay marriage will "take us down a slippery slope to legalized polygamy and 'polyamory' [group marriage]. Marriage will be transformed into a variety of relationship contracts, linking two, three, or more individuals . . . in every conceivable combination of male and female."[34]

The religious debate over same-sex marriage rests on personal faith and can't be settled by comparing the social science evidence, pro and con. But from a historical perspective, the claim that we stand on the brink of legalizing polygamy is a bit farfetched. In fact, the historical trend has been running in the opposite direction. Most countries where polygamy is still legal are moving to repeal those laws. Young women in cultures that practice polygamy are defying their parents and community leaders in order to make their own choices. It is also hard to imagine any government agreeing to pay pensions to three or four survivors instead of one or any employer paying medical insurance for three spouses.

Some of the agitation on the issue of same-sex marriage strikes me as a case of trying to lock the barn door after the horses have already gone. The demand for gay and lesbian marriage was an inevitable result of the previous revolution in heterosexual marriage. It was heterosexuals who had already created many alternative structures for organizing sexual relationships or raising children and broken down the primacy of two-parent families based on a strict division of labor between men and women.

In the short run, the United States is unlikely to join Belgium, the Netherlands, and Canada in legalizing same-sex marriage. By the end of 2004, forty-three states had passed statutes limiting marriage to a man and a woman, and eleven had enshrined this defiintion in their constitutions. The United States is one of the most sexually conservative countries in the industrial world. In 2002, 42 percent of Americans told pollsters that homosexuality was morally wrong. Only 16 percent of Italians, 13 percent of the French, and 5 percent of Spaniards felt that way.[35]

Still, even in America attitudes toward homosexuality have changed immensely over the past fifteen years. Since the end of the 1990s support for same-sex marriage has bobbed back and forth between a low of 31 percent and a high of 40 percent. This is a minority of the population, to be sure, but half of the eighteen- and nineteen-year-olds polled by *USA Today* in March 2004 supported legalization of gay marriage, compared with just 19 percent of respondents over sixty-five. And ironically, as views have polarized over the question of whether gays and lesbians should be able to use the word *marriage* to describe their relationships, the once-radical demand for same-sex civil unions has become a compromise position. "Let them have the same rights as me and my wife," one businessman told me. "Just don't call it marriage."[36]

Constitutional amendments or not, gay and lesbian families are not going back into the closet. One-third of female same-sex households and more than one-fifth of male same-sex households include biological children under eighteen. Eight U.S. states and the District of Columbia currently allow a child to have two legal mothers or two legal fathers. And 40 percent of the nation's adoption agencies report that they have placed children with gay or lesbian parents. This is a reality that won't go away. In 2002 the American Academy of Pediatrics called for legalizing partner adoptions in families where the biological parent of a child lives with a same-sex partner. In 2004 the American Psychological Association endorsed same-sex marriage.[37]

Only a small minority of gays and lesbians are interested in marrying at this point. But those who do seek that right are not the main threats to the stable male breadwinner family system or the primacy of marriage in social and personal life. Divorce, single parenthood, and cohabitation among heterosexuals have already reshaped the role of marriage in society and its meaning in people's lives. Marriage has also been fundamentally transformed by the behavior of married people who will never divorce and by single people who would never consider having children out of wedlock.

The reproductive revolution has shaken up all the relationships once taken for granted between sex, marriage, conception, childbirth, and parenting. People who could not become parents before can now do so in such bewildering combinations that a child can potentially have five different parents: a sperm donor, an egg donor, a birth mother, and the social father and mother who raise the child. On the other hand, some married couples use new reproductive technologies to avoid having children altogether. Seen in this light, a childless marriage is just as much a challenge to the tradition that children are the central purpose and glue of a wedded relationship as is a gay union.

The many young people who delay marrying until their late twenties or early thirties also contribute to the diminishing role of marriage in organizing social and personal life. Today, in contrast with medieval Europe and colonial America, most young people go through an extended period when they do not live with and are not under the control of their parents or any other married people. However, as singles they can exercise most of the political and economic privileges of adulthood when they turn eighteen and twenty-one.

This large pool of single youth, along with the extension of the life span, has contributed to a stunning explosion of solitary living in Western societies. More than one-quarter of all U.S. households now contain only one person. At various times and in various places in history, rates of nonmarital sex, divorce, cohabitation, or out-of-wedlock childbearing have been higher than they are today.[38] But never before have so many people lived alone. And never before have unmarried people, living alone or in couples, had the same rights as married adults. The spread of solitary living and cohabitation reduces the social weight of marriage in the economy and polity, creating tastes, habits, expectations, and voting blocs that are not tied to the role of wife or husband.

In the 1950s married couples represented 80 percent all households in the United States. By the beginning of the twenty-first century they were less than 51 percent, and married couples with children were just 25 percent of all households. For the first time ever, there were more single-person households than those with a married couple and children. Married persons were still a majority of the workforce and of the home buyers in 2001, but unmarried individuals were gaining fast, accounting for 42 percent of the workforce and 40 percent of home buyers.[39]

Single men and women today also exercise much more personal discretion about whether and when to get married. In the 1950s the average age of marriage was also the age at which most people actually married. Today the average age of marriage is the product of some very early marriages, some very late ones, and lots of variations in between. European demographer Anton Kuijsten comments that rather than ordering from "the standard life course menu, as people used to do," an individual now "composes his or her history *à la carte.*" And marriage, "the obligatory entrée" during the 1950s, "has become the optional dessert."[40]

Marriage was once part of the credentialing process that people had to go through to gain adult responsibility and respectability. It was like completing high school today. Few young people go to high school because they expect it to be a deeply fulfilling experience. They go because they need that piece of paper to get entry-level jobs or gain admittance to the more selective and prestigious credentials provided by college.

Marriage used to be like that. It was the gateway to adulthood and respectability and the best way for people to maximize their resources and pool labor. This is no longer the case. Marriage still allows two people to merge resources, divide tasks, and accumulate more capital than they could as singles.

But it is not the only way they can invest in their future. In fact, it's a riskier investment than it was in the past. The potential gains of getting married need to be weighed against the possibilities offered by staying single to pursue higher education or follow a better job. And the greater likelihood of eventual divorce reinforces the appeal of leaving your options open while investing in your own personal skills and experience.

Moving lockstep through a series of predictable transitions is no longer a route to personal security. Each man and woman must put together a highly individualized sequence of transitions in and out of school, work, and marriage in order to take advantage of shifting opportunities and respond to unexpected setbacks—a "do-it-yourself biography."[41]

All these changes have profoundly and irreversibly transformed modern marriage. This revolution is not confined to the United States. Despite cultural variations, almost all industrial countries have experienced similar changes. Divorce rates tripled in France and Holland and quadrupled in Britain between 1970 and 1990. As in the United States, divorce rates began to fall in Western Europe in the 1990s, but rates of marriage fell even faster. By the late 1990s 40 percent of all births in France and Britain were to unmarried women. In Iceland, in 1999, more than 60 percent of all births were to unwed parents.[42]

The trend toward solitary living is likewise widespread. In 1950 just 10 percent of all households in Europe contained only one person. Five decades later one-person households made up a third of all British households and 40 percent of Swedish households. Even in Greece, which had the lowest percentage of one-person households in Europe at the end of the twentieth century, such households represented almost 20 percent of the total, twice the 1950 average for Europe as a whole.[43]

Changes in marital norms are spreading even to countries that were holdouts in the 1980s and early 1990s. In Spain, Italy, and Japan, the number of two-earner marriages has soared since the mid-1990s. Although divorce is still stigmatized, there has also been a huge fall in the rate of marriage, suggesting we are looking at a massive historical tide that, when blocked in one direction, simply seeks another place to flow. More than half of Spanish women aged twenty-five to twenty-nine are single. The rate of marriage in Italy is much lower than in the United States. Japan shares with Scandinavia the distinction of having the highest percentage of unmarried women between age twenty and forty of anywhere in the world.[44]

Recognition of same-sex unions is another global trend. Between 2000 and 2004 same-sex marriage was legalized in Belgium, the Netherlands, and Canada. Countries as diverse as Spain, Iceland, Germany, Hungary, South

Africa, Portugal, Taiwan, and Argentina gave same-sex couples many of the same legal rights as married heterosexuals.[45]

Finally, the role of women has been transformed in the past thirty years. Between 1970 and 1997 women's representation in the total labor force increased in every sector of the globe.[46] About the only place where it was rolled back during the 1990s was in Afghanistan, where the Taliban regime forced women out of the schools and jobs they had entered under the previous Soviet-backed governments.

The change in women's work patterns has been both a cause and an effect of the revolution in fertility, not only in the industrialized countries but in the developing world as well. In the late 1960s a woman in the poorer countries of the world typically had six children. Today the average is fewer than three. In fact, demographers now project that the world's population will begin to decline before 2050.[47]

The "Disestablishment" of Marriage

Despite all these changes, marriage is not doomed. In most countries, heterosexual marriage still has a privileged legal status. In the United States, for example, it confers more than a thousand legal and tax benefits unavailable to single people. And for most Americans, marriage is the highest expression of commitment they can imagine. Americans are more likely than Europeans or Japanese to tell pollsters they value marriage highly, and they still marry at higher rates than most other industrial countries.

Nor have people lost respect for the marriage vows. Even as divorce and nonmarriage have increased, our standards for what constitutes a "good" marriage have risen steadily. The percentage of people who believe it is okay to cheat, lie, or keep secrets in a marriage has fallen over the past forty years. Many couples work hard to enrich their relationship and deepen their intimacy, with a dedication that would astonish most couples of the past. Marriage as a relationship between two individuals is taken more seriously and comes with higher emotional expectations than ever before.[48]

But marriage as an institution exerts less power over people's lives than it once did. In the 1930s Mae West quipped: "Marriage is a great institution. But I ain't ready for an institution." My grandmother was profoundly shocked by that comment. Most people today would not be. Now people want to live in a relationship, not an institution.

And unlike my grandmother's generation, they no longer *have* to live in an institution. In most Western countries there has been a blurring of the distinctions between the legal responsibilities and rights of married and unmarried individuals. Domestic partnership laws have been adopted by governments or employers in most Western countries, and in some non-Western ones as well. These grant unmarried couples the same insurance benefits, inheritances, and other legal privileges as married partners.

Nearly half the five hundred largest companies in America now extend benefits to unmarried partners who live together. My husband works for an airline that allows unmarried employees to designate one individual as their domestic travel partner, with the same rights to free travel as a spouse. That person can be a boyfriend, girlfriend, nephew, or neighbor. Some of the most tradition-bound golf clubs now offer family memberships to unmarried men and women.

In France and Canada, an individual can establish a legally recognized care-giving or resource-pooling relationship with any other person and receive many legal and financial benefits that used to be reserved for married couples. Two sexual partners can take advantage of this arrangement. So can two sisters, two army buddies, or a celibate priest and his housekeeper. The United States has resisted extending marriage's legal benefits this far. But it has joined the international trend giving children the right to support and recognition from both parents, whether or not they were ever married. Marriage has lost its legal monopoly over the rules organizing people's personal rights and obligations.

Few of these changes in the rights and privileges of marriage were imposed by "activist judges." In some cases, extending marriagelike rights was a legislative response to pressure from unmarried heterosexual partners or gays and lesbians. In other cases, businesses had to respond to the 42 percent of their employees who were unmarried. The courts generally stepped in only when faced with urgent new problems posed by the already existing changes in living habits—for example, when an unmarried man walked away from a long-term relationship, refusing to help support his children or the woman who sacrificed her career to do the child rearing and housekeeping in the partnership.

In response to such problems, courts in the United States and some Western European countries began to rule that cohabiting heterosexual partners who built up substantial assets over the years must divide them fairly, even if all the assets were in one person's name. And many attorneys and judges have come to support legal recognition for same-sex unions because they are already having to deal with the division of assets and similar issues in de facto gay and lesbian *divorces.*

The breakdown of the wall separating marriage from nonmarriage has been described by some legal historians and sociologists as the deinstitutionalization or delegalization of marriage or even, with a French twist, as *demariage*. I like historian Nancy Cott's observation that it is akin to what happened in Europe and America when legislators disestablished their state religion.[49]

With disestablishment, the state no longer conferred a whole set of special rights and privileges on one particular denomination while denying those rights to others. When this happened, religion itself did not disappear. But many different churches and new religious groups proliferated. Similarly, once the state stopped insisting that everyone needed a government-sanctioned marriage license to enjoy the privileges and duties of parenthood or other long-term commitments, other forms of intimate relationships and child-rearing arrangements came out from underground. And just as people's motives for joining a church changed when there was no longer one official religion, so people began deciding whether or not to marry on a new basis.

We may personally like or dislike all these changes. But there is a certain inevitability about most of them. For better or worse, marriage has been displaced from its pivotal position in personal and social life. No matter how much society values marriage, it cannot afford to ignore the fact that many children are being raised and many obligations are being incurred in alternative settings. A perfect storm has reshaped the landscape of married life, and few things about marriage will ever be the same.

Chapter 17

———◆———

Uncharted Territory:
How the Transformation of Marriage
Is Changing Our Lives

In the 1950s the rules for "making marriage work" were clear-cut. Psychologist Clifford Adams wrote that "the bride who wants to do her full job will plan from the start to create the kind of home her husband wants, and to do it with no more assistance from him than he willingly offers." Adams, whose "Making Marriage Work" columns appeared in the *Ladies' Home Journal,* believed with most marital counselors of the day that the husband's job came first, "not only because of its importance but also because it occupies most of his waking hours, leaving only a narrow margin for other duties and pleasures." Therefore, he warned wives, don't treat your husband "as a kitchen helper, errand boy or handy man." And if hubby "offers to dry the dishes, thank him for the favor, rather than regard it as your right."[1]

The rules for catching and keeping a mate were equally simple—and all directed at women. Advice books told teenage girls to keep a list of a boy's likes and dislikes in food, movies, and recreation. As a pop song put it in the early 1960s, "wear your hair just for him; do the things he likes to do." Wives were urged to get up early enough to do their hair and makeup before serving breakfast. "Indulge his whims when possible, even when they strike you as foolish," said Adams.

In one of his columns in the *Journal,* Adams recounted how one wife was able to save her marriage. "She encouraged him to try a new card game, then played poorly herself so his score would look good." She also "pretended ineptitude" at such household tasks as balancing the checkbook. "Occasionally she even invented troubles for him to cope with (replacing a good fuse with a dud, fraying a lamp cord to produce a short) so he would feel needed."[2]

Not many women today have the time, energy, or inclination to engage in such elaborate manipulation of their boyfriends or husbands. Nor do most men find female helplessness charming. As the roles of men and women become more equal, people have grown impatient with such games.

But couples today do have to work to keep their marriages healthy and mutually fulfilling. The fact that individuals can now lead productive lives outside marriage means that partners need to be more "intentional" than in the past about finding reasons and rituals to help them stay together.[3] A marriage that survives and thrives in today's climate of choice is likely to be far more satisfying, fair, and effective for the partners and their children than in the past. However, couples have to think carefully about what it takes to build, deepen, and sustain commitments that are now almost completely voluntary. Modern marriages cannot just glide down the well-worn paths of the past.

Figuring out what makes for a good partner and sustains a marriage is particularly hard today because the revolution in family life that began in the 1970s forces us to rethink nearly everything we used to think we knew about how marriage works—or doesn't work. In chapter 16 I pointed out that pressures flowing from many different directions converged in the 1970s, 1980s, and 1990s to create a perfect storm in marriage and family life. But the havoc wreaked by storms is usually temporary. Even uprooted trees eventually grow back. Perhaps an earthquake better describes the stunning transformation of marriage we have to deal with in the new millennium.

Over a period of two centuries, subtle shifts in economics, politics, and reproductive patterns gradually detached the married couple from the bedrock of institutions, laws, and customs that had encased them in rigid roles. Beneath the seeming continuities of marriage and family life, new fault lines opened up. In the late 1960s these changes began triggering a series of tremors that toppled familiar landmarks of family life and permanently altered the social landscape on which we build our lives. We are still feeling the aftershocks today.

Like it or not, today we are all pioneers, picking our way through uncharted and unstable territory. The old rules are no longer reliable guides to work out modern gender roles and build a secure foundation for marriage. Wherever it is that people want to end up in their family relations today, even if they are totally committed to creating a so-called traditional marriage, they have to get there by a different route from the past.

There are many people who claim they can provide you with a road map. But in fact, on virtually every issue concerning marriage today, most personal advice gurus and policy makers lag behind the real changes transforming marriage. My local bookstore has shelf after shelf of marital advice books. The titles range from *The Surrendered Wife* to *The Fifty-Fifty Marriage* to *Remaining Single and Loving It*. In 1995 *The Rules: Time-Tested Secrets for Capturing the Heart of Mr. Right* became an international bestseller. So did its 2002 follow-up, *The Rules for Marriage: Time-Tested Secrets for Making Your Marriage Work*—despite the fact that one of the two authors filed for divorce on the eve of its publication.

Unlike scholarly journals, mass-market advice books are rarely reviewed by experts in the field. Instead of getting tested research findings, most of the time you get what some author claims worked for him or her, or what someone thinks *might* work for you, or what some publisher's marketing department hopes *you* will think might work for you, all mixed in with "time-tested rules" that might have worked in the past but no longer hold true.[4]

I am not a psychologist, and I won't play one in this book. But for the last several years, I have served first as cochair and now as director of research and public education for the Council on Contemporary Families, a group of respected family scholars and practitioners from various fields who compare their research results and clinical experience. So I've had the privilege of seeing the cutting-edge work that my colleagues in sociology and psychology are doing on contemporary family dynamics.

When I look at their research through the lens of my historical studies, I am struck by how many of the things researchers used to be able to say about marriages are no longer true. For example, it *truly* used to be good advice for a woman to "play dumb" to catch a man. Not anymore. Women used to be attracted to older, powerful men who earned more money than they did. That is no longer the case. In the past, marriages in which both spouses worked were less stable than male breadwinner marriages. That's changing too. Yet many people still plan their personal lives and policy makers still draw up social policies on the basis of these and other outmoded assumptions.

Take the question that torments many single women who have postponed marriage to pursue higher education or careers: "Will all the good men already be taken by the time I'm ready to marry?" In 1986 a *Newsweek* cover story titled "Too Late for Prince Charming" claimed that a woman's marriage prospects plummeted after age thirty, so that a single woman of forty had a better chance of being killed by a terrorist than of finding a husband. In a 2002 book, economist Sylvia Ann Hewlett wrote that "nowadays the rule of thumb seems to be that the more successful a woman, the less likely it is that she will find a husband or bear a child." Hardly a month goes by that I don't receive a call from a reporter wanting my views about the "crisis" facing educated career women in their thirties who haven't found husbands and for whom time is running out.[5]

But the *Newsweek* claim was wrong even back in 1986. And by 2002 Hewlett's "nowadays" was already three decades out-of-date. More women than ever before are marrying for the first time at age thirty, forty, fifty, and even sixty. Feminist icon Gloria Steinem married for the first time at the age of sixty-six. It is simply not true that high-achieving women are especially at risk for a lonely old age.[6]

So why do people assume that highly educated women or women with professional careers are less likely than other women to find a man? Because it used to be true, and there was a very elegant theory to explain it. For years many family researchers subscribed to economist Gary Becker's idea that marriage decisions were made on the basis of the advantages of specialization and exchange. Becker noted that men had greater earning power and women greater expertise in homemaking and child rearing. Therefore, he argued, a male breadwinner/female homemaker marriage produced an "efficient" team. According to Becker, a man maximized his earning power by focusing his energies on paid work, while a woman maximized her well-being by handling all the domestic matters that otherwise would distract her husband from earning the biggest possible family income.[7]

This updated version of the male hunter theory of marriage postulates that men want to marry partners who will take over home front activities that divert attention away from making money. So they look for women who are good homemakers. Women, the theory goes, search for mates who are good providers. But what if a woman has good earning possibilities of her own? A related theory, called the independence effect, predicts that she will have less incentive to marry, and men will also find her a less attractive mate. Moreover, if such a woman does marry, she will be more likely to divorce than other women.

For centuries, the independence effect did have considerable predictive power in Western Europe and North America. Until the 1950s highly educated women *were* less likely to marry than less educated women.[8]

But for women born since 1960, things are different. College graduates and women with higher earnings are now *more* likely to marry than women with less education and lower wages, although they generally marry at an older age. The legal profession is one big exception to this generalization. Female attorneys are less likely to ever marry, to have children, or to remarry after divorce than women in other professions. But an even higher proportion of *male* attorneys are childless, suggesting there might be something about this career that is unfriendly to everyone's family life, not just women's. For career women in other fields the independence effect has evaporated.[9]

Despite these general trends, many women tell me they feel "desperate" to find a man. Running into potential partners gets harder once you're out of school and no longer spend most of your waking hours in a concentrated pool of singles in your own age-group. Also, when women work in predominantly female work settings, as many still do, they have few opportunities to meet potential partners at work.

So it's understandable that many women are anxious about the prospect of finding a good husband. But few modern women are actually *desperate* to marry. Historically, desperate is agreeing to marry a much older man whom you find physically repulsive. Desperate is closing your eyes to prostitutes and mistresses and praying you don't get a venereal disease. Desperate is having child after child because your husband won't let you use birth control or covering the bruises you got last night when you hurry to the market to shop for his evening meal. Women today may be anxious about finding a mate, but most could not even imagine being that desperate.

Some observers worry that as women get better educated, men are the ones who will have a harder time finding mates. Traditionally women looked for men who were older and more successful than they. So some think that men may soon face a marriage crisis, as educated women turn up their noses at suitors who are less successful than they, or even only equally successful.

Women in the past did tend to prefer older men with greater wealth or earning power. But this preference was based on social and economic necessity, not on genetic programming. And this "rule" of marriage formation is also changing. Recently two researchers compared women's views on the ideal mate in a number of societies with differing levels of equality between men and women. In societies where women were approaching equality with men in economic and political affairs, females were much less likely to seek older, high-earning men as husbands than were women in societies that offered females fewer options for independence.[10]

In the United States the difference in the ages of men and women at first marriage has been narrowing for the past eighty years and has now reached a historic low. In fact, by the late 1990s more than one-third of women aged thirty-five to forty-four were living with younger men. High male earnings have also become less important to women. A 2001 poll in the United States found that 80 percent of women in their twenties believed that having a husband who can talk about his feelings was more important than having one who makes a good living.[11]

If women today are less likely to choose husbands on the basis of "success appeal," men are shedding older ideas about what makes for sex appeal. Men still rate youth and good looks higher than women do when looking for mates, but those criteria no longer outweigh others. Modern men tend to want mates who are on a similar level in terms of education or earnings potential. "I don't want someone I have to help with her homework," a male friend of mine said when a mutual acquaintance offered to fix him up with a woman fifteen years his junior. Being a smart, achieving woman used to be perceived as a liability in the marriage market, says sociologist Pepper Schwartz, but is now a big asset. As they grow up, young men today are used to seeing women in many different roles. "She's your doctor, your teacher, your professor. These models can be quite erotic."[12]

But what about the chance of high-achieving women having children? The conventional wisdom is humorously summed up in the poster depicting a sophisticated career woman slapping her forehead and exclaiming "Oh, no, I forgot to have kids!" Stories about women who wait too long and then discover they cannot have children are a staple in the media. Some people even attribute America's high out-of-wedlock childbearing to career women who suddenly realize they have priced themselves out of the marriage market but decide to have children anyway.

Here again conventional wisdom lags behind the changes in reality. High-achieving women are actually much less likely to have children out of wedlock than any other group of women. And once they marry, they are as likely as all other married working women to have children, although they tend to have their kids at an older age.[13]

At this point—and this trend is more pronounced in the United States than in most other industrial countries—low-income women are more likely to have children out of wedlock than other groups and less likely ever to marry. This leads some people to argue that America's high poverty levels, especially among African Americans, are due to falling marriage rates and that encouraging low-income individuals to marry would be an effective anti-poverty program.

In 1996 the federal government officially threw its weight behind the marriage promotion movement, adopting a welfare reform bill that made getting poor people married one of its central goals. Some states have implemented their own programs to boost marriage rates. Oklahoma paid a married couple to go around the state organizing "marriage rallies." The West Virginia welfare department offered single mothers an extra $100 a month if they got married. By 2003 nearly every state was funding programs to promote marriage, and President George W. Bush had promised to earmark $1.5 billion in federal funds to promote marriage.[14]

Here again, ignorance of actual trends in marriage has produced many misconceptions. Marriage promoters began with the assumption that low-income people were not marrying because they did not value marriage. But the relationship between people's attitudes toward marriage and their actual behavior turned out to be much more complicated. In this, as in many other aspects of family life, the connection between what people believe in the abstract and what they do in real life is often tenuous at best.

In the United States, for example, highly educated people are much more likely than any other group to think that remaining single or having a child out of wedlock is an acceptable choice. Yet they are also more likely to marry than their less educated counterparts and are much less likely to have children out of wedlock.

By contrast, men and women with lower incomes and less education, whatever their racial background, are much more likely to view marriage as the preferred state, but they are also less likely to get married. African Americans are more disapproving of cohabitation than white Americans but are nonetheless more likely to cohabit. Born-again Christians are as likely to divorce as Christians who are not born again, and the divorce rate of both is only 2 percentage points below the divorce rate of atheists and agnostics. Similarly, in America's Bible Belt, the low-income areas of the South, out-of-wedlock births and divorce rates are higher than anywhere else in the country, even though polls indicate that the region has the highest disapproval of "nontraditional" family behaviors.[15]

So why are low-income, less educated Americans less likely to marry? Some researchers argue that gender mistrust leads to lower marriage rates. Such mistrust is in fact widespread in low-income communities and, for a complex mix of reasons, is especially evident in low-income African American communities.[16] But in the past, under different historical conditions, gender mistrust actually *encouraged* marriage formation. In the 1950s a woman's distrust of men stopped her from having sex with her boyfriend or living with him before marriage because everyone knew that "no man is going to buy the cow if he can get the milk for free." Sure enough, the girls who "held out" were most likely to get their boyfriends to propose.

But there is a critical difference between then and now. To push this insulting analogy a little further, cows need someone to feed them every day, and back then even a low-income husband could provide more food for his wife than she could get on her own. A bad marriage was usually a better option for a woman, especially if she had a child, than no marriage at all.

This isn't true anymore, especially for low-income women. Cinderella may have been a scrub girl rescued by a prince, but in real life a low-income woman is likely to find her relationships in the pool of men in her own neighborhood, where secure blue-collar jobs have disappeared and been replaced by jobs that pay wages too low to support families. A woman who marries a man with few job prospects may end up having to support him as well as their children. Even if the marriage does improve her economic well-being, its stability may be undermined by chronic economic and neighborhood stress. Low-income women who marry and divorce later have higher poverty rates than women who never marry at all, and their children may suffer more emotionally as well.[17] In these circumstances, getting married can be risky.

Impoverished women understand these risks better than many of the marriage promoters trying to convince them of the benefits of marriage. When sociologist Kathy Edin conducted in-depth interviews with nearly three hundred low-income mothers, they consistently told her they couldn't afford to marry a man with a less than stable job history, or poor job skills. Some women said that they had truly loved a partner but had forced themselves to break off the relationship when it looked as if the man couldn't pull his own economic weight.[18]

Sociologists Andrew Cherlin and Linda Burton are studying low-income families in three American cities. They report that most women they interview hold marriage in high regard. But these women see marriage as something you have to work your way up to. A woman who waited to marry her partner until quite a while after having a child with him explained that her most vivid memory of growing up was that the gas and electricity kept getting turned off. "When I got pregnant, we agreed we would marry someday in the future because we loved each other and wanted to raise our child together. But we would not get married until we could afford to get a house and pay all the utility bills on time." Another explained that she would marry her partner only when he realized that the first priority after getting paid should be taking care of the household bills, "not going out and getting new clothes or doing this and that."[19]

In earlier times this woman would probably have married the father of her child anyway, hoping that both she and the social pressures of the day would help him grow up. And right up through the 1960s many wives accepted that marriage was an unequal relationship in which a husband would first treat himself to a few beers and some bets on the horses before turning the rest of his pay over to his wife to feed and clothe the family.

But many women today see no point in marrying unless their prospective husband has both the economic prospects and the emotional dependability to make pooling their resources worthwhile. "I don't need a husband to help me scrape by," a welfare recipient told me. "I can scrape by on my own. Find me a man who's got a steady job and a mortgage and no jail time in his past, and I'll marry him pretty damn quick." Another chimed in: "I got two kids, and the last thing I need is a man who's gonna be a drain on my wallet *and* my heart."

Sociologist Frank Furstenberg comments that "it's as if marriage has become a luxury consumer item, available only to those with the means to bring it off. Living together or single-parenthood has become the budget way to start a family."[20] At the very least, marriage is now a discretionary item that must be weighed against other options for self-protection or economic mobility.

This is true for women and men in higher income brackets as well. Today people from all walks of life often invest in their own individual skills and resources before hooking up with a partner. Most young adults tell pollsters they want "to be economically set" before they get married. In the 1950s and 1960s young men and women thought that marriage was the way people settled down and made relationships work. Today most young people see marriage as something you do only when you're already sure your partner has settled down and the relationship is working. You enter marriage, they say, only after you have maneuvered past the risks and begun to rake in the rewards of life.[21]

Some marriage advocates, recognizing these realities, have shifted their attention from marriage promotion to marriage preparation, offering classes to low-income individuals who want to get married, so they can start on a sounder footing. This approach avoids pressuring people into marriage and could potentially offer low-income couples useful counseling. But it is not a panacea. Psychologist Thomas Bradbury, director of the UCLA Marriage and Family Development Project, notes that no marriage education or relationship skills program can permanently immunize couples against the effects of chronic economic and neighborhood stress. Among women without high school degrees, about 60 percent of marriages end in divorce, compared with one-third of the marriages of female college graduates. Poverty, unemployment, and having children by a previous relationship (as almost 40 percent of low-income partners do) all raise the risk of marital failure.[22]

The corrosive effects of unemployment and poverty in a land of abundance help explain why even though low-income unmarried parents say they want to wed, most of them break up before they actually do. Sociologists Kristin Seefeldt and Pamela Smock found that an unmarried couple in this income bracket who have a child together have only a 9 percent chance of marrying within a year of the child's birth. If any one of four aspects of the couple's life improves—their supportive attitude toward each other; their favorable attitude toward marriage; their feelings of trust; the amount of the man's wages—the chance they will marry increases by just over three percentage points. If all four improve, the probability they will marry goes up by more than ten points, to about 20 percent, meaning that even under optimal circumstances only one in five such couples will marry within a year.[23]

That kind of jump in marriage rates for low-income parents might well be worth striving for. But historical trends suggest that since marriage is no longer the primary way that all individuals organize their sex lives and child rearing, we ought not to put all our eggs into the basket of promoting marriage. We should be offering resources to promote healthy relationships, whether married or unmarried, and to improve people's parenting, whatever their marital status. At a conference on marriage education a young African American woman I met told me, "I don't think classes would have saved our marriage. But classes might have helped us handle the divorce and the coparenting of our kids better."[24]

Divorce is another issue on which the pronouncements of policy makers and personal advice gurus generally lag behind the changing dynamics of marriage. Much has been written about how to protect women from being left by their husbands. But one of the ways that the song of courtship is out of sync with the dance of marriage is that although women still tend to be more eager than men to enter marriage, they are also more likely to become discontented once married. A survey conducted in the United States during the mid-1990s found that a majority of divorced wives said they were the ones who wanted out of the marriage. Fewer than one-quarter said their husbands had unilaterally wanted to get out of the marriage. These women weren't putting up brave faces. Divorced men reported the same pattern. A recent study of divorces that occur after age forty found that two-thirds were initiated by wives.[25]

Women's greater dissatisfaction with marriage is not in fact new. But there has been an important shift in the characteristics of women who actually seek divorces. Historically, women with higher levels of education and earnings, the ones better able to support themselves, were much more likely than other women to leave a marriage. But today women at lower socioeconomic levels can better support themselves than in the past and are therefore more willing to divorce, especially if they are married to men who subscribe to "traditional" gender roles. At the same time, higher-income women have more leverage in marriage than in the past and are more likely to have husbands who at least in principle support gender equality. They can often persuade their husbands to change behaviors that make them unhappy rather than just call it quits.

Here, then, is yet another "rule" that is changing. During the 1980s and 1990s the marriages of college-educated women became more stable compared with the 1970s, while the marriages of women with less education became less stable. By the mid-1990s, among Americans younger than forty-five, men and women who had bachelor's degrees or higher had considerably lower divorce rates than those in any other educational category.[26]

Another area where many marriage pundits have been unable to stay current is in the relationship between women's work and the likelihood of divorce. Studies in the 1960s, 1970s, and 1980s showed that as wives worked more hours and earned more income, marital quality declined and the risk of divorce rose. But those studies, says sociologist Stacy Rogers, often confused cause and effect. Many women increased their work hours precisely because marital tensions were high, wanting to get out of the house or to protect themselves in case the marriage ended in divorce. If such women did eventually divorce, the breakups were usually a response to the same marital problems that first motivated them to get a job and build up an emotional and economic safety net outside marriage.[27]

However, a woman who finds increased satisfaction at work may sometimes also find her marriage improves. She may start by working more hours outside the home to escape marital discord and then discover that her work adds enough satisfaction to her life to revive her interest in the marriage rather than simply enable her to leave it. I spoke to a woman last year who told me that her husband thought there was more tension in their marriage now that she was working. But her take on it was that her greater economic independence made her more willing to address tensions that had been there all along. "He doesn't like that he has to give in more often now," she said, "but I would have left him if I hadn't gone out and gotten that job."

Today working wives report fewer feelings of distress than wives who stay at home, and they are more likely to believe that their marriages are egalitarian. And unlike the past, marital equality is now associated with greater marital satisfaction for men as well as women.[28]

This isn't true for every marriage, of course. As old rules and generalizations change, they don't change in the same way for everyone. A woman who wants to work and has a husband who agrees can have a much happier marriage than she could have had in the past. But a woman who doesn't want to work but has to may not be happier. And if she wants to work but her husband does not want her to, they have to deal with a conflict that did not exist when a man could simply forbid his wife to take a job.

These kinds of differences make one-size-fits-all social policies or instruction manuals for marriage unhelpful. For example, is getting an education a plus or a minus for marital stability? Highly educated couples usually make more money and have less traditional attitudes toward gender roles. Both these attributes generally increase marital satisfaction. But educated women are more likely to have demanding jobs, which can put additional stress on marriage. More education is also associated with less agreement that lifelong marriage is a moral imperative, increasing the likelihood that highly educated couples may turn to divorce if they become dissatisfied.[29]

Similarly, in marriages where wives work there is still a higher chance of divorce than in male breadwinner marriages, if only because wives who are self-supporting can leave marriages they find unsatisfying. But when a wife works, the couple tends to share child rearing more equally, which makes wives happier and less likely to leave.

All these changes create trade-offs and tough choices. A woman has a slightly better shot at a stable marriage if she is a full-time homemaker, for example, but she still faces a much higher chance of divorce than she did fifty years ago. And when a male breadwinner marriage does break up, a homemaker is far more likely to be impoverished by the divorce and find it harder to regain her financial footing than a woman who worked prior to the divorce.[30]

Every man and woman must weigh these pros and cons according to their individual values and options. And contrary to what many marriage promotion activists believe, these dilemmas cannot be sidestepped by making divorce less accessible.

The enactment of no-fault divorce laws reduced the bargaining power of a partner who does not want to end the marriage. This has often worked against women, especially economically vulnerable full-time homemakers. But when a wife can get a divorce over her husband's objections, that *increases* a woman's bargaining power in a marriage the husband wants to maintain.[31]

The availability of unilateral divorce provides an important escape mechanism in seriously troubled marriages. Economists Betsey Stevenson and Justin Wolfers found that in states that adopted unilateral divorce, this was followed, on average, by a 20 percent reduction in the number of married women committing suicide, as well as a significant drop in domestic violence for both men and women. Criminologists William Bailey and Ruth Peterson report that higher rates of marital separation lead to lower homicide rates against women. But a woman's right to leave a marriage can also be a lifesaver for *men*. The Centers on Disease Control reports that the rate at which husbands were killed by their wives fell by approximately two-thirds between 1981 and 1998, in part because women could more easily leave their partners.[32]

Thankfully, most unhappy marriages don't lead to murder or suicide, even where divorce is hard to get. In most cases, divorce is not a lifesaver, but a traumatic process that inflicts painful, sometimes long-lasting wounds on everyone involved. It is especially stressful for children. Although 75 to 80 percent of children recover well and function within normal ranges after divorce, children from divorced families have twice the risk of developing behavioral and emotional problems as children from continuously married families.[33]

But children in high-conflict marriages are often better off if their parents divorce than if they stay together. Children also suffer when exposed to constant and chronic low-level friction in a marriage, such as parents not talking to each other, being critical or moody, exhibiting jealousy, or being domineering.

A well-functioning, continuous, and happily married two-parent family provides an optimal environment for children. But a well-functioning marriage with two cooperating parents is not always what you get. When it's not, divorce can be an escape hatch for the children as well as the adults. Sociologist Paul Amato estimates that divorce lowers the well-being of 55 to 60 percent of the children involved. But it actually *improves* the well-being of 40 to 45 percent.[34] It is not very helpful to give people hard-and-fast personal advice, far less to pass sweeping laws, on the basis of the averages obtained from such variable outcomes.

Just as the impact of divorce varies from family to family and even from sibling to sibling in the same family, the differences *within* male breadwinner marriages, two-earner marriages, cohabiting partners, divorced couples, and unwed parents are now often greater than the differences *between* those categories.

Consider the experience of living in a male breadwinner family today.

Most married couples with children have both partners in the labor force, but male breadwinner families are not about to disappear. Some couples organize their entire married lives in that pattern. Others adopt the male breadwinner form for a few years while the children are young. In 2002 about one-quarter of all children under age fifteen lived in families where the mothers did not work for pay.

Here too, however, the dynamics are shifting. And here too policy makers and pundits have not kept up with the change. In the 1950s two-earner couples were concentrated in lower-income families, scrambling to earn enough to survive. In nearly all middle-class and most working-class families, wives did not have paid jobs, at least until the children left home. Today, by contrast, stay-at-home mothers are concentrated in the poorest and richest rungs of the population. The only two segments of the population in which male bread-winner families predominate are the bottom 25 percent of the income distribution and the top 5 percent.[35]

The fact that both groups have large numbers of families in which wives do not work outside the home for pay does not in any way imply that the dynamics of family life are similar for the richest and poorest families. In high-income male breadwinner marriages, couples can reap big advantages from gender specialization. Managers and top executives with stay-at-home wives generally earn more than their counterparts with working wives. The wife's activities free her husband to focus on his job, and she can cultivate the social networks that enhance his status.[36] Wives in such marriages usually have the resources and time to develop skills that earn them respect from their communities and their husbands even though they don't bring in income.

Once on a flight back from Europe my seat mate was an executive whose wife had never worked outside the home. He was a trove of information about Italian architecture and art. "How did you ever learn so much about art?" I asked. "I'm completely ignorant," he replied. "I'm just repeating what my wife told me. She gets to learn all about art," he said, "because I take care of the money. And I get the benefit of her knowledge when we travel." The man's wife is a prominent patron of the arts who probably never feels devalued as "just a housewife."

Unlike many homemakers, this woman would probably not face deep financial stress if her marriage fell apart. When an affluent male breadwinner marriage breaks up, courts generally recognize the important contribution a nonworking wife makes in such unions and assign more financial value to a wealthy wife's homemaking and child rearing than to that of a woman married to a low-earning husband.

The story is very different for low-earning male breadwinner marriages. In many of these families, a woman stays home because she cannot *afford* to go out to work. Studying one rural county in the United States, researchers Margaret Nelson and Joan Smith found that when a husband earned a wage that was barely enough for the family to scrape by, the family usually didn't have enough money to pay for things like child care or a second car or suitable clothes for the workplace that would allow the wife to work and contribute additional income to the family. Also, the kinds of jobs available for the wife typically did not pay enough for the family to recoup those costs.[37]

Today low-income families in which only the husbands work for wages are at a much greater disadvantage now than were families who adopted this arrangement in the early twentieth century. At that time there were still many ways for wives to supplement the family livelihood outside the official labor market. Today, a wife who stays home may be able to avoid spending money, but she's rarely able to earn money by selling homemade products, sewing, or taking in boarders. At best she can put in a stint selling cosmetics or cookware to friends and neighbors. But this rarely provides long-term income.

It is also harder than in the past for a stay-at-home wife to save substantial money by self-provisioning, because it is now often cheaper to buy clothing and canned goods at cut-rate outlets than to sew and can yourself. The old equation has changed. Most families no longer save money by keeping wives at home. They lose by not having wives in the workplace, where women have more opportunities than in the past to earn decent wages.

The internal dynamics of low-income families in which wives stay home have also changed. Housewives today are rarely impressed if a husband occasionally offers to dry the dishes, and the male breadwinners in these marriages don't get the *Father Knows Best* respect from their wives and children that men with higher earnings and more secure jobs might receive. There are new tensions in these marriages because the prerogatives that used to go with being the male breadwinner in a male-dominant culture are no longer uncontested.

In most middle-class marriages, arrangements in which the husband works and the wife stays home are short-lived adjustments to the birth of a child. But changing expectations give even these short-term male breadwinner marriages a new twist. Most contemporary couples expect to share breadwinning and child-rearing roles more equally than their parents or grandparents did. When they adopt a more "traditional" division of labor after the birth of a child, this often *destabilizes* their relationship and increases their stress rather than relieving it. A wife who formerly worked outside the home feels isolated, lonely, and undervalued. Her husband doesn't understand why she isn't more grateful that he is putting in extra hours at work to support the new addition to the family. When such a couple adopts a traditional division of labor after the birth of a child, *both* parents usually end up dissatisfied. The more traditional the roles, the more dissatisfaction.[38]

Many women enjoy staying home while their children grow up and therefore postpone even starting a career until the kids leave home. But this too can have unexpected consequences down the road. Often a wife who starts working late stays on the job after her husband retires. But working women with retired husbands tend to be more dissatisfied with their marriages than any other type of wife.[39]

The impact of a couple living together without being married is also changing faster than many people realize. Fifty years ago, if a couple decided to live together outside marriage, they were choosing an unconventional course that pigeonholed them into a tiny and suspect segment of the population. Their lives would likely be much less stable than those of people who followed the accepted rules.

Today, however, there are many different kinds of cohabitation. Young people still in college or just beginning to establish job credentials may live together to reap some of the benefits of married life, like income pooling, companionship, and expectations of fidelity, even though they see the relationship as temporary. There are also people who consciously choose cohabitation as an alternative to marriage because they don't want their commitment to be a matter of legal record. For example, many seniors lose economic benefits if they remarry. In addition, an older couple, each with grown children, may not want to complicate separate inheritance arrangements.

Some cohabiting couples have philosophical objections to involving the state in their relationship. Some just don't see a need to get married. A growing minority of cohabiting couples have relationships that are hard to distinguish from marriage. They may live together for decades and raise children together. Many other people move in together as a step toward marriage. Indeed, in a majority of marriages today the couple has already lived together.[40]

Lumping all these different situations together to make overarching generalizations about "the" consequences of living together is a mistake. Cohabiting couples, for example, are more likely, on average, to experience infidelity or domestic violence than married couples. But again we have to disentangle cause and effect. Cohabitation is sometimes an uneasy compromise between one partner who wants to marry and one who doesn't. Or an individual may hesitate to marry because the partner has a history of infidelity, a drinking or drug problem, or a wicked temper. These problems are not caused by the couple's failure to marry. They are the reasons a couple doesn't get married. There is no evidence that a violent man will stop abusing his partner just because she agrees to marry him.[41]

In the United States and Britain, living together before marriage is associated with an increased risk of divorce later on. That's not the case in France or Germany. Because attitudes toward unmarried sex are still more disapproving in the United States and Britain than in France or Germany, it may well be that Americans and Britons who decide to live together before marriage are already more open to nontraditional arrangements, including divorce, than the general population. In Germany, where fewer people disapprove of premarital sex, cohabitation before marriage is associated with a slightly *lower* risk of divorce down the line.

There are many differences in cohabitation patterns across Western Europe and North America, but in general unmarried couples who live together divide housework more evenly than married couples, while men who live with their partners before marrying them do more housework than men who move directly into marriage. Perhaps men who are more egalitarian and more likely to share housework are also more likely to cohabit. But some researchers maintain that because living together does not come with the same package of traditional gender scripts as does marriage, it is easier for a woman to get her partner to do more housework.[42]

All these new patterns in marriage, cohabitation, and childbearing also create new categories of stepfamilies. Some stepfamilies don't involve marriage at all. Sometimes even a first marriage by both partners creates a stepfamily because one or both partners come with children they had outside marriage. There are also big differences among traditional stepfamilies. Do the wife's or husband's children by a former marriage live in the household? Are children from the new marriage living with children from a previous marriage? Each of these stepfamilies faces special issues not covered by any list of "time-tested rules."[43]

When people try to figure out their best shot at a stable, happy marriage—or, for that matter, a contented single life—they may get frustrated trying to balance the differences in what makes men and women happy or successful in marriage. For example, a woman who holds conventional ideas about gender roles and marriage is, on average, less likely to divorce than a woman who is less traditional. But a woman with traditional views also has a slightly lower chance of marrying in the first place. A wife whose attitudes become more egalitarian during the course of her marriage often reports a decline in her marital happiness and an increase in conflict.[44]

For men the patterns are reversed. Men who have traditional gender attitudes are more likely to marry, but also more likely to end up divorced, than men with more egalitarian views. Husbands whose attitudes become more egalitarian during the marriage report increased happiness and fewer marital problems.

Some commentators believe men and women are becoming ever more different in their values and desires. The subtitle of a recent book by political scientist Andrew Hacker was *The Growing Gulf Between Women and Men.* Hacker argues that men and women today are less willing to make the concessions and take on the obligations that make marriage work.[45]

But less willing to make concessions and take on obligations than when? For thousands of years every wife was compelled to acknowledge her husband as her lord and master, and he had the right to beat her if she disobeyed or talked back to him. Until the 1970s a husband could force his wife to have sex whenever he wanted. He had complete authority over family finances and, under most legal codes, didn't even have to consult her about where the couple lived. Until the mid-twentieth century, many families in Europe and America had two separate standards of living: one for the husband that included meat and beer and a lower one for the wife and children.[46]

Conversely, for thousands of years women chose suitors by the size of their landholdings or inheritance prospects instead of their individual qualities and often made cruel sport of them behind their backs. Wives who had no choice but to accept their husbands' domination in the big things might retaliate in thousands of little ways that made their husbands miserable.

I don't see a growing estrangement or widening gender gap in what women and men want from each other. Most men and women are moving in the same direction in their values. It's true that women's attitudes, behaviors, and expectations are changing faster than men's, and this can lead to marital conflict or make some people wary of getting married at all. But most men are much more accepting of equal rights for women than their fathers were and even than they themselves used to be.

Of course some still cling to older norms of marriage, especially in the abstract. In 1998 the sixteen-million-member Southern Baptist Church approved a code for marital conduct that harks right back to the 1950s. The code says a husband should "provide for, protect, and lead his family." A wife is to "submit herself graciously" to her husband's leadership and "serve as his helper in managing their household."[47]

But even many American women who think they accept this definition of marriage are unlikely to practice it every day. So some men resort to mail-order bride catalogs, seeking women from countries where females still have lower expectations of equality. More than five thousand women from the Philippines come to the United States each year in this capacity. Thousands more come from the former Soviet Union, Eastern Europe, and other impoverished regions. One online matchmaking organization assures its clientele that these "are not the cosmopolitan women that threaten you with divorce each and every time they do not get their own way." Another Web site promises: "She is the weaker gender and knows it."[48]

But most American men no longer want a weaker, subservient partner. Men may not have the same exact definition of equality as women, and they may still have trouble living up to their own ideals, but there is a steady convergence between men and women in their support for mutual respect, fidelity, honesty, and shared tasks.

Take the question of who does how much around the house. Wives still do considerably more household work than husbands, and men usually overestimate what percentage of the chores they do. It is tempting for women to interpret this exaggeration as a sign of male hypocrisy. But I think it reflects a gigantic change in social values. Until fifty years ago, men typically *underreported* how much household work or child care they did because they did not want to admit to doing "women's work." It is a huge step forward that men think they should say they do more than they actually do. Moreover, even if men are not doing as much as they think, they're doing a lot more than they used to. During the 1970s and 1980s wives cut back on time spent in routine cooking and cleaning, while husbands *increased* the time they devoted to those chores. During the late 1980s and the 1990s both husbands and wives increased the time they spent with their children. Men today are much more likely than in the past to report that they enjoy cooking and cleaning, and this is especially true for men under thirty.[49]

So I don't think that men and women are growing farther apart in what they want. In sociologist Kathleen Gerson's interviews with young adults who came of age in the 1980s and 1990s, she found that only one-third of the young men wanted a "traditional" marriage in which the man was the main breadwinner and the woman did most of the nurturing. There are still more young men than women who prefer male breadwinner marriages, but the gap has been closing. Most young people of both sexes want good jobs with the flexibility to have fulfilling family lives and loving marriages in which each spouse shares child rearing and breadwinning.[50]

The big problem doesn't lie in differences between what men and women want out of life and love. The big problem is how hard it is to achieve equal relationships in a society whose work policies, school schedules, and social programs were constructed on the assumption that male breadwinner families would always be the norm. Tensions between men and women today stem less from different aspirations than from the difficulties they face translating their ideals into practice.

Gerson found that when the demands of daily living and the organization of work make it hard to live out egalitarian ideals, men and women have different fallback positions. Of the young men who wanted egalitarian marriages, 60 percent said that if this was out of reach, they would choose some kind of modified male breadwinner marriage, in which they earned the bulk of family income and their partner took care of most family obligations. The reaction of young women, however, was strikingly different. Eighty percent of them told Gerson they would rather go it alone than be in a traditional or even a modified traditional marriage.

In practice, most women continue to compromise their egalitarian ideals. From 1996 to 2000 Peggy Orenstein interviewed women across the country about their hopes and dreams. She found that many, even as they dreamed about an equal marriage, "were tracking themselves into lower-paying, more flexible jobs than their male peers," assuming that they would have to do most of the child rearing. Yet she also found that many women said they would consider "bypassing the middle man" and having a baby on their own if they hadn't found a man they considered good marriage material by the time they were thirty-five or forty.[51]

A significant historical reversal is occurring in the attitudes of men and women toward marriage. During the first three-quarters of the twentieth century women needed and also wanted marriage much more than men did. Men were more reluctant to enter marriage than women and more likely to complain of its burdens. During the 1980s and 1990s, however, men began to rate marriage much more highly than in previous decades, and by the end of the century more men than women said that marriage was their ideal lifestyle.[52]

There has also been a subtle but momentous gender shift in attitudes toward having children. Most women have always loved their children. But women were also more aware of the sacrifices involved in child rearing and much more interested than their husbands in limiting the number of children they bore. This is not surprising since through most of history a woman not only risked death in childbirth but bore most of the burdens of child rearing, even cutting back on her own food, but not her husband's, if a new child arrived and money was tight.[53]

This began to change in the twentieth century, and by the end of the century many men had discovered the joys of involved parenthood. Because they were more involved, however, they began to feel the restrictions children place on one's freedom. As men's involvement in child rearing relieved their responsibilities, women became *less* likely to say that children restrict parental freedom but men became *more* likely to do so.[54]

Once upon a time almost all men and women accepted that their lives had to be a package deal: You get married and then you have kids. Now men and women can customize their life course. They can pick and choose whether they want to marry at all, when they want to marry, whether they want children, how many children they want, and when they want them. Some males and females have become more involved parents and partners than ever before, while others now say that they are not interested in being parents or partners at all.

For most people, there are pros and cons to each of these decisions. And those are now different from the pros and cons for men and women in the past. Men must grapple with new questions: "Do I really want children if I have to do half the work of raising them?"; "Am I willing to stay involved with my children if I'm not still with the mother and getting the benefits of having a wife?"[55]

Women, on the other hand, grapple with different questions: "What does marriage really offer?"; "What are its costs compared to its benefits?"; "How would marriage be a help to me in raising any children I choose to have?"

The answers that men and women come up with vary from individual to individual, as do the consequences of the choices they make. The democratization of marriage has been messy. People with more choices have more chances to make bad decisions as well as good ones. When a couple has to negotiate because the husband cannot simply impose his will, there is a chance that negotiations will break down. When both partners can have equally important but conflicting career trajectories or life goals, even the most loving couple may come to a parting of the ways. The bad news is that the institution of marriage will never again be as universal or stable as it was when marriage was the only viable option. But that is also the good news.

Over the past century, marriage has steadily become more fair, more fulfilling, and more effective in fostering the well-being of both adults and children than ever before in history. It has also become more optional and more fragile. The historical record suggests that these two seemingly contradictory changes are inextricably intertwined. Even more than love and marriage, fulfilling and fragile seem to "go together like a horse and carriage."

Conclusion

---•◦•---

Better or Worse?
The Future of Marriage

Conclusion

———— ⟫◉⟪ ————

A
s I was considering how to wrap up a book that has covered so many centuries and taken me through so many changes in my own thinking, I realized that my historical studies have taken me to the very place I have ended up in my personal life. Like many women who grew up in the 1950s and 1960s, I went through a number of stages in my attitude toward marriage. As a teenager I thought getting married meant living happily ever after. During boring classes in junior high school, I doodled hearts in my notebook, coupling my initials with those of whatever boy I currently had a crush on. I would write out my first name in front of his last, trying to see how they looked when prefixed with the magical title "Mrs."

But in college, my interest in getting married took a backseat to the excitement of campus life and my involvement in the outside world. Around that time I also became more critical of my parents' marriage. My dad, whom I loved dearly and who was a wonderful father, was not a wonderful husband. He could be impatient, demanding, and occasionally condescending toward my mother (though never to his daughters). Even as a self-centered eighteen-year-old I saw that when my mother finally left my dad, after nineteen years of marriage, there was a dramatic improvement in her self-confidence. She went back to college; she traveled; she regaled my friends with her adventures, including a night spent club-hopping with Frank Sinatra. Suddenly she was as interesting to me as my dad had always been. She was interesting to other people too. She founded the first women's center in Washington state and developed an independent identity as a respected and caring English teacher.

Marriage, a History

My mother's experience, combined with a few heartbreaks of my own, made me wonder if I might be better off staying single, and my ambivalence about marriage was reinforced by the historical and anthropological research on male-female relations that I was encountering in my studies. Eventually, though, my mother married again, entering a joyful relationship that outlasted her first marriage. My stepfather's selfless devotion to her, which never flagged through easy times or hard, showed me just how great a good marriage could be.

Even with this positive model, I long resisted the idea of marriage for myself. I worried that being married would rob me of my hard-earned independent identity, just as it had, the first time around, for my mom. When I finally tied the knot, it was with enough trepidation that my husband-to-be announced to our assembled friends and families, only half in jest, that his sister would stand beside me throughout the wedding ceremony to prevent me from bolting. For the first year of marriage the word *husband* came out of my mouth in a self-conscious stutter, as in "My huh-huh-husband will be over later."

With time, however, the word began to roll easily and frequently off my tongue. For one thing, it was nice to have something less cumbersome to call my partner than my "significant other" or my "live-in boyfriend." I also came to see the word as a public signal to friends and family that I was in a committed relationship and as an invitation for them to take an interest in our well-being as a *couple*. Still, I am quite sure that my marriage would not be nearly as satisfying if I had gotten married in the years when I most wanted to or if I had entered marriage without knowing I had the option to leave and could therefore ask for the changes I wanted.

The historical transformation in marriage over the ages has created a similar paradox for society as a whole. Marriage has become more joyful, more loving, and more satisfying for many couples than ever before in history. At the same time it has become optional and more brittle. These two strands of change cannot be disentangled.

For thousands of years, marriage served so many economic, political, and social functions that the individual needs and wishes of its members (especially women and children) took second place. Marriage was not about bringing two individuals together for love and intimacy, although that was sometimes a welcome side effect. Rather, the aim of marriage was to acquire useful in-laws and gain political or economic advantage.

Only in the last two hundred years, as other economic and political institutions began to take over many of the roles once played by marriage, did Europeans and Americans begin to see marriage as a personal and private relationship that should fulfill their emotional and sexual desires. Once that happened, free choice became the societal norm for mate selection, love became the main reason for marriage, and a successful marriage came to be defined as one that met the needs of its members.

But each of these changes had negative as well as positive implications for the stability of marriage as an institution. No sooner did the ideal of marrying for love triumph than its most enthusiastic supporters started demanding the right to divorce if love died. Once people came to believe that families should nurture children rather than exploit their labor, many began to feel that the legal consequences of illegitimacy for children were inhumane. And when people started thinking that the quality of the relationship was more important than the economic functions of the institution, some men and women argued that the committed love of two unmarried individuals, including those of the same sex, deserved at least as much social respect as a formal marriage entered into for mercenary reasons.

For 150 years, four things kept people from pushing the new values about love and self-fulfillment to their ultimate conclusion: that people could construct meaningful lives outside marriage and that not everything in society had to be organized through and around married couples.

The first impediment to such beliefs and behavior was the conviction that there were enormous and innate differences between men and women, one of which was that women had no sexual desires. This crumbled in the 1920s, as people rejected the notion of separate spheres and emphasized the importance of sexual satisfaction for women as well as men.

The second thing that held back the subversive potential of the love revolution was the ability of relatives, neighbors, employers, and government to regulate people's personal behavior and penalize nonconformity. The influence of these individuals and institutions was eroded by the growth of urbanization, which allowed more anonymity in personal life, and the development of national corporations, banks, and other impersonal institutions that cared more about people's educational credentials and financial assets than their marital status and sexual histories.

The third factor that kept the love revolution from undermining the centrality of marriage in society was the combination of unreliable birth control and harsh penalties for illegitimacy. Then, in the 1960s, birth control became reliable enough that the fear of pregnancy no longer constrained women's sexual conduct. And in the 1970s reformers abolished the legal category of illegitimacy, successfully arguing that it was unfair to penalize a child whose mother was unable or unwilling to wed.

Marriage, a History

Women's legal and economic dependence on men and men's domestic dependence on women was the fourth factor that had long driven people to get and stay married. But during the 1970s and 1980s women won legal autonomy and made huge strides toward economic self-sufficiency. At the same time, the proliferation of laborsaving consumer goods such as permanent-press fabrics, ready-made foods, and automatic dishwashers undercut men's dependence on women's housekeeping.

As all these barriers to single living and personal autonomy gradually eroded, society's ability to pressure people into marrying, or keep them in a marriage against their wishes, was drastically curtailed. People no longer needed to marry in order to construct successful lives or long-lasting sexual relationships. With that, thousands of years of tradition came to an end.

Today we are experiencing a historical revolution every bit as wrenching, far-reaching, and irreversible as the Industrial Revolution. Like that huge historic turning point, the revolution in marriage has transformed how people organize their work and interpersonal commitments, use their leisure time, understand their sexuality, and take care of children and the elderly. It has liberated some people from restrictive, inherited roles in society. But it has stripped others of traditional support systems and rules of behavior without establishing new ones.

The marriage revolution has brought personal turmoil in its wake. But we cannot turn the clock back in our personal lives any more than we can go back to small-scale farming and artisan production in our economic life. The Industrial Revolution exacted an enormous personal toll on people who were uprooted from traditional communities and whose old ways of organizing their lives were destroyed. While some entrepreneurs thrived during the transition, there were farmers and craftsmen who lost everything. But individuals and society as a whole had to come to grips with the fact that the new system of wage labor and the free market was here to stay. We face a similar situation with the revolution in marriage.

This is a recurring pattern in periods of massive historical change. The gains that social change produces in some areas of life are usually inseparable from the losses it produces in others. It would be wonderful if we could pick and choose what historical changes we will and won't accept, but we are not that lucky. Just as many people found new sources of employment in the industrial world even after the factories had displaced old ones, many people will be able to carve out satisfying and stable marriages on a new basis. But many others will live their lives and construct their personal commitments outside marriage.

Conclusion

When I make this point in talks, some people accuse me of not appreciating the advantages of marriage. That is not so. A successful marriage can be remarkably beneficial. But researching this book has convinced me that many of these benefits would disappear if we tried to reimpose the societal norm of lifelong marriage for everyone.

When a modern marriage is stable, it is so in a more appealing way than in the past. Marriage no longer gives husbands the right to abuse wives or sacrifice their children's education in order to benefit from their labor. Modern marriages no longer feature two standards of living, one for the man and a lower one for the wife and children. There is also no longer a rigid sexual double standard that turns a blind eye to a man's adultery and tars a woman for life if she has sex outside marriage.

Today married people in Western Europe and North America are generally happier, healthier, and better protected against economic setbacks and psychological depression than people in any other living arrangement.[1] Some of these benefits of marriage are due to what sociologists call selection effects. That is, people who are already good-natured, healthy, socially skilled, and emotionally stable are more likely to get married and stay married than individuals with fewer of these qualities. Similarly, individuals who can make a good impression in job interviews and can manage their finances and time successfully are more likely to have stable marriages than men and women without such skills.

But I believe marriage itself adds something extra, over and above its selection effects. It remains the highest expression of commitment in our culture and comes packaged with exacting expectations about responsibility, fidelity, and intimacy. Married couples may no longer have a clear set of rules about which partner should do what in their marriage. But they do have a clear set of rules about what each partner should *not* do. And society has a clear set of rules for how everyone else should and should not relate to each partner. These commonly held expectations and codes of conduct foster the predictability and security that make daily living easier.

Arrangements other than marriage are still treated as makeshift or temporary, however long they last. There is no consensus on what rules apply to these relationships. We don't even know what to call them. Divorced families may be labeled "broken" families, even when they actually work very well. Until recently children born to unwed parents were called illegitimate—and treated as such in law and social life. The relationship between a cohabiting couple, whether heterosexual or same sex, is unacknowledged by law and may be ignored by the friends and relatives of each partner. Marriage, in contrast, gives people a positive vocabulary and public image that set a high standard for the couple's behavior and for the respect that outsiders ought to give to their relationship.

If we withdrew our social acceptance of alternatives to marriage, marriage itself might suffer.[2] The very things that make marriage so potentially satisfying are for the most part inseparable from the things that make unsatisfying marriages less bearable. The same personal freedoms that allow people to expect more from their married lives also allow them to get more out of staying single and give them more choice than ever before in history about whether or not to remain together.

There are those who believe that because married people are, on average, better off than divorced or single people, society should promote lifelong marriage for everyone and lead a campaign against divorce and cohabitation. But using averages to give personal advice to individuals or to construct social policy for all is not wise. On average, marriage has substantial benefits for both husbands and wives. That's because most marriages are pretty happy. But individuals in unhappy marriages are *more* psychologically distressed than people who stay single, and many of marriage's health benefits fade if the marriage is troubled. A three-year study of married couples in which one partner had mild hypertension found that in happy marriages, the blood pressure of the at-risk partner dropped when couples spent even a couple of extra minutes together. But for those who were unhappily married, a few extra minutes of time together raised the blood pressure of the at-risk spouse. Having an argumentative or highly critical spouse can seriously damage a person's health, raising blood pressure, lowering immune functions, and even worsening the symptoms of chronic illnesses like arthritis.[3]

Women are at particular risk in a bad marriage. A man in a bad marriage still gets some health benefits compared with single men, because even a miserable wife tends to feed her husband more vegetables, schedule his medical checkups, and shoulder much of the housework and the emotional work that make life function smoothly. But there are no such compensations for an unhappily married woman. Unhappy wives have higher rates of depression and alcohol abuse than single women. A bad marriage raises a woman's cholesterol readings and decreases her immune functioning. Researchers at the University of Pittsburgh found that unhappily married women in their forties were more than twice as likely to have medical symptoms that put them at risk for heart attacks and strokes as happily married or never-married females. A long-term study of patients in Oregon even found that unequal decision-making power in marriage was associated with a higher risk of death for women.[4]

Conclusion

Promoting good marriages is a worthwhile goal, and we can help many marriages work better than they currently do. I argued in the last chapter that in today's changing world, one-size-fits-all advice books and glib formulas for marital success are of little value. But sociologists and psychologists have found a few general principles that seem to help most kinds of modern marriage flourish.

Because men and women no longer face the same economic and social compulsions to get or stay married as in the past, it is especially important that men and women now begin their relationship as friends and build it on the basis of mutual respect. You can no longer force your partner to conform to a predetermined social role or gender stereotype or browbeat someone into staying in an unsatisfying relationship. "Love, honor, and negotiate" have to replace the older rigid rules, say psychologists Betty Carter and Joan Peters.[5]

But negotiation will not resolve every difference of opinion or interest. As men and women marry later, they come to marriage with a lot of life experience and many previously formed interests and skills. It's no longer possible to assume that two people can merge all their interests and beliefs. When two grownups get together and neither has the whip hand, both must learn to live with their differences.

Accepting differences does not mean putting up with everything a partner dishes out. It is certainly not the same thing that psychologists meant in the 1950s, when this advice was directed only at the wife. Today acceptance in a relationship must be a two-way street. To be effective, it has to be based on *real* friendship and respect, not the counterfeit interest that so many 1950s marriage manuals recommended when they told the wife to pretend to be interested in his work and the husband to pretend to be interested in her day. And in a world where marriages are no longer held together by the compulsion of in-laws and society or the mutual dependence of two individuals who cannot do each other's jobs, on-going emotional investments in a marriage have to replace external constraints in providing ballast for the relationship.

Another important principle that flows from the historical changes in marriage is that husbands have to respond positively to their wives' requests for change. This is not female favoritism or male bashing. For thousands of years marriage was organized in ways that reinforced female subservience. Today, even though most of the legal and economic basis for a husband's authority over his wife and her deference to his needs is gone, we all have inherited unconscious habits and emotional expectations that perpetuate female disadvantage in marriage. For example, it is still true that when women marry, they typically do more housework than they did before marriage. When men marry, they do less. Marriage decreases free time for women, but not for men. In many cases, write researchers Marybeth Mattingly and Suzanne Bianchi, being married places women "constantly on call," lessening the quantity and often the quality of their leisure time.[6]

Women are more likely to bring up marital issues for discussion because they have more to gain from changing these traditional dynamics of marriage. According to psychology researcher John Gottman and his collaborators, if a man responds positively to his wife's request for change, that is one of the best indicators that they will stay together and have a happy marriage. It helps a lot, they note, if the wife asks nicely. But it does not help if she keeps quiet for fear of provoking conflict. Constructive, nonviolent anger does not usually lead to divorce, but stonewalling a partner's request for change poses a big risk to a marriage.[7]

In the thirty years I have been researching family life, I have read many women's diaries, written over the last four-hundred years. Reading these records of women's lives and marriages, I was struck by how often entries focused not on the joy of their marriages but on wives' struggle to accept their lot. Many women did write about their love and respect for their husbands, of course, but many others filled their diaries with reminders to themselves to cultivate patience, self-restraint, and forgiveness. One woman's refrain was that her husband's behavior was "the cross I have to bear," another's, the reminder that her husband had never beaten her and that she should "be more grateful for what I have." Others would pray for the forbearance to put up with a husband's drinking or foul temper.

"Give me strength"; "Make me realize how fortunate I am"; "Help me not to provoke him"; "Give me patience." These pleas occur over and over, even in the journals of women who were satisfied with their marriages. Men's journals dwelled less on the need to accommodate themselves to their wives' shortcomings, but they too reflected the frustration of living in a fixed institution in which there was no sense that problems could be worked through and relationships renegotiated.

What might I write if I had time to keep a daily diary? It would undoubtedly be infused by the greater sense of choice that my husband and I now have in comparison with the past. As with any marriage, there are times we have to search for patience and forbearance. But the choice to stay and work things out is a conscious one and a mutual process, not a unilateral resignation to accept the inevitable. My diary would record a lot more active delight in my daily married life than most journals of the past and a lot less talk about "resigning myself to my lot." Yet as a modern woman I live with an undercurrent of anxiety that is absent from the diaries of earlier days. I know that if my husband and I stop negotiating, if too much time passes without any joy, or if a conflict drags on too long, neither of us *has* to stay with the other.

What is true for individual marriages is also true for society. As a result of centuries of social change, most people in the Western world have a choice about whether or not to enter marriage and, if they do marry, whether or not to stay in it for the rest of their lives. The structure of our economy and the values of our culture also encourage or even force people to make much more individualistic decisions than in the past. Today, as never before, decisions about marriage and family life rest with the individuals involved, not with society as a whole.

Married people may be able to reach out to friends and counselors for help, and our employers and political leaders could make it easier for us to sustain our relationships by instituting family-friendly work policies and social programs to help us juggle our many roles. But the most effective support systems for married couples, such as subsidized parental leaves, flexible work schedules, high-quality child care, and access to counseling when a relationship is troubled, would also make things easier for those people who are constructing relationships outside marriage. Conversely, any measures that significantly limited social support or freedom of choice for the unmarried would probably backfire on the quality of life for the married as well.

We can certainly create more healthy marriages than we currently do, and we can save more marriages that are in trouble. But just as we cannot organize modern political alliances through kinship ties or put the farmers' and skilled craftsmen's households back as the centerpiece of the modern economy, we can never reinstate marriage as the primary source of commitment and caregiving in the modern world. For better or worse, we must adjust our personal expectations and social support systems to this new reality.

Notes

==•(()•==

Introduction

1. Amy Kaler, "'Many Divorces and Many Spinsters': Marriage as an Invented Tradition in Southern Malawi, 1946–1999," *Journal of Family History* 26 (2001), pp. 547, 548.

2. On record high divorce rates of Malaysia and Indonesia in the 1930s, 1940s, and 1950s, see William Goode, *World Changes in Divorce Patterns* (New Haven: Yale University Press, 1993). On high rates of illegitimacy, which accounted for more than 80 percent of total births in some sections of Austria in the second half of the nineteenth century, see André Burguière, "The Formation of the Couple," *Journal of Family History* 12 (1987). For the rest of this paragraph, see the notes to chapter 2.

3. Claude Martin and Irene Thèry, "The Pacs and Marriage and Cohabitation in France," *International Journal of Law, Public Policy and the Family* 15 (April 2001); Kathleen Kiernan, "The Rise of Cohabitation and Childbearing Outside Marriage in Western Europe," *International Journal of Law, Policy and the Family* 15 (2001); Ilona Ostner, "Cohabitation in Germany—Rules, Reality and Public Discourses," *International Journal of Law, Policy and the Family* 15 (2001); Karen Mason, Noriko Tsuya, and Manja Choe, eds. *The Changing Family in Comparative Perspective: Asia and the United States* (Honolulu: East-West Center, 1998); Sonni Efron, "Baby Bust Has Japan Fearing for Its Future," *Los Angeles Times,* June 24, 2001; Paul Wiseman, "No Sex Please, We're Japanese," *USA Today,* June 23, 2004.

4. Barbara Crossette, "UN Agency Sets Sights on Curbing Child Marriage," *New York Times,* March 8, 2001; Constanzia Tobio, "Marriage, Cohabitation and the Residential Independence of Young People in Spain," *International*

Journal of Law, Policy and the Family 15 (2001); Chan Wai Kong, "Stupid Cupid?," *New Straits Times,* November 18, 2001; Dinah Spritzer, "More People Say, 'We Don't,'" *Prague Post,* April 15, 2004.

5. Saudi Women Advise on Marriage Crisis, BBC News, December 31, 2001 (http: news.bbc.co.uk/hi/english/world/middle_east/ newsid1735000/1735965.stm); Alan Riding, "Italian Court Rules that Son Knows Best About Leaving Home," *New York Times,* April 6, 2002.

6. Wade Mackey and Ronald Immerman, "Cultural Viability and Gender Egalitarianism," *Journal of Comparative Family Studies* 33 (2002); Ariek Eckholm, "Desire for Sons Drives Use of Prenatal Scans in China," *New York Times,* June 21, 2002; Paul Wiseman, "China Thrown Off Balance as Boys Outnumber Girls," *USA Today,* June 19, 2002.

7. Margaret Hunt, *The Middling Sort: Commerce, Gender, and the Family in England, 1680–1780* (Berkeley: University of California Press, 1996).

8. Even as late as 1967, almost three-quarters of female college students in America said they would consider marrying someone they didn't love if he had all the other qualities they wanted in a mate. It is only since the unprecedented expansion of women's economic independence in the 1970s, 1980s, and 1990s that women have begun to hold out for a "soul mate." Daniel Albas and Cheryl Albas, "Love and Marriage," in K. Ishwaran, ed., *Family and Marriage: Cross-cultural Perspectives* (Toronto: Thompson Educational Publishing, 1992), p. 138; David Popenoe et al., *The State of Our Unions, 2002* (New Brunswick, NJ: The National Marriage Project, June 2001).

9. George Peter Murdock, *Ethnographic Atlas* (Pittsburgh: University of Pittsburgh Press, 1967).

10. My thanks to Joanna Radbord, associate at Epstein Cole LLP, Toronto, and co-counsel to the applicant couples in *Halpern v. Canada,* for providing me with access to the affidavits filed in the case. *Halpern v. Canada* (2002): 60 O.R. (3d) 321 (Div Ct_; (2003) 225D.L.R. (4th) 529 (Ont. CA) The Ontario Supreme Court unanimously ruled that denying equal marriage rights to gays and lesbians was unconstitutional and gave the government two years to rewrite the common law definition of marriage so that it includes two persons, not necessarily one man and one woman. The decision can be accessed online at http://www. sgmlaw.com/userfiles/ filesevent/file_1413620_halpern.PDF. 10. Amy Kaler, "'Many Divorces and Many Spinsters.'"

Chapter 1. The Radical Idea of Marrying for Love

1. Quoted in John Jacobs, *All You Need Is Love and Other Lies About Marriage* (New York: HarperCollins, 2004), p. 9.

2. William Jankowiak and Edward Fischer, "A Cross-Cultural Perspective on Romantic Love," *Ethnology* 31 (1992).

3. Ira Reiss and Gary Lee, *Family Systems in America* (New York: Holt, Rinehart and Winston, 1988), pp. 91–93.

4. Karen Dion and Kenneth Dion, "Cultural Perspectives on Romantic Love," *Personal Relationships* 3 (1996); Vern Bullough, "On Being a Male in the Middle Ages," in Clare Less, ed., *Medieval Masculinities* (Minneapolis: University of Minnesota Press, 1994); Hans-Werner Goetz, *Life in the Middle Ages, from the Seventh to the Thirteenth Century* (Notre Dame, Ind.: University of Notre Dame Press, 1993).

5. Francis Hsu, "Kinship and Ways of Life," in Hsu, ed., *Psychological Anthropology* (Cambridge, U.K.: Schenkman, 1972), and *Americans and Chinese: Passage to Differences* (Honolulu: University Press of Hawaii, 1981); G. Robina Quale, *A History of Marriage Systems* (Westport, Conn.: Greenwood Press, 1988); Marilyn Yalom, "Biblical Models," in Yalom and Laura Carstensen, eds., *Inside the American Couple* (Berkeley: University of California Press, 2002).

6. Andreas Capellanus, *The Art of Courtly Love* (New York: W. W. Norton, 1969), pp.106–07.

7. Ibid., pp.106–07, 184. On the social context of courtly love, see Theodore Evergates, ed., *Aristocratic Women in Medieval France* (Philadelphia: University of Pennsylvania Press, 1999); Montaigne, quoted in Olwen Hufton, *The Prospect Before Her: A History of Women in Western Europe, 1500–1800* (New York: Alfred A. Knopf, 1996), p. 148.

8. Betty Radice, trans., *Letters of Abelard and Heloise* (Harmondsworth, U.K.: Penguin, 1974).

9. The philosopher Seneca, quoted in Philippe Aries, "Love in Married Life," in Aries and André Bejin, *Western Sexuality* (Oxford, U.K.: Blackwell, 1985), p. 134.

10. Sarah Pomeroy, *Plutarch's Advice to the Bride and Groom and a Consolation to His Wife* (New York: Oxford University Press, 1990), p. 7.

11. P. Grimal, *Love in Ancient Rome* (Norman: University of Oklahoma Press, 1986), p. 252; Yan Thomas, "Fathers as Citizens of Rome," in André Burguière et al., *A History of the Family, vol. 1: Distant Worlds, Ancient Worlds* (Cambridge, Mass.: Belknap Press, 1996), p. 265; Abdelwahab Bouhdida, *Sexuality in Islam* (London: Routledge and Kegan Paul, 1985); Fatima Mernissi, *Beyond the Veil: Male-Female Relationships in a Modern Muslim Society* (Bloomington: Indiana University Press, 1987); Beth Baron, "Marital Bonds in Modern Egypt," in Nikki Keddie and Baron, eds., *Women in Middle Eastern History: Shifting Boundaries in Sex and Gender* (New Haven: Yale University Press, 1991).

12. Helen Regis, "The Madness of Excess," in William Jankowiak, ed., *Romantic Passion: A Universal Experience?* (New York: Columbia University Press, 1995), p. 144; Hans Medick and David Sabean, *Interest and Emotion: Essays on the Study of Family and Kinship* (New York: Cambridge University Press, 1984), pp. 11–13.

13. Jim Bell, "Notions of Love and Romance Among the Taita," in Jankowiak, *Romantic Passion,* p. 161. Some polygamous societies, however, strongly disapprove of a man's showing preference for any of his wives. See Jack Goody and S. J. Tambiah, *Bridewealth and Dowry in Africa and Eurasia* (Cambridge, U.K.: Cambridge University Press, 1973), p. 38.

14. David and Vera Mace, *Marriage East & West* (New York: Doubleday, 1960), p. 132; V. V. Prakasa Rao and V. Nandini Rao, *Marriage, the Family, and Women in India* (New Delhi: Heritage Publishers, 1982), pp. 222–24; Monisha Pasupathi, "Arranged Marriages," in Yalom and Carstensen, eds., *Inside the American Couple.*

15. Steven Ozment, *When Fathers Ruled: Family Life in Reformation Europe* (Cambridge, Mass.: Harvard University Press, 1983).

16. Suzanne Dixon, *The Roman Family* (Baltimore: Johns Hopkins University Press, 1992); Marilyn Yalom, *A History of the Wife* (New York: HarperCollins, 2002).

17. Anne Bradstreet, "To My Dear and Loving Husband," in Adelaide Amore, ed., *A Woman's Inner World: Selected Poetry and Prose of Anne Bradstreet* (New York: University Press of America, 1982), p. 24. For other examples of love letters and poetry of the past, see Barbara Watterson, *Women in Ancient Egypt* (New York: St. Martin's Press, 1991).

18. Anthony Fletcher, *Gender, Sex, and Subordination in England, 1500–1800* (New Haven: Yale University Press, 1995), p. 413.

19. The phrase is from Chiara Saraceno, who argues that until the end of the nineteenth century, Italian families defined love as the development of such feelings over the course of a marriage. Saraceno, "The Italian Family," in Antoine Prost and Gerard Vincent, eds., *A History of Private Life: Riddles of Identity in Modern Times* (Cambridge, Mass.: Belknap Press, 1991), p. 487.

20. Michel Cartier, "China: The Family as a Relay of Government," in Burguière, ed., *Distant Worlds, Ancient Worlds;* Richley Crapo, *Cultural Anthropology: Understanding Ourselves and Others* (New York: McGraw-Hill, 1995); Burton Pasternak, Carol Ember, and Melvin Ember, eds., *Sex, Gender, and Kinship: A Cross-Cultural Perspective* (Upper Saddle River, N.J.: Prentice Hall, 1997); Melvyn Goldstein, "When Brothers Share a Wife," *Natural History* 96 (1987); J. P. Singh Rana, *Marriage and Customs of Tribes of India* (New Delhi: MD Publications, 1998).

21. Nancy Levine, *The Dynamics of Polyandry: Kinship, Domesticity, and Population on the Tibetan Border* (Chicago: University of Chicago Press, 1988).

22. Kristin Mann, *Marrying Well: Marriage, Status and Social Change Among the Educated Elite in Colonial Lagos* (Cambridge, U.K.: Cambridge University Press, 1985), p. 72; Connie Anderson, "The Persistence of Polygyny as an Adaptive Response to Poverty and Oppression in Apartheid South Africa," *Cross-Cultural Research* 34 (2000); J. S. Solway, "Affines and Spouses, Friends and Lovers: The Passing of Polygyny in Botswana," *Journal of Anthropological Research* 46 (1990); Karl Llewellyn and E. A. Hoebel, *The Cheyenne Way* (Norman: University of Oklahoma Press, 1941), p. 186.

23. Patricia Ebrey, *The Inner Quarters: Marriage and the Lives of Chinese Women in the Sung Period* (Berkeley: University of California Press, 1993), p. 156; Cartier, "China: The Family as a Relay of Government," p. 520.

24. Ellen Rothman, *Hands and Hearts: A History of Courtship in America* (New York: Basic Books, 1984), footnote, p. 43.

25. Jane Collier, *Marriage and Inequality in Classless Societies* (Palo Alto, Calif.: Stanford University Press, 1988), p. 164; Jan Collins and Thomas Gregor, "The Boundaries of Love," in Jankowiak, ed., *Romantic Passion,* p. 90. For more on the relatively low value placed on marriage in comparison to siblings or extended family members, see Susan Rogers, "Woman's Place: A Critical Review of Anthropological Theory," *Comparative Studies in Society and History* 20 (1982); Nicera Suderkasa, "Female Employment and Family Organization in West Africa," in Dorothy McGuigan, *New Research on Women and Sex Roles* (Ann Arbor: University of Michigan Press, 1976); Karen Sacks, *Sisters and Wives: The Past and Future of Sexual Equality* (Westport, Conn.: Greenwood Press, 1979); George P. Murdock, *Social Structure* (New York: Free Press, 1949), pp. 2–3; Jane Guyer, "Household and Community in African Studies," *African Studies Review* 24 (1981); Ogbomo, *When Men and Women Mattered: A History of Gender Relations Among the Owan of Nigeria* (New York: University of Rochester Press, 1997).

26. Ebrey, *Inner Quarters,* p. 193; Douglas Martin and Yang Huanyi, "The Last User of a Secret Woman's Code," *New York Times,* October 7, 2004; Edward Cody, "A Language by Women for Women," *Washington Post,* February 24, 2004.

27. D. R. White, *Cultural Diversity Data Base* (La Jolla, Calif.: National Collegiate Software Clearinghouse, 1987), pp. 31, 22.

28. Pasternak, Ember, and Ember, *Sex, Gender, and Kinship;* Françoise Zonabend, "An Anthropological Perspective on Kinship and the Family," in Burguière et al., *Distant Worlds, Ancient Worlds,* p. 58; Lila Leibowitz, *Females, Males, Families* (Scituate, Mass.: Duxbury Press, 1978). In the classical world and through most of European history, women were regarded as having a stronger sex drive than men. Not until the nineteenth

century did American writers begin to express the opinion that women had little interest in sex. See Elyzabeth Abbott, *A History of Celibacy* (New York: Scribners, 2001) and Carol Groneman, *Nymphomania: A History* (New York: W. W. Norton, 2001).

29. Pamela Stern and Richard Condon, "A Good Spouse Is Hard to Find: Marriage, Spouse Exchange, and Infatuation Among the Copper Inuit," in Jankowiak, *Romantic Passion*.

30. Quale, *A History of Marriage Systems*.

31. Stephen Beckerman et al., "The Bari Partible Paternity Project: Preliminary Results," *Current Anthropology* 39 (1998), p. 165. See also A. C. Roosevelt, "Gender in Human Evolution," in Sarah Nelson and Myriam Rosen-Ayalon, eds., *In Pursuit of Gender: Worldwide Archaeological Approaches* (Walnut Creek, Calif.: Rowan and Littlefield Publishers, 2002), pp. 367–68.

32. Beckerman et al., "Bari Partible Paternity Project," p. 166.

Chapter 2. The Many Meanings of Marriage

1. Natalie Angier, "Mating Dances Go On and On," *New York Times,* July 10, 2001, pp. D1, D2.

2. Pioneering anthropologist Ernest Crawley argued that marriage is simply an extension or elaboration of the biological functions of mating. Evolutionary psychologists Martin Daly and Margo Wilson maintain that the essence of marriage in both animals and humans is the individual relationship between a male and a female, who join together to mate, produce children, and divide tasks. Ernest Crawley (1902), cited in Ronald Fletcher, "Mating, the Family and Marriage: A Sociological View," in Vernon Reynolds and John Kelly, eds., *Mating and Marriage* (New York: Oxford University Press, 1991); Martin Daly and Margo Wilson, "The Evolutionary Psychology of Marriage and Divorce," in Linda Waite, ed., *The Ties that Bind: Perspectives on Marriage and Cohabitation* (New York: Aldine de Gruyter, 2000).

3. Helen Fisher, *Anatomy of Love* (New York: W. W. Norton, 1992). People who argue that pair-bonding in humans springs from the same sources as pair-bonding among birds are making quite an evolutionary leap. Our closest ancestors on the evolutionary ladders are primates, and only 10 to 15 percent of primate species live in monogamous pair bonds. Primate social groups are sometimes organized around females and their young, sometimes around one male with several females, and sometimes around three or more adults of both sexes, but very seldom around the couple. Even among monogamous primates, the pair bond does not organize most food gathering, sharing, or defense. Barbara Smuts, "Social Relationships and Life Histories of Primates," in Mary Ellen Morbeck, Alison Galloway,

and Adrienne L. Zihlman, eds., *The Evolving Female: A Life-History Perspective* (Princeton: Princeton University Press, 1997), p. 64; Augustin Fuentes, "Re-Evalutating Primate Monogamy," *American Anthropologist* 100 (1999); Adrienne Zihlman, "Pygmy Chimps, People and the Pundits," *New Science* 104 (1984); Susan Sperling, "Baboons with Briefcases: Feminism, Functionalism, and Sociobiology in the Evolution of Primate Gender," *Signs* 17, no. 1 (1991); Meredith Small, *Female Choices* (Ithaca, N.Y.: Cornell University Press, 1993), pp. 110–13; Linda Marie Fedigan, "The Changing Role of Women in Models of Human Evolution," *Annual Review of Anthropology* 15 (1986), pp. 34–41; Adrienne Zihlman, "Sex Differences and Gender Hierarchies Among Primates: An Evolutionary Perspective," in Barbara Miller, ed., *Sex and Gender Hierarchies* (New York: Cambridge University Press, 1993), pp. 37–41; Jane Goodall, *The Chimpanzees of Gombe: Patterns of Behavior* (Cambridge, Mass.: Belknap Press, 1986); Linda Wolfe, "Human and Nonhuman Primates' Social Relationships," *Anthropology News* (May 2004).

4. Meyer Fortes, *Rules and the Emergence of Society* (London: Royal Anthropological Institute of Great Britain and Ireland, Occasional Paper No. 39, 1983), p. 6.

5. Murdock, *Social Structure* (see chap. 1, n. 25).

6. For this and the following paragraph, see Guyer, "Household and Community in African Studies," (see chap. 1, n. 25); Ernestine Friedl, *Women and Men: An Anthropologist's View* (New York: Holt, Rinehart and Winston, 1975), pp. 103, 122–23; Evelyn Blackwood, "Marriage and the 'Missing' Man," *Anthropology News* (May 2004); Michael Mitterauer, "Marriage Without Co-Residence: A Special Type of Family Form in Rural Carinthia," *Journal of Family History* 6 (Summer 1981); Patrick Beillevaire, "Japan: A Household Society," in Burguière et al., *Distant Worlds, Ancient Worlds* (see chap. 1, n. 11); Françoise Zonabend, "An Anthropological Perspective on Kinship and the Family," ibid.

7. Edmund Leach, *Rethinking Anthropology* (London: Athlone Press, 1961); A. R. Radcliffe-Brown and Daryll Forde, eds., *African Systems of Kinship and Marriage* (Oxford, U.K.: Oxford University Press, 1950); Kathleen Gough, "The Nayars and the Definition of Marriage," *Journal of the Royal Anthropology Institute* 89 (1959); Reynolds and Kellett, eds., *Mating and Marriage;* Leibowitz, *Females, Males, Families* (see chap 1, n. 28).

8. Royal Anthropological Institute, *Notes and Queries on Anthropology* (1951), p. 110.

9. Kathleen Gough, "The Nayar: Central Kerala," in David Schneider and Gough, eds., *Matrilineal Kinship* (Berkeley: University of California Press, 1961), and Gough, "The Nayars and the Definition of Marriage"; Eileen Krige, "Woman-Marriage, with Special Reference to the Lovedu—Its

Significance for the Definition of Marriage," *Africa* 44 (1974); Evelyn Blackwood, "Sexuality and Gender in Certain Native American Tribes: The Case of Cross-Gender Females," *Signs* 10 (1984); E. Evans-Pritchard, *Kinship and Marriage Among the Nuer* (New York: Oxford University Press, 1951); Alan Barnard and Anthony Good, *Research Practices in the Study of Kinship* (London: Academic Press, 1984), p. 90; Denise O'Brien, "Female Husbands in Southern Bantu Societies," in Alice Schegal, ed., *Sexual Stratification: A Cross-Cultural View* (New York: Columbia University Press, 1977); Ifi Amadiume, *Male Daughters, Female Husbands: Gender and Sex in an African Society* (London: Zed Books, 1987).

10. Janice Stockard, *Daughters of the Canton Delta: Marriage Patterns and Economic Strategies in South China, 1860–1930* (Palo Alto, Calif.: Stanford University Press, 1989), pp. 92–95; Crapo, *Cultural Anthropology*, pp. 220–31 (see chap. 1, n. 20).

11. Richley Crapo, *Cultural Anthropology*, pp. 106–07.

12. Suzanne Frayser, *Varieties of Sexual Experience: An Anthropological Perspective on Human Sexuality* (New Haven: HRAF Press, 1985), p. 248.

13. Pasternak, Ember, and Ember, *Sex, Gender, Kinship*, p. 85 (see chap. 1, n. 20).

14. Edmund Leach, "The Social Anthropology of Marriage and Mating," in Reynolds and Kellett, eds., *Mating and Marriage*, p. 93.

15. Edmund Leach, *Social Anthropology* (New York: Oxford University Press, 1982), pp. 206, 203.

16. Ibid., p. 210; Nikki Keddie, "Introduction," in Keddie and Baron, eds., *Women in Middle Eastern History*, p. 8 (see chap. 1, n. 11); Fatima Mernissi, *Women and Islam* (Oxford, U.K.: Basil Blackwell, 1991), p. 53; Judith Tucker, *Gender and Islamic History* (Washington, D.C.: American Historical Association, 1993), p. 6; Michael Satlow, *Jewish Marriage in Antiquity* (Princeton: Princeton University Press, 2001), p. 194.

17. Eleanor Leacock, "Montagnais Women and the Program for Jesuit Colonization," in Mona Etienne and Leacock, eds., *Women and Colonization: Anthropological Perspectives* (New York: Praeger, 1980), pp. 30–31.

18. Goody and Tambiah, *Bridewealth and Dowry*, p. 14.

19. Akira Hayami, "Illegitimacy in Japan," in Peter Laslett, Karla Oosterveen and Richard Smith, eds., *Bastardy and its Comparative History* (Cambridge, Mass.: Harvard University Press, 1980), p. 397.

20. Colin Turbull, "The Mbuti Pygmies: An Ethnographic Survey," *Anthropological Papers of the American Museum of Natural History* 18 (1965).

21. Maria Lepowsky, "Gender in an Egalitarian Society," in Peggy Sanday and Ruth Goodenough, eds., *Beyond the Second Sex* (Philadelphia: University of Pennsylvania Press, 1990), p. 192; Frayser, *Varieties of Sexual Experience*, p. 27.

22. Leach, *Social Anthropology;* Friedl, *Women and Men: An Anthropologist's View* (New York: Holt, Rinehart and Winston, 1975).

23. In many societies, adopting the role of the other sex or blurring elements of each was seen as creating a third gender and conferred high spiritual status. Leach, *Rethinking Anthropology,* pp. 107–08; Nancy Shoemaker, ed., *Negotiators of Change: Historical Perspectives on Native American Women* (New York: Routledge, 1995), p. 5; Evelyn Blackwood, ed., *The Many Faces of Homosexuality: Anthropological Approaches to Homosexual Behavior* (New York: Harrington Park Press, 1986); Walter Williams, *The Spirit and the Flesh: Sexual Diversity in American Indian Culture* (Boston: Beacon Press, 1988); Sue-Ellen Jacobs, Wesley Thomas, and Sabine Lang, eds., *Two-Spirit People: Native American Gender Identity, Sexuality, and Spirituality* (Urbana: University of Illinois Press, 1997).

24. Lucy Mair, *Marriage* (Middlesex, U.K.: Penguin, 1971), p. 78; Friedl, *Women and Men*; Alan Barnard and Anthony Good, *Research Practices in the Study of Kinship,* p. 139; Allen Johnson and Timothy Earle, *The Evolution of Human Societies: From Foraging Group to Agrarian State* (Palo Alto, Calif.: Stanford University Press, 2000); Allen Johnson, personal communication, March 14, 2003.

25. Claude Lévi-Strauss, "Introduction," Burguière et al., *Distant Worlds, Ancient Worlds,* pp. 4, 25–26 (see chap. 1, n. 11).

26. Edmund Leach, "The Social Anthropology of Marriage and Mating," in Reynolds and Kellett, eds., *Mating and Marriage;* Brian Hayden, "Pathways to Power: Principles for Creating Socioeconomic Inequities," in T. Douglas Price and Fary Feinman, eds., *Foundations of Social Inequality* (New York: Plenum Press, 1995).

27. Leach, *Social Anthropology.*

28. Friedl, *Women and Men,* p. 21.

29. Cai Hua, *A Society Without Fathers or Husbands: The Na of China,* trans. Asti Hustevdt (New York: Zone Books, 2001), p. 146 and passim. For those wondering if this is a reputable source, see the review by eminent anthropologist Clifford Geetz in *New York Review of Books* (October 18, 2001) and Tami Blumenfield, "Walking Marriages," *Anthropology News* (May 2004). See also Yang Erche Namu and Christine Matthieu, *Leaving Mother Lake: A Girlhood at the Edge of the World* (Boston: Little, Brown and Company, 2003).

Chapter 3. The Invention of Marriage

1. C. C. Uhlenbeck, *A New Series of Blackfoot Texts from the Southern Piegans Blackfoot Reservation, Teton County, Montana* (Amsterdam: Johannes Muller, 1912), p. 167.

Notes

2. Robin Fox, *The Red Lamp of Incest* (New York: E. P. Dutton, 1980), p. 147. For other versions, see Sherwood Washburn, "Tools and Human Evolution," *Scientific American* 203 (1960); Sherwood Washburn and Chet Lancaster, "The Evolution of Hunting," in Richard Lee and DeVore, eds., *Man the Hunter* (Chicago: Aldine de Gruyter Press, 1968); Lionel Tiger, *Men in Groups* (New York: Random House, 1969, 1971); Robert Ardrey, *African Genesis* (New York: Dell, 1961) and *The Hunting Hypothesis* (New York: Atheneum, 1976); Desmond Morris, *The Naked Ape* (New York: McGraw-Hill, 1967); C. Owen Lovejoy, "The Origins of Man," *Science* 211 (1981) and "Modeling Human Origins: Are We Sexy Because We Are Smart, or Smart Because We Are Sexy?," in D. T. Rasmussen, ed., *The Origin and Evolution of Humans and Humanness* (Sudbury, Mass.: Jones and Bartlett, 1993); Lionel Tiger and Robin Fox, *The Imperial Animal* (New York: Holt, Rinehart and Winston, 1971); C. Knight, *Blood Relations* (New Haven: Yale University Press, 1991). A more recent retelling argues that women manipulated their sexuality because their bodies needed the iron from the meat that the men provided. Leonard Shlain, *Sex, Time and Power* (New York: Viking, 2003).

3. E. O. Wilson, *Sociobiology: The New Synthesis* (Cambridge, Mass.: Harvard University Press, 1975), p. 553.

4. For more work disputing the male protector explanation of either primate or early hominid behavior, see Smuts, "Social Relationships and Life Histories of Primates," p. 64 (see chap. 2, n. 3); Fuentes, "Re-Evaluating Primate Monogamy," (see chap. 2, n. 3); A. C. Roosevelt, "Gender in Human Evolution," p. 366 (see chap. 1, n. 31); Zihlman, "Women's Bodies, Women's Lives," in Morbeck et al., *The Evolving Female;* Jane Balme and Wendy Beck, "Archaeology and Feminism: Views on the Origins of the Division of Labour," in Hilary du Cros and Laurajane Smith, eds., *Women in Archaeology* (Canberra: Australian National University Press, 1993); Glenn Conroy, *Reconstructing Human Origins: A Modern Synthesis* (New York: W. W. Norton, 1997); W. G. Runciman, John Maynard Smith, and R. I. M. Dunbar, eds., *Evolution of Social Behaviour Patterns in Primates and Man* (Oxford, U.K.: Oxford University Press, 1996); Dean Falk, "Brain Evolution in Females," in Lori Hager, ed., *Women in Human Evolution* (New York: Routledge, 1997), p. 128; Sally Linton, "Woman the Gatherer," in Sue-Ellen Jacobs, ed., *Women in Perspective: A Guide for Cross-cultural Studies* (Urbana: University of Illinois Press, 1971); Zihlman, "Pygmy Chimps, People and the Pundits" (see chap. 2, n. 3); Susan Sperling, "Baboons with Briefcases" (see chap. 2, n. 3); Small, *Female Choices,* 110–13 (see chap. 2, n. 3); Linda Marie Fedigan, "The Changing Role of Women in Models of Human Evolution," *Annual Review of Anthropology* 15 (1986), pp. 34–41; Zihlman, "Sex Differences and Gender Hierarchies

Among Primates" (see chap. 2, n. 3); Goodall, *The Chimpanzees of Gombe* (see chap. 2, n. 3); Adrienne Zihlman, "Did the Australopithecines Have a Division of Labor?," in Dale Walde and Norren Willows, eds., *The Archaeology of Gender: Proceedings of the Twenty-second Annual Conference of the Archaeological Association of the University of Calgary* (Calgary: University of Calgary, 1991), p. 67; Sally McBrearty and Marc Monitz, "Prostitutes or Providers? Hunting, Tool Use and Sex Roles in Earliest Homo," in Walde and Willows, *Archaeology of Gender*, p. 74; Conroy, *Reconstructing Human Origins*; Margaret Power, *The Egalitarians, Human and Chimpanzee: An Anthropological View of Social Organization* (New York: Cambridge University Press, 1991). Recently, Craig Stanford has revived the notion that meat acquisition was a very important determinant of human evolution, but he emphasizes the high degree of female choice in both subsistence activities and mating. Stanford, *The Hunting Apes and the Origins of Human Behavior* (Princeton: Princeton University Press, 1999) and *Significant Others* (New York: Basic Books, 2003). See also Christophe Boesch and Hedwige Boesch-Achermann, *The Chimpanzees of the Tai Forest: Behavioural Ecology and Evolution* (Oxford, U.K.: Oxford University Press, 2000). My thanks to Adrienne Zihlman for pointing me to many of these references and to Peta Henderson for helping me work through the recent work on hunting.

5. For this and the next two paragraphs, see Lee and DeVore, eds., *Man the Hunter.* Friedl, *Women and Men* (see chap. 2, n. 22); Nancy Tanner and Adrienne Zihlman, "Women in Evolution, Part 1: Innovation and Selection in Human Origins," *Signs* 1, no. 3 (Spring 1976); Heather Pringle, "New Women of the Ice Age," *Discover* 19 (1998); Richard Lee, *The !Kung San: Men, Women and Work in a Foraging Society* (Cambridge, U.K.: Cambridge University Press, 1979); Colin Turnbull, *The Forest People: A Study of the Pygmies of the Congo* (New York: Clarion, 1962); Richard Lee, "Population Growth and the Beginnings of Sedentary Life Among the !Kung Bushman," in Brian Spooner, ed., *Population Growth: Anthropological Implications* (Cambridge: Massachusetts Institute of Technology Press), pp. 329–42; Francis Dahlberg, *Woman the Gatherer* (New Haven: Yale University Press, 1981); Linton, "Woman the Gatherer," in Jacobs, ed., *Women in Perspective*; Patricia Draper, "!Kung Women," in Rayna Reiter, ed., *Toward an Anthropology of Women* (New York: Monthly Review Press, 1975); Sally Slocum, "Woman the Gatherer: Male Bias in Anthropology," ibid.; Paula Webster: "Matriarchy: A Vision of Power," ibid.; Eleanor Leacock and R. B. Lee, eds., *Politics and History in Band Societies* (Cambridge, U.K.: Cambridge University Press, 1982); Colin Turnbull, *Wayward Servants: The Two Worlds of the African Pygmies* (Garden City, N.Y.: Natural History Press, 1978); Lee and DeVore, eds.,

Notes

Man the Hunter; M. Goodman, P. Griffin, A. Estioko-Griffin, and J. Grove, "The Compatibility of Hunting and Mothering Among the Agta Hunter-Gatherers of the Philippines," *Sex Roles* 12 (1985); Agnes Estioko-Griffin and P. Bion Griffin, "Women Hunters: The Implications for Pleistocene Prehistory and Contemporary Ethnography," in Madeleine Goodman, ed., *Women in Asia and the Pacific: Towards an East-West Dialogue* (Honolulu: University of Hawaii Press, 1985), p. 70. Meat may be valued above its proportionate weight in the diet, and may create high status for male hunters and in some cases increase male power, but as I explain in the discussion of food sharing, women were seldom dependent on their husbands for all the meat they received, even if they were often dependent on the hunting of men as a group.

6. Christine Gailey, "Evolutionary Perspectives on Gender Hierarchy," in Beth Hess and Myra Marx Ferree, eds., *Analyzing Gender: A Handbook of Social Science Research* (Newbury Park, Calif.: Sage, 1987); Tanner and Zihlman, "Women in Evolution, Part 1"; Nancy Tanner, *On Becoming Human* (Cambridge, U.K.: Cambridge University Press, 1981); Fedigan, "Changing Role of Women." For debates on the very existence of home bases, see Richard Potts, "Home Bases and Early Hominids," *American Scientist* 72 (1984); Lewis Binford, *Bones: Ancient Men and Modern Myths* (New York: Academic Press, 1981); Walde and Willows, *Archaeology of Gender;* Chris Stringer and Clive Gamble, *In Search of the Neanderthals* (New York: Thames and Hudson, 1993); Roosevelt, "Gender in Human Evolution"; Klein, *Human Career;* Lisa Rose and Fiona Marshall, "Meat Eating, Hominid Sociality, and Home Bases Revisited," along with several comments on the paper, in *Current Anthropology* 37 (1996); Jane Lancaster, "A Feminist and Evolutionary Biologist Looks at Women," *Yearbook of Physical Anthropology* 34 (1991); M. Landau, *Narratives of Human Evolution* (New Haven: Yale University Press, 1991). See also chapter 1, note 4. A nicely constructed popular critique of the male hunting view of gender roles can be found in Rosalind Barnett and Caryl Rivers, *Same Differences* (New York: Basic Books, 2004).

7. Lila Leibowitz, "In the Beginning . . . : The Origins of the Sexual Division of Labour and the Development of the First Human Societies," in Stephanie Coontz and Peter Henderson, eds., *Women's Work, Men's Property* (London: Verso, 1986) and *Females, Males, Families* (see chap. 1, n. 28); Estioko-Griffin and Griffin, "Women Hunters"; Thomas Patterson, *Archaeology: The Historical Development of Civilizations* (Englewood Cliffs, N.J.: Prentice-Hall, 1993); Rose and Marshall, "Meat Eating, Hominid Sociality, and Home Bases Reconsidered." Robert Foley argues that early hominids had polygynous mating patterns, or male harems, with a clear division of functions between males and females. But he too agrees that

pair-bonding was an outcome, not a cause, of human evolution, and he does not argue that it was a response to female dependence on males for food or child rearing, which no single male could provide for an entire harem. He suggests that the egalitarian sexual relations and pair bonds that emerged among anatomically modern humans were a sharp break—and an evolutionary step forward—from an earlier tradition of male sexual dominance. Many other commentators do not even accept the scenario of early male dominance. Foley, "Hominids, Humans and Hunter-Gatherers: An Evolutionary Perspective" in Tim Ingold, David Riches, and James Woodburn, eds., *Hunters and Gatherers 1: History, Evolution and Social Change* (Oxford, U.K.: Berg, 1988). For more on current evolutionary theory, see Richard Leakey and Roger Lewin, *Origins Reconsidered: In Search of What Makes Us Human* (New York: Doubleday, 1992); Adrienne Zihlman, "The Paleolithic Glass Ceiling" in Hager, *Women in Human Evolution*; Tanner and Zihlman, "Women in Evolution, Part 1"; Tanner, *On Becoming Human*; Fedigan, "Changing Role of Women"; Paul Mellars, "Major Issues in the Emergence of Modern Humans," *Current Anthropology* 30 (1989); Olga Soffer, "Ancestral Lifeways in Eurasia," in Matthew Nitecki and Doris Nitecki, eds., *Origins of Anatomically Modern Human Beings* (New York: Plenum Press, 1994); Barry Cunliffe, ed., *The Oxford Illustrated Prehistory of Europe* (New York: Oxford University Press, 1994); Ofer Bar-Yosef, "The Contribution of Southwest Asia to the Study of the Origin of Modern Humans," in Nitecki and Nitecki, eds., *Origins;* Controy, *Reconstructing Human Origins;* Brian Hayden et al., "Fishing and Foraging," in Olga Soffer, ed., *The Pleistocene Old World: Regional Perspectives* (New York: Plenum Press, 1987); Patterson, *Archaeology*; Steven Mithen, "The Early Prehistory of Human Social Behaviour," in Runciman, Smith, and Dunbar, *Evolution of Social Behaviour Patterns in Primates and Man*; Colin Renfrew and Paul Bahn, *Archaeology: Theories, Methods and Practice* (New York: Thames and Hudson, 2000); Roosevelt, "Gender in Human Evolution."

8. Richard Potts, "Home Bases and Early Hominids," *American Scientist* 72 (1984); Binford, *Bones.* For recent research and debate on home bases, hearths, and nuclear family living arrangements, see Walde and Willows, *Archaeology of Gender;* Stringer and Gamble, *In Search of Neanderthals;* Roosevelt, "Gender in Human Evolution"; Klein, *Human Career;* Rose and Marshall, "Meat Eating, Hominid Sociality, and Home Bases Revisited."

9. Christopher Tilley, *An Ethnography of the Neolithic: Early Prehistoric Societies in Southern Scandinavia* (New York: Cambridge University Press, 1996); Roberta Gilchrist, *Gender and Archaeology: Contesting the Past* (New York: Routledge, 1999); Jenny Moore and Eleanor Scott, eds., *Invisible People and Processes: Writing Gender and Childhood into European Archaeology* (New

York: Leicester University Press, 1997); du Cros and Smith, *Women in Archaeology;* Hager, *Women in Human Evolution;* Leibowitz, *Females, Males, Families;* Rhoda Halperin, "Ecology and Mode of Production: Seasonal Variation and the Division of Labor by Sex Among Hunter-Gatherers," *Journal of Anthropological Research* 36 (1980), p. 391; Joan Gero, "Genderlithics: Women's Roles in Stone Tool Production," in Gero and Margaret Conkey, eds., *Engendering Archaeology: Women and Prehistory* (Oxford, U.K.: Basil Blackwell, 1991).

10. Renfrew and Bahn, *Archaeology;* Jared Diamond, *Guns, Germs and Steel: The Fates of Human Societies* (New York: W. W. Norton, 1999); Zihlman, "Sex Differences and Gender Hierarchies Among Primates." See also Allen Johnson and Timothy Earle, *The Evolution of Human Societies: From Foraging Group to Agrarian State* (Palo Alto, Calif.: Stanford University Press, 1987 and 2000). Author Robert Foley argues that early hominids lived in male-headed harems and that the invention of bands and pair bonds did not occur until modern humans replaced Neanderthals, but even in this scenario, humans lived in bands longer than any other social formation. Foley, "Hominids, Humans and Hunter-Gatherers." Allen Johnson and Timothy Earle make the case for focusing on camps rather than bands in the 2000 edition of their book.

11. In reconstructing the social life of early humans, many archaeologists supplement their fossil evidence with observations from foraging groups that were observed in more recent times. For a thoughtful discussion of what we may and may not extrapolate from recent hunter-gatherers to the past, see Johnson and Earle. Even Robert Kelly, who warns against attempts to reconstruct prehistoric foraging life from ethnographies of more recent foraging bands, agrees that similar ecological and social constraints created some patterns in the past that would have been similar to those of more recent foragers. Kelly, *The Foraging Spectrum: Diversity in Hunter-Gatherer Lifeways* (Washington, D.C.: Smithsonian Institution, 1995). My discussion of life in band-level societies draws on many of the works cited earlier, along with James Woodburn, "Egalitarian Societies," *Man* 17 (1982); "Stability and Flexibility in Hadza Residential Groupings," in Lee and DeVore, eds., *Man the Hunter;* and Peter Gardner, "Foragers' Pursuit of Individual Autonomy," *Current Anthropology* 32 (1991), pp. 550, 556. See also Lee, *The !Kung San;* Colin Turnbull, "The Mbuti Pygmies of the Congo," in J. L. Gibbs, ed., *Peoples of Africa* (New York: Holt, Rinehart and Winston, 1965); Lynne Bevan, "Skin Scrapers and Pottery Makers, 'Invisible' Women in Prehistory," in Moore and Scott, eds., *Invisible People and Processes;* Turnbull, *The Forest People.* See also Mark Cohen and Sharon Bennett, "Skeletal Evidence for Gender ·

Hierarchies in Prehistory," in Miller, *Sex and Gender Hierarchies;* Gerhard Lenski and Jean Lenski, *Human Societies: An Introduction to Macrosociology* (New York: McGraw-Hill, 1974); Naomi Quinn, "Anthropological Studies on Women's Status," *American Review of Anthropology* 6 (1977), p.18; Shelton Davis and Robert Matthews, *The Geological Imperative* (Cambridge, U.K.: Anthropology Research Centre, 1976).

12. Brian Hayden, "Pathways to Power: Principles for Creating Socioeconomic Inequalities," in T. Douglas Price and Gary Feinman, *Images of the Past* (New York: Plenum Press, 1995); Polly Wiener, "Risk, Reciprocity and Social Influences on !Kung San Economics," in Leacock and Lee, *Politics and History in Band Societies;* J. O'Shea, "Coping with Scarcity: Exchange and Social Storage," in Alison Sheridan and G. N. Bailey, eds., *Economic Anthropology: Towards an Integration of Ecological and Social Approaches* (Oxford, U.K.: British Archaeological Reports, International Series 96, 1981); Richard Lee, "Politics, Sexual and Non-Sexual, in Egalitarian Society," in Leacock and Lee, *Politics and History in Band Societies.*

13. Bruce Winterhalder, "Open Field, Common Pot: Harvest Variability and Risk Avoidance in Agricultural and Foraging Societies," in Elizabeth Cashdan, ed., *Risk and Uncertainty in Tribal and Peasant Economies* (Boulder, Colo.: Westview Press, 1990), p. 82, and "Optimal Foraging: Simulation Studies of Diet Choice in a Stochastic Environment," *Journal of Ethnobiology* 6 (1986); Brian Hayden and Rob Gargett, "Big Man, Big Heart?: A Mesoamerican View of the Emergence of Complex Society," *Ancient Mesoamerica* 1 (1990), p. 4; Elizabeth Cashdan, "Egalitarianism Among Hunters and Gatherers," *American Anthropologist* 82 (1980). See also Hillard Kaplen, Kim Hill, and A. Magdalena Hurtado, "Risk, Foraging, and Food Sharing Among the Ache," in Cashdan, ed., *Risk and Uncertainty;* Paul Graves-Brown, "Their Commonwealths Are Not as We Supposed: Sex, Gender, and Material Culture in Human Evolution," in James Steele and Stephen Shennan, eds., *The Archaeology of Human Ancestry: Power, Sex, and Tradition* (London: Routledge, 1996).

14. The *!* indicates a click sound not present in European languages. More recently, anthropologists have taken to calling the Bushmen the name they apply to themselves, the Dobe Ju/'hoansi. Lorna Marshall, "Sharing, Talking and Giving: Relief of Social Tensions Among !Kung Bushmen," *Africa* 30 (1961), p. 236; Albert Myers, ed., *William Penn's Own Account of the Lanni Lenape or Delaware Indians* (Somerset, N.J.: Middle Atlantic Press, 1970 [1683]), p. 333. For more on the sharing and hospitality traditions of the Indians of northeastern America, see my *Social Origins of Private Life: A History of American Families, 1600–1900* (London: Verso, 1988) and Eleanor Leacock, "The Montagnais-Naskapi Band," in

D. Damas, ed., *Contributions to Anthropology: Band Societies* (Ottawa: National Museum of Canada Bulletin 228, 1969).

15. Polly Wiessner, "Leveling the Hunter: Constraints on the Status Quest in Foraging Societies," in Wiessner and Wulf Schiefenhovel, eds., *Food and the Status Quest: An Interdisciplinary Perspective* (Providence: Berg Books, 1996), pp. 182–83.

16. Brian Hayden, *Archaeology: The Science of Once and Future Things* (New York: W. H. Freeman and Company, 1993).

17. Quoted in Claude Lévi-Strauss, *The Elementary Structures of Kinship* (Boston: Beacon Press, 1969 [1949]), p. 481.

18. Richley Crapo, *Cultural Anthropology* (see chap. 1, n. 20); G. Robina Quale, *A History of Marriage Systems* (New York: Greenwood Press, 1988).

19. Marvyn Meggitt, *Desert People: A Study of the Walbiri Aborigines of Central Australia* (Chicago: University of Chicago Press, 1965). In addition to the reading cited in my other notes, I was helped in my understanding of this by personal communications from Brian Hayden, Simon Fraser University, and Allen Johnson, University of California at Los Angeles, in March 2003.

20. Johnson and Earle, *Evolution of Human Societies;* Henry Sharp, "Women and Men Among the Chippewyan," in Laura Klein and Lillian Ackerman, eds., *Woman and Power in Native North America* (Norman: University of Oklahoma Press, 1995). See also Peter Gardner, "Foragers' Pursuit of Individual Autonomy," *Current Anthropology* 32 (1991); James Woodburn, "Egalitarian Societies," *Man* 17 (1982) and "Stability and Flexibility in Hadza Residential Groupings," in Lee and DeVore, eds., *Man the Hunter.*

21. Lévi-Strauss, *Elementary Structures of Kinship,* pp. 485, 116.

22. For women's important productive and reproductive value, see Margaret Ehrenberg, *Women in Prehistory* (Norman: University of Oklahoma Press, 1989); Rita Wright, "Women's Labor and Pottery Production in Prehistory," in Gero and Conkey, *Engendering Archaeology.* On the use of marriage to control and exploit women, see Gayle Rubin, "The Traffic in Women: Notes on the 'Political Economy' of Sex," in Reiter, *Toward an Anthropology of Women,* p. 175; Collier, *Marriage and Inequality;* Heidi Hartmann, "The Unhappy Marriage of Marxism and Feminism," in Lydia Sargent, ed., *Women and Revolution,* (Boston: South End Press, 1981), p. 18; Elizabeth Moen, "What Does 'Control over Our Bodies' Really Mean?," *International Journal of Women's Studies* 2 (1979); Lisette Josephides, *The Production of Inequality: Gender and Exchange Among the Kewa* (London: Tavistock, 1985). See also the articles in Zillah Eisenstein, ed., *Capitalist Patriarchy and the Case for Socialist Feminism* (New York: Monthly Review Press, 1979); Shulameth Firestone, *The Dialectic of Sex: The Case for Feminist Revolution* (New York: Morrow, 1970); Heidi

Hartmann, "The Family as the Locus of Gender, Class, and Political Struggle," *Signs* 6, no. 3 (Spring 1981); Ulku Bates, Florence Denmark, Virginia Held, et al., *Women's Realities, Women's Choices: An Introduction to Women's Studies* (New York: Oxford University Press, 1983), pp. 249–50.

23. Christine Delphy and Diana Leonard, *Familiar Exploitation: A New Analysis of Marriage in Contemporary Western Societies* (Cambridge, U.K.: Polity Press, 1992), pp. 1, 100, 258–60; Iris Marion Young, *Intersecting Voices: Dilemmas of Gender, Political Philosophy, and Power* (Princeton: Princeton University Press, 1997), p. 102, 105–06; Jaclyn Geller, *Here Comes the Bride: Women, Weddings, and the Marriage Mystique* (New York: Four Walls Eight Windows, 2001), pp. 18–19.

24. Alan Klein, "Adaptive Strategies and Process on the Plains: The 19th Century Cultural Sink" Ph.D dissertation, State University of New York at Buffalo, 1976, p. 103.

25. Pekka Hamalainen, "The Rise and Fall of Plains Indian Horse Cultures," *Journal of American History* (December 2003); Klein, "Adaptive Strategies" and "The Political Economy of Gender: A 19th Century Plains Indian Case Study," in Patricia Albers and Beatrice Medicine, eds., *The Hidden Half: Studies of Plains Indian Women* (Washington, D.C.: University Press of America, 1983); Oscar Lewis, "Effects of White Contact upon Blackfoot Culture," *Monographs of the American Ethnological Society* 6 (1942); George Catlin, *Letters and Notes on the Manners, Customs and Condition of the North American Indians* (New York: Gramercy, 1973) 1; Klein, "Political Economy of Gender"; Patricia Albers, "Sioux Women in Transition: A Study of Their Changing Status in Domestic and Capitalist Sectors of Production," in Albers and Medicine, *The Hidden Half.*

26. Karen Sacks, *Sisters and Wives: The Past and Future of Gender Inequality* (Westport, Conn.: Greenwood Press, 1979); Diane Bell, "Desert Politics: Choices in the Marriage Market," in Mona Etienne and Eleanor Leacock, *Women and Colonization* (see chap. 2, n. 17); Christine Gailey, "Evolutionary Perspectives on Gender Hierarchy," in Hess and Ferree, eds., *Analyzing Gender,* p. 48; Jack Goody, "Marriage Prestations, Inheritance and Descent in Pre-Industrial Societies," *Journal of Comparative Family Studies* 1 (1971), p. 4; Peggy Reeves Sanday, "The Reproduction of Patriarchy in Feminist Anthropology," in Mary McGanney Gigen, ed., *Feminist Thought and the Structure of Knowledge* (New York: NewYork University Press, 1988), pp. 55–56; Kathleen Gough, "Variation in Residence," in David Schneider and Gough, *Matrilineal Kinship* (see chap. 2, n. 9); Karla Poewe, "Matriliny in the Throes of Change," *Africa* 48 (1978); C. Lancaster, "Gwembe Valley Marriage Prestations in Historical Perspective," *American Anthropologist* 83 (1981); Kay Martin and Barbara Voorhies, *Female of the Species* (New York: Columbia University Press, 1975); Jill Nash, "A Note

on Groomprice," *American Anthropologist,* 80 (1978); Alice Schlegal, *Sexual Stratification: A Cross-cultural View* (see chap. 2, n. 9).

27. Suzanne Frayser, *Varieties of Sexual Experience,* p. 27 (see chap. 2, n. 12); Cashdan, "Egalitarianism Among Hunters and Gatherers"; Lepowsky, "Gender in an Egalitarian Society" (see chap. 2, n. 21); John Noble Wilford, "Sexes Equal on South Sea Isle," *New York Times,* March 29, 1994, pp. C1, C11; Barry Hewlett, "Husband–Wife Reciprocity and the Father-Infant Relationship Among Aka Pygmies," in Barry Hewlett, ed., *Father-Child Relations: Cultural and Biosocial Contexts* (New York: Aldine de Gruyter, 1992); Karen Endicott, "Fathering in an Egalitarian Society" ibid.; Barry Hewlett, *Intimate Fathers: The Nature and Context of Aka Pygmy Paternal Infant Care* (Ann Arbor: University of Michigan Press, 1992); Eleanor Leacock, "Introduction," in Leacock and Nancy Oestreich Lurie, eds., *North American Indians in Historical Perspective* (New York: Random House, 1971), p. 23; Frederick Eggan, *Social Organization of the Western Pueblos* (Chicago: University of Chicago Press, 1969); Lurie, "Indian Women: A Legacy of Freedom," in Charles Jones, ed., *Look to the Mountain Top* (San Jose, Calif.: H. M. Gousha, 1972); Karen Anderson, *Chain Her by One Foot* (New York: Routledge, 1991); Baron LaHontan, *New Voyages to North America,* [1703], ed. Reuben Thwaites, (New York: B. Franklin, 1970) vol. 2, p. 463; Cornelius Jaenan, *Friend and Foe: Aspects of French-Amerindian Cultural Contact in the Sixteenth and Seventeenth Centuries* (New York: Columbia University Press, 1976) p. 86; Theda Purdue, *Cherokee Women: Gender and Culture Change, 1700–1835* (Lincoln: University of Nebraska Press, 1999); Marvin K. Opler, "The Ute and Paiute Indians of the Great Basin Southern Rim," in Leacock and Lurie, *North American Indians.*

28. Pasternak, Ember, and Ember, *Sex, Gender, and Kinship* (see chap. 1, n. 20); Friedl, *Women and Men;* Jane Collier, *Marriage and Inequality in Classless Societies* (see chap. 1, n. 25); Karen Brodkin Sacks, review of Collier, *American Anthropologist* 92 (1990); Marshall Sahlins, "The Segmentary Lineage: An Organization of Predatory Expansion," *American Anthropologist* 63 (1961); Alan Barnard and Anthony Good, *Research Practices in the Study of Kinship* (see chap. 1, n. 9); Anderson, *"Chain Her by One Foot";* Richard Sattler, "Muskogee and Cherokee Women's Status," in Laura Klein and Lillian Ackerman, eds., *Women and Power in Native North America* (Norman: University of Oklahoma Press, 1995), p. 226; Christine Gailey, *Kinship to Kinship: Gender Hierarchy and State Formation in the Tongan Islands* (Austin: University of Texas, 1987), pp. 11–13. Jane Collier, *Marriage and Inequality in Classless Society* argues that the dependence of men on marriage among the Plains Indian groups she studied led them to restrict female autonomy and force women into marriage. But she

admits that husbands and parents were usually unable to prevent a woman from leaving a husband, taking a lover, or running off with another man.

29. The most widely accepted outlines of such social change usually draw on Elman Service's account of a historical transition from bands to tribes and from tribes to chiefdoms and states. This is often combined with Morton Fried's categorization of social evolution as proceeding from egalitarian societies, where social status was acquired individually and did not confer power to command the labor or tribute of others, to ranked societies, which involved some inheritance of property and social status by leading lineages, and then to stratified societies, marked by strong, largely inherited differences in wealth and power. Allen Johnson and Timothy Earle believe that the earliest human societies were small collections of families that congregated together in camps or hamlets but periodically dispersed into smaller units in reaction to disputes within the camp or for the purpose of spreading out over more territory during certain times of the year. Only later in history, they argue, did a larger number of families form a more permanent association based on such shared interests as defense or food storage. Only later still, under very specific circumstances, did there emerge a regional polity, in which larger groups were incorporated under the leadership or control of a hereditary elite. Elman Service, *Primitive Social Organization* (New York: Random House, 1962) and *Origins of the State and Civilization* (New York: W. W. Norton, 1975); Morton Fried, *The Evolution of Political Society* (New York: Random House, 1967); Johnson and Earle, *The Evolution of Human Societies.* Many scholars argue that change did not evolve in a linear way, but that complex chiefdoms or empires periodically arose and then collapsed, creating a variety of hybrid political, ecological, and social forms. Susan Gregg, *Foragers and Farmers: Population Interaction and Agricultural Expansion in Prehistoric Europe* (Chicago: University of Chicago Press, 1988); Mark Cohen, "Prehistoric Hunter-Gatherers: The Meaning of Cultural Complexity," in Price and Brown, *Prehistoric Hunter-Gatherers;* K. Ekholm and J. Friedman, "'Capital' Imperialism and Exploitation in Ancient World Systems," in Andre Gunder Frank and Barry Gills, *The World System: Five Hundred Years or Five Thousand?* (New York: Routledge, 1991); Ernest Burch and Linda Ellana, *Key Issues in Hunter-Gatherer Research* (Oxford, U.K.: Berg, 1994); Price and Brown, *Prehistoric Hunter-Gatherers* (see chap. 2, n. 12); Harry Lourandos, "Pleistocene Australia," in Soffer, ed., *The Pleistocene Old World;* Claude Meillasoux, *Maidens, Meal and Money: Capitalism and the Domestic Community* (Cambridge, U.K.: Cambridge University Press, 1981); Lewis Binford, "Post-Pleistocene Adaptations," in Stuart Struever, ed., *Prehistoric Agriculture* (Garden City, N.Y.: Natural History Press, 1971); Kelly, *The Foraging Spectrum;* Crapo, *Cultural Anthropology;* Peter Mitchell, Royden Yates,

and John Parkington, "At the Transition: The Archaeology of the Pleistocene-Holocene Boundary in Southern Africa," in Lawrence Strauss et al., *Humans at the End of the Ice Age: The Archaeology of the Pleistocene-Holocene Transition* (New York: Plenum Press, 1996).

30. Stephen Plog, "Social Dynamics in the Pueblo Southwest," in Price and Feinman, *Foundations of Social Inequality,* pp. 196–97. For more on the processes described in this and the next paragraph, see Marie Louise Stig, *Gender Archaeology* (Cambridge: Polity Press, 2000), p. 165; Michelle Hegman, "The Risks of Sharing and Sharing as Risk Reduction: Interhousehold Food Sharing in Egalitarian Societies," in Susan Gregg, ed., *Between Bands and States* (Carbondale: Southern Illinois University, 1991); Christopher Tilley, *An Ethnography of the Neolithic;* Mithen, "The Mesolithic Age," in Cunliffe, *Oxford Illustrated Prehistory of Euope;* Renfrew and Bahn, *Archaeology;* Grahame Clark and Stuart Piggott, *Prehistoric Societies* (New York: Alfred A. Knopf, 1972); John Robb, "Gender Contradictions, Moral Coalitions, and Inequality in Prehistoric Italy," *Journal of European Archaeology* 2 (1994); Richard Pearson, "Social Complexity in Chinese Coastal Neolithic Sites," *Science* 213 (1981); John Bintliff, "The Neolithic in Europe and Social Evolution," in Bintliff, ed., *European Social Evolution: Archaeological Perspectives* (London: University of Bradford, 1984); Russell Handsman, "Whose Art Was Found at Lepenski Vir: Gender Relations and Power in Archaeology," in Gero and Conkey, eds., *Engendering Archaeology;* Harry Lourandos, "Intensification and Australian Prehistory," in Price and Brown, *Prehistoric Hunter-Gatherers;* Brenda Kennedy, *Marriage Patterns in an Archaic Population: A Study of Skeletal Remains from Port au Choic, Newfoundland* (Ottawa: National Museums of Canada, 1981); Ian Hodder, *Symbols in Action* (Cambridge, U.K.: Cambridge University Press, 1982); R.W. Hutchinson, *Prehistoric Crete* (Baltimore: Penguin, 1962); Susan Pollock, *Ancient Mesopotamia: The Eden that Never Was* (New York: Cambridge University Press, 1999).

31. Dolores Jewsiewicki, "Lineage Mode of Production: Social Inequalities in Equatorial Africa," in Donald Crummey and C. C. Steward, eds. *Modes of Production in Africa: The Precolonial Era* (Beverly Hills, Calif.: Sage, 1981); Suzanne Wemple, *Women in Frankish Society: Marriage and the Cloister, 500–900* (Philadelphia: University of Pennsylvania Press, 1981); Collier, *Marriage and Inequality in Classless Societies;* H. K. Schneider, *The Wahi Wanyaturu: Economics in an African Society,* (Chicago: Aldine, 1970); Schneider and Gough, eds., *Matrilineal Kinship* (see chap. 2, n. 9); Jonathan Friedman and M. J. Rowlands, "Notes Towards an Epigenetic Model of the Evolution of 'Civilization,'" in Friedman and Rowlands, eds., *The Evolution of Social Systems* (Pittsburgh: University of Pittsburgh Press, 1978), pp. 207–13; Hayden, "Pathways to Power," pp. 42–44;

Kristian Kristiansen and Michael Rowlands, *Social Transformations in Archaeology: Global and Local Perspectives* (New York: Routledge, 1998); Colin Haselgrove, "Wealth, Prestige and Power: The Dynamics of Late Iron Age Political Centralisation in South-East England," in Colin Renfrew and Stephen Shennan, eds., *Ranking, Resource, and Exchange: Aspects of the Archaeology of Early European Society* (New York: Cambridge University Press, 1982), p. 81. I thank Brian Hayden for his helpful clarification of the role of bridewealth in putting junior men in debt to elders.

32. Studies of genetic material from the remains of prehistoric people show that many populations interbred much more widely than would be expected if marriage was occurring between the same communities and kin groups over and over again, as happens once marriage becomes a way of concentrating people and resources in a few linked kin groups and excluding others from participation in the exchange. Only over time did highly restrictive marriage systems develop. Archaeologist Kristian Kristiansen suggests that exogamous and endogamous forms of marriage alternated in Europe during the Neolithic Era and the Bronze Age. In times of expansion based on raiding or war, elites constructed marriage alliances with distant kingdoms, whereas during periods of territorial consolidation or intensification of agriculture, marriage was more likely to take place with neighbors and local kin, in order to concentrate and preserve property. Lawrence Straus, "The Last Glacial Maximum in Cantabrian Spain," in Olga Soffer and Clive Gamble, eds., *The World at 18,000 BC* (London: Unwin Hyman, 1990), vol. 1, p. 106; Janette Deacon, "Changes in the Archaeological Record in South Africa," ibid., vol. 2, p. 183. John Bintliff, "Iron Age Europe in the Context of Social Evolution from the Bronze Age Through to Historic Times," in Bintliff, ed., *European Social Evolution;* Brenda Kennedy, *Marriage Patterns in an Archaic Population;* Strauss et al., *Humans at the End of the Ice Age;* William Marquardt, "Complexity and Scale in the Study of Fisher-Gatherer-Hunters: An Example from the Eastern United States," in Price and Brown, *Prehistoric Hunter-Gatherers;* Stringer and Gamble, *In Search of the Neanderthals;* Whittle, *Europe in the Neolithic;* Silvana Tarli and Elena Repetto, "Sex Differences in Human Populations: Change Through Time," in Mary Ellen Morbeck, Alison Galloway, and Adrienne Zihlman, eds., *The Evolving Female* (see chap. 2, n. 3); Cohen and Bennett (1993), cited in Roosevelt, "Gender in Human Evolution"; Kristiansen, *Europe Before History.* The ultimate endogamous marriage is between brother and sister, a practice that was surprisingly common (and was considered sacred rather than sinful) among aristocrats and rulers in several ancient kingdoms, such as Egypt, Hawaii, and the Inca Empire in Peru. See Keith Hopkins, "Brother-Sister Marriage in Roman Egypt," *Comparative Studies in*

Society and History 22 (1980); Roger Middleton, "Brother–Sister and Father–Daughter Marriage in Ancient Egypt," *American Sociological Review* 27 (1962); W. H. Davenport, "The Hawaiian 'Cultural Revolution': Some Political and Economic Considerations," *American Anthropologist* 71 (1969).

33. Roland Lardinois, in Burguière et al., *Distant Worlds, Ancient Worlds.*

34. Frank Alvarez-Pereyre and Florence Heymann, "The Hebrew Family Model," ibid., p. 181.

35. Yan Thomas, "Fathers as Citizens of Rome," ibid., pp. 230–32; Karen Lang, "Women in Ancient Literature," in Bella Vivante, ed., *Women's Roles in Ancient Civilizations: A Reference Guide* (Westport, Conn.: Greenwood Press, 1999), p. 44. Unlike European Christians, Romans and Greeks had no objection to adopting unrelated children or adults in order to perpetuate their family succession. But they were downright paranoid about the possibility that their *wives* might present them with children they hadn't fathered. The difference was logical. An adopted heir had to relinquish all ties to his family of origin. But when a child was born into a family under false pretenses, there was always the danger that the mother might someday activate the child's ties with the biological father or his family.

36. Joan Huber, "Comparative Gender Stratification," in Janet Chafetz, ed., *Handbook of the Sociology of Gender* (New York: Kluwer, 1999), pp. 70–76; Marvin Harris, "The Evolution of Human Gender Hierarchies," in Barbara Miller, ed., *Sex and Gender Hierarchies* (New York: Cambridge University Press, 1993); Claire Robertson and Iris Berger, "Introduction," in Robertson and Berger, eds., *Woman and Class in Africa* (New York: Africana Publishing Company, 1986), p. 5; Gerda Lerner, *The Creation of Patriarchy* (New York: Oxford University Press, 1986), p. 83. On the variety of gender systems, see Peter Stearns, *Gender in World History* (New York: Routledge, 2000), pp. 8–37. For a description of changing gender roles with the development of the plow and of warrior aristocracies in prehistoric Italy, see Robb, "Gender Contradictions."

37. Hayden, "Pathways to Power," 59; Nikki Keddie, "Introduction," in Keddie and Baron, eds., *Women in Middle Eastern History,* p. 2 (see chap. 1, n. 11); Howard Levy, *Chinese Foot Binding* (New York: W. Rawls, 1966).

38. Leila Ahmed, *Women and Gender in Islam* (New Haven: Yale University Press, 1992), pp. 14–15; Karen Nemet-Nejat, "Women in Ancient Mesopotamia," in Vivante, *Women's Roles,* p. 91.

39. Peta Henderson, "Women in Mesopotamia," unpublished paper, the Evergreen State Colllege, 1978; Stephanie Dalley, *Mari and Karana: Two Old Babylonian Cities* (Piscataway, New Jersey: Gorgias Press, 2002); Peter Stearns, *Gender in World History* (London: Routledge, 2000), pp. 9–18; Jerry Bentley and Herbert Ziegler, *Traditions and Encounters: A Global Perspective on the Past, vol. 1, From the Beginnings to 1500* (Boston:

McGraw-Hill, 2000); Barbara Lesko, "Women of Ancient Egypt and Western Asia," in Renate Bridenthal, Susan Stuard, and Merry Wiesner, eds., *Becoming Visible: Women in European History,* 3d ed. (Boston: Houghton Mifflin, 1998), pp. 39–40.

40. Ebrey, *The Inner Quarters,* pp. 45, 50 (see chap. 1, n. 23).
41. Karen Sacks, "Engels Revisited: Women, the Organization of Production, and Private Property," in Michelle Rosaldo and Louise Lamphere, eds., *Women, Culture, and Society* (Palo Alto, Calif.: Stanford University Press, 1974). On the varying costs and benefits of marriage in different ancient states, see Barbara Lesko, "Women of Ancient Egypt and Western Asia," in Bridenthal, Stuard, and Wiesner, eds., *Becoming Visible.*
42. Harry Willekens, "Is Contemporary Western Family Law Historically Unique?," *Journal of Family History* 28 (2003).

Chapter 4. Soap Operas of the Ancient World

1. For information on Mari, see Jean-Jacques Glassner, "From Sumer to Babylon," in André Burguière et al., *Distant Worlds, Ancient Worlds* (see chap. 1, n. 11); B. F. Batto, *Studies on Woman at Mari* (Baltimore: Johns Hopkins University Press, 1974); Stephanie Dalley, *Mari and Karana* (Piscataway, N.J.: Gorgias Press, 2002). For other examples of marriage politics in the ancient Middle East, see William Hallo and William Simpson, *The Ancient Near East: A History* (New York: Harcourt College Publishers, 1998), p. 33; Annie Forgeau, "The Pharaonic Order," in Burguière et al., *Distant Worlds, Ancient Worlds,* p. 132; *Letters from Mesopotamia: Official, Business, and Private Letters on Clay Tablets from Two Millennia,* trans. and with an introduction by A. Leo Oppenheim (Chicago: University of Chicago Press, 1967).
2. The quotation is from Dalley, *Mari and Karana,* pp. 108–09.
3. For this and the next paragraph, see Anne Kinney, "Women in Ancient China," in Vivante, *Women's Roles in Ancient Civilizations,* p. 25 (see chap. 3, n. 35).
4. Retha Warnicke, *The Marrying of Anne of Cleves: Royal Protocol in Early Modern England* (Cambridge, UK: Cambridge University Press, 2000), pp. 3–4.
5. *Letters from Mesopotamia,* p. 120. For an account of how the Incas used the same techniques in Peru many centuries later, see Irene Silverblatt, *Moon, Sun, and Witches: Gender Ideologies and Class in Inca and Colonial Peru* (Princeton: Princeton University Press, 1987); Susan Niles, "Women in the Ancient Andes," in Vivante, ed., *Women's Roles,* pp. 323–26.
6. Barbara Watterson, *Women in Ancient Egypt* (see chap. 1, n. 17).
7. Gay Robins, *Women in Ancient Egypt* (Cambridge, U.K.: Cambridge University Press, 1993), pp. 34–35.

8. Kristian Kristiansen and Michael Rowlands, *Social Transformations in Archaeology: Global and Local Perspectives* (New York: Routledge, 1998); Daniel Ogden, *Polygamy, Prostitutes and Death: The Hellenistic Dynasties* (London: Duckworth Press, 1999).

9. Beverly Bossler, *Powerful Relations: Kinship, Status, and the State in Sung China (960–1279)* (Cambridge, Mass.: Council on East Asian Studies, Harvard University Press, 1998).

10. Melvin Thatcher, "Marriages of the Ruling Elite in the Spring and Autumn Period," in Rubie Watson and Patricia Buckley Ebrey, *Marriage and Inequality in Chinese Society* (Berkeley: University of California Press, 1991), pp. 66–67.

11. Watterson, *Women in Ancient Egypt.*

12. Thatcher, "Marriages of the Ruling Elite in the Spring and Autumn Period."

13. Jacques Soustelle, *Daily Life of the Aztecs on the Eve of the Spanish Conquest* (Palo Alto, Calif.: Stanford University Press, 1961), p 183.

14. Lerner, *Creation of Patriarchy* (see chap. 3, n. 31), p. 113; Watterson, *Women in Ancient Egypt,* p. 157; Soustelle, *Daily Life of the Aztecs,* pp. 65 and note 59, p. 264.

15. For this and the next two paragraphs, see Watterson, *Women in Ancient Egypt,* p. 151; Robins, *Women in Ancient Egypt,* p. 32; Glassner, "From Sumer to Babylon"; Forgeau, "The Pharaonic Order"; Elizabeth Carney, "The Reappearance of Royal Sibling Marriage in Ptolemaic Egypt," *La Parola del Passato* 237 (1987).

16. Rubie Watson, "Marriage and Gender Inequality," in Watson and Ebrey, eds., *Marriage and Inequality in Chinese Society.*

17. Robins, *Women in Ancient Egypt.*

18. Ogden, *Polygamy, Prostitutes and Death.*

19. Ibid.

20. Sarah Pomeroy, *Goddesses, Whores, Wives, and Slaves: Women in Classical Antiquity* (New York: Schocken, 1975).

21. Plutarch, "Life of Marcus Antonius," in William Shakespeare, *Antony and Cleopatra* (New York: New American Library, 1964), p. 195.

22. The material in this and the following paragraphs is based on Pomeroy, *Goddesses, Whores;* Ogden, *Polygamy;* J. P. V. D. Balsdon, *Roman Women: Their History and Habits* (New York: John Day Co., 1963); Susan Treggiari, *Roman Marriage: Iusti Coniuges from the Time of Cicero to the Time of Ulpian* (Oxford, U.K.: Oxford University Press, 1991).

23. Jo Ann McNamara, "Matres Patriae/Matres Ecclesiae: Women of Rome," in Renate Bridenthal, Susan Stuard, and Merry Wiesner, eds., *Becoming Visible* (see chap. 3, n. 39).

24. Ivan Morris, *The World of the Shining Prince: Court Life in Ancient Japan* (New York: Alfred A. Knopf, 1964).

25. Patricia Tsurimi, "Japan's Early Female Emperors," *Historical Reflections* 8 (1981).

26. Giulia Sissa, "The Family in Ancient Athens," in Burguière, *Distant Worlds, Ancient Worlds;* Pomeroy, *Goddesses, Whores.*

27. Yan Thomas, "Fathers as Citizens of Rome," in Burguière et al., *Distant Worlds, Ancient Worlds;* Treggiari, *Roman Marriage.*

28. Marilyn Katz, "Daughters of Demeter: Women in Ancient Greece," in Bridenthal, Stuard, and Wiesner, eds., *Becoming Visible,* p. 65; Dixon, *The Roman Family,* p. 67 (see chap. 1, n. 16).

29. Bruce Thornton, *Eros: The Myth of Ancient Greek Sexuality* (Boulder, Colo.: Westview Press, 1997), pp. 167–68; W. K. Lacey, *The Family in Classical Greece* (Ithaca, N.Y.: Cornell University Press, 1968) p. 115.

30. Elaine Fantham et al., *Women in the Classical World: Image and Text* (New York: Oxford University Press, 1994), p. 123; Lacey, *The Family in Classical Greece,* pp. 71–72.

31. Forgeau, "The Pharaonic Order."

32. Susan Niles, "Women in the Ancient Andes," in Vivante, ed., *Women's Roles;* Gailey, *Kinship to Kingship* (see chap. 3, n. 28); Johnson and Earle, *Evolution of Human Societies* (see chap. 3, n. 10). Slaves, however, were frequently forbidden to marry. Marc Van de Mierop, "Women in the Economy of Sumer," in Barbara Lesko, ed., *Women's Earliest Records from Ancient Egypt and Western Asia* (Atlanta: Scholars Press, 1989); Lerner, *The Creation of Patriarchy;* Rita Wright, "Technology, Gender and Class: Worlds of Difference in Ur III Mesopotamia," in Wright, ed., *Gender and Archaeology* (Philadelphia: University of Pennsylvania Press, 1996).

33. Judith Evans Grubbs, "'Marriage More Shameful than Adultery': Slave-Mistress Relationships, 'Mixed Marriages,' and Late Roman Law," *Phoenix* XLVII (1993), p. 125; Pomeroy, *Goddesses, Whores,* pp. 193–95; Dixon, *Roman Family,* pp. 92, 124; Jo Ann McNamara, "Matres Patriae/Matres Ecclesiae: Women of Rome," in Bridenthal, Stuard, and Wiesner, eds., *Becoming Visible,* p. 88.

34. David Cherry, ed., *The Roman World: A Sourcebook* (Malden, Mass.: Blackwell Publishing, 2001), pp. 70–78.

Chapter 5. Something Borrowed . . .

1. My sources for the discussion of Greece, unless otherwise noted, include Sarah Pomeroy, *Families in Classical and Hellenistic Greece* (Oxford: Clarendon Press, 1997); Lacey, *Family in Classical Greece;* Katz, "Daughters of Demeter" (see chap. 4, n. 28); Marilyn Arthur, "'Liberated' Women: The Classical

Era," in Bridenthal et al., eds., *Becoming Visible* (see chap. 3, n. 39); Victor Ehrenberg, *The Greek State* (New York: W. W. Norton, 1964); M. T. W. Arnheim, *Aristocracy in Greek Society* (London: Thames and Hudson, 1977); Chester Starr, *The Economic and Social Growth of Early Greece, 800–500 B.C.* (New York: Oxford University Press, 1977); Gustave Glotz, *The Greek City and Its Institutions* (New York: Barnes and Noble, 1969); Victor Ehrenberg, *The People of Aristophanes* (New York: Schocken, 1962); Pomeroy, *Goddesses, Whores* (see chap. 4, n. 20); Giula Sissa, "The Family in Ancient Athens," in Burguière et al., *Distant Worlds, Ancient Worlds* (see chap. 1, n. 11); Cynthia Patterson, *The Family in Greek History* (Cambridge, Mass.: Harvard University Press, 1998); Cheryl Anne Cox, *Household Interests: Property, Marriage Strategies, and Family Dynamics in Ancient Athens* (Princeton: Princeton University Press, 1998).

2. Aeschylus, *The Oresteian Trilogy,* trans. Philip Vellacott (London: Penguin Books, 1969), p. 47. The quotes in the next few paragraphs come from pp. 50, 147, 168, 169, and 176 respectively. For a somewhat different reading of the play, but one that I believe complements my analysis, Cynthia Patterson, *Family in Greek History.*

3. Katz, "Daughters of Demeter"; Thornton, *Eros* (see chap. 4, n. 29).

4. Eva Cantarella, *Pandora's Daughters: The Role and Status of Women in Greek and Roman Antiquity* (Baltimore: Johns Hopkins University Press, 1981), p. 46; Fantham et al., *Women in the Classical World* (see chap. 4, n. 30).

5. Thornton, *Eros.*

6. Cantarella, *Pandora's Daughters.*

7. For the first argument, see Arthur, "Liberated Women," p. 79. For the second, see Pomeroy, *Goddesses, Whores,* pp. 179–85. See also Peter Stearns, *Gender in World History* (New York: Routledge, 2000), p. 15.

8. Unless otherwise noted, the information about Roman marriage comes primarily from Dixon, *The Roman Family* (see chap. 1, n. 16); Treggiari, *Roman Marriage* (see chap. 4, n. 22).

9. Mary Lefkowitz and Maureen Fant, *Women's Lives in Greece & Rome: A Source Book in Translation* (London: Duckworth Press, 1992), p. 187.

10. K. R. Bradley, *Discovering the Roman Family: Studies in Roman Social History* (New York: Oxford University Press, 1991); Dixon, *Roman Family;* Treggiari, *Roman Marriage;* David Herlihy, *Medieval Households* (Cambridge, Mass.: Harvard University Press, 1985).

11. Ulpian's *Rules,* excerpted in Emilie Ant, ed., *Women's Lives in Medieval Europe: A Sourcebook* (New York: Routledge, 1993), p. 34.

12. Treggiari, *Roman Marriage,* p. 54.

13. David Cherry, ed., *The Roman World: A Sourcebook* (Malden, Mass.: Blackwell Publishing, 2001), p. 55.

14. Ibid., p. 53.

15. Lefkowitz and Fant, *Women's Life,* p. 112; Dixon, *Roman Family,* p. 51; Treggiari, *Roman Marriage,* pp. 441–65.

16. Philip Reynolds, *Marriage in the Western Church: The Christianization of Marriage During the Patristic and Early Medieval Periods* (Leiden: E. J. Brill, 1994).

17. In addition to Dixon and Treggiari, see A. S. Gatwick, "Free or Not So Free? Wives and Daughters in the Late Roman Republic," in Elizabeth Craik, ed., *Marriage and Property* (Aberdeen, U.K.: Aberdeen University Press, 1984).

18. Ibid.; Jo-Marie Claassen, "Documents of a Crumbling Marriage: The Case of Cicero and Terentia," *Phoenix* 50 (1996); Judith Evans Grubbs, "'Pagan' and 'Christian' Marriage," *Journal of Early Christian Studies* 2 (1994).

19. Lefkowitz and Fant, *Women's Life,* pp. 164–65. See also Judith Hallett, *Fathers and Daughters in Roman Society: Women and the Elite Family* (Princeton: Princeton University Press, 1984). Studies of connubial epitaphs show that Roman husbands' description of their departed wives were much more individualized than Greeks', recording specific endearing qualities rather the conventional phrases. R. B. Lattimore, *Themes in Greek and Latin Epitaphs* (Urbana: University of Illinois Press, 1942).

20. Quoted in Craig Williams, *Roman Homosexuality: Ideologies of Masculinity in Classical Antiquity* (New York: Oxford University Press, 1999), p. 52.

21. For this and the following paragraphs, see Gordon Williams, "Representations of Roman Women in Literature," in Diana Kleiner and Susan Matheson, eds., *I Claudia: Women in Ancient Rome* (New Haven: Yale University Art Gallery, 1996), p. 133; Donna Hurley, "Livia (Wife of Augustus)," in Online Encyclopedia of Roman Emperors, www.romanemperors.org/livia.htm#N_2.(1999). Accessed April 25, 2002.

22. Suetonius Tranquillus, *Lives of the Caesars,* Book III, *Tiberius,* VII:2, trans. J. C. Rolfe (Cambridge, Mass.: Harvard University Press, 1964–65), pp. 302–03; Treggiari, *Roman Marriage,* p. 47.

23. The Augustan legislation discussed here and in the following paragraphs is described in detail in Treggiari, *Roman Marriage,* and Dixon, *Roman Family.* See also Will Durant, *Caesar and Christ* (New York: Simon & Schuster, 1944).

24. Grubbs, "'Pagan' and 'Christian' Marriage."

25. Treggiari, *Roman Marriage.*

26. Durant, *Caesar and Christ,* p. 230 and note 40, p. 686.

27. Williams, "Representations of Roman Women," p. 133.

28. On Hindu beliefs, see Mani Ram Sharma, *Marriage in Ancient India* (Delhi: Agam Kala Prakashan, 1993); V. V. Prakasa Rao and V. Nandini Rao, *Marriage, the Family and Women in India* (New Delhi: Heritage

Publishers, 1982). On marriage and the history of Judaism, see Carol Meyers, *Discovering Eve: Ancient Israelite Women in Context* (New York: Oxford University Press, 1988); Alan Segal, *Rebecca's Children: Judaism and Christianity in the Roman World* (Cambridge, Mass.: Harvard University Press, 1986); Norman Gottwald, *The Tribes of Yahweh: A Sociology of the Religion of Liberated Israel* (Maryknoll, NY: Orbis Press, 1979); Michael Coogan, ed., *The Oxford History of the Biblical World* (New York: Oxford University Press, 1998); Naomi Steinberg, *Kinship and Marriage in Genesis: A Household Economics Perspective* (Minneapolis: Augsburg Fortress, 1993); Arlene Swidler, ed., *Marriage Among the Religions of the World* (Lewiston, Maine: Edward Mellen Press, 1990); Satlow, *Jewish Marriage in Antiquity,* pp. 131–61 (see chap. 2, n. 16).

29. There were dissenting voices. In the late fourth century the monk Jovian scandalized most other Christian scholars by arguing that there was no real difference in the virtue of a virgin and that of a married person. "Be not proud," Jovian admonished the virgin, for "you and your married sisters are members of the same church" and share the same merit. But Jovian's beliefs were officially repudiated by church synods in Rome and Milan. David Hunter, *Marriage in the Early Church* (Minneapolis: Fortress Press, 1992), pp. 16–21. Pope Gregory, quoted in Pierre Guichard and Jean-Pierre Cuviller, "Barbarian Europe," in Burguière et al., *Distant Worlds, Ancient Worlds,* p. 331. My sources for the discussion of Greece, unless otherwise noted, include Sarah Pomeroy, *Families in Classical and Hellenistic Greece;* Lacey, *The Family in Classical Greece;* Katz, "Daughters of Demeter"; Marilyn Arthur, "'Liberated' Women: The Classical Era," in Bridenthal and Koonz, eds., *Becoming Visible;* Ehrenberg, *The Greek State;* Arnheim, *Aristocracy in Greek Society;* Starr, *The Economic and Social Growth of Early Greece;* Glotz, *The Greek City and its Institutions;* Ehrenberg, *The People of Aristophanes;* Pomeroy, *Goddesses, Whores;* Giula Sissa, "The Family in Ancient Athens"; Patterson, *The Family in Greek History;* Cox, *Household Interests.*

Chapter 6. Playing the Bishop, Capturing the Queen

1. On Byzantium, see Angeliki Laiou, "Sex, Consent, and Coercion in Byzantium," in Laiou, ed., *Consent and Coercion to Sex and Marriage in Ancient and Medieval Societies* (Washington, D.C.: Dumbarton Oaks Research Library and Collection, 1993); Dion Smythe, "Behind the Mask: Empresses and Empire in Middle Byzantium," in Anne Duggan, ed., *Queens and Queenship in Medieval Europe* (Woodbridge, U.K.: Boydell Press, 1995); Keith Hopkins, *Conquerors and Slaves* (New York: Cambridge University Press, 1978); Lynda Garland, *Byzantine Empresses: Women and Power in Byzantium AD 527–1204* (New York: Routledge,

Notes

1999); Janet Nelson, "Gender, Memory and Social Power," *Gender & History* 12 (2000). On royal wives in the West, see Duggan, *Queens and Queenship* and Pauline Stafford, *Queens, Concubines, and Dowagers: The King's Wife in the Early Middle Ages* (Athens: University of Georgia Press, 1983).

2. For an in-depth study of eunuchs, see Katherine Ringrose, *The Perfect Servant* (Chicago: University of Chicago Press, 2003).

3. Among the works I have drawn on for this and the following discussion, in addition to those cited in specific notes, are: Lisa Bitel, *Women in Early Medieval Europe, 400–1100* (Cambridge, U.K.: Cambridge University Press, 2002); John Bernhardt, *Itinerant Kingship and Royal Monasteries in Early Medieval Germany, c. 936–1075* (New York: Cambridge University Press, 1993); Goetz, *Life in the Middle Ages* (see chap. 1, n. 4); Julia Smith, "Did Women Have a Transformation of the Roman World?," *Gender and History* 12 (2000); John Parsons, ed., *Medieval Queenship* (New York: St. Martin's Press, 1993); Joyce Hill and Mary Swan, eds., *The Community, the Family and the Saint: Patterns of Power in Early Medieval Europe* (Brepols, Belgium: University of Leeds, 1998); Stafford, *Queens, Concubines;* Francis and Joseph Gies, *Marriage and the Family in the Middle Ages* (New York: Harper & Row, 1987); Georges Duby, *The Early Growth of the European Economy* (Ithaca, N.Y.: Cornell University Press, 1974); Susan Stuard, *Women in Medieval Society* (Philadelphia: University of Pennsylvania Press, 1976); Wemple, *Women in Frankish Society* (see chap. 3, n. 31); David Herlihy, *Medieval Households* (Cambridge, Mass.: Harvard University Press, 1985) and *Women, Family and Society in Medieval Europe* (Providence: Bergmahn Books, 1995); C. Warren Hollister, *Henry I* (New Haven: Yale University Press, 2001); Jenny Jochens, *Women in Old Norse Society* (Ithaca, N.Y.: Cornell University Press, 1995); Perry Anderson, *Passages from Antiquity to Feudalism* (London: New Left Books, 1974); Mark Bloch, *Feudal Society* (London: Routledge and Kegan Paul, 1961); Maurice Keen, *The Pelican History of Medieval Europe* (New York: Penguin Books, 1978); Derek Baker, ed., *Medieval Women* (Oxford, U.K.: Basil Blackwell, 1978); Jacqueline Murray, ed., *Conflicted Identities and Multiple Masculinities: Men in the Medieval West* (New York: Garland Publishing, 1999); Lees, *Medieval Masculinities* (see chap. 1, n. 4); Linda Mitchell, ed., *Women in Medieval Western European Culture* (New York: Garland Publishing, 1999).

4. F. L. Attenborough, ed., *The Laws of the Earliest English Kings* (New York: Russell and Russell, 1963), p. 85 and passim.

5. For example, the Norman aristocracy that conquered England in 1066 had been methodically constructed through local "peace-weaving" marriages between the feuding Viking families that had settled in northern France during the ninth century. Eleanor Searle, *Predatory*

Kinship and the Creation of Norman Power, 840–1066 (Berkeley: University of California Press, 1988).

6. Stafford, *Queens, Concubines,* p. 50.
7. See, for example, Wemple, *Women in Frankish Society.*
8. Pauline Stafford, "Sons and Mothers: Family Politics in the Early Middle Ages," in Baker, *Medieval Women.*
9. For the story of Charlemagne and his family, see Wemple, *Women in Frankish Society,* pp. 76–80; Livingstone, "Powerful Allies," in Mitchell, ed., *Women in Medieval Western European Culture,* p. 18; Stafford, *Queens, Concubines,* pp. 60–62.
10. Scott Waugh, *The Lordship of England: Royal Wardships and Marriages in English Society and Politics, 1217–1327* (Princeton: Princeton University Press, 1988); Ivan Ermakoff, "Prelates and Princes," *American Sociological Review* 62 (1997).
11. For more on this story, see Charles Edward Smith, *Papal Enforcement of Some Medieval Marriage Laws* (Port Washington, N.Y.: Kenniket Press, 1940); Wemple, *Women in Frankish Society;* Searle, *Predatory Kinship;* Stafford, *Queens, Concubines.*
12. Searle, *Predatory Kinship,* p. 249.
13. Mayke de Jong, "To the Limits of Kinship," in Jan Cremmer, ed., *From Sappho to de Sade: Moments in the History of Sexuality* (New York: Routledge, 1991); Peter Fleming, *Family and Household in Medieval England* (New York: Palgrave, 2001).
14. Jean-Louis Flandrin, *Families in Former Times* (New York: Cambridge University Press, 1979), p. 24. As historian Christopher Brooke remarks, these rules "were at once a marvelous excuse for cynics and a sad burden on tender consciences." Brooke, *The Medieval Idea of Marriage* (Oxford, U.K.: Oxford University Press, 1989), p. 125. Why did the church support such unrealistic rules? Anthropologist Jack Goody suggests that the multiplication of such barriers to marriage was part of a deliberate strategy to limit the number of male heirs among the aristocracy, thus maximizing the chance that individuals would leave their property to the church. Goody, *The Development of the Family and Marriage in Europe* (Cambridge, U.K.: Cambridge University Press, 1983). But whatever its material interests, the church had sincere reasons for encouraging people to broaden their marriage networks. Beginning with Jesus himself, Christianity encouraged people to build a community of love and fellowship that reached beyond the tightly defined loyalties of family ties. Islam also tried to widen the circles of cooperation by establishing categories of people with whom one could not mate. Although marriage between cousins was accepted, there was an incest taboo for "milk relatives," people who had been wet-nursed by the same woman. Steven Epstein,

"The Medieval Family: A Place of Refuge and Sorrow," in Samuel Cohn and Epstein, eds., *Portraits of Medieval and Renaissance Living* (Ann Arbor: University of Michigan Press, 1996), p. 168.

15. Smith, *Papal Enforcement,* p. 163.
16. Constance Bouchard, *"Those of My Blood": Constructing Noble Families in Medieval France* (Philadelphia: University of Pennsylvania Press, 2001).
17. Georges Duby, Dominique Barthelemy, and Charles de la Ronciete, "The Aristocratic Households of Feudal France," in Arthur Goldhammer and Georges Duby, *A History of Private Life,* vol. 2, *Revelations of the Medieval World* (Cambridge, Mass.: Belknap Press, 1987), pp. 135–36; Bouchard, *"Those of My Blood,"* pp. 40, 56; Stafford, *Queens, Concubines,* p. 81.
18. Smith, *Papal Enforcement.*
19. During the seventh century, Arab Muslims conquered most of the former Roman territories in the Middle East, as well as North Africa, most of Spain, and the former Persian Empire, leaving the Byzantine Empire with control of only Asia Minor. In Arab society, marriage conferred important economic and political benefits on men. The first four political successors to Muhammad all were linked to him by marriage, either as father of one of his wives or as husband of one of his daughters. But as in Byzantium, marriage in Islam was much less important in building political alliances than in the West. Descent was more rigidly traced along the paternal side, and the aim of marriage was to keep wealth and property within the family rather than to create wider alliances. Even today women are often expected to marry their paternal first cousins. This pattern creates tight, male-based solidarity networks rather than far-flung political alliances.

    The role of marriage alliances in Islamic politics constricted further as Islam extended its empire into the Middle East and adopted the already widespread pre-Islamic customs of veiling and female seclusion. By the middle of the eighth century upper-class women were sequestered entirely from the public life of the court. They could sometimes manipulate the men around them by force of personality or by temporarily acting in the place of men, but their own political ties or bloodlines counted for little. Paradoxically, however, women in Islam had significant economic rights. They could draw up prenuptial contracts, and they could inherit property that they held separately from their husbands. For sources on Islam, see Tucker, *Gender and Islamic History* (see chap. 2, n. 16) and "The Arab Family in History," in Tucker, ed., *Arab Women: Old Boundaries, New Frontiers* (Bloomington: Indiana University Press, 1993); Arnold, *A History of Celibacy* (see chap. 1, n. 28); Arlene Swidler, *Marriage Among the Religions of the World* (Lewiston, ID: E. Mellen Press, 1990), p. 80; Eric Wolf, "The Social Organization of Mecca and the Origins of Islam," *Southwest Journal of Anthropology* 7 (1951); Thierry Blanquis, "The Family in Arab Islam," in Burguière et al., *Distant Worlds, Ancient Worlds;* Stearns, *Gender in World History,* pp. 38–42; Amira El Azhary Sonbol, *Women, the Family, and Divorce Laws in Islamic History* (Syracuse, NY: Syracuse University Press, 1991); Ahmed, *Women and Gender in Islam* (see chap. 3, n. 38); Jonathan Berkey, "Women in Medieval Islamic Society," in Mitchell, ed., *Women in Medieval Western European Culture;* Albert Hourani, *A History of the Arab Peoples* (New York: Warner Books, 1991); Denise Spellberg, *Politics, Gender, and the Islamic Past* (New York: Columbia University Press, 1994).

20. Guinevere quote from Constance Bouchard, *Strong of Body, Brave and Noble: Chivalry and Society in Medieval France* (Ithaca, N.Y.: Cornell University Press, 1998), p. 4.

21. Stafford, *Queens, Concubines.*

22. Ibid.

23. Duby, Barthelemy, and La Ronciete, "The Aristocratic Households of Feudal France."

24. W. S. Mackie, ed., *The Exeter Book,* Part II, Poems IX–XXXII (London: Oxford University Press, 1934); Marion Facinger, "A Study of Medieval Queenship: Capetian France, 987–1237," *Studies in Medieval Renaissance History* 5 (1968).

25. John Parsons, "Mothers Daughters, Marriage, Power," in Parsons, ed., *Medieval Queenship;* Constance Owens, "Noblewomen and Political Activity," in Mitchell, ed., *Women in Medieval Western Culture.*

26. Bitel, *Women in Early Medieval Europe.*

27. Stafford, *Queens, Concubines.*

28. John Gillingham, "Love, Marriage and Politics in the Twelfth Century," *Forum for Modern Language Studies: Interdisciplinary Medieval Studies* 25 (1989).

29. Georges Duby, *The Chivalrous Society* (Berkeley: University of California Press, 1977), *Medieval Marriage: Two Models from Twelfth-Century France* (Baltimore: Johns Hopkins University Press, 1978), and *The Knight, the Lady, and the Priest: The Making of Modern Marriage in Medieval France* (New York: Pantheon, 1983); Bitel, *Women in Early Medieval Europe.*

30. In 1328 the Capetians forbade female inheritance of the kingdom through the Salic Law, which they claimed was a traditional Germanic law. It was in fact a new invention. For more on the complex history of women's inheritance rights, see Sarah Lambert, "Queen or Consort: Rulership and Politics in the Latin East, 1118–1228," in Duggan, ed., *Queens and Queenship;* Bitel, *Women in Early Medieval History;* Susan Stuard, "The Dominion of Gender," in Bridenthal, Stuard, and Wiesner, eds., *Becoming Visible;* See also Janet Nelson, "Medieval Queenship," in

Mitchell, ed., *Women in Medieval Western European Culture;* Stafford, *Queens, Concubines;* Searle, *Predatory Kinship;* Theodore Eversgate, ed., *Aristocratic Women in Medieval France* (Philadelphia: University of Pennsylvania Press, 1999) and "The Feudal Imaginary of Georges Duby," *Journal of Medieval and Early Modern Studies* 27 (1997); David Herlihy, "The Making of the Medieval Family," *Journal of Family History* 18 (Summer 1983); Thomas Bisson, ed., *Cultures of Power: Lordship, Status, and Process in Twelfth-Century Europe* (Philadelphia: University of Pennsylvania Press, 1995).

31. Janet Nelson, "Medieval Queenship," in Mitchell, ed., *Women in Medieval Western European Culture,* p. 205.

Chapter 7. How the Other 95 Percent Wed

1. Stafford, *Queens, Concubines,* p. 80 (see chap. 6, n. 1); Gies, *Marriage and the Family,* p. 56 (see chap. 6, n. 3); Wemple, *Women in Frankish Society,* p. 87 (see chap. 3, n. 31). See also Grubb, " 'Pagan' and 'Christian' Marriage" (see chap. 5, n. 18).

2. For this and the next paragraph, see Bitel, *Women in Early Medieval Europe* (see chap. 6, n. 3).

3. For this and the following paragraphs on church history, see Anne Barstow, *Married Priests and the Reforming Papacy* (New York: Edwin Mellen Press, 1982); James Brundage, *Law, Sex, and Christian Society in Medieval Europe* (Chicago: University of Chicago Press, 1987); Michael Sheehan, *Marriage, Family and Law in Medieval Europe: Collected Studies* (Toronto: University of Toronto Press, 1996); R. M. Helmholz, *Marriage Litigation in Medieval England* (Cambridge, U.K.: Cambridge University Press, 1974); Brooke, *The Medieval Idea of Marriage* (see chap. 6, n. 14); James Brundage, "Concubinage and Marriage in Medieval Canon Law," *Journal of Medieval History* 1 (1975); Martin Ingram, "Spousal Litigation in the English Ecclesiastical Courts, c1350–1640," in R. B. Outhwaite, *Marriage and Society: Studies in the Social History of Marriage* (New York: St. Martin's Press, 1981) and *Church Courts, Sex and Marriage in England, 1570–1640* (Cambridge, U.K.: Cambridge University Press, 1987); Constance Rousseau and Joel Rosenthal, eds., *Women, Marriage and Family in Medieval Christendom* (Kalamazoo: Western Michigan University, 1998); Philip Reynolds, *Marriage in the Western Church: The Christianization of Marriage During the Patristic and Early Medieval Periods* (New York: E. J. Brill, 1994); Georges Duby, *Love and Marriage in the Middle Ages* (Chicago: University of Chicago Press, 1994); Vern Bullough and James Brundage, eds., *Handbook of Medieval Sexuality* (New York: Garland Publishing, 1996); Janice Norris, "Nuns and Other Religious Women and Christianity

in the Middle Ages," in Mitchell, *Women in Medieval Western European Culture* (see chap. 6, n. 3); Pauline Stafford, "Queens, Nunneries and Reforming Churchmen," *Past and Present* 163 (1999); Fleming, *Family and Household in Medieval England* (see chap. 6, n. 13).

4. Ingram, "Spousal Litigation in the English Ecclesiastical Courts," p. 40.
5. The legal cases in this and the next paragraph are reported in Henrietta Leyser, *Medieval Women: A Social History of Women in England, 450–1500* (New York: St. Martin's Press, 1995), pp. 112–16.
6. The examples in this and the following paragraph are taken from Shannon McSheffrey, *Love and Marriage in Late Medieval London* (Kalamazoo: Western Michigan University, 1995), passim, and Leyser, *Medieval Women,* pp. 112–13. I thank Professor McSheffrey for clarifying the stories and their outcomes for me (personal communication, December 3, 2003). For more accounts of such suits and the predominance of male plaintiffs in them, see Jeffrey Watt, *The Making of Marriage: Matrimonial Control and the Rise of Sentiment in Neuchâtel, 1550–1800* (Ithaca, N.Y.: Cornell University Press, 1992) and Ingram, *Church Courts, Sex and Marriage.*
7. Paul Griffiths, *Youth and Authority: Formative Experiences in England, 1560–1640* (Oxford, U.K.: Clarendon Press, 1996).
8. Werner Rosener, *Peasants in the Middle Ages* (Cambridge, U.K.: Polity Press, 1985); Leyser, *Medieval Women.* My discussion of peasant marriage is based largely on Rosener, *Peasants;* G. G. Coulton, *Medieval Village, Manor, and Monastery* (New York: Harper & Row, 1960); Beatrice Gottlieb, *The Family in the Western World from the Black Death to the Industrial Age* (New York: Oxford University Press, 1993); G. C. Homans, *English Villagers of the Thirteenth Century* (Cambridge, Mass.: Harvard University Press, 1942); Mary Erler and Maryanne Kowalski, eds., *Women and Power in the Middle Ages* (Athens: University of Georgia Press, 1988); Mavis Mate, *Women in Medieval English Society* (Cambridge, U.K.: Cambridge University Press, 1999); Barbara Hanawalt, *The Ties that Bound: Peasant Families in Medieval England* (New York: Oxford University Press, 1986); Judith Bennett, *Women in the Medieval English Countryside: Gender and Household in Brigstock Before the Plague* (New York: Oxford University Press, 1987); Emmanuel Le Roy Ladurie, *Montaillou: The Promised Land of Error* (New York: Vintage, 1979); Zvi Razi, *Life, Marriage and Death in a Medieval Parish: Economy, Society and Demography in Halesowen, 1270–1400* (Cambridge, U.K.: Cambridge University Press, 1980); Bouchard, *Strong of Body, Brave and Noble* (see chap. 6, n. 20); Fleming, *Family and Household in Medieval England;* and Christopher Dyer, *Making a Living in the Middle Ages* (New Haven: Yale University Press, 2002). David Cressy, *Birth, Marriage, and Death: Ritual, Religion, and the Life-cycle in Tudor and Stuart*

England (Oxford, U.K.: Oxford University Press, 1997) provides a wealth of information on both rural and urban family life.

9. Madonna Hettinger, "So Strategize: The Demands in the Day of the Peasant Women in Medieval Europe," in Mitchell, ed., *Women in Medieval Western European Culture.*

10. Judith Bennett, *A Medieval Life: Cecilia Penifader of Brigstock, c. 1295–1344* (Boston: McGraw-Hill, 1998).

11. Ladurie, *Montaillou,* p. 180.

12. Homans, *English Villagers;* Razi, *Life, Marriage and Death.*

13. John Gillis, *For Better, for Worse: British Marriages, 1600 to the Present* (New York: Oxford University Press, 1985).

14. Cressy, *Birth, Marriage, Death;* Homans, *English Villagers;* Judith Bennett, "Public Power and Authority in the Medieval English Countryside," in Erler and Kowalski, eds., *Women and Power.* For an Italian example of the responsibilities that husbands gained, both over and for other people, as a result of marriage, see Susan Stuard, "Burdens of Matrimony," in Lees, ed., *Medieval Masculinities* (see chap. 1, n. 4).

15. Bennett, *A Medieval Life.*

16. Amy Erickson, *Women and Property in Early Modern England* (New York: Routledge, 1993).

17. Pierre Bonnassie, "A Family of the Barcelona Countryside and Its Economic Activities Around the Year 1000," in Sylvia Thrupp, ed., *Early Medieval Society* (New York: Appleton-Century-Crofts, 1967).

18. Hanawalt, *Ties that Bound;* Homans, *English Villagers;* Leyser, *Medieval Women;* Judith Bennett, "Medieval Women, Modern Women," in David Aers, ed., *Culture and History 1350–1600: Essays on English Communities, Identities and Writing* (New York: Harvester Wheatsheaf, 1992); Linda Mitchell, *Portraits of Medieval Women* (London: Palgrave, 2003).

19. Shannon McSheffrey, "Men and Masculinity in Late Medieval London Civic Culture," in Jacqueline Murray, ed., *Conflicted Identities and Multiple Masculinities: Men in the Medieval West* (New York: Garland Publishing, 1999), p. 245.

20. Susan Stuard, "The Dominion of Gender" and Merry Wiesner, "Spinning out Capital," in Bridenthal, Stuard, and Wiesner, eds., *Becoming Visible* (see chap. 3, n. 39).

21. Gottlieb, *Family in the Western World,* p. 54.

22. Martha Howell, *Women, Production and Patriarchy in Late Medieval Cities* (Chicago: University of Chicago Press, 1986); Marion Kaplan, ed., *The Marriage Bargain: Women and Dowries in European History* (New York: Haworth Press, 1985); Mark Angelos, "Urban Women, Investment, and the Commercial Revolution of the Middle Ages," in Mitchell, ed.,

Women in Medieval Western European Culture; P. J. P. Goldberg, *Women, Work, and Life Cycle in a Medieval Economy: Women in York and Yorkshire, c 1300–1520* (Oxford, U.K.: Clarendon Press, 1992).

23. Bennett, "Medieval Women, Modern Women."

24. Fleming, *Family and Household;* Louise Collis, *Memoirs of a Medieval Woman: The Life and Times of Margery Kempe* (New York: Harper & Row, 1964).

25. Michael Sheehan, "The Formation and Stability of Marriage in Fourteenth-Century England: Evidence of an Ely Register," *Mediaeval Studies* 33 (1971); Alan Macfarlane, *Marriage and Love in England: Modes of Reproduction 1300–1840* (Oxford, U.K.: Oxford University Press, 1986).

26. Jacqueline Murray, "Individualism and Consensual Marriage: Some Evidence from Medieval England," in Rousseau and Rosenthal, eds., *Women, Marriage and Family;* Geneviève Ribordy, "The Two Paths to Marriage: The Preliminaries of Noble Marriage in Late Medieval France," *Journal of Family History* 26 (2001).

27. Anthony Molho, *Marriage Alliance in Late Medieval Florence* (Cambridge, Mass.: Harvard University Press, 1994), pp.128–29.

28. Fleming, *Family and Household.*

29. For this and the other Paston family stories described below, see H. S. Bennett, *The Pastons and Their England* (London: Cambridge University Press, 1975), along with Gies and Gies, *Marriage and the Family,* pp. 258–68.

30. Diana O'Hara, *Courtship and Constraint: Rethinking the Making of Marriage in Tudor England* (Manchester, U.K.: Manchester University Press, 2000), p. 32; Shannon McShreffrey, "I Will Never Have None Ayenst My Faders Will": Consent and the Making of Marriage in the Late Medieval Diocese of London," in Rousseau and Rosenthal, eds., *Women, Marriage, Family,* p. 156. See also David Hopkin, "Love Riddles, Couple Formation, and Local Identity in Eastern France," *Journal of Family History* 28 (2003).

31. See, for example, *A Medieval Home Companion,* trans. and ed. Tania Bayard (New York: Harper Perennial, 1992).

32. Sara Mendelson and Patricia Crawford, *Women in Early Modern England, 1550–1720* (Oxford, U.K.: Clarendon Press, 1998), p. 10.

33. The tale was written down in Italian by Boccaccio in 1353, as well as retold and translated into Latin by Petrarch. Latin was still the international language of Western Europe, so the tale spread across Germany and France into England. Griselda's story appeared in several French versions, one of which was a treatise on domestic economy entitled *The Goodman of Paris* (c. 1393). The quote comes from the version in *The Goodman of Paris,* by A Citizen of Paris (c. 1393), translated by Eileen Power (London: George Routledge & Sons, 1928), p. 140.

34. Ibid., pp. 137, 140.
35. Geoffrey Chaucer, *The Canterbury Tales,* trans. into modern English by Nevill Coghill (Baltimore: Penguin Books, 1966), pp. 370–71.
36. Ibid., pp. 288–96.
37. "The Book of Vices and Virtues," in Emilie Amt, *Women's Lives in Medieval Europe: A Sourcebook* (New York: Routledge, 1993), p. 89.
38. Quoted in Barstow, *Married Priests and the Reforming Papacy,* pp. 61–62. See also Pauline Stafford, "Queens, Nunneries and Reforming Churchmen," *Past and Present* 163 (1999); Louise Mirrer, "Women's Representation in Male-Authored Works of the Middle Ages," in Mitchell, ed., *Women in Medieval Western European Culture,* p. 316; Katharine Rogers, *The Troublesome Helpmate: A History of Misogyny in Literature* (Seattle: University of Washington Press, 1966).
39. "Holy Maidenhood," in Amt, *Women's Lives,* pp. 91–92.
40. As late as 1617 Lady Grace Mildmay, meditating on her fifty years of marriage, declared of her husband: "I carried always that reverent respect towards him . . . that I could not find it in my heart to challenge him for the worst word or deed which ever he offered me in all his life." Jacqueline Eales, *Women in Early Modern England, 1500–1700* (London: UCL Press, 1998).
41. Russell Dobash and R. Emerson Dobash, "Community Response to Violence Against Wives," *Social Problems* 28 (1981); Mendelson and Crawford, *Women,* p. 128; Anthony Fletcher, *Gender, Sex, and Subordination in England, 1500–1800* (New Haven: Yale University Press, 1995), p. 192.

Chapter 8. Something Old, Something New

1. For divergent views on the origins of affectionate, love-based marriage, see MacFarlane, *The Origins of English Individualism: The Family, Property and Social Transition* (New York: Cambridge University Press, 1979) and *Marriage and Love in England* (see chap. 7, n. 25); Ozment, *When Fathers Ruled* (see chap. 1, n. 15); Simon Schama, *The Embarrassment of Riches: An Interpretation of Dutch Culture in the Golden Age* (New York: Alfred A. Knopf, 1988), p. 426; André Burguière, "The Formation of the Couple," *Journal of Family History* 12 (1987); Lawrence Stone, *The Family, Sex, and Marriage in England, 1500–1800* (New York: Harper & Row, 1977); Gillis, *For Better, for Worse* (see chap. 7, n. 13); Carl Degler, *At Odds: Women and the Family in America from the Revolution to the Present* (New York: Oxford University Press, 1980); Michael Mitteraur and Reinhard Sieder, *The European Family: Patriarchy to Partnership from the Middle Ages to the Present* (Chicago: University of Chicago Press, 1986); Jean-Louis Flandrin, *Families in Former Times: Kinship, Household, and Sexuality* (New

York: Cambridge University Press, 1979); Randolph Trumbach, *The Rise of the Egalitarian Family: Aristocratic Kinship and Domestic Relations in Eighteenth-Century England* (New York: Academic Press, 1978); Edward Shorter, *The Making of the Modern Family* (New York: Basic Books, 1975); Leonore Davidoff, *Family Fortunes: Men and Women of the English Middle Class, 1780–1850* (Chicago: University of Chicago Press, 1987); G. R. Quaife, *Wanton Wenches and Wayward Wives: Peasants and Illicit Sex in Early Seventeenth-Century England* (New Brunswick, N.J.: Rutgers University Press, 1979).

2. On the distinctive marriage pattern described in the following pages, see John Hajnal, "European Marriage Patterns in Perspective," in D. V. Glass and D. E. C. Eversley, eds., *Population and History* (New York: McGraw-Hill, 1969); Bennett, "Medieval Women, Modern Women" (see chap. 7, n. 15); Peter Laslett and Richard Wall, eds., *Household and Family in Past Time* (Cambridge, U.K.: Cambridge University Press, 1972); Katherine Lynch, "The European Marriage Pattern in the Cities," *Journal of Family History* 16 (1991); Zvi Razi, "The Myth of the Immutable English Family," *Past and Present,* 40 (1993); Lloyd Bonfield, Richard Smith, and Keith Wrightson, *The World We Have Gained: Histories of Population and Social Structure* (London: Basil Blackwell, 1986); Heide Wunder, *"He Is the Sun, She Is the Moon": Women in Early Modern Germany* (Cambridge, Mass.: Harvard University Press, 1998); Goody, *The Development of the Family and Marriage in Europe* (see chap. 7, n. 14) and *The European Family: An Historico-Anthropological Essay* (London: Blackwell Publishers, 2000); Goody and Tambiah, *Bridewealth and Dowry* (see chap. 1, n. 13); Scott Waugh, *The Lordship of England: Royal Wardships and Marriage in English Society and Politics* (Princeton: Princeton University Press, 1988); Fleming, *Family and Household in Medieval England* (see chap. 6, n. 13); Richard Smith, "Geographical Diversity in the Resort to Marriage in Late Medieval Europe," in P. J. P. Goldberg, ed., *Woman Is a Worthy Wight: Women in English Society c. 1200–1500* (Wolfeboro Falls, NH: Alan Sutton Publishing, 1992); P. J. P. Goldberg, *Women, Work and Life Cycle in a Medieval Economy* (New York: Oxford University Press, 1992); Judith Bennett and Amy Froide, eds., *Singlewomen in the European Past, 1250–1800* (Philadelphia: University of Pennsylvania Press, 1998); André Burguière et al., *A History of the Family* (Cambridge, Mass.: Harvard University Press, 1996), vols. 1 *Distant Worlds, Ancient Worlds* and 2 *The Impact of Modernity;* E. A. Wrigley and Roger Schofield, eds., *The Population History of England, 1541–1871: A Reconstruction* (Cambridge, Mass.: Harvard University Press. 1981); E. A. Wrigley et al., *English Population History from Family Reconstitution* (New York: Cambridge University Press, 1997);

Amy Erickson, *Women and Property in Early Modern England* (London: Routledge, 1993); John Brewer and Susan Staves, eds., *Early Modern Conceptions of Property* (New York: Routledge, 1995); Bullough and Brundage, eds., *Handbook of Medieval Sexuality* (see chap. 7, n. 3); Jacqueline Eales, *Women in Early Modern England, 1500–1700* (London: UCL Press, 1998).

3. Lyndal Roper, "'Going to Church and Street': Weddings in Reformation Augsburg," *Past and Present* 106 (1988), pp. 83–84; Gillis, *For Better, for Worse;* Cressy, *Birth, Marriage, and Death* (see chap. 7, n. 8).

4. There were, however, many exceptions to the general rule of one married couple per household. In central Italy there were significant numbers of joint families, in which two married brothers lived together and owned their land in common. Nuclear families accounted for only about half the households in southern France during the late seventeenth and early eighteenth centuries. In central Europe and around the Pyrenees, it was common for the inheriting son to bring his bride to his parents' home and gradually take over full control of the farm in his father's declining years. Such stem families, as historians and demographers call them, may have been more common in England and northern France than census data reveal. Since an inheriting son in these regions did not normally marry and move in with his father until the latter thought that he could no longer work the land himself, and since people in that time did not normally live long after their strength had begun to fail, most households would be composed of nuclear families for all but a few overlapping years, but many individuals would experience a brief amount of time in a stem family. For more on these variations, see Flandrin, *Families in Former Times,* p. 65; Peter Laslett, "Mean Household Size in England Since the Sixteenth Century," in Laslett and Wall, eds., *Household and Family in Past Time;* Stephanie Coontz, *The Social Origins of Private Life: A History of American Families, 1600–1900* (London: Verso, 1988); Wally Seccombe, *A Millennium of Family Change* (London: Verso, 1992).

5. For the discussion of singles, age of marriage, and service, see Ingram, *Church Courts, Sex and Marriage in England* (see chap. 7, n. 3); Bennett and Froide, "A Singular Past," p. 16; Peter Laslett, *Family Life and Illicit Love in Earlier Generations* (New York: Cambridge University Press, 1977), p. 43; David Reher, "Family Ties in Western Europe: Persistent Contrasts," *Population and Development Review* 24 (1998); Seccombe, *Millennium.*

6. Olwen Hufton, *The Prospect Before Her: A History of Women in Western Europe* (New York: Alfred A. Knopf, 1996) and "Women, Work and Marriage in Eighteenth-Century France," in Outhwaite, *Marriage and Society* (see chap. 7, n. 3).

7. Vivian Elliott, "Single Women in the London Marriage Market," in Outhwaite, *Marriage and Society.*

8. Gottlieb, *Family in the Western World,* p. 52; Mitterauer and Sieder, *European Family,* p. 127.

9. Steven Ozment, *Ancestors: The Loving Family in Old Europe* (Cambridge, Mass.: Harvard University Press, 2001), p. 25.

10. For the story of one such woman, see Judith Bennett, *A Medieval Life* (chap. 7, n. 10). See also Olwen Huften, *The Poor of Eighteenth-Century France* (Oxford, 1974); Bennett and Froide, "A Singular Past," p. 23.

11. Ron Lesthaeghe, "On the Social Control of Human Reproduction," *Population and Development Review* 6 (1980); Richard Wall, "The Transformation of the European Family Across the Centuries," in Wall, Tamara Hareven, and Josef Ehmer, eds., *Family History Revisited: Comparative Perspectives* (Newark: University of Delaware, 2001). For a description of this interdependence in Sweden as late as the eighteenth century, see Orvar Lofgren, "Family and Household: Images and Realities," in Robert McC. Netting, Richard Wilk, and Eric Arnould, eds., *Households: Comparative and Historical Studies of the Domestic Group* (Berkeley: University of California Press, 1984); Gillis, *For Better, for Worse;* Naomi Tadmore, *Family and Friends in Eighteenth-Century England* (Cambridge, U.K.: Cambridge University Press, 2001).

12. David Sabean, *Property, Production, and Family in Neckherhausen, 1700–1870* (Cambridge, U.K.: Cambridge University Press, 1990); Emmanuel Ladurie, *Montaillou* (see chap. 7, n. 3).

13. Seccombe, *Millennium.*

14. E. A. Wrigley, "Marriage, Fertility and Population Growth in Eighteenth-Century England," in Outhwaite, *Marriage and Society;* Seccombe, *Millennium.*

15. Jack Goldstone, "Gender, Work and Culture: Why the Industrial Revolution Came Early to England but Late to China," *Sociological Perspectives* 39 (1996). Interestingly, Japan's marriage patterns were closer to those of Western Europe than to China until the late nineteenth century. Marriage was not universal for women, and lower-class women, especially in the more commercial western region of Japan, often left their villages for several years before marriage to work in rural handicraft centers or in more distant cities as servants, cooks, brewers, and entertainers. Many rural women left their home at about age thirteen or fourteen and returned ten to fifteen years later, after more than a decade working outside the home. This tradition had a significant economic impact during the early years of industrialization in the late nineteenth century, when female workers were the major source of labor in the new mills and factories. The participation of women in Japanese economic

modernization was reversed at the very end of the nineteenth century, when the Meiji government (1868–1898) pushed through laws and policies that strengthened male control over property, barred women from political meetings, attacked traditional means of birth control, and redefined women's activities under the rubric of "good wives, good mothers." However, these actions did not stimulate a widespread women's rights movement in Japan, possibly because the Japanese extended family discouraged the independence of the married couple unit and encouraged individuals to see themselves as working for the ancestors and for the future of the family as a whole. L. L. Cornell, "Hajnal and the Household in Asia," *Journal of Family History* 12 (1987); Susan Mann, *Women's and Gender History in Global Perspective: East Asia (China, Japan, Korea)* (Washington, D.C.: American Historical Association, 1999); Akira Hayami, "Another *Fossa Magna:* Proportion Marrying and Age at Marriage in Late-Nineteenth-Century Japan," *Journal of Family History* 12 (1987); E. Patricia Tsurimi, *Factory Girls: Women in the Thread Mills of Meiji Japan* (New Haven: Yale University Press, 1990).

16. Anthropologist Jack Goody has argued that the European dowry system created a conjugal fund that elevated the married couple household over the extended family or lineage. This in turn, he suggests, led to more equality between husbands and wives, especially in combination with the church's support for a woman's right to refuse an unwanted marriage and its lack of support for a man's right to *leave* one. But there was nothing inherent in the European dowry system that gave wives increased bargaining power within marriage. In England, for instance, the husband legally had complete control over his wife's dowry. In northern France, historian Martha Howell has argued, the move to dowries replaced a system of community property rights that had given women greater security. Furthermore, among the very rich, a woman's dowry was often mobilized in the interest in family alliances, and a rich man's daughter might find herself married off against her will to a nobleman whose family offered social status in exchange for ready cash. Goody, *Development of Family and Marriage;* Rubie Watson and Patricia Ebrey, *Marriage and Inequality in Chinese Society* (Berkeley: University of California Press, 1991); Anthony Molho, *Marriage Alliance in Late Medieval Florence* (Cambridge, Mass.: Harvard University Press, 1994); Kaplan, *The Marriage Bargain;* Martha Howell, *The Marriage Exchange: Property, Social Place, and Gender in Cities of the Low Countries, 1300–1550* (Chicago: University of Chicago Press, 1998).

17. Deniz Kandiyoti, "Bargaining with Patriarchy," *Gender & Society* 2 (1988); Mann, *Women's and Gender History,* p. 5: Margery Wolf, *Women and the Family in Rural Taiwan* (Palo Alto, Calif.: Stanford University Press, 1972).

Notes

18. Steve Derne, "Hindu Men Talk About Controlling Women," *Sociological Perspectives* 37 (1994).

19. Leon Battista Alberti, *The Family in Renaissance Florence* tr. Renee Watkins (Columbia: University of South Carolina Press, 1969), p. 98; Von Eyb, quoted in Ozment, *When Fathers Ruled,* p. 7. See also Joan Kelly, "Early Feminist Theory and the *Querelle des Femmes,* 1400–1789," *Signs* 8 (1982).

20. Unless otherwise noted, my discussion of the Reformation is drawn from Ozment, *When Fathers Ruled;* Joel Harrington, *Reordering Marriage and Society in Reformation Germany* (New York: Cambridge University Press, 1997); Eric Carlson, *Marriage and the English Reformation* (Oxford, U.K.: Blackwell Publishers, 1994); Kathleen Davis, "Continuity and Change in Literary Advice on Marriage," in Outhwaite, *Marriage and Society;* William and Marilyn Haller, "The Puritan Art of Love," *Huntington Library Quarterly* 5 (1941–42); Christopher Hill, *Society and Puritanism in Pre-Revolutionary England* (New York: St. Martin's Press, 1997); Wunder, *"He Is the Sun";* Flandrin, *Families in Former Times;* Lyndal Roper, *The Holy Household: Women and Morals in Reformation Augsburg* (Oxford, U.K.: Clarendon Press, 1989); Thomas Robisheaux, *Rural Society and the Search for Order in Early Modern Germany* (Cambridge, U.K.: Cambridge University Press, 1989); Merry Wiesner, *Working Women in Renaissance Germany* (New Brunswick, N.J.: Rutgers University Press, 1986); James Farr, *Authority and Sexuality in Early Modern Burgundy* (New York: Oxford University Press, 1995); Sherrin Marshall, ed., *Women in Reformation and Counter-Reformation Europe: Public and Private Worlds* (Bloomington: Indiana University Press, 1989); Hufton, *The Prospect Before Her;* Susan Karnet-Nunn, "The Reformation of Women," in Bridenthal, Stuard, and Wiesner, *Becoming Visible* (see chap. 3, n. 39).

21. Luther quoted in Ozment, *When Fathers Ruled,* pp. 3; other quotes from Wunder, *"He Is the Sun,"* pp. 45, 50.

22. Yalom, *A History of the Wife* (see chap. 1, n. 16).

23. For more details on Henry's various wives and mistresses, see Karen Lindsey, *Divorced, Beheaded, Survived: A Feminist Reinterpretation of the Wives of Henry VIII* (Reading, Mass.: Addison-Wesley, 1995).

24. Rosemary O'Day, *The Family and Family Relationships, 1500–1900: England, France and the United States of America* (New York: St. Martin's Press, 1994), p. 43.

25. Quoted in Ozment, *Ancestors,* p. 35.

26. Flandrin, *Families in Former Times;* André Burguière, "The Formation of the Couple," *Journal of Family History* 12 (1987).

27. Eales, *Women in Early Modern England,* p. 64.

28. Ozment, *When Fathers Ruled,* pp. 50–55; Kathleen Davies, "Continuity

and Change in Literary Advice on Marriage," in Outhwaite, *Marriage and Society,* pp. 76–77.

29. Cressy, *Birth, Marriage, and Death,* p. 376.

30. Wally Seccombe estimates that 85 percent of the population growth in Europe between 1500 and 1800 took place among people who made all or a good part of their livings from wages. *Millennium,* p. 166. For other sources on this and the following paragraphs on economic change, see: David Levine, *Family Formation in an Age of Nascent Capitalism* (New York: Academic Press 1977); Peter Kriedte, Hans Medick, and Jurgen Schlumbohm, *Industrialization Before Industrialization: Rural Industry in the Genesis of Capitalism* (Cambridge, U.K.: Cambridge University Press, 1981); Franklin F. Mendels, "Proto-industrialization: The First Phase of the Industrialization Process," *Journal of Economic History* 32 (1972); Hans Medick, "The Proto-industrial Family Economy," *Social History* 3 (1976); Rudolph Braun, "Early Industrialization and Demographic Change in the Canton of Zurich," in Charles Tilly, ed., *Historical Studies of Changing Fertility* (Princeton: Princeton University Press, 1978); Myron Gutmann and Rene Leboutte, "Rethinking Protoindustrialization and Family," *Journal of Interdisciplinary History* 14 (1971); Michael Mitterauer, "Peasant and Non-Peasant Family Forms in Relation to the Physical Environment and the Local Economy," *Journal of Family History* 17 (1992); Ulrich Pfister, "The Protoindustrial Household Economy: Toward a Formal Analysis," *Journal of Family History* 17 (1992).

31. Wiesner, *Working Women,* pp. 6, 192; Karant-Nunn, "Reformation of Women," p. 196; Wiesner, "Spinning Out Capital," p. 210; Henry Kamen, *European Society, 1500–1700* (London: Hutchinson, 1984), p. 167; Ingram, *Church Courts,* p. 131.

32. Ozment, *When Fathers Ruled,* pp. 30–39; Burguière, "Formation of the Couple," p. 44.

33. Pavla Miller, *Transformations of Patriarchy in the West, 1500–1900* (Bloomington: Indiana University Press, 1998); Trevor Dean and K. J. P. Lowe, "Introduction," in Dean and Lowe, eds., *Marriage in Italy, 1300–1650* (Cambridge, U.K.: Cambridge University Press, 1998).

34. For the examples in this and the following paragraph, see Sarah Hanley, "Engendering the State: Family Formation and State Building in Early Modern France," *French Historical Studies* 16 (1989). See also Julie Hardwick, *The Practice of Patriarchy: Gender and the Politics of Household Authority in Early Modern France* (Philadelphia: Pennsylvania State University Press, 1998).

35. For this and the following two paragraphs, see Ozment, *When Fathers Ruled;* Hanley, "Engendering the State"; André Burguière and François

Lebrun, "Priest, Prince, and Family," in Burguière et al., *The Impact of Modernity,* p. 130; R. M. Smith, "Marriage Processes in the English Past," in Lloyd Bonfield, Richard Smith, and Keith Wrightson, *The World We Have Gained: Histories of Population and Social Structure* (Oxford: Basil Blackwell, 1986), p. 72.

36. Schama, *Embarrassment of Riches.*
37. Carole Shammas, *A History of Household Government in America* (Charlotteville: University of Virginia Press, 2002), p. 98. Shammas says that "exclusion of one-fifth of the population from any kind of marital legislation" suggests that the marriage system was not "parent-run" (p. 106). But the inclusion of four-fifths and the pattern of children marrying in birth order do not indicate anything even close to a system of purely individual choice.
38. For cases where young people who defied their parents were left in the lurch, see Cressy, *Birth, Marriage, and Death.*
39. Ibid., pp. 242–43.
40. Quoted in Ozment, *When Fathers Ruled,* pp. 73–74.
41. Hufton, *Prospect Before Her.*
42. Claire Tomalin, *Samuel Pepys: The Unequalled Self* (New York: Alfred A. Knopf, 2002), p. 201; Margaret Hunt, *The Middling Sort: Commerce, Gender, and the Family in England, 1680–1780* (Berkeley: University of California Press, 1996), p. 152; Martha Sexton, *Being Good: Woman's Moral Values in Early America* (New York: Hill and Wang, 2003), p. 136.
43. O'Day, *Family and Family Relationships.*
44. Cressy, *Birth, Marriage, and Death,* pp. 249–50. The son held a grudge longer than most young men who recorded their initial disappointments in their letters and diaries. He refused other "great matches" and finally took a bride in Ireland without consulting his parents. In this he was comparatively atypical.
45. Barbara Harris, "Marriage Sixteenth-Century Style," *Journal of Social History* 15 (1982).
46. Miriam Slater, *Family Life in the Seventeenth Century: The Verneys of Claydon House* (London: Routledge and Kegan Paul, 1984), p. 72.
47. Alberti, *The Family,* p. 210.
48. Ingram, *Church Courts,* p. 144 (emphasis added); Kathleen Davies, "Continuity and Change in Literary Advice on Marriage," in Outhwaite, *Marriage and Society;* Saxton, *Being Good,* p. 52; Margaret Ezell, *The Patriarch's Wife* (Chapel Hill: University of North Carolina Press, 1987), p. 2.
49. Wunder, *"He Is the Sun,";* Anthony Fletcher, *Gender, Sex and Subordination in England, 1500–1800* (New Haven: Yale University Press, 1995), pp. 198–201; David Underdown, "The Taming of the Scold," in Anthony

Fletcher and John Stevenson, eds., *Order and Disorder in Early Modern England* (Cambridge, U.K.: Cambridge University Press, 1985); Jeffrey Watt, "The Impact of the Reformation and Counter-Reformation," in David Kertzer and Marzio Barbagli, eds., *The History of the European Family, Vol. 1: Family Life in Early Modern Times* (New Haven: Yale University Press, 2001).

50. Ann Little, "'Shee Would Bump his Mouldy Britch': Authority, Masculinity, and the Harried Husbands of New Haven Colony," in Michael Bellesiles, ed., *Lethal Imagination: Violence and Brutality in American History* (New York: New York University Press, 1999).

51. *The Book of Common Prayer,* 1559, http://justus.anglican.org/resources/bcp/1559/Marriage_1559.htm.

Chapter 9. From Yoke Mates to Soul Mates

1. Watt, *The Making of Marriage* (see chap. 8, n. 6). For more on the Enlightenment, see Susan Bell and Karen Offen, eds., *Women, the Family, and Freedom: The Debate in Documents,* vol. 1, *1750–1880* (Palo Alto, Calif.: Stanford University Press, 1983); Dena Goddman, *The Republic of Letters: A Cultural History of the French Enlightenment* (Ithaca, N.Y.: Cornell University Press, 1994); Thomas Munck, *The Enlightenment: A Comparative Social History, 1721–1794* (New York: Oxford University Press, 2000).

2. Michael Grossberg, *Governing the Hearth: Law and the Family in Nineteenth-Century America* (Chapel Hill: University of North Carolina Press, 1985).

3. Amanda Vickery, *The Gentleman's Daughter: Women's Lives in Georgian England* (New Haven: Yale University Press, 1998); Susan Staves, "British Seduced Maidens," *Eighteenth-Century Studies* 14 (1980); French bourgeoisie, quote from Marion Kaplan, "Introduction," in Kaplan, ed., *The Marriage Bargain* (see chap. 7, n. 16); Gillis, *For Better, for Worse* (see chap. 7, n. 13).

4. Amy Erickson, *Women and Property in Early Modern England* (London: Routledge, 1993); Bridget Hill, *Women Alone: Spinsters in England, 1660–1850* (New Haven: Yale University Press, 2001); Marlene LeGates, "The Cult of Womanhood in Eighteenth-Century Thought," *Eighteenth-Century Studies* 10 (1976). See also Leonore Davidoff, *Worlds Between: Historical Perspectives on Gender and Class* (New York: Routledge, 1995).

5. Gottlieb, *The Family in the Western World* (see chap. 7, n. 8); Roderick Phillips, *Untying the Knot: A Short History of Divorce* (New York: Cambridge University Press, 1991).

6. Lisa Wilson, *Ye Heart of a Man: The Domestic Life of Men in Colonial New England* (New Haven: Yale University Press, 1999); Daniel Scott Smith, "Parental Control and Marriage Patterns: An Analysis of Historical Trends in Higham, Massachusetts," *Journal of Marriage and the Family* 35

(1973); Joan Gundersen, *To Be Useful to the World: Women in Revolutionary America, 1740–1790* (New York: Twayne Publishers, 1996).

7. Natalia Pushkareva, *Women in Russian History from the Tenth to the Twentieth Century* (Armonk, N.Y.: M. E. Sharpe. 1997), pp. 121–86.

8. For this and the next paragraph, see Watt, *The Making of Marriage.*

9. Ian Watt, *The Rise of the Novel* (Berkeley: University of California Press, 1957).

10. Fletcher, *Gender, Sex and Subordination,* pp. 202–03 (see chap. 8, n. 49).

11. William Hubbard, "The Happiness of a People," election sermon, May 3, 1676 (Boston: no publisher listed, 1702).

12. Quoted in Sara Mendelson and Patricia Crawford, *Women in Early Modern England, 1550–1720* (New York: Oxford University Press, 1998), p. 444.

13. Jean Jacques Rousseau, *Everyman's Library: Essays & Belles-Lettres* (New York: E. P. Dutton, 1957), pp. 322, 333; J. G. Fichte, *The Science of Rights,* excerpted in Julia O'Faolain and Lauro Martines, eds., *Not in God's Image: Women in History* (New York: Harper & Row, 1973), p. 288.

14. Asa Briggs, *Social History of England* (New York: Viking, 1984), p. 199.

15. Thomas Laquer, *Solitary Sex: A Cultural History of Masturbation* (New York: Zone Books, 2003).

16. Anthony Giddens, *The Transformation of Intimacy: Sexuality, Love, and Eroticism in Modern Societies* (Palo Alto, Calif.: Stanford University Press, 1992), p. 46.

17. Roderick Phillips, *Putting Asunder: A History of Divorce in Western Society* (Cambridge, U.K.: Cambridge University Press, 1988); Nancy Cott, "Eighteenth-Century Family and Social Life Revealed in Massachusetts Divorce Records," *Journal of Social History* 10 (1976).

18. L. H. Butterfield, ed., *Adams Family Correspondence* (Cambridge, Mass.: Belknap Press of Harvard, 1963), vol. 1, p. 370.

19. F. Dexter, ed., *The Literary Diary of Ezra Stiles [1769–1795]* (New York: C. Scribner's Sons, 1901), vol. 2, p. 490; vol. 3, pp. 15, 167.

20. Charles Brockden Brown, *Alcuin: A Dialogue,* ed. Lee Edwards (Northampton, Mass.: Gehanna Press, 1970), pp. 13–14; Coontz, *Social Origins,* p. 147 (see chap. 8, n. 4).

21. Jane Abray, "Feminism in the French Revolution," *American Historical Review* 80 (1975); Sarah Hanley, "Social Sites of Political Practice in France," *American Historical Review* 102 (1997), pp. 27–28; Olympe des Gourge, *Les Droits de la Femme,* excerpted in O'Faolain and Martines, eds., *Not in God's Image,* p. 308.

22. Graham Robb, *Strangers: Homosexual Love in the Nineteenth Century* (New York: W. W. Norton, 2003), p. 176; A. X. van Naerssen, *Gay Life in Dutch Society* (New York: Harrington Park Press, 1987), p. 9; James Steakley,

The Homosexual Emanicpation Movement in Germany (Salem, N.H.: Ayer Company, 1975), p. 12.

23. Suzanne Desan, *The Family on Trial in Revolutionary France* (Berkeley: University of California Press, 2004), pp. 220, 248.

24. Alison Sulloway, *Jane Austen and the Province of Womanhood* (Philadelphia: University of Pennsylvania Press, 1989); Robb, *Strangers,* p. 177.

25. Desan, *Family on Trial,* pp. 220, 242, 255.

26. Quoted in Steven Mintz, *Huck's Raft: A History of American Childhood* (Cambridge, Mass.: Belknap Press, 2004), p. 54.

27. Abray, "Feminism in the French Revolution"; Miller, *Transformations of Patriarchy in the West,* p. 105 (see chap. 8, n. 33); Coontz, *Social Origins of Private Life,* pp. 148–52; Gunderson, *To Be Useful,* p. 171.

28. Carole Pateman, *The Sexual Contract* (Cambridge: Polity Press, 1988); Desan, *Family on Trial* p. 306.

29. Karin Hausen, "Family and Role-Division: The Polarisation of Sexual Stereotypes in the Nineteenth Century," in Richard Evans and W. R. Lee, eds., *The German Family: Essays on the Social History of the Family in Nineteenth- and Twentieth-Century Germany* (London: Croom Helm, 1981); Fletcher, *Gender, Sex and Subordination.* See also Thomas Laquer, *Making Sex: Body and Gender from the Greeks to Freud* (Cambridge, U.K.: Harvard University Press, 1990).

30. Quoted in Dorothee Sturkenboom, "Historicizing the Gender of Emotions," *Journal of Social History* 20 (2000), p. 68.

31. Mary Philbrook, "Women's Suffrage in New Jersey Prior to 1807," *New Jersey Historical Proceedings* 97 (1939), p. 96.

32. Lendol Calder, *Financing the American Dream: A Cultural History of Consumer Credit* (Princeton: Princeton University Press, 1999), p. 76; Nancy Cott, *The Bonds of Womanhood* (New Haven: Yale University Press, 1977), p. 43; Catherine Kelly, *In the New England Fashion: Reshaping Women's Lives in the Nineteenth Century* (Ithaca, N.Y.: Cornell University Press, 1997), p. 43.

33. Bengt Ankerloo, "Agriculture and Women's Work: Directions of Change in the West, 1700–1900," *Journal of Family History* 4 (1979); E. A. Hammond, Sheila Johansson, and Caren Ginsberg, "The Value of Children During Industrialization," *Journal of Family History* 8 (1983); Sara Horrell and Jane Humphries, "Women's Labour Force Participation and the Transition to the Male Breadwinner Family, 1790–1865," in Pamela Sharpe, ed., *Women's Work: The English Experience 1650–1914* (New York: Arnold, 1998); K. D. M. Snell, "Agricultural Seasonal Unemployment, the Standard of Living, and Women's Work, 1690–1860," ibid.; Jane Humphries, "Enclosures, Common Rights and Women: The

Proletarianization of Families in the Late Eighteenth and Early Nineteenth Centuries," *Journal of Economic History* 50 (1990).

34. Marion Gray, *Productive Men, Reproductive Women: The Agrarian Household and the Emergence of Separate Spheres During the German Enlightenment* (New York: Berghahn Books, 2000), pp. 301–02.

35. Deborah Simonton, *A History of European Women's Work: 1700 to the Present* (New York: Routledge, 1998), pp. 91–93. See also Lenore Davidoff, *Family Fortunes: Men and Women of the English Middle Class, 1780–1850* (Chicago: University of Chicago Press, 1987); Wunder, *"He Is the Sun, She Is the Moon,"* p. 203. For the same transition, slightly later, in France, see Martine Segalen, *Love and Power in the Peasant Family: Rural France in the Nineteenth Century* (Oxford, U.K.: Basil Blackwell, 1983), pp. 8–9.

36. Boydston, *Home and Work;* Cott, *Bonds of Womanhood;* Kelly, *New England Fashion,* p. 44.

37. Some historians see the explosion of unwed childbearing as a result of women's increased liberation, some as a result of their increased vulnerability. Both of course could be at work at once. For various interpretations, see Seccombe, *Millennium* (see chap. 8, n. 4); Shorter, *Making of the Modern Family;* Louise Tilly, Joan Scott, and Miriam Cohen, "Women's Work and European Fertility Patterns," *Journal of Interdisciplinary History* 6 (1976).

38. Hugh Cunningham, *Children and Childhood in Western Society Since 1500* (Harlow, U.K.: Longman, 1995).

39. Mintz, *Huck's Raft.*

40. Richard Godbeer, *Sexual Revolution in Early America* (Baltimore: Johns Hopkins University Press, 2002), p. 265.

41. Seccombe, *Millennium.* For other sources on this and the following paragraphs on economic change, see: Levine, *Family Formation in an Age of Nascent Capitalism* (see chap. 8, n. 30); Kriedte, Medick, and Schlumbohm, *Industrialization Before Industrialization* (see chap. 8, n. 30); Mendels, "Proto-industrialization" (see chap. 8, n. 30); Medick, "The Proto-industrial Family Economy" (see chap. 8, n. 30); Braun, "Early Industrialization and Demographic Change in the Canton of Zurich" (see chap. 8, n. 30); Gutmann and Leboutte, "Rethinking Protoindustrialization and Family" (see chap. 8, n. 30); Mitterauer, "Peasant and Non-Peasant Family Farms (see chap. 8, n. 30); Pfister, "The Protoindustrial Household Economy" (see chap. 8, n. 30).

42. For an excellent description of how middle-class marital and family strategies changed during the early phases of wage labor and industrialization, see Mary Ryan, *Cradle of the Middle Class: The Family in Oneida County, New York, 1790–1865* (New York: Cambridge University Press, 1983).

43. D'Emilio and Freedman, *Intimate Matters,* p. 45. For the early eighteenth-

century history of the new emphasis on chastity, see Ingrid Tague, *Women of Quality* (Rochester, N.Y.: Boydell, 2002).

Chapter 10. "Two Birds Within One Nest"

1. T. Walter Herbert, *Dearest Beloved: The Hawthornes and the Making of the Middle-Class Family* (Berkeley: University of California Press, 1993), pp. 12–13.
2. Nancy Cott, *The Bonds of Womanhood: Women's Sphere in New England, 1780–1835* (New Haven: Yale University Press, 1977), p. 68; "Empire of Woman," reprinted in Mary Beth Norton, ed., *Major Problems in American Women's History* (Lexington, Mass.: D. C. Heath, 1989), p. 114; Gail Collins, *America's Women* (New York: William Morrow, 2004), p. 87.
3. John Tosh, *A Man's Place: Masculinity and the Middle-Class Home in Victorian England* (New Haven: Yale University Press, 1999), p. 47; Herbert, *Dearest Beloved*, p. 14.
4. Asa Briggs, *A Social History of England* (London: Penguin, 1999); Daniel Scott Smith, "The Long Cycle in American Illegitimacy and Prenuptial Pregnancy," in Laslett, Oosterveen, and Smith, eds., *Bastardy* (see chap. 2, n. 19); John D'Emilio and Estelle Freedman, *Intimate Matters: A History of Sexuality in America* (New York: Harper & Row, 1988).
5. Laslett, Oosterveen, and Smith, *Bastardy;* André Burguière and François Lebrun, "Priest, Prince, and Family," in Burguière et al., *Impact of Modernity,* vol. 2, p. 129; Mark Abrahamson, *Out-of-Wedlock Births: The United States in Comparative Perspective* (Westport, Conn.: Praeger, 1998); Smith, "Long Cycle"; Judith Flanders, *Inside the Victorian Home* (New York: W. W. Norton, 2004).
6. D'Emilio and Freedman, *Intimate Matters,* p. 70; Smith, *Changing Lives,* p. 181; G. J. Barker-Benfield, *The Horrors of the Half-Known Life: Male Attitudes Toward Women and Sexuality in Nineteenth-Century America* (New York: Harper Colophon, 1976), pp. 275, 278.
7. Quoted in Leonore Davidoff, *Worlds Between: Historical Perspectives on Gender and Class* (New York: Routledge, 1995), p. 41.
8. Steven Ruggles, *Prolonged Connections: The Rise of the Extended Family in Nineteenth-Century England and America* (Madison: University of Wisconsin Press, 1987).
9. Quotes from Gottlieb, *The Family in the Western World* pp. 252, 254 (see chap. 7, n. 8). On the peasant attachment to the *domus,* see Ladurie, *Montaillou* (see chap. 7, n. 8).
10. Kirk Jeffrey, "The Family as Utopian Retreat from the City," *Soundings* 55 (1972), p. 28. For the other quotes, see *Ladies Book* 1 (1840), p. 331; *Southern Literary Messenger* 1 (1835), p. 508; John Todd, *The Moral*

Influence, Dangers and Duties, Connected with Great Cities (Northampton, Mass.: 1841).

11. Leonore Davidoff, *Family Fortunes: Men and Women of the English Middle Class, 1780–1850* (Chicago: University of Chicago Press, 1987), p. 187; Taine quoted in John Tosh, *A Man's Place*, p. 28.

12. Leonore Davidoff, "The Family in Britain," in F. M. L. Thompson, ed., *The Cambridge Social History of Britain 1750–1950* (Cambridge, U.K.: Cambridge University Press, 1990), vol. 2, p. 71. Pockels, quoted in Smith, *Changing Lives*, p. 183. See also Peter Gay, *The Bourgeois Experience, Victoria to Freud*, vol. 4: *The Naked Heart* (New York: W. W. Norton, 1995).

13. Hale quotes, from G. R. Searle, *Morality and the Market in Victorian Britain* (Oxford: Clarendon Press, 1998), p. 156, and Nancy Woloch, *Women and the American Experience* (New York: McGraw-Hill, 1994), vol. 1, pp. 102–03.

14. Searle, *Morality and the Market*, p. 156; Barbara Pope, "Angel's in the Devil's Workshop," in Bridenthal et al., *Becoming Visible* (see chap. 3, n. 39).

15. Woloch, *Women and the American Experience*, p. 105.

16. Michael Kimmel, *Manhood in America: A Cultural History* (New York: Free Press, 1996), pp. 54–55; Tosh, *Man's Place*, p. 55; Barker-Benfield, *Horrors of the Half-Known Life*, p. 198. Another minister advised businessmen that despite a wife's ignorance of practical matters, she could often serve as a moral "mentor."

17. Mary Ryan, "The Power of Women's Networks," *Feminist Studies* 5 (1979); Barbara Epstein, *The Politics of Domesticity: Women, Evangelism, and Temperance in Nineteenth-Century America* (Middletown, Conn.: Wesleyan University Press, 1981). On domestic feminism, see Daniel Scott Smith, "Family Limitation, Sexual Control, and Domestic Feminism in Victorian America," in Mary Hartmann and Lois Banner, eds., *Clio's Consciousness Raised* (New York: Harper and Row, 1974).

18. E. Anthony Rotundo, *American Manhood: Transformations in Masculinity from the Revolution to the Modern Era* (New York: Basic Books, 1993), p. 107. For more on men's acceptance of domesticity in the United States, see Stephen Frank, *Life with Father: Parenthood and Masculinity in the Nineteenth-Century American North* (Baltimore: Johns Hopkins University Press, 1998).

19. Tosh, *A Man's Place*, p. 5.

20. Orvar Lofgren, "Families and Households: Images and Reality," in Robert McC. Netting, Richard Wilk, and Eric Arnould, eds., *Households: Comparative and Historical Studies of the Domestic Group* (Berkeley: University of California Press, 1984), p. 456. Laborer quoted in Gillis, *For Better, for Worse*, p. 112 (see chap. 7, n. 13). On the evolution of the word *family*

and the resentment of servants and hired hands at being excluded from it in the early nineteenth century, see Raymond Williams, *Keywords: A Vocabulary of Culture and Society* (New York: Oxford University Press, 1983), p. 132.

21. Lawrence Stone quoted in Gillis, *For Better, for Worse,* p. 138; Ellen Rothman, *Hands and Hearts: A History of Courtship in America* (New York: Basic Books, 1984), pp. 81–82, 175–76; Peter Ward, *Courtship, Love, and Marriage in Nineteenth-Century English Canada* (Montreal: McGill-Queen's University Press, 1990), p. 117.

22. This custom persisted in some areas until the second half of the nineteenth century. In 1856 a surprised northern observer described a typical "Christmas Serenade" in St. Augustine, Texas. A band of "pleasant spirits . . . blowing tin horns and beating tin pans," he reported, visited every house in town, "kicking in doors and pulling down fences until every male member of the family had appeared with appropriate instruments and joined the merry party." Penne Restad, *Christmas in America: A History* (New York: Oxford University Press, 1995); Peter Stearns, "The Making of the Domestic Occasion: The History of Thanksgiving in the United States," *Journal of Social History* 32 (1999). On the invention of the Sunday dinner, see John Gillis, *A World of Their Own Making: Myth, Ritual, and the Quest for Family Values* (New York: Basic Books, 1997). For a good description of the sentimentalization and privatization of celebrations in the nineteenth century, see Elizabeth Pleck, *Celebrating the Family* (Cambridge, Mass.: Harvard University Press, 2000). For a contrasting description of the dense ties beyond the nuclear family prevailing in the eighteenth century, see Naomi Tadmor, *Family and Friends in Eighteenth-Century England: Household, Kinship, and Patronage* (Cambridge: Cambridge University Press, 2001).

23. Gillis, *World of Their Own Making,* p. 101; Restad, *Christmas,* p. 41; Stearns, "Domestic Occasion."

24. Pleck, *Celebrating the Family.*

25. Mark Fann, *A Republic of Men: The American Founders, Gendered Language, and Patriarchal Politics* (New York: New York University Press, 1998); Adams quoted in W. Norton Grubb and Marvin Lazerson, *Broken Promises: How America Fails Its Children* (New York: Basic Books, 1982), p. 283.

26. Coontz, *Social Origins,* pp. 226–29, 235; Kathryn Sklar, *Catharine Beecher* (New York: Norton, 1976); Mary Ryan, *Women in Public: Between Banners and Ballots, 1825–1880* (Baltimore: Johns Hopkins University Press, 1990), pp. 37, 52–53; Russell Conwell, *Acres of Diamonds* (New York: Pyramid, 1966), p. 22.

27. William McLoughlin, *The Meaning of Henry Ward Beecher: An Essay on the*

Shifting Values of Mid-Victorian America, 1840–1870 (New York: Alfred A. Knopf, 1970), pp. 115–16.

28. Rosemary O'Day, *The Family and Family Relationships, 1500–1900: England, France and the United States* (New York: St. Martin's Press, 1994); James Riley, *Rising Life Expectancy: A Global History* (Cambridge, U.K.: Cambridge University Press, 2001); Cynthia Comacchio, *The Infinite Bonds of Family: Domesticity in Canada, 1850–1940* (Toronto: University of Toronto Press, 1999). On the struggles of slave families, see Emily West, *Chains of Love: Slave Couples in Antebellum South Carolina* (Urbana: University of Illinois Press, 2004) and Brenda Stevenson, "Distress and Discord in Virginia Slave Families," in Carol Bleser, ed., *In Joy and in Sorrow: Women, Family, and Marriage in the Victorian South* (New York: Oxford University Press, 1991).

29. Stephanie Coontz, *The Way We Never Were: American Families and the Nostalgia Trap* (New York: Basic Books, 2000); Faye Dudden, *Serving Women: Household Service in 19th-Century America* (Middletown, Conn.: Wesleyan University Press, 1983); David Katzman, *Seven Days a Week: Women and Domestic Service in Industrializing America* (New York: Oxford University Press, 1978); Christine Stansell, *City of Women: Sex and Class in New York, 1789–1860* (Urbana: University of Illinois, 1987); Flanders, *Inside the Victorian Home.*

30. James McMillan, *Housewife or Harlot: The Place of Women in French Society 1870–1940* (New York: St. Martin's Press, 1981), p. 9; Deborah Simonton, *A History of European Women's Work: 1700 to the Present* (London: Routledge, 1998), pp. 87–88; D'Emilio and Freedman, *Intimate Matters,* p. 70.

31. Josef Ehmer, "Marriage," in David Kertzer and Mario Barbagli, eds., *The History of the European Family,* vol. 2, *Family Life in the Long Nineteenth Century, 1789–1913* (New Haven: Yale University Press, 2001), p. 320; Charles Rosenberg, "Sexuality, Class and Role in 19th-Century America," *American Quarterly* 25 (1973), p. 139.

32. Carroll Smith-Rosenberg and Charles Rosenberg, "The Female Animal: Medical and Biological Views of Woman and Her Role in Nineteenth Century America," *Journal of American History* 60 (1973); *Ladies' Companion* 9 (1838); William and Robin Haller, *The Physician and Sexuality in Victorian America* (Chicago: University of Chicago Press, 1974); Susan Phinney Conrad, *Perish the Thought: Intellectual Women in Romantic America, 1830–1860* (New York: Oxford University Press, 1976).

33. Amy Erickson, *Women's Property in Early Modern England* (London: Routledge, 1993); Fletcher, *Gender, Sex, and Subordination* (chap. 7, n. 41); Susan Okin, "Women and the Making of the Sentimental Family," *Philosophy and Public Affairs* 11 (1982).

34. Nancy Cott, "Passionlessness: An Interpretation of Victorian Sexual

Ideology," in Nancy Cott and Elizabeth Pleck, eds., *A Heritage of Her Own* (New York: Simon and Schuster, 1979); Duby, *Love and Marriage in the Middle Ages,* pp. 27–28 (see chap. 7, n. 3).

35. John Demos, "The American Family in Past Time," *American Scholar,* 43 (1974); Dr. John Cowan, in Ronald Walters, ed., *Primers for Prudery: Sexual Advice to Victorian America* (Baltimore: Johns Hopkins University Press, 2000).

36. Peter Laipson, "'Kiss Without Shame, for She Desires It,'" *Journal of Social History* (1996), p. 507; Norton, *Major Problems,* p. 228.

37. D'Emilio and Freedman, *Intimate Matters,* p. 180.

38. Cormany quoted in Shawn Johansen, *Family Men: Middle-Class Fatherhood in Early Industrializing America* (New York: Routledge, 2001), p. 51.

39. Walters, *Primers for Prudery;* Cott, "Passionless"; James Mohr, *Abortion in America: The Origins and Evolution of National Policy, 1800–1900* (New York: Oxford University Press, 1978); Janet Brodie, *Contraception and Abortion in Nineteenth-Century America* (Ithaca, N.Y.: Cornell University Press, 1994).

40. Estelle Freedman, *The History of the Family and the History of Sexuality* (Washington, D.C.: American Historical Association, 1998); D'Emilio and Freeman, *Intimate Matters;* Daniel Scott Smith, "'Early' Fertility Decline in America," *Journal of Family History* 12 (1987). Michael Anderson, "The Social Implications of Demographic Change," in Thompson, *Cambridge Social History,* vol. 2; Alison Prentice et al., *Canadian Women: A History* (Toronto: Harcourt Brace, 1996); Miller, *Transformations of Patriarchy in the West* (see chap. 8, n. 33).

41. David Pivar, *Purity Crusade: Sexual Morality and Social Control, 1868–1900* (Westport, Conn.: Greenwood Press, 1973).

42. Mary Ann Glendon, *The Transformation of Family Law* (Chicago: University of Chicago Press, 1989), p. 238.

43. Jennine Hurl-Eamon, "Domestic Violence Prosecuted: Women Binding over their Husbands for Assault at Westminster Quarter Sessions, 1685–1720," *Journal of Family History* 26 (2001); M. Hunt, "Wife Beating, Domesticity and Women's Independence in Eighteenth-Century London," *Gender and History,* 4 (1992); R. P. Dobash and R. E. Dobash, "Community Response to Violence Against Wives: Charivari, Abstract Justice, and Patriarchy," *Social Problems* 28 (1981); Leah Leneman, *Alienated Affections: The Scottish Experience of Divorce, 1684–1830* (Edinburgh: Edinburgh University Press, 1998); A. James Hammerton, *Cruelty and Companionship: Conflict in Nineteenth-Century Married Life* (London: Routledge, 1992); Shani D'Cruze, *Crimes of Outrage: Sex, Violence and Victorian Working Women* (DeKalb: Northern Illinois University Press, 1998); Leah Leneman, "'A Tyrant and Tormentor': Violence Against Wives in Eighteenth- and

Early Nineteenth-Century Scotland," *Continuity and Change* 12 (1997); Linda Hirshman and Jane Larson, *Hard Bargains: The Politics of Sex* (New York: Oxford University Press, 1998); Steven Mintz, "Regulating the American Family," in Joseph Hawes and Elizabeth Nybakken, eds., *Family and Society in American History* (Urbana: University of Illinois Press, 2001).

44. Riley, *Rising Life Expectancy*, pp. 172–79.

45. Anderson, "Social Implications," p. 27; Phillips, *Putting Asunder*, p. 393 (see chap. 9, n. 17).

46. For this and the next paragraph, see Jeanne Boydston, *Home and Work: Housework, Wages, and the Ideology of Work in the Early Republic* (New York: Oxford University Press, 1990); Francis Early, "The French-Canadian Family Economy and Standard-of-Living in Lowell, Massachusetts, 1870," *Journal of Family History* 7 (1982), p. 184; Michael Haines, "Industrial Work and the Family Life Cycle, 1889–1890," *Research in Economic History* 4 (1979), p. 291; Claudia Goldin, *Understanding the Gender Gap: On the Economic History of American Women* (New York: Oxford University Press, 1990); Michael Anderson, *Family Structure in Nineteenth-Century Lancashire* (Cambridge, U.K.: Cambridge University Press, 1971); Colin Creighton, "The Rise of the Male Breadwinner Family," *Comparative Studies in Society and History* 38 (1996); Joanna Bourke, "Housewifery in Working-Class England," in Pamela Sharpe, ed., *Women's Work: The English Experience, 1650–1914* (London: Arnold Publishers, 1998), p. 339; Sara Horrell and Jane Humphries, "Women's Labour Force Participation and the Transition to the Male Breadwinner Family," *Economic History Review* 48 (1995).

47. Simonton, *History of European Women's Work*, p. 262; Wally Seccombe, *Weathering the Storm: Working-Class Families from the Industrial Revolution to the Fertility Decline* (London, New York: Verso, 1993), pp. 111–24.

48. Riley, *Rising Life Expectancy;* Ute Frevert, "The Civilizing Tendency of Hygiene," in John Fout, ed., *German Women in the Nineteenth Century* (London: Holmes & Meier, 1984); S. D. Chapman, ed., *The History of Working Class Housing* (London: David & Charles, 1971); Anna Clark, "The New Poor Law and the Breadwinner Wage," *Journal of Social History* (2000).

49. Thomas Hine, *The Rise and Fall of the American Teenager* (New York: Perennial Books, 1999), p. 125; Amy Dru Stanley, *From Bondage to Contract: Wage Labor, Marriage, and the Market in the Age of Slave Emancipation* (Cambridge, Mass.: Harvard University Press, 1998), p. 147.

Chapter 11. "A Heaving Volcano"

1. The quotes from Franklin and Sedgwick in the following paragraphs are from Zsuzsa Berend, "'The Best or None!' Spinsterhood in Nineteenth-Century New England," *Journal of Social History* 33 (2000), p. 937.

2. For more on this transformation, see Rotundo, *American Manhood,* p.110 *(see chap. 10, n. 18);* Peter Gay, *The Bourgeois Experience, Victoria to Freud: The Naked Heart* (New York: Oxford University Press, 1984), p. 100.

3. Karen Lystra, *Searching the Heart: Women, Men, and Romantic Love in Nineteenth-Century America* (New York: Oxford University Press, 1989), pp. 22–23, 45, 50.

4. Catherine Kelly, *In the New England Fashion: Reshaping Women's Lives in the Nineteenth Century* (Ithaca, N.Y.: Cornell University Press, 1999), p. 147; Peter Ward, *Courtship, Love, and Marriage in Nineteenth-Century English Canada* (Buffalo: McGill-Queens University Press, 1990), p. 156. Historian Peter Gay notes that Americans of that era reversed the judgment of earlier generations and came to think that an inability to fall in love was a worse flaw in an individual than a tendency to fall in love too easily. Gay, *The Bourgeois Experience,* p. 100.

5. The rival quote and the lovers' exchanges in the next two paragraphs come from Lystra, *Searching the Heart,* pp. 235–49.

6. Lee Chambers-Schiller, *Liberty, A Better Husband* (New Haven: Yale University Press), p. 38; Gail Collins, *America's Women* (New York: HarperCollins, 2003), p. 138; Nancy Cott, *The Bonds of Womanhood* (New Haven: Yale University Press, 1977).

7. Herbert, *Dearest Beloved,* p. 186 (see chap. 10, n. 1).

8. O'Faolain and Martines, *Not in God's Image,* p. 315 (see chap. 9, n. 13).

9. W. R. Greg, "Prostitution," *Westminster Review* 53 (1850). Free love advocates in the United States made the same point, arguing that law and custom forced women to marry and submit to unwanted sex in order to ensure their livelihood and respectability. In 1870 the novelist Henry James argued that marriage came into "dishonor" when it was forced on people; only when it was based on free sentiment rather than constraints could it be "holy." Nicola Beisel, *Imperiled Innocents: Anthony Comstock and Family Reproduction in Victorian America* (Princeton: Princeton University Press, 1997), pp. 79, 87–88; Joanne Passet, *Sex Radicals and the Quest for Women's Equality* (Urbana: University of Illinois Press, 2003); James quotes, in David Kennedy, "The Family, Feminism and Sex," in Thomas Frazier, ed., *The Private Side of American History* (New York: Harcourt Brace Jovanovich, 1979), p. 125.

10. James Talbot, "Miseries of Prostitution," *Westminster Review* 53 (1850), p. 472.

11. Rotundo, *American Manhood.* On the inherent push toward both equality and the right to divorce, see James Traer, *Marriage and the Family in Eighteenth-Century France* (Ithaca, N.Y.: Cornell University Press, 1980); Lynn Hunt, "Forgetting and Remembering: The French Revolution Then and Now," *American Historical Review* 100 (1995).

12. Phillips, *Putting Asunder* (see chap. 9, n. 17); Briggs, *Social History* (see chap. 9, n. 14); Josef Ehmer, "Marriage," in David Kertzer and Mario Barbagli, eds., *The History of the European Family,* vol. 2: *Family Life in the Long Nineteenth Century, 1789–1913* (New Haven: Yale University Press, 2001); Carole Shammas, *A History of Household Government in America* (Charlottesville: University of Virginia Press, 2002); Hendrik Hartog, *Man and Wife in America* (Cambridge, Mass.: Harvard University Press, 2000).

13. Cited in E. J. Goldthorpe, *Family Life in Western Societies: A Historical Sociology of Family Relationships in Britain and North America* (New York: Cambridge University Press, 1987).

14. Lystra, *Searching the Heart,* pp. 235–36.

15. Taylor Stoehr, *Free Love in America: A Documentary History* (New York: AMS Press, 1979), p. 270.

16. Tosh, *A Man's Place,* pp. 161, 168 (see chap. 10, n. 3); Maeve Doggett, *Marriage, Wife-Beating and the Law in Victorian England* (Columbia: University of South Carolina Press, 1993), p. 144.

17. Carroll Smith-Rosenberg, "Beauty, the Beast, and the Militant Woman: A Case Study in Sex Roles and Social Stress in Jacksonian America," *American Quarterly* 23 (1971). On how adherents to the doctrine of true womanhood could become converts to feminism, see Nancy Cott, *The Bonds of Womanhood: "Woman's Sphere" in New England* (New Haven: Yale University Press, 1977).

18. Nancy Woloch, *Women and the American Experience* (New York: McGraw-Hill, 1994), vol. 2.

19. Kirk Jeffrey, "Marriage, Career, and Feminine Ideology in Nineteenth Century America," *Feminist Studies* 2 (1975), p. 123.

20. Phillips, *Putting Asunder;* Briggs, *Social History;* Ehmer, "Marriage."

21. Steven Ruggles, *Prolonged Connections: The Rise of the Extended Family in Nineteenth-Century England and America* (Madison: University of Wisconsin Press, 1987). Furthermore, among the highest levels of the bourgeoisie, there was a temporary resurgence of economic marriage. Because raising capital still depended on family connections, marriages between cousins became as desirable to expanding business entrepreneurs as they had been to members of the aristocracy and royalty in earlier centuries. Marriages with kin were common among coal and iron industrialists in the Rhineland and English Midlands, financiers and merchants in Belgium, France, Germany, and Britain, and the rural bourgeoisie in Italy. Over the course of the nineteenth century there was actually a temporary increase in the proportion of marriages that took place between first cousins, with the greatest number of such marriages occurring between 1880 and 1920. David Sabean, "Aesthetic of Marriage Alliance: Class Codes and Endogamous Marriage in the Nineteenth-Century Propertied

Classes," in Richard Wall, Tamara Hareven, and Josef Ehmer, eds., *Family History Revisited: Comparative Perspectives* (Newark: University of Delaware Press, 2001); Ehmer, "Marriage." For similar trends slightly down the social scale, see David Sabean, *Property, Production, and Family in Neckarhausen, 1700–1870* (Cambridge, U.K.: Cambridge University Press, 1990).

22. Http://65.66.134.201/cgi-bin/webster/webster.exe?search_fortexts_web1828=Love.

23. Harvey Graff, *Conflicting Paths: Growing Up in America* (Cambridge, Mass.: Harvard University Press, 1995), p. 219.

24. Carroll Smith-Rosenberg, *Disorderly Conduct: Visions of Gender in Victorian America* (New York: Oxford University Press, 1985), pp. 35–36, 53–89; D'Emilio and Freedman, *Intimate Matters,* pp. 125–27 (see chap. 10, n. 6); Lilian Faderman, *Surpassing the Love of Men: Romantic Friendship and Love Between Women from the Renaissance to the Present* (New York: William Morrow, 1981).

25. Anthony Rotundo, "Romantic Friendship: Male Intimacy and Middle-Class Youth in the Northern United States, 1800–1900," *Journal of Social History* 23 (Fall 1989); Rotundo, *American Manhood.* On the long history of intense male bonds prior to this time, see Alan Bray, *The Friend* (Chicago: University of Chicago Press, 2003).

26. D'Emilio and Freeman, *Intimate Matters,* pp. 127–29; Joathan Katz, *The Invention of Homosexuality* (New York: Plume, 1996); Martin Duberman, Martha Vicinus, and George Chauncey, Jr., eds., *Hidden from History* (New York: Meridian, 1990); Peter Boag, *Same-Sex Affairs, Constructing and Controlling Homosexuality in the Pacific Northwest* (Berkeley: University of California Press, 2003).

27. Graham Robb, *Strangers: Homosexual Love in the Nineteenth Century* (New York: Norton, 2003), p. 107. See also Jonathon Katz, ed., *Gay American History: Lesbians and Gay Men in the USA* (New York: Crowell, 1976); John Ibson, *Picturing Men: A Century of Male Relationships in Everyday American Photography* (Washington: Smithsonian Institution, 2002) and David Deitcher, *Dear Friends: American Photographs of Men Together* (New York: Harry Abrams, 2001).

28. Sulloway, *Jane Austen,* p. 17 (chap. 9, n. 24).

29. Jo Freeman, "The Legal Basis of the Sexual Caste System," *Valparaiso University Law Review* 5 (1971), p. 210; Norma Basch, *In the Eyes of the Law: Women, Marriage and Property in Nineteenth-Century New York* (Ithaca, N.Y.: Cornell University Press, 1982).

30. Katharine Rogers, *The Troublesome Helpmate: A History of Misogyny in Literature,* (Seattle: University of Washington Press, 1966), pp. 190, 211 (emphasis added).

31. Michael Grossberg, "Who Gets the Child? Custody, Guardianship, and the Rise of a Judicial Patriarchy in Nineteenth-Century America," *Feminist Studies* 9 (1983), pp. 247, 250.

32. Debra Viles, "Disabilities of Marriage," *Michigan Historical Review* 28 (2001); Hartog, *Man and Wife in America;* Basch, *In the Eyes of the Law;* Jo Freeman, "The Legal Revolution," in Freeman, ed., *Women: A Feminist Perspective* (Mountain View, Calif.: Mayfield, 1989).

33. Nancy Cott, *Public Vows: A History of Marriage and the Nation* (Cambridge, Mass.: Harvard University Press, 2000), p. 162.

34. Quoted in Davidoff, *Family Fortunes,* p. 183 (see chap. 8, n. 1).

35. William Kristol, "Women's Liberation: The Relevance of Tocqueville," in Ken Masugi, ed., *Interpreting Tocqueville's* Democracy in America (Savage, Maryland: Rowman & Littlefield, 1999), p. 491.

36. Francis J. Grund, *Aristocracy in America* (Gloucester, Mass.: Peter Smith, 1968 [1840]), p. 40.

37. Michael Roper and John Tosh, "Introduction," in Roper and Tosh, eds., *Manful Assertions: Masculinities in Britain Since 1800* (London: Routledge, 1991).

38. Anya Jabour, *Marriage in the Early Republic: Elizabeth and William Wirt and the Companionate Ideal* (Baltimore: Johns Hopkins University Press, 1998); Rotundo, *American Manhood,* p. 165; Orvar Lofgren, "Family and Household: Images and Realities," in Robert McC. Netting, Richard Wilk, and Eric Arnould, eds., *Households: Comparative and Historical Studies of the Domestic Group* (Berkeley: University of California Press, 1984), p. 462.

39. Mary Ryan, "Femininity and Capitalism in Antebellum America," in Zillah Eisenstein, ed., *Capitalist Patriarchy and the Case for Socialist Feminism,* (New York: Monthly Review, 1979), p. 158; Beecher quoted in Lendol Calder, *Financing the American Dream: A Cultural History of Consumer Credit* (Princeton: Princeton University Press, 1999) p. 97. On women's inability to recognize the love that men performed in daily life, see Francesca Cancian, "The Feminization of Love," *Signs* 11 (1986).

40. "Essay on Marriage," *Universalist and Ladies' Repository* (1834), p. 371.

41. Woloch, *Women and the American Experience,* vol. 1, p. 104.

42. Tosh, *A Man's Place,* p. 173; Howard Chudacoff, *The Age of the Bachelor: Creating an American Subculture* (Princeton: Princeton University Press, 1999).

43. David G. Pugh, *Sons of Liberty: The Masculine Mind in Nineteenth-Century America,* (Westport, Conn.: Greenwood Press, 1983), p. 88; Peter Gabriel Filene, *Him/Her/Self* (New York: New American Library, 1974), p. 83; John Demos, "The American Family in Past Time," *American Scholar,* 43 (1974); Charles Rosenberg, "Sexuality, Class and Role in Nineteenth-

Century America," *American Quarterly* 25 (1973), p. 139; John Haller and Robin Haller, *The Physician and Sexuality in Victorian America* (Urbana: University of Illinois Press, 1974), p. 203; G. J. Barker-Benfield, *The Horrors of the Half-Known Life: Male Attitudes Toward Women and Sexuality in Nineteenth-Century America* (New York: Harper & Row, 1976), p. 159; Rotundo, *American Manhood*, p. 125; D'Emilio and Freedman, *Intimate Matters*, pp. 110, 180. For an argument that many couples overcame their inhibitions and had good sex lives, see Carl Degler, "What Ought to Be and What Was: Women's Sexuality in the Nineteenth Century," *American Historical Review* 79 (1974).

44. D'Emilio and Freedman, *Intimate Matters*, p. 179; Tosh, *A Man's Place*, p. 68.

45. D'Emilio and Freedman, *Intimate Matters*, pp. 174–78.

46. Ibid., p. 110.

47. Rachel Maines, *The Technology of Orgasm* (Baltimore: Johns Hopkins University Press, 1999).

48. Michel Foucault, *The History of Sexuality* (New York: Vintage, 1988); Paul Rabinow, ed., *The Foucault Reader* (New York: Pantheon, 1984); Steven Marcus, *The Other Victorians: A Study of Sexuality and Pornography in Mid-Nineteenth-Century England* (New York: New American Library, 1974).

49. The information and quotations in this and the following paragraphs are drawn from Tosh, *A Man's Place*, pp. 68–71, 98, 100.

50. Lesley Hall, *Hidden Anxieties: Male Sexuality 1900–1950* (Oxford, U.K.: Polity Press, 1991), pp. 10, 43–49, 100–06.

51. Joanne Meyerowitz, *Women Adrift: Independent Women Wage Earners in Chicago, 1880–1930* (Chicago: University of Chicago Press, 1988); Lewis Ehrenberg, *Steppin' Out: New York City Nightlife and the Transformation of American Culture, 1890–1930* (Westport, Conn.: Greenwood Press, 1981); Kathy Peiss, *Cheap Amusements: Working Women and Leisure in Turn-of-the-Century New York* (Philadelphia: Temple University Press, 1989); Randy McBee, *Dance Hall Days: Intimacy and Leisure Among Working-Class Immigrants in the United States* (New York: New York University Press, 2000); Kathy Peiss, " 'Charity Girls' and City Pleasures: Historical Notes on Working-Class Sexuality," in Christina Simmons and Kathy Peiss, eds., *Passion and Power: Sexuality in History* (Philadelphia: Temple University Press, 1989); Nancy Cott, *The Grounding of Modern Feminism* (New Haven: Yale University Press, 1987); Barbara Melosh, ed., *Gender and American History Since 1890* (New York: Routledge, 1993).

52. Jane Hunter, *How Young Ladies Became Girls: The Victorian Origins of American Girlhood* (New Haven: Yale University Press, 2002); Filene, *Him/Her/Self.*

53. Andrea Tone, *Devices and Desires: A History of Contraception in America* (New York: Hill & Wang, 2000).

54. Yalom, *History of the Wife* (see chap. 1, n. 16); Jane Lewis, *The End of Marriage? Individualism and Intimate Relations* (Northampton, Mass.: Edward Elgar, 2001).

55. Ginger Frost, "A Shock to Marriage? The Clitheroe Case and the Victorians," in George Robb and Nancy Erber, eds., *Disorder in the Court: Trials and Sexual Conflict at the Turn of the Century* (New York: New York University Press, 1999).

56. *Loc sit;* Lesley Hall, *Sex, Gender and Social Change in Britain Since 1880* (London: Macmillan, 2000), p. 58.

57. Mary Ann Glendon, *The Transformation of Family Law* (Chicago: University of Chicago Press, 1989).

58. For this and the next paragraph, see Collins, *America's Women.*

59. James Weir, Jr., "The Effect of Female Suffrage on Posterity," *American Naturalist* 29 (1895), p. 825. Other quotes in this and the next paragraph from Katharine Rogers, *The Troublesome Helpmate: A History of Misogyny in Literature* (Seattle: University of Washington Press, 1966), pp. 214, 221.

Chapter 12. "The Time When Mountains Move Has Come"

1. This poem was translated for me and presented as a parting gift by members of a history class I taught at the Kobe University of Commerce. There are many other translations of Yosano's poetry available in English. See Laurel Rodd, "Yosano Akiko and the Taisho Debate over the 'New Woman,'" in Gail Bernstein, ed., *Recreating Japanese Women, 1600–1945* (Berkeley: University of California Press, 1991), p. 180.

2. Edith Hurwitz, "The International Sisterhood," in Bridenthal et al., *Becoming Visible* (see chap. 3, n. 39).

3. Daniel Scott Smith, "The Dating of the American Sexual Revolution," in Michael Gordon, ed., *The American Family in Social-Historical Perspective* (New York: St. Martin's Press, 1978); William Leuchtenburg, *The Perils of Prosperity* (Chicago: University of Chicago Press, 1993), p. 171.

4. Birgitte Soland, *Becoming Modern: Young Women and the Reconstruction of Womanhood in the 1920s* (Princeton: Princeton University Press, 2000); June Hahner, *Emancipating the Female Sex: The Struggle for Women's Rights in Brazil* (Durham, N.C.: Duke University Press, 1990); Robert Tignor et al., *Worlds Together, Worlds Apart* (New York: W. W. Norton, 2002); Gisela Block, *Women in European History* (Oxford, U.K.: Blackwell Publishers, 2002); Miriam Silverberg, "The Modern Girl as Militant," in Bernstein, ed., *Recreating Japanese Women.* See also James McGovern, "The American Woman's Pre–World War I Freedom in Manners and Morals," *Journal of American History* 55 (1968).

5. Bonnie Smith, *Changing Lives: Women in European History Since 1700*

(Lexington, Mass.: D. C. Heath, 1989); Renate Bridenthal, "Something Old, Something New," in Bridenthal et al., *Becoming Visible.*

6. D'Emilio and Freedman, *Intimate Matters,* p. 223–35 (see chap. 10, n. 6); William Carson, *The Marriage Revolt: A Study of Marriage and Divorce* (New York: Hearst's International Library Co., 1915); Havelock Ellis, "Introduction," in V. F. Calverton and S. D. Schmalhausen, *Sex in Civilization* (New York: Macaulay Company, 1929), p. 28; Lesley Hall, *Sex, Gender and Social Change in Britain Since 1880* (London: Macmillan Press, 2000), p. 121; Atina Grossman, "*Girlkultur* or Thoroughly Rationalized Females: A New Woman in Weimar Germany?," in Judith Friedlander et al., *Women in Culture and Politics* (Bloomington: Indiana University Press, 1986).

7. Quoted in Mary Jo Buhle, *Women and American Socialism, 1870–1920* (Urbana: University of Illinois, 1981).

8. Raoul de Roussy de Sales, "Love in America" [1938], in Warren Sussman, ed., *Culture and Commitment, 1929–1945* (New York: George Braziller, 1973), pp. 96–97.

9. Robert and Helen Lynd, *Middletown: A Study in Modern American Culture* (New York: Harcourt Brace Jovanovich, 1956 [1929]), p. 266; Mary Ryan, "The Projection of a New Womanhood," in Jean Friedman and William Shade, eds., *Our American Sisters* (Boston: Allyn & Bacon, 1976), p. 46; Frederick Lewis Allen, *Only Yesterday: An Informal History of the 1920s* (New York: Harper & Row, 1964), p. 96.

10. Ellen Rothman, *Hands and Hearts: A History of Courtship in America* (New York: Basic Books, 1984).

11. Quoted in Beth Bailey, *From Front Porch to Back Seat: Courtship in Twentieth-Century America* (Baltimore: Johns Hopkins University Press, 1989), p. 20.

12. Paula Fass, *The Damned and the Beautiful* (New York: Oxford University Press, 1977); Bailey, *From Front Porch to Back Seat.*

13. Laura Hirshbein, "The Flapper and the Fogy," *Journal of Family History* 26 (2001), p. 126; D'Emilio and Freedman, *Intimate Matters,* p. 257.

14. Ryan, "Projection of a New Womanhood," p. 46; John Spurlock and Cynthia Magistro, *New and Improved: The Transformation of Women's Emotional Culture* (New York: New York University Press, 1998), pp. 24, 42.

15. Fass, *Damned and Beautiful;* D'Emilio and Freedman, *Intimate Matters;* Linda Hirshman and Jane Larson, *Hard Bargains: The Politics of Sex* (New York: Oxford University Press, 1998).

16. In 1906, Americans consumed almost eleven tons of cocaine, reports Jill Jonnes, *Hep-Cats, Narcs, and Pipe Deans: A History of America's Romance with Illegal Drugs* (New York: Scribners, 1996).

17. E. S. Martin, "Mothers and Daughters," *Good Housekeeping* 64 (1917), p. 27; Spurlock and Magistro, *New and Improved,* pp. 123–24; Mary

Louise Roberts, *Civilization Without Sexes: Reconstructing Gender in Postwar France, 1917–1927;* (Chicago: University of Chicago Press, 1994), p. 9; John McMahon, "The Jazz Path of Degradation," *Ladies' Home Journal* (January 1922). I am indebted to my student Brianna Oliver for drawing the McMahon article to my attention.

18. Joseph Krutch, writing in the 1928 *Atlantic Monthly,* quoted in John Modell, *Into One's Own* (Berkeley: University of California Press, 1989), p. 98

19. Filene, *Him/Her/Self,* p. 42 (see chap. 11, n. 43); Thomas Hine, *The Rise and Fall of the American Teenager* (New York: Perennial, 1999), p.178.

20. William Sumner, "Modern Marriage," *Yale Review* 13 (1924), p. 274.

21. Ernest Groves, *The Marriage Crisis* (New York: Longmans, Green, and Co., 1928). Hundreds of books and articles were published in America on the "crisis" of marriage. The same fears were raised in Europe. In 1925 a French author asked readers to consider if the institution of marriage had "suddenly and irrevocably become outdated." In Germany, commentators discussed *Die Sexual-Revolution,* the "marriage crisis," the "fiasco of monogamy," and the "birth strike" of women. Maurice Duval, "The Crisis of Marriage" (1924), quoted in Roberts, *Civilization Without Sexes; Grossman, "Girlkultur";* Atina Grossman, *Reforming Sex: The German Movement for Birth Control and Abortion Reform, 1920–1950* (New York: Oxford University Press, 1995); John Martin, "Structuring the Sexual Revolution," *Theory and History* 25 (1996).

22. Nathan Miller, *New World Coming: The 1920s and the Making of Modern America* (New York: Scribner, 2003); Lynd, *Middletown;* Andrew Cherlin, *Marriage, Divorce, Remarriage* (Cambridge, Mass.: Harvard University Press, 1992); William O'Neill, *Divorce in the Progressive Era* (New Haven: Yale University Press, 1967). Again, the United States was not unique. In Britain, petitions for divorce tripled between 1916 and 1920. Even in European countries with lower divorce rates, the percentage increases were just as striking. Hall, *Sex, Gender and Social Change.*

23. Elaine Tyler May, *Great Expectations: Marriage and Divorce in Post-Victorian America* (Chicago: University of Chicago Press, 1980); Roosevelt and Shaw, quoted in Carson, *Marriage Revolt,* pp. 377, 427.

24. Carson, *Marriage Revolt,* pp. 74, 389.

25. Christina Simmons, "Women's Power in Sex; Radical Challenges to Marriage in the Early 20th Century," *Feminist Studies* 29 (2003); Graham Robb, *Strangers: Homosexual Love in the Nineteenth Century* (New York: W. W. Norton, 2003), p. 191; Lilian Faderman, *Surpassing the Love of Men* (New York: William Morrow, 1981), p. 315.

26. George Chauncey, *Gay New York: Gender, Urban Culture, and the Making of the Gay Male World, 1890–1940* (New York: Basic Books, 1994); Sharon

Ullman, *Sex Seen: The Emergence of Modern Sexuality in America* (Berkeley: University of California Press, 1997), p. 49.

27. Charlotte Perkins Gilman, *Herland* (New York: Pantheon, 1979). Feminist ideas were also raised across Europe and in such seeming bastions of male dominance as Muslim areas of India and Confucian China. In 1905 Rokeya Sakhawat Hossain, a Bengali Muslim woman, published a satirical story in which women keep men in seclusion. A 1904 novel in China, *The Stone of the Goddess Nuwa,* portrayed an all-female organization that observed a radically different version of the "three obediences" ordained by traditional Confucian thought. Rather than successively obey their father, husband, and son, women who resided in the Heavenly Fragrant Court had to obey three principles: Understand international politics; assert their independence from men; and develop China's arts, science, and culture. The women in this novel bore children through artificial insemination, harvesting sperm from breeder men whom they maintained in a special apartment complex. See Rokeya Sakhawat Hossain, *Sultana's Dreams and Selections from the Secluded Ones* (New York: Feminist Press, 1988); David Der-wei Wang, *Fin-de-Siècle Splendor: Repressed Modernities of Late Qing Fiction, 1849–1911* (Palo Alto, Calif.: Stanford University Press, 1997).

28. Filene, *Him/Her/Self,* p. 42; Freda Kirchway, ed., *Our Changing Morality: A Symposium* (New York: Boni, 1924); McGovern, "American Woman's Pre-World War I Freedom"; Watson, quoted in Richard Gelles, *Contemporary Families: A Sociological View* (Thousand Oaks, Calif.: Sage, 1995); Walter Lippmann quoted in Jane Lewis, *The End of Marriage? Individualism and Intimate Relations* (Northampton, Mass.: Edward Elgar, 2001).

29. Floyd Dell, *Love in the Machine Age: A Psychological Study of the Transition from Patriarchal Society* (New York: Farrar & Rinehart, 1930).

30. Ibid., pp. 6–7, 117–82. 364.

31. Helena Wright, *The Sex Factor in Marriage* (New York: Vanguard Press, 1931), p. 31; Robinson and Fielding quoted in Laipson, "'Kiss Without Shame," p. 509 (see chap. 10, n. 36). For discussions of attempts to sexualize marriage in order to save it, see Christina Simmons, "Modern Sexuality and the Myth of Victorian Repression," in Melosh, *Gender and American History.*

32. Miller, *New World Coming.* Paula Fass points out that the sexual revolution in the 1920s "was not a revolt against marriage but a revolution within marriage," marked by "the sexualization of love and the glorification of sex." Fass, *The Damned and the Beautiful.*

33. Cott, *Grounding;* Mary Ryan, "The Projection of a New Womanhood:

The Movie Moderns in the 1920s," in Lois Scharf and John Jenson, eds., *Decades of Discontent* (Boston: Northeastern University Press, 1987).

34. Collins, *America's Women,* p. 332.

35. Faderman, *Surpassing the Love of Men,* pp. 297–99.

36. Spurlock and Magistro, *New and Improved,* p. 60; Nancy Sahli, "Smashing: Women's Relationships Before the Fall," *Chrysalis* 8 (1979); Cynthia Comacchio, *The Infinite Bonds of Family: Domesticity in Canada, 1850–1940* (Toronto: University of Toronto Press, 1999), p. 60.

37. Christina Simmons, "Companionate Marriage and the Lesbian Threat," in Kathryn Sklar and Thomas Dublin, *Woman and Power in American History* (Englewood Cliffs, N.J.: Prentice-Hall, 1991), vol. 2, p. 188; Spurlock and Magistro, *New and Improved,* p. 45.

38. Spurlock and Magistro, *New and Improved,* pp. 94–95.

39. Gail Bederman, *Manliness and Civilization* (Chicago: University of Chicago Press, 1995); Chauncey, *Gay New York;* Ullman, *Sex Seen;* Jonathan Ned Katz, *The Invention of Heterosexuality* (New York: E. P. Dutton, 1995).

40. Dell, *Love in the Machine Age,* p. 10; Spurlock and Magistro, *New and Improved,* pp. 122–24.

41. Spurlock and Magistro, *New and Improved,* pp. 118–19.

42. For the information in this and the following two paragraphs, see Modell, *Into One's Own;* Spurlock and Magistro, *New and Improved;* Bailey, *From Front Porch to Back Seat.* Rates of marriage also rose, and the age of marriage fell, in most of Europe during this period. Michael Mitterauer and Richard Sieder, *The European Family: Patriarchy to Partnership from the Middle Ages to the Present* (Chicago: University of Chicago Press, 1982); Comacchio, *Infinite Bonds of Family;* Nancy Christie, *Engendering the State: Family, Work, and Welfare in Canada* (Buffalo, N.Y.: University of Toronto Press, 2000). Hall, *Sex, Gender and Social Change;* Anita Grossmann, " 'Satisfaction Is Domestic Happiness,' " in Michael Dobkowski and Isidor Walliman, eds., *Towards the Holocaust* (Westport, Conn.: Greenwood Press, 1983); Peter Laslett, *The World We Have Lost* (New York: Scribner, 1973).

43. Lynd, *Middletown,* p. 111.

44. Edward Strecker, *Their Mothers' Sons: The Psychiatrist Examines an American Problem* (Philadelphia: J. B. Lippincott, 1946), pp. 13, 30, 43, 209.

45. Dorothy Bromley, "Feminist—New Style," in Mary Beth Norton, ed., *Major Problems in American Women's History* (Lexington, Mass.: D. C. Heath, 1989), p. 324; Rayna Rapp and Ellen Ross, "The 1920s," in Judith Friedlander et al., eds., *Women in Culture and Politics* (Bloomington: Indiana University Press), p. 59; Collins, *America's Women,* p. 329.

46. Modell, *Into One's Own,* p. 99.

47. Bailey, *From Front Porch to Back Seat,* pp. 88, 90.

48. Groves, quoted in Simmons, "Modern Sexuality and the Myth of Victorian Repression," p. 27; Dell, *Love in the Machine Age,* p. 311; Simmons, "Companionate Marriage," p. 191; Rapp and Ross, "The 1920s," p. 56.

49. Donald Hernandez, *America's Children* (New York: Russell Sage, 1993).

50. Cott, *Grounding of Modern Feminism;* Alice Kessler-Harris, *Out to Work: A History of Wage Earning Women in the United States* (New York: Oxford University Press, 1982).

51. Claudia Goldin, *Understanding the Gender Gap* (New York: Oxford University Press, 1990); Leslie Tentler, *Wage-Earning Women: Industrial Work and Family life in the United States, 1900–1930* (New York: Oxford University Press, 1979); Leuchtenburg, *Perils of Prosperity.*

52. Shelley MacDermid and Denna Targ, "A Call for Greater Attention to the Role of Employers," *Journal of Family and Economic Issues* 16 (1995).

53. Clair (Vickery) Brown, "Home Production for Use in a Market Economy," in Barrie Thorne and Marilyn Yalom, *Rethinking the Family* (New York: Longmans, 1982); Ruth Schwartz Cowan, *More Work for Mother: The Ironies of Household Technology from the Open Hearth to the Microwave* (New York: Basic Books, 1983); Nancy Cott, *Public Vows: A History of Marriage and the Nation* (Cambridge, Mass.: Harvard University Press, 2000).

54. Cott, *Grounding of Modern Feminism,* pp. 164–65; Bromley, "Feminist—New Style," p. 324; Rapp and Ross, "The 1920s," p. 59.

55. For the quotes in this and the next paragraph, see Felix Adler, *Marriage and Divorce* (New York: D. Appleton and Company, 1915), pp. 12–13, 20–21, 47–48.

56. Modell, *Into One's Own,* p. 116.

57. Elaine Tyler May, *Homeward Bound: American Families in the Cold War Era* (New York: Basic Books, 1988).

58. Dell, *Love in the Machine Age,* pp. 117–82.

59. Ruth Alexander, *The "Girl Problem": Female Sexual Delinquency in New York, 1900–1930* (Ithaca, N.Y.: Cornell University Press, 1996); Mary Odem, *Delinquent Daughters: Protecting and Policing Adolescent Female Sexuality in the United States* (Chapel Hill: University of North Carolina Press, 1995); Ellen Ryerson, *The Best-Laid Plans: America's Juvenile Court Experiment* (New York: Hill & Wang, 1978); Anthony Platt, *The Child-Savers,* pp. 69, 99, 135–45; John Sutton, *Stubborn Children: Controlling Delinquency in the United States, 1640–1981* (Berkeley: University of California Press, 1988); Susan Tiffin, *In Whose "Best Interest": Child Welfare Reform in the Progressive Era* (Westport, Conn.: Greenwood Press, 1982); Constance Nathanson, *Dangerous Passage: The Social Control of Sexuality in Women's Adolescence* (Philadelphia: Temple University Press, 1991).

60. Carson, *Marriage Revolt,* pp. 443–44.

61. Wendy Kline, *Building a Better Race: Gender, Sexuality and Eugenics from the*

Turn of the Century to the Baby Boom (Berkeley: University of California Press, 2001); Molly Ladd-Taylor, "Eugenics, Sterilisation and Modern Marriage in the USA: The Strange Career of Paul Popenoe," *Gender & History* 13 (2002), pp. 305–06; Linda Gordon, *The Moral Property of Women: A History of Birth Control Politics in America* (Urbana: University of Illinois Press, 2002), p. 219.

62. Peter Wallenstein, *Tell the Court I Love My Wife: Race, Marriage, and Law* (New York: Palgrave, 2002); Randall Kennedy, *Interracial Intimacies* (New York: Pantheon, 2003).

63. Groves, *Marriage Crisis,* pp. 66, 175, 185.

64. Popenoe, quoted in Ladd-Taylor, "Eugenics, Sterilisation and Modern Marriage," p. 300; Kline, *Building a Better Race,* p. 132.

65. Norma Basch, *Framing American Divorce* (Berkeley: University of California Press, 1999); Hartog, *Man and Wife in America.*

66. Maurer v. Maurer, 42 P, 186, Or 150, Oregon Supreme Court, April 1935. See also Hengen v. Hengen, 166 P. 525, 85 Or 155, Oregon Supreme Court, July 17, 1917. I am indebted to attorney William J. Howe III for calling my attention to these cases.

67. Samuel Schmalhausen, "The Sexual Revolution," in Calverton and Schmalhausen, eds., *Sex in Civilization,* pp. 418–19.

Chapter 13. Making Do, Then Making Babies

1. I conducted interviews with Cora Winslow Archer (not her real name) in 1990 and 1991. This reconstruction of her life is drawn from my notes.

2. Robert Tignor et al., *Worlds Together, Worlds Apart* (New York: W. W. Norton, 2002), p. 60; Steven Mintz and Susan Kellogg, *Domestic Revolutions: A Social History of American Family Life* (New York: Free Press, 1988), pp. 134–37.

3. Susan Ware, *Holding Their Own: American Women in the 1930s* (Boston: Twayne Publishers, 1982), p. 6; Wendy Kline, *Building a Better Race: Gender, Sexuality and Eugenics from the Turn of the Century to the Baby Boom* (Berkeley: University of California Press, 2001), p. 125; Mintz and Kellogg, *Domestic Revolutions,* p. 136.

4. Jeane Westin, *Making Do: How Women Survived the 1930s* (Chicago: Follett, 1976), pp. 46, 52, 77.

5. Ware, *Holding Their Own;* Nancy Cott, *Public Vows* (Cambridge, Mass.: Harvard University Press, 2000). Almost all the trends I describe for America held for Europe as well. While I don't have space to detail them in the text, I include citations in this and other notes for those interested in comparing the American experience with that of Europe. Bonnie Smith, *Changing Lives: Women in European History Since 1700* (Lexington, Mass.: D. C. Heath, 1989; Kline, *Building a Better Race;* Hanna Diamond, *Women*

and the Second World War in France, 1939–48 (Harlow, U.K.: Longmans, 1999).

6. Ellen Dubois, *The United States After 1865* (Washington, D.C.: American Historical Association, 2000); Kessler-Harris, *Women Have Always Worked;* Elaine Tyler May, "Myths and Realities of the American Family," in Antoine Prost and Gerard Vincent, eds., *A History of Private Life,* vol. 5: *Riddles of Identity in Modern Times* (Cambridge, Mass.: Belknap Press, 1991); Claudia Goldin, *Understanding the Gender Gap* (New York: Oxford University Press, 1990). For Europe, see Renate Bridenthal, "Something Old, Something New: Women Between the Two World Wars," in Bridenthal et al., eds., *Becoming Visible* (see chap. 3, n. 39).

7. Westin, *Making Do,* p. 27.

8. Glenn Elder, *Children of the Great Depression* (Chicago: University of Chicago Press, 1974); William Chafe, *The American Woman* (New York: Oxford University Press, 1972); Francesca Cancian, *Love in America* (New York: Cambridge University Press, 1987).

9. Steven McLaughlin et al., *The Changing Lives of American Women* (Chapel Hill: University of North Carolina Press, 1988); Cott, *Public Vows;* Dubois, *United States After 1865;* Ruth Milkman, "Women's Work and Economic Crisis: Some Lessons of the Great Depression," *Review of Radical Political Economics* 81 (1976). Similar measures were enacted in Europe, except for Sweden, which in 1939 passed a law protecting the right of women to work, regardless of marital status. Jane Lewis, "Gender and the Development of Welfare Regimes," *Journal of European Social Policy* 2 (1992); Peter Stachura, ed., *Unemployment and the Great Depression in Weimar Germany* (New York: St. Martin's Press, 1986); Wolfgang Voegeli, "Nazi Family Policy," *Journal of Family History* 28 (2003); Christina Florin and Bengt Nilsson, "'Something in the Nature of a Bloodless Revolution . . . ,'" in Rolf Torstendahl, ed., *State Policy and Gender System in the Two German States and Sweden 1945–1989* (Uppsala, Sweden: Lund, 1999).

10. Nancy Cott, "Marriage and Women's Citizenship in the United States," *American Historical Review* 103 (1998); Gwendolyn Mink, *The Wages of Motherhood: Inequality in the Welfare State, 1917–42* (Ithaca, N.Y.: Cornell University Press, 1995); Linda Gordon, *Pitied but Not Entitled: Single Mothers and the History of Welfare* (New York: Free Press, 1994).

11. Cott, *Public Vows.*

12. Anita Grossmann, "'Satisfaction Is Domestic Happiness,'" in Dobkowski and Walliman, *Towards the Holocaust* (see chap. 12, n. 42); Voegeli, "Nazi Family Policy."

13. Linda Gordon, *The Moral Property of Women: A History of Birth Control Politics in America* (Urbana: University of Illinois Press, 2002); D'Emilio and

Freedman, *Intimate Matters* (see chap. 10, n. 6); Kline, *Building a Better Race,* p. 4.

14. Rothman, *Hands and Hearts,* p. 299 (see chap. 10, n. 21); John Modell, *Into One's Own: From Youth to Adolescence in the United States, 1920–1975* (Berkeley: University of California, 1989), pp. 172–74; NCFR quote, in Bailey, *From Front Porch to Back Seat,* p. 132 (see chap. 12, n. 11).

15. Unless otherwise noted, the material on American women and World War II is drawn from Susan Hartmann, *The Home Front and Beyond: American Women in the 1940s* (Boston: Twayne Publishers, 1982); Mary Ryan, *Womanhood in America* (New York; New Viewpoints, 1975), p. 317; Amy Kesselman, *Fleeting Opportunities: Women Shipyard Workers in Portland and Vancouver During World War II and Reconversion* (Albany: State University of New York Press, 1990); Ruth Milkman, *Gender at Work: The Dynamics of Job Segregation by Sex During World War II* (Urbana: University of Illinois Press, 1987); Karen Anderson, *Wartime Women: Sex Roles, Family Relations, and the Status of Women During World War Two* (Westport, Conn.: Greenwood, 1981); Alan Cline, "Women Workers in World War II," *Labor History* 20 (1979); Nancy Gabin, "'They Have Placed a Penalty on Womanhood,'" *Feminist Studies* 8 (1982); Emily Yellin, *Our Mothers' War* (New York: Free Press, 2004). On Canadian and European trends, see Ruth Pierson, *"They're Still Women After All": The Second World War and Canadian Womanhood* (Toronto: McClelland and Steward, 1986) and Gisela Bock, *Women in European History* (Oxford, U.K.: Blackwell Publishers, 2002).

16. Letter quoted in Yalom, *History of the Wife,* p. 329 (see chap. 1, n. 16).

17. Sherna Gluck, *Rosie the Riveter Revisited: Women, the War and Social Change* (New York: New American Library, 1987).

18. Quoted in Yalom, *History of the Wife,* p. 351.

19. Pierson, *"They're Still Women,"* p. 216.

20. Doug Owram, *Born at the Right Time: A History of the Baby Boom in Canada* (Toronto: University of Toronto Press, 1996), p.12.

21. Rotundo, *American Manhood* (see chap 10, n. 18); Modell, *Into One's Own;* Bailey, *From Front Porch to Back Seat.*

22. For this and the next paragraph, see Edwin Amenta, *Bold Relief: Institutional Politics and the Origins of Modern Social Policy* (Princeton: Princeton University Press, 1998); Keith Olson, *The G.I. Bill, the Veterans, and the Colleges* (Louisville: University Press of Kentucky, 1974); Paul Simon, "A GI Bill for Today," *Chronicle of Higher Education* (October 31, 2003). Britain adopted a more universal welfare policy than the American model, but one that was similar in its gender distinctions. For example, a royal commission rejected calls for equal pay, saying that "individual justice" had to take a backseat to the "social advantage" of preserving jobs for

men and making sure that motherhood remained a desirable occupation for women. For more on European postwar family policies, see Karen Offen, *European Feminisms 1700–1950: A Political History* (Palo Alto, Calif.: Stanford University Press, 2000), pp. 388–89; Gail Braybon and Penny Summerfield, *Out of the Cage: Women's Experiences in Two World Wars* (London: Pandora Press, 1987); Jane Lewis, *Women in England 1870–1950* (Sussex, U.K.: Wheatsheaf Books, 1984), pp. 204–05; Heineman, *What Difference Does a Husband Make?;* Torstendahl, *State Policy and Gender System;* Ute Frevert, *Women in German History* (New York: St. Martin's Press, 1989); Robert Moeller, *Protecting Motherhood: Women and the Family in the Politics of Postwar West Germany* (Berkeley: University of California Press, 1993).

23. Hartmann, *Home Front and Beyond,* p. 44; June Willenz, *Women Veterans: America's Forgotten Heroines* (New York: Continuum, 1983); Margot Canaday, "Building a Straight State: Sexuality and Social Citizenship Under the 1944 GI Bill," *Journal of American History* (December 2003).

24. Stanley Surrey, "Federal Taxation of the Family—The Revenue Act of 1948" *Harvard Law Review* 61 (1948), p. 1112; Edward McCaffrey, *Taxing Women* (Chicago: University of Chicago Press, 1997). In 1969, following complaints from single taxpayers about having to pay more than married colleagues making the same income, Congress modified the law to provide that a single person's tax liability could not amount to more than 120 percent of that owed by a couple with the same total income. The 1969 law preserved the male breadwinner marriage bonus. But as the employment and earnings of working wives expanded during the 1980s, many married couples with two earners ended up paying *more* taxes than two single people with the same respective incomes. By 1999, 41 percent of all couples got a marriage bonus while 48 percent paid a marriage penalty. The marriage penalty for two-earner couples was an unintended consequence of the original male breadwinner bonus established in 1948. McCaffrey, *Taxing Women;* Virginia Postrel, "Wives' Tale," *Boston Globe,* April 13, 2003, p. E1.

25. "Marriage and Divorce," *March of Time,* series 14, 1948; William Tuttle, Jr., *"Daddy's Gone to War": The Second World War in the Lives of America's Children* (New York: Oxford University Press, 1993).

26. Since few men seemed to be interested in teaching elementary school, Farnham and Lundberg allowed for one exception to their objection to wives working outside the home. They proposed that married women with children take over elementary school teaching, but that the school day should be shortened enough that the mother/teachers would have plenty of time at home. Edward Strecker, *Their Mothers' Sons: The Psychiatrist Examines an American Problem* (Philadelphia: J. B. Lippincott,

1946); Marynia Farnham and Ferdinand Lundberg, *Modern Woman: The Lost Sex* (New York: Harper and Brothers, 1947), pp. 143, 167, 221, 241, 365.

27. For the whole passage, which includes all quotes used in the following paragraphs, see John Sirjamaki, "Cultural Configurations in the American Family," *American Journal of Sociology* 53 (1948).

28. Claire Duchen, *Women's Rights and Women's Lives in France, 1944–1968* (London: Routledge, 1994).

29. For the figures in this and the next several paragraphs, see: Modell, *Into One's Own;* Kline, *Building a Better Race;* Bailey, *From Front Porch to Back Seat;* Sandra Hofferth, "The American Family: Changes and Challenges," in Helen Wallace, Gordon Green, and Kenneth Jaros, eds., *Health and Welfare for Families in the 21st Century* (Sudbury, Mass.: Jones and Bartlett, 2003); *Historical Statistics of the United States: Colonial Times to 1970* (Washington, D.C.: U.S. Department of Commerce, 1975); Jessica Weiss, *To Have and to Hold: Marriage, the Baby Boom and Social Change* (Chicago: University of Chicago Press, 2000); Braybon and Summerfield, *Out of the Cage;* Gillis, *For Better, for Worse* (see chap. 7, n. 13); William J. Goode, *World Revolution in Family Patterns* (New York: Free Press, 1963); James Ponxetti, ed., *International Encyclopedia of Marriage and Family* (New York: Macmillan Reference USA, 2003).

30. Italy and Switzerland were among the few exceptions. Italian marriage rates dropped after the war and did not begin to rise until late in the 1950s. Switzerland's marriage rates, which had long been lower than most other regions of Europe, remained so right up through the 1980s. But in both West and East Germany, the rate of marriage rose so much during the 1950s that by the early 1960s even women of the World War II generation, who had experienced the massive loss of men in their age categories during the war, were as likely to be married as women of the same age had been before the war. And younger women were much *more* likely to be married than their prewar counterparts. In France, the marriage rate peaked between 1946 and 1950 and remained at historically high levels until the mid-1960s. Heineman, *What Difference Does a Husband Make?;* Duchen, *Women's Rights.* For other variations, see Olga Toth and Peter Robert, "Sociological and Historical Aspects of Entry into Marriage," *Journal of Family History* 19 (1994); Pier Paolo Viazza, "Illegitimacy and the European Marriage Pattern," in Lloyd Bonfield, Richard Smith, and Keith Wrightson, eds., *The World We Have Gained: Histories of Population and Social Structure* (Oxford, U.K.: Basil Blackwell, 1986).

31. Patrick Festy, "On the New Context of Marriage in Western Europe," *Population and Development Review* 6 (1980); Chiara Saraceno, "The Italian Family: Paradoxes of Privacy," in Prost and Vincent, eds., *Riddles of Identity*

in Modern Times; Sheila Kamerman and Alfred Kahn, *Family Change and Family Policies in Great Britain, Canada, New Zealand and the United States* (Oxford, U.K.: Clarendon Press, 1997); R. L. Cliquet, *The Second Demographic Transition: Fact or Fiction?* (Strasbourg: Council of Europe Population Studies No. 23, 1991); Michael Young and Peter Willmott, *The Symmetrical Family* (New York: Penguin, 1975); Martine Segalen, *Love and Power in the Peasant Family* (Oxford, U.K.: Basil Blackwell, 1983).

32. Rothman, *Hands and Hearts,* p. 301; Weiss, *To Have and to Hold,* p. 23; Goode, *World Revolution,* p. 48.

33. Weiss, *To Have and to Hold,* p. 23; Modell, *Into One's Own,* pp. 48–49, 248–49.

34. Weiss, *To Have and to Hold;* Kline, *Building a Better Race,* p. 125; Owram, *Born at the Right Time;* Goode, *World Revolution and Family Patterns;* Jennifer Loehlin, *From Rugs to Riches: Housework, Consumption and Modernity in Germany* (Oxford, U.K.: Berg, 1999).

35. Michael Anderson, "The Social Implications of Demographic Change," in F. M. L. Thompson, ed., *The Cambridge Social History of Britain 1750–1950,* vol. 2: *People and Their Environment,* (Cambridge, U.K.: Cambridge University Press, 1990); Daniel Scott Smith, "Recent Change and the Periodization of American Family History," *Journal of Family History* 20 (1995); Cliquet, *Second Demographic Transition;* M. Nabil El-Khorazaty, "Twentieth-Century Family Life Cycle," *Journal of Family History* 22 (1997).

36. John Modell details this speeding up and converging of life transitions for the United States, in *Into One's Own,* but it also occurred throughout Western Europe and in Canada. For more on the convergence of marriage patterns across social classes and ethnic groups, see Michael Young and Peter Willmot, *Family and Kinship in East London* (London: Routledge and Kegan Paul, 1957); John Goldthorpe et al., *The Affluent Worker in the Class Structure* (Cambridge, U.K.: Cambridge University Press, 1969); Peter Willmott and Michael Young, *Family and Class in a London Suburb* (London: Routledge and Kegan Paul, 1960); Erica Carter, *How German Is She?: Postwar West German Reconstruction and the Consuming Woman* (Ann Arbor: University of Michigan Press, 1997); Deborah Simonton, *A History of European Women's Work* (New York: Routledge, 1998); Duchen, *Women's Rights;* Karen Anderson, *Changing Woman: A History of Racial Ethnic Women in Modern America* (New York: Oxford University Press, 1996); Valerie Matsumoto, *Farming the Home Place: A Japanese American Community in California, 1919–1982* (Ithaca, N.Y.: Cornell University Press, 1993); Denise Segura, "Working at Motherhood," in Evelyn Glenn, Grace Chang and Linda Forcey, eds., *Mothering: Ideology, Experience, and Agency* (New York: Routledge, 1994). Of course, this convergence in

marriage behavior and ideals by no means lessened the huge gap between the economic and social options of different social groups or eliminated cultural differences in their interpretation of marriage and gender.

37. Mintz and Kellogg, *Domestic Revolutions;* Goode, *World Revolution and Family Patterns;* Hanna Diamond, *Women and the Second World War in France* (Harlow, U.K.: Longmans, 1999); Simonton, *A History of European Women's Work;* Owram, *Born at the Right Time;* Melanie Nolan, "A Subversive State?: Domesticity in Dispute in 1950s New Zealand," *Journal of Family History* 27 (2002); Colin Creighton, "The Rise of the Male Breadwinner Family: A Reappraisal," *Comparative Studies in Society and History* 38 (1996); Donald Hernandez, *America's Children: Resources from Family, Government, and the Economy* (New York: Russell Sage, 1993); Daphne Spain and Suzanne Bianchi, *Balancing Act: Motherhood, Marriage, and Employment Among American Women* (New York: Russell Sage, 1996).

Chapter 14. The Era of Ozzie and Harriet

1. Owram, *Born at the Right Time,* p. 22 (see chap. 13 n. 20); Elaine Tyler May, *Homeward Bound: American Families in the Cold War Era* (New York: Basic Books, 1988); Barbara Ehrenreich, *The Hearts of Men: American Dreams and the Flight from Commitment* (Garden City, N.Y.: Anchor Press, 1983), pp. 14–28; Douglas Miller and Marson Nowak, *The Fifties: The Way We Really Were* (Garden City, N.Y.: Doubleday, 1977), p. 154; Duchen, *Women's Rights* (see chap. 13, n. 28); Marjorie Ferguson, *Forever Feminine: Women's Magazines and the Cult of Femininity* (London: Heinemann, 1983); Moeller, *Protecting Motherhood* (see chap. 13, n. 22); Martine Segalen, "The Family in the Industrial Revolution," in Burguière et al., p. 401 (see chap. 8, n. 2).

2. Daniel Yankelovich, *New Rules: Searching for Self-Fulfillment in a World Turned Upside Down* (New York: Random House, 1981); Lois Gordon and Alan Gordon, *American Chronicle: Seven Decades in American Life, 1920–1989* (New York: Crown, 1990).

3. Coffin et al., *Western Civilizations* (see chap. 10, n. 29); Stephanie Coontz, *The Way We Never Were* (New York; Basic Books, 1992); Andrew Hurley, *Diners, Bowling Alleys and Trailer Parks: Chasing the American Dream in the Postwar Consumer Culture* (New York: Basic Books, 2001) William Chafe, *The Unfinished Journey: America Since World War II* (New York: Oxford University Press, 1986).

4. Ferguson, *Forever Feminine,* p. 31.

5. I remember watching this show once when I was twelve and sobbing because all the women deserved to win. My mother was furious at the whole concept. "They're using other people's poverty to advertise their goods to the rest of us," she fumed. For a detailed analysis of the show,

confirming my mother's instincts, see Georganne Scheiner, "Would You Like to Be Queen for a Day?," *Historical Journal of Film, Radio and Television* 23 (2003).

6. Alan Ehrenhalt, *The Lost City: Discovering the Forgotten Virtues of Community in the Chicago of the 1950s* (New York: Basic Books, 1995), p. 233; modernity quote from the French woman's magazine *Marie-Claire,* in Duchen, *Women's Rights and Women's Lives,* p. 73 (see chap. 13, n. 28).

7. Quoted in Ruth Rosen, *The World Split Open: How the Modern Women's Movement Changed America* (New York: Viking, 2000), p. 44.

8. Coontz, *The Way We Never Were,* p. 25; Rosenteur, quoted in Bailey, *From Front Porch to Back Seat,* p. 76 (see chap. 12, n. 11).

9. Martha Wolfenstein, "Fun Morality" [1955], in Warren Susman, ed., *Culture and Commitment, 1929–1945* (New York: George Braziller, 1973), pp. 84, 90; Coontz, *The Way We Never Were,* p. 171.

10. Ernest Burgess and Harvey Locke, *The Family: From Institution to Companionship* (New York: American Book Company, 1960), pp. 479, 985, 538.

11. Molly Ladd-Taylor, "Eugenics, Sterilisation and Modern Marriage in the USA," *Gender & History* 13 (2001), pp. 312, 318.

12. Nisbet, quoted in John Scanzoni, "From the Normal Family to Alternate Families to the Quest for Diversity with Interdependence," *Journal of Family Issues* 22 (2001); Mirra Komarovsky, *Women in the Modern World: Their Education and Their Dilemmas* (Boston: Little, Brown, 1953).

13. Talcott Parsons, "The Kinship System of the United States" in Parsons, *Essays in Sociological Theory* (Glencoe, Ill.: Free Press, 1954); Parsons and Robert Bales, *Family, Socialization, and Interaction Processes* (Glencoe, Ill.: Free Press, 1955).

14. Ladd-Taylor, "Eugenics."

15. *Historical Statistics of the United States: Colonial Times to the Present* (Washington, D.C.: U.S. Department of Commerce, Bureau of the Census, 1975); Sheila Tobias and Lisa Anderson, "What Really Happened to Rosie the Riveter," *Mss Modular Publications* 9 (1973).

16. Ruth Pierson, *"They're Still Women After All": The Second World War and Canadian Womanhood* (Toronto: McClelland and Stewart, 1986); Penny Summerfield, "Women in Britain Since 1945," in James Obelkevich and Peter Catterall, eds., *Understanding Post-War British Society* (London: Routledge, 1994); Loehlin, *From Rugs to Riches* (see chap. 13, n. 34); Eva Kolinsky, *Women in Contemporary Germany* (Oxford, U.K.: Berg, 1989); *United Nations Demographic Yearbooks* (New York: United Nations, 1953, 1962, 1968).

17. Beth Bailey, "Scientific Truth . . . and Love: The Marriage Education Movement in the United States," *Journal of Social History* 20 (1987).

18. Steven D. McLaughlin et al., *The Changing Lives of American Women* (Chapel Hill: University of North Carolina, 1988); William Chafe, *The Paradox of Change: American Women in the Twentieth Century* (New York: Oxford University Press, 1991).

19. M. Therese Seibert, Mark Fossett, and Dawn Baunach, "Trends in Male-Female Inequality, 1940–1990," *Social Science Research* 26 (1997).

20. Rosen, *World Split Open,* pp. 41–42, 26; Myra Strober and Agnes Miling Kaneko Chan, *The Road Winds Uphill All the Way: Gender, Work, and Family in the United States and Japan* (Cambridge, Mass.: MIT Press, 1999), pp. 16–17; Mintz and Kellogg, *Domestic Revolutions,* p. 181 (see chap. 13, n. 2).

21. Craig Heinicke, "One Step Forward: African-American Married Women in the South, 1950–1960," *Journal of Interdisciplinary History* 31 (2000); Bart Landry, *Black Working Wives: Pioneers of the American Family Revolution* (Berkeley: University of California Press, 2000).

22. Miller and Nowak, *The Fifties,* pp. 164–65; Weiss, *To Have and to Hold,* p. 19 (see chap. 13, n. 29); Rosen, *World Split Open,* p. 41.

23. Glenna Mathews, *"Just a Housewife": The Rise and Fall of Domesticity in America* (New York: Oxford University Press, 1987); Betty Friedan, *The Feminine Mystique* (New York: Dell, 1963).

24. Bailey, *From Front Porch to Back Seat,* p. 111.

25. Mirra Komarovsky, *Blue-Collar Marriage* (New Haven: Vintage, 1962), p. 331. Mintz and Kellogg, *Domestic Revolutions,* p. 194; Norval Glenn, "Marital Quality," in David Levinson, ed., *Encyclopedia of Marriage and the Family* (New York: Macmillan, 1995), vol. 2, p. 449.

26. Mary Ann Glendon, *The Transformation of Family Law* (Chicago: University of Chicago Press, 1989), p. 88. On Europe, Gisela Bock, *Women in European History* (Oxford, U.K.: Blackwell Publishers, 2002), p. 248; Bonnie Smith, *Changing Lives: Women in European History Since 1700* (Lexington, Mass.: D. C. Heath, 1989), p. 492.

27. Sara Evans, *Tidal Wave: How Women Changed America at Century's End* (New York: Free Press, 2003), pp. 1–20; John Ekelaar, "The End of an Era?," *Journal of Family History* 28 (2003), p.109. See also Lenore Weitzman, *The Marriage Contract* (New York: Free Press, 1981).

28. Ehrenhalt, *Lost City,* p. 233.

29. Quoted in Michael Kimmell, *Manhood in America: A Cultural History* (New York: Free Press, 1996), p. 246.

30. Ladd-Taylor, "Eugenics," p. 319.

31. Ralph LaRossa, "The Culture of Fatherhood in the Fifties," *Journal of Family History* 29 (2004).

32. D'Emilio and Freedman, *Intimate Matters,* p. 246 (see chap. 10, n. 6).

33. Historian Rickie Solinger points out that while a whole set of public policy initiatives encouraged white women to relinquish their babies for

adoption in the 1950s, legislators assumed black women would keep theirs and focused instead on preventing them from having more. Solinger, *Wake Up Little Susie: Single Pregnancy and Race before Roe v. Wade* (New York: Routledge, 1992).

34. Penalties were even more severe for men and women who acted on same-sex desires. During the 1950s there was a huge crackdown on the homosexual subcultures that had grown up in early-twentieth-century cities and gained more visibility during World War II. See Angus McLaren, *Twentieth-Century Sexuality* (Malden, Mass.: Blackwell, 1999).

35. Pierson, *"They're Still Women,"* pp. 217–18; Veronica Strong-Boag, "Home Dreams: Women and the Suburban Experient," in Strong-Boag and Anita Fellman, eds., *Rethinking Canada: The Promise of Women's History* (Toronto: Oxford University Press, 1997), p. 392.

36. Weiss, *To Have and to Hold.*

37. Ibid., p. 32; Robert Rutherdale, "Fatherhood, Masculinity, and the Good Life During Canada's Baby Boom," *Journal of Family History* 24 (1999), p. 367.

38. May, *Homeward Bound,* p. 202; Weiss, *To Have and to Hold,* pp. 136–38.

39. Marilyn Van Derbur Atler, "The Darkest Secret," *People* (June 10, 1991); Doss Darin, *The Magnificent Shattered Life of Bobby Darin and Sandra Dee* (New York: Warner Books, 1995); Elizabeth Pleck, *Domestic Tyranny* (New York: Oxford University Press, 1987); Linda Gordon, *Heroes of Their Own Lives: The Politics and History of Family Violence, 1880–1960* (New York: Viking, 1988).

40. Coontz, *The Way We Never Were,* p. 35; Leonore Davidoff et al., *The Family Story* (London: Longmans, 1999), p. 215.

41. Obituary for Coya Knutson, *New York Times,* October 12, 1996, p. 52; "Coya Knutson," in Karen Foerstel, *Biographical Dictionary of Congressional Women* (Westport, Conn.: Greenwood Press, 1999), pp. 152–53.

42. Benita Eisler, *Private Lives: Men and Women of the Fifties* (New York: Franklin Watts, 1986); Friedan, *Feminine Mystique.*

43. Parsons, "The Kinship System of the United States"; Parsons, "The Normal American Family," in Seymour Farber, Piero Mustacchi, and Roger Wilson, eds., *Man and Civilization: The Family's Search for Survival* (New York: McGraw-Hill, 1965); Parsons and Bales, *Family, Socialization, and Interaction Processes.* For similar theories in British sociology, see Michael Young and Peter Willmott's *The Symmetrical Family* (London: Pelican, 1973), pp. 28–30; *Family and Kinship in East London* (Glencoe, Ill.: The Free Press, 1957); and *Family and Class in a London Suburb.*

44. The quotations and figures in this and the following paragraphs are from Goode, *World Revolution.*

45. Research since the 1960s confirms that Goode was right in noting the

spread of the new marriage system to other industrializing countries, such as Japan. At the beginning of the twentieth century, Japan had comparatively high rates of divorce and extramarital births, and women played an important role in both the agricultural and the industrial labor force. But divorce and unwed childbearing decreased as Japan industrialized in the first third of the twentieth century, and after World War II, sociologist Yamada Masahiro argues, the "domestication of women" became national policy, with social welfare legislation, tax policies, and informal hiring practices all giving special advantages to families consisting of a salaried husband and a full-time housewife.

While less widespread than in the West, the number of Japanese marriages based on love rather than parental arrangement began to increase in the 1950s, as did the value that individuals placed on domesticity, a pattern that came to be called my-home-ism by the Japanese. Almost all women in the postwar era got married between the ages of twenty-one and twenty-five and bore two or three children before they reached thirty.

Important cultural differences remained between male breadwinner marriages in the West and in Japan during the 1950s, however. The Japanese nuclear family ideal was more centered on the children than on the couple. In addition, the social responsibilities of Japanese salaried workers, on top of their long work hours, meant that wives and children often took their "family" meals without the husband present. In addition, ties to parents remained strong, inhibiting free choice of marriage partners and the development of a couple's privacy after the wedding. Even today, older parents are much more likely to live with one of their married adult children in Japan than in Europe and North America. Furthermore, although the frequency of love matches grew rapidly after 1940, it was not until 1965 that the number of love matches exceeded the number of arranged marriages in Japan. Louise Tilly, *Industrialization and Gender Inequality* (Washington, D.C.: American Historical Association, 1993), p. 38; Noriko Iwai, "Divorce in Japan," in R. Robin Miller, ed., *With This Ring: Divorce, Intimacy, and Cohabitation from a Multicultural Perspective* (Stamford, Conn.: JAI Press, 2001); Yamada Masahiro, *The Japanese Family in Transition* (Tokyo: Foreign Press Center, 1998); Yamada Masahiro, "The Housewife: A Dying Breed?" *JapanEcho* (April 2001), p. 56; Kathleen Uno, *Passages to Modernity: Motherhood, Childhood, and Social Reform in Early Twentieth Century Japan* (Honolulu: University of Hawaii Press, 1999); Peter Stearns, *Gender in World History* (New York: Routledge, 2000), pp. 108–10; Susan Mann, *East Asia (China, Japan, Korea)* (Washington, D.C.: American Historical Association, 1999), p. 35; Gail Lee Bernstein, ed., *Recreating Japanese Women, 1600–1945* (Berkeley: University of California Press,

1991); Larry Carney and Charlotte O'Kelly, "Women's Work and Women's Place in the Japanese Economic Miracle," in Kathryn Ward, ed., *Women Workers and Global Restructuring* (Ithaca, N.Y.: ILR Press, 1990).

46. Susan de Vos, "Nuptiality in Latin America," in Miller, ed., *With This Ring.*

47. For the quotes in this and the next paragraph, see Goode, *World Revolution,* pp. 16, 62–65, 372–73.

Chapter 15. Winds of Change

1. Frank Furstenberg, Jr., "Family Change and Family Diversity," in Neil Smelser and Jeffrey Alexander, eds., *Diversity and its Discontents* (Princeton: Princeton University Press, 1999).

2. Nena McNeil and George McNeil, *Open Marriage: A New Life Style for Couples* (New York: M. Evans, 1972); Shulameth Firestone, *The Dialectic of Sex: The Case for Feminist Revolution* (New York: William Morrow, 1970). For an account of the women's movement, see Sara Evans, *Rising Tide: How Women Changed America at Century's End* (New York: Free Press, 2003).

3. Quoted in Arlene Skolnick, *Embattled Paradise* (New York: Basic Books, 1991), p. 139.

4. McLaughlin et al., *The Changing Lives of American Women* (see chap. 13, n. 9).

5. Quoted in D'Emilio and Freedman, *Intimate Matters,* pp. 346–47 (see chap. 10, n. 6).

6. McLaughlin et al., *The Changing Lives of American Women,* p. 169; Cliff Jahr, "Anita Bryant's Startling Reversal," *Ladies' Home Journal* (December 1980), p. 68.

7. Generally, the new ideas and behaviors were accepted first by people with other criticisms of the status quo, such as student activists. But they soon lost their early association with radicalism and even with secularism. In the 1960s, Catholics accepted the pill as readily as Protestants; Ronald Reagan, the first president to make family values a central campaign theme, was also the first divorced president in history; by the 1980s, acceptance of casual sex was as widespread among people who supported U.S. foreign policy as those who opposed it; and by the 1990s, evangelical Christians had as high a divorce rate as the population as a whole.

8. Abraham Maslow, *Motivation and Personality* (New York: Harper & Row, 1954). On the dress rehearsal of the 1920s in terms of individualistic values and desires for sexual fulfillment, see Francesca Cancian, *Love in America: Gender and Self-Development* (New York: Cambridge University Press, 1987).

9. For an extended argument about how modernization and industrialization raise people's expectations for personal satisfaction and individual autonomy, see Ronald Inglehart and Pippa Norris, *Rising Tide: Gender Equality and*

Cultural Change Around the World (New York: Cambridge University Press, 2003).

10. John Clausen, *American Lives: Looking Back at the Children of the Great Depression* (New York: Free Press, 1993). The quotes in this paragraph and the poll in the next paragraph are from Jessica Weiss, *To Have and to Hold,* pp. 108, 206, and note 7, p. 278 (see chap. 13, n. 29).

11. Barbara Ehrenreich, *The Hearts of Men: American Dreams and the Flight from Commitment* (New York: Anchor Press, 1983), pp. 12, 30; Keats, quoted in Donald Katz, *Home Fires* (New York: HarperCollins, 1992), p. 121.

12. Ehrenreich, *Hearts of Men,* pp. 30, 42, 47.

13. "'It's Good to Blow Your Top': Women's Magazines and a Discourse of Discontent, 1945–1965," *Journal of Women's History* 8 (1996).

14. Andrew Cherlin, "Should the Government Promote Marriage?," *Contexts* (Fall 2003); Weiss, *To Have and to Hold.*

15. Maxine Virtue, *Family Cases in Court* (1956), quoted in Katherine Caldwell, "Not Ozzie and Harriet: Postwar Divorce and the American Liberal Welfare State," *Law and Social Inquiry* 23 (1998).

16. Mary Ann Glendon, *The Transformation of Family Law: State, Law, and Family in the United States and Western Europe* (Chicago: University of Chicago Press, 1989).

17. For discussion of the complex interaction between women's employment and women's rights described in the following paragraphs, see Janet Chafetz, "Chicken or Egg? A Theory of the Relationship between Feminist Movements and Family Change," in Mason and Jensen, *Gender and Family;* Robert Jackson, *Destined for Equality: The Inevitable Rise of Women's Status* (Cambridge, Mass.: Harvard University Press, 1998); Julia Blackwelder, *Now Hiring: The Feminization of Work in the United States, 1900–1995* (College Station: Texas A&M University Press, 1997); Valerie Oppenheimer, *The Female Labor Force in the United States* (Berkeley: University of California Population Monograph Series, 1970); Alice Kessler-Harris, *Out to Work: A History of Wage-Earning Women in the United States* (New York: Oxford University Press, 1982); Cynthia Harrison, *On Account of Sex: The Politics of Women's Issues, 1945–1968* (Berkeley: University of California Press, 1988); William Chafe, *The Paradox of Change: American Women in the Twentieth Century* (New York: Oxford University Press, 1991); Sara Evans, "The Rebirth of the Women's Movement in the 1960s," in Kathryn Sklar and Thomas Dublin, eds., *Women and Power in American History, vol. 2: From 1870* (Englewood Cliffs, N.J.: Prentice-Hall, 1991). For a recent account of how changes in the 1950s undergirded the expansion of women's work and the women's movement after the 1960s, see Nancy MacLean, "Postwar Women's History: The 'Second Wave'" or the End of the

Family Wage?" in Jean-Christophe Agnew and Roy Rosenzweig, eds., *A Companion to Post-1945 America* (Malden, Mass.: Blackwell Publishing, 2002).

18. Helen Gurley Brown, *Sex and the Single Girl* (New York: Bernard Geis Associates, 1962), p. 4.

19. Hans-Peter Blossfeld, "Changes in the Process of Family Formation and Women's Growing Economic Independence," and Jenny de Jong Gierveld and Aat Liefbroer, "The Netherlands," in Blossfeld, *New Role of Women: Family Formation in Modern Societies* (Boulder, Colo.: Westview Press, 1995).

20. Susan Householder Van Horn, *Women, Work, and Fertility, 1900–1986* (New York: New York University Press, 1988); Lynn Weiner, *From Working Girl to Working Mother* (Chapel Hill: University of North Carolina, 1985); Glendon, *Transformation of Family Law;* Woloch, *Women and the American Experience* (see chap. 10, n. 13).

21. Ronald Lesthaeghe, "The Second Demographic Transition," in Mason and Jensen, eds., *Gender and Family Change,* p. 17; R. L. Cliquet, "The Second Demographic Transition: Fact or Fiction?," *Population Studies* 23 (1992), p. 22; Daniel Scott Smith, "The Dating of the American Sexual Revolution," in Michael Gordon, ed., *The American Family in Social-Historical Perspective* (New York: St. Martin's Press, 1978); Rothman, *Hands and Hearts,* pp. 307–08 (see chap. 10, n. 21).

22. Quoted in Andrea Tone, *Devices and Desires: A History of Contraceptives in America* (New York: Hill & Wang, 2001), pp. 234–35. See also Angus McLaren, *Twentieth-Century Sexuality: A History* (Malden, Mass.: Blackwell Publishers, 1999), p. 174; Beth Bailey, *Sex in the Heartland* (Cambridge, Mass.: Harvard University Press, 1999).

23. Steven Nock, "The Divorce of Marriage and Parenthood," *Journal of Family Therapy* 22 (2000). For a history of how the pill spread and became available to single as well as married women, see Beth Bailey, "Prescribing the Pill: Politics, Culture, and the Sexual Revolution in America's Heartland," *Journal of Social History* 30 (1997); Casper and Bianchi, *Continuity and Change in the American Family* (Thousand Oaks, Calif.: Sage, 2002); Kuijsten, "Changing Family Patterns in Europe," *European Journal of Population* 12 (1996).

24. Mary Ann Mason, Mark Fine, and Sarah Carnochan, "Family Law in the New Millennium," *Journal of Family Issues* 22 (2001).

25. Susan Douglas and Meredith Michaels, *The Mommy Myth* (New York: Free Press, 2004), pp. 42–43.

26. Wallerstein, *Tell the Court I Love My Wife,* pp. 189–219 (see chap. 12, n. 62).

27. Glendon, *Transformation of Family Law,* pp. 75–81.

28. Quoted in Wallerstein, *Tell the Court,* p. 240.

29. Rolf Nygren, "Interpreting Legitimacy," *Journal of Family History* 28 (2003).

30. Linda Hantrais and Marie-Therese Letablier, *Families and Family Policies in Europe* (New York: Longmans, 1996).

31. Ron Lesthaeghe and Dominique Meekers, "Values Changes and the Dimensions of Familism in the European Community," *European Journal of Population* 2 (1988); Ronald Inglehart, "The Silent Revolution in Europe: Intergenerational Change in Post-Industrial Societies," *American Political Science Review* 65 (1971); Ronald Inglehart, *The Silent Revolution: Changing Values and Political Styles Among Western Publics* (Princeton: Princeton University Press, 1977); Ronald Inglehart, *Culture Shift in Advanced Industrial Society* (Princeton: Princeton University Press, 1990); Joseph Veroff, Elizabeth Douvan, and Richard Kulka, *The Inner American: A Self-Portrait from 1957 to 1976* (New York: Basic Books, 1981); Daniel Yankelovich, *The New Morality* (New York: McGraw-Hill, 1974).

32. Veroff, Douvan, and Kulka, *Inner American,* pp. 191–92; Daniel Yankelovich, *New Rules: Searching for Self-Fulfillment in a World Turned Upside Down* (New York: Random House, 1981).

33. Inglehart and Norris, *Rising Tide.*

34. Andrew Sum, Neal Fogg, and Robert Taggert, "The Economics of Despair," *American Prospect* 27 (1996), pp. 83–84. I describe the earnings crisis of 1973–1992 and its effect on family life in more depth in *The Way We Never Were* (see chap. 10, n. 29) and *The Way We Really Are: Coming to Terms with America's Changing Families* (New York: Basic Books, 1997). See also R. M. Rubin and B. J. Riney, *Working Wives and Dual Earner Families* (Westport, Conn.: Praeger, 1994) and Ellman, "Divorce Rates, Marriage Rates." A recent discussion of the international dimensions of this crisis can be found in Oliver Zunz, Leonard Schoppa, and Nobuhiro Hiwatari, eds., *Social Contracts Under Stress: The Middle Classes of America, Europe, and Japan at the Turn of the Century* (New York: Russell Sage, 2002). Barbara Risman and Pepper Schwartz, "After the Sexual Revolution: Gender Politics in Teen Dating," *Contexts* 1 (2002); Ira Ellman, "Divorce Rates, Marriage Rates, and the Problematic Persistence of Traditional Marital Roles," *Family Law Quarterly* 34 (2000), p. 6; Thornton and Young-DeMarco, "Four Decades of Trends," p. 1028.

35. Janet Chafetz and Jacqueline Hagan, "The Gender Division of Labor and Family Change in Industrial Societies," *Journal of Comparative Family Studies* 27 (1996); Peter Li, "Labor Reproduction and the Family Under Advanced Capitalism," *Journal of Comparative Family Studies* 24 (1993); Susan McCrae, "Introduction," in McRae, ed., *Changing Britain: Families and Households in the 1990s* (New York: Oxford University Press, 1999); Chiara Saraceno,

"Changing Gender and Family Models," in Zunz, Schoppa, and Hiwatari, *Social Contracts;* Ponzetti, *International Encyclopedia.*

36. In the United States, for example, one study found that only one-third of women who graduated from high school in 1960 still had full-time jobs five years later. But by 1980, that number had increased to nearly two-thirds. Kristin Smith, "Maternity Leave and Employment Patterns, 1961–1995," U.S. Census Bureau, Public Information Office, December 5, 2001; Marlis Buchmann, *The Script of Life in Modern Society* (Chicago: University of Chicago Press, 1989).

37. Suzanne Bianchi and Daphne Spain, "Women in the Labor Force, 1950–1980," in Sklar and Dublin, eds., *Women and Power in American History,* vol. 2. For similar trends in Europe, see Hantrais and Letablier, *Families and Family Policies in Europe.*

38. Yankelovich, *New Rules.*

39. Elizabeth Beck-Gernsheim, *Reinventing the Family* (Cambridge, Mass.: Blackwell, 2002); Ulrich Beck, *Risk Society: Toward a New Modernity* (London: Sage, 1986); Ulrich Beck and Elizabeth Beck-Gernsheim, *The Normal Chaos of Love* (Cambridge, U.K.: Polity, 1995).

40. Norval Glenn, "Marital Quality," in David Levinson, ed., *Encyclopedia of Marriage and the Family* (New York: Simon & Schuster Macmillan, 1995), vol. 2.

Chapter 16. The Perfect Storm

1. Amitai Etzioni, "The Family: Is It Obsolete?" *Journal of Current Social Issues* 14 (1977), p. 4. Measuring divorce rates is very complicated. The crude divorce rate is the number of divorces per thousand married people. But one can also measure the ratio of divorces to marriages in any particular year or track trends over the past decade and project into the past. Because the 50 percent rate was a projection of how many marriages would end before the couple reached their fortieth wedding anniversary, it may have overstated the rate of marital breakdown. Nevertheless, almost 40 percent of first marriages contracted in the 1970s ended in divorce before their fifteenth anniversaries, so the 50 percent estimate was certainly reasonable.

2. Casper and Bianchi, *Continuity and Change* (see chap. 15, n. 23); Helen Rumbelow, "Women Less Likely to Remarry," *Washington Post,* July 24, 2002.

3. Christopher Marquis, "Total of Unmarried Couples Surged in U.S. Census," *New York Times,* March 13, 2003; Andrew Hacker, "How Are Women Doing?," *New York Review of Books* (April 11, 2002); Jane Lewis and Kathleen Kiernan, "The Boundaries Between Marriage, Nonmarriage, and Parenthood," *Journal of Family History* 21 (1996);

Kathleen Seltzer, "Cohabitation and Family Change," in Marilyn Coleman and Lawrence Ganong, eds., *Handbook of Contemporary Families* (Thousand Oaks, Calif.: Sage, 2004).

4. Pamela Smock and Sanjiv Gupta, "Cohabitation in Contemporary North America," in Alan Booth and Ann Crouter, eds., *Just Living Together: Implications for Children, Families, and Public Policy* (Mahwah, N.J.: Lawrence Erlbaum, 2002); Wendy Manning and Pamela Smock, "First Comes Cohabitation and Then Comes Marriage," *Journal of Family Issues* 23 (2002); Heath Foster, "More Moms and Dads Aren't Tying the Knot," *Seattle Post-Intelligencer,* May 1, 2003.

5. Joshua Goldstein, "The Leveling of Divorce in the United States," *Demography* 36 (1999); demographer Steven Nock at the University of Virginia, personal communication, July 23, 2003; BBC News, "UK Divorce Rate Lowest for 22 Years," August 21, 2001; Lois Brady, "Why Marriage Is Hot Again," *Redbook* (September 1996). Unless otherwise noted, the sources for other figures on stabilization in the United States (and the later discussion of similar trends in Europe) come from Casper and Bianchi, *Continuity and Change*; Linda Hantrais and Marie-Therese Letablier, *Families and Family Policies in Europe* (New York: Longmans, 1996); Hans-Peter Blossfeld, ed., *The New Role of Women: Family Formation in Modern Societies* (Boulder, Colo.: Westview Press, 1995); Karen Mason and An-Magritt Jensen, eds., *Gender and Family Change in Industrialized Societies* (Oxford, U.K.: Clarendon Press, 1995); Chiara Saraceno, "Changing Gender and Family Models," in Oliver Zunz, Leonard Schoppa, and Nobuhiro Hiwatari, eds., *Social Contracts Under Stress: The Middle Classes of America, Europe, and Japan at the Turn of the Century* (New York: Russell Sage, 2002); Karin Brewster and Irene Padavic, "Changes in Gender-Ideology, 1977–1996," *Journal of Marriage and the Family* 62 (2000); Tom Smith, "The Emerging 21st Century American Family, General Social Survey Social Change Report," no. 42, National Opinion Research Center, University of Chicago, November 24, 1999; Arland Thornton and Linda Young-Demarco, "Four Decades of Trends in Attitudes Toward Family Issues in the United States: The 1960s Through the 1990s," *Journal of Marriage and Family* 63 (2001); James Q. Wilson, *The Marriage Problem* (New York: HarperCollins, 2002); Mark Gillespie, "Americans Consider Infidelity Wrong," Gallup News Service, July 10, 2001, SeniorJournal.com; Vern Bengston, Timothy Biblarz, and Robert Roberts, *How Families Still Matter* (New York: Cambridge University Press, 2002); "Facts at a Glance," *Child Trends* (William and Flora Hewlett Foundation and Charles Stewart Mott Foundation, November 2003); U.S. Census Bureau, "Living Arrangements of Children Under 18 Years Old: 1960 to Present," Internet release date, June 29, 2001; Allen Dupree and

Wendell Primus, "Declining Share of Children Lived with Single Mothers in the Late 1990s" (Washington, D.C.: Center on Budget and Policy Priorities, June 15, 2001); Sharon Vandivere, Kristen Moore, and Martha Zaslow, *Children's Family Environments: Findings from the National Survey of America's Families* (Washington, D.C.: Urban Institute, 2001).

6. For this and the next paragraph, see Tamar Lewin, "More Mothers of Babies Under 1 Are Staying Home," *New York Times,* October 19, 2001; Stephanie Armour, "More Moms Make Kids Their Career of Choice," *USA Today,* March 12, 2002; Census Press Release CB03-166, October 23, 2003.

7. Lisa Belkin, "The Opt-Out Revolution," *New York Times Magazine,* October 26, 2003; Claudia Wallis, "The Case for Staying Home," *Time* (March 22, 2004), p. 51.

8. In the 1980s, juvenile crime rates and teen pregnancies rose hand in hand with the number of single-parent families, leading many commentators to fear that changing family forms were creating a generation of "superpredators." But although the number of single-parent homes continued to rise in the 1990s, teen violence and teen birthrates plummeted after 1992. By the end of the century the violent crime rate among teenagers had reached its lowest level in more than twenty years, and the teen birthrate was at an all time historic low. "Juvenile Homicides Decline," *New York Times,* December 15, 2000; Lina Guzman et al., "How Children Are Doing: The Mismatch Between Public Perception and Statistical Reality," *Child Trends Research Brief,* Publication 2003-12 (July 2003); Stephanie Ventura et al., "Estimate Pregnancy Rates for the United States, 1990–2000" (New York: Alan Guttmacher Institute, June 14, 2004).

9. Jeff Madrick, "Still a Gender Wage Gap," *New York Times,* June 10, 2004; Teresa Carson, "Lesbian Moms a Growing U.S. Phenomenon," Reuters News Service, May 25, 2004.

10. *Fertility of American Women, June 2002* (U.S. Census Bureau, Current Population Survey, October 2003); Stephanie Armour, "Some Moms Quit as Offices Scrap Family-Friendliness," *USA Today,* May 4, 2004.

11. Paula England, Carmen Garcia-Beaulieu, and Mary Rose, "Women's Employment Among Blacks, Whites, and Three Groups of Latinas," *Gender & Society* 18 (2004).

12. Kathleen Gerson, "Moral Dilemmas, Moral Strategies, and the Transformation of Gender: Lessons for Two Generations of Work and Family Change," *Gender & Society* 16 (2002), pp. 17–18.

13. Donald Hernandez, *America's Children: Resources from Family, Government and the Economy* (New York: Russell Sage, 1993).

14. David Leonhardt, "Wage Gap Between Men and Women Closes to Narrowest," *New York Times,* February 17, 2003.

15. Arleen Leibowitz and Jacob Klerman, "Explaining Changes in Married Mothers' Employment over Time," *Demography* 32 (1995).

16. Families and Work Institute, *2002 National Study of the Changing Workforce* (New York: 2002); Ellen Galinsky et al., *Feeling Overworked: When Work Becomes Too Much* (New York: Families and Work Institute, 2001).

17. Amy Goldstein, "When Wives Bring Home More Bacon," *Washington Post* National Weekly Edition, March 6, 2000; Peg Tyre and Daniel McGinn, "She Works, He Doesn't," *Newsweek* (May 12, 2003); Jason Fields, "Children's Living Arrangements and Characteristics, March 2002," *Current Population Reports* P20-547 (June 2002); Henry Bellows, "Domestic Dads," Tacoma *News Tribune,* June 24, 2004.

18. Louise Lamphere, Patricia Zavella, and Felipe Gonzales, with Peter Evans, *Sunbelt Working Mothers: Reconciling Family and Factory* (Ithaca, N.Y.: Cornell University Press, 1993); Tamar Lewin, "More Women Earn Half Their Household Income," *New York Times,* May 11, 1995; Francine Deutsch, "Halving It All," in Naomi Gerstel, Dan Clawson, and Robert Zussman, *Families at Work: Expanding the Boundaries* (Nashville: Vanderbilt University Press, 2002), p. 127.

19. Phillip Blumstein and Pepper Schwartz, *American Couples: Money, Work, Sex* (New York: William Morrow, 1983); Richard Gelles, *Contemporary Families: A Sociological View* (Thousand Oaks, Calif.: Sage, 1995), p. 344.

20. Andrew Cherlin, "By the Numbers," *New York Times Magazine,* April 5, 1998; L. Johnston, J. Bachman, and P. O'Malley, "Monitoring the Future: Questionnaire Responses from the Nation's High School Seniors" (Ann Arbor, Mich.: Survey Research Center, Institute for Social Research, 1998).

21. Thomas Bradbury, "Understanding and Altering the Longitudinal Course of Marriage," *Journal of Marriage and Family* 66 (November 2004).

22. John Rowe and Robert Kahn, *Successful Aging* (New York: Pantheon Books, 1992); Susan Cohen, "Generation Next," *Washington Post Magazine,* June 1, 1997; Casper and Bianchi, *Continuity and Change;* Teresa Cooney and Kathleen Dunne, "Intimate Relationships in Later Life: Current Realities, Future Prospects," *Journal of Family Issues,* 22 (2001); Phillips, *Putting Asunder* (see chap. 9, n. 17).

23. Joshua Goldstein, "The Leveling of Divorce in the United States," *Demography* 36 (1999); Norval Glenn, "Feedback: A Reconsideration of the Effect of No-Fault Divorce," *Journal of Marriage and the Family* 59 (1997); Ira Ellman, "Divorce Rates, Marriage Rates, and the Problematic Persistence of Traditional Marital Roles," *Family Law Quarterly* 34 (2000). For a dissenting view, see Margaret Brinig and F. H. Buckley, "No-Fault Laws and at-Fault People," *International Review of Law and Economics* 18 (1998).

24. Frank Furstenberg, *Unplanned Pregnancy: The Social Consequences of Teenage*

Childbearing (New York: Free Press, 1976). See also Frank Furstenberg, Jeanne Brooks-Gunn, and S. Philip Morgan, *Adolescent Mothers in Later Life* (New York: Cambridge University Press, 1987).

25. Gabrielle Raley, "No Good Choices," in Stephanie Coontz, Maya Parson, and Gabrielle Raley, eds., *American Families: A Multicultural Reader* (New York: Routledge, 1999); Ted Huston and Heidi Malz, "The Case for (Promoting) Marriage: The Devil Is in the Details," *Journal of Marriage and Family* 66 (November 2004).

26. Lawrence Wu and Barbara Wolfe, "Introduction," in Wu and Wolfe, eds., *Out of Wedlock: Causes and Consequences of Nonmarital Fertility* (New York: Russell Sage, 2001).

27. Larry Muhammad, "Adopting Solo," *Louisville Courier-Journal,* March 30, 2003; Joy Thompson, "Wanted: Single, Female Mom?," *USA Today,* April 9, 2004.

28. Larry Bumpass and Hsien-Hen Lu, "Cohabitation: How the Families of U.S. Children Are Changing," *Focus* 21 (2000); personal communication, Andrew J. Cherlin, Johns Hopkins University, July 30, 2003.

29. Risman and Schwartz, "Gender Politics."

30. Nina Bernstein, "In a Culture of Sex, More Teenagers Are Striving for Restraint," *New York Times,* March 7, 2004.

31. For the cohabitation behaviors and values discussed in the next paragraphs, see Kathleen Kiernan, "Cohabitation in Western Europe," in Booth and Crouter, eds., *Just Living Together;* Celine Le Bourdais and Evelyne Lapierre-Adamcyk, "Changes in Conjugal Life in Canada," *Journal of Marriage and Family* 66 (2004); Seltzer "Cohabitation"; Smock and Gupta, "Cohabitation in Contemporary North America," in Booth and Crouter, *Just Living Together;* Kathleen Kiernan, "The Rise of Cohabitation and Childbearing Outside Marriage in Western Europe," *International Journal of Law, Policy and the Family* 15 (2001); Seltzer, "Cohabitation and Family Change," in Coleman and Ganong, *Handbook of Contemporary Families;* William Axinn and Arland Thornton, "The Relationship Between Cohabitation and Divorce," *Demography* 29 (1992); Casper and Bianchi, *Continuity and Change;* John Haskey, "Demographic Aspects of Cohabitation in Great Britain," *International Journal of Law, Policy, and the Family* 15 (2001); Pamela Smock, "Cohabitation in the United States," *Annual Review of Sociology* 26 (2000); Claude Martin and Irene Thery, "The Pacs and Marriage and Cohabitation in France," *International Journal of Law, Public Policy and the Family* 15 (April 2001); David Coleman and Tarani Chandola, "Britain's Place in Europe's Population," in Susan McRae, ed., *Changing Britain: Families and Households in the 1990s* (New York: Oxford University Press, 1999).

32. For this and the following paragraphs, see David Von Drehle and Alan

Cooperman, "A Fast-Moving Movement," *Washington Post* National Weekly Edition, March 15–21, 2004; "Quebec Court Declares Same-Sex Marriage Legal," *The Olympian,* March 20, 2004; Typh Tucker, "Out-of State Travelers Boost Same-Sex Marriage Crowds," *The Olympian,* March 20, 2004; "Gay? NO Marriage License Here: Straight? Ditto," *New York Times,* March 27, 2004; Karen Breslau and Brad Stone, "Outlaw Vows," *Newsweek* (March 1, 2004).

33. Evelyn Nieves, "Family Values Groups and Gay Marriage," *Washington Post,* August 17, 2003; James Dobson, *Focus on the Family Newsletter,* September 2003; James Dobson, *Focus on the Family Newsletter,* April 2004.

34. Stanley Kurtz, "The Road to Polyamory," *Weekly Standard* (August 4–11, 2003).

35. Eric Widmer, Judith Treas, and Robert Newcomb, "Attitudes Toward Nonmarital Sex in 24 Countries," *Journal of Sex Research* 35 (1998); John Fetto, "Gay Friendly?" *American Demographics* (May 2002).

36. Cathy Grossman, "Is the Recent Backlash Against Homosexuality Just a 'Blip'?," *USA Today,* July 31, 2003; Adam Goodheart, "Change of Heart," *AARP Magazine* (May and June, 2004), p. 44; John Ritter, "Gay-Marriage Backers Seize Opportunity," *USA Today,* March 22, 2004; Dennis Cauchon, "Civil Unions Gain Support," *USA Today,* March 10, 2004.

37. Bonnie Powell, "Former Law Dean Examines Same-Sex Marriage," University of California News Center, February 27, 2003; Joan Laird, "Lesbian and Gay Families," in Froma Walsh, ed., *Normal Family Processes: Growing Diversity and Complexity* (New York: Guilford, 2003); Karen Peterson, "Adoption Groups Opening Doors to Gays," *USA Today,* November 4, 2003; Marilyn Elias, "Psychologists to Endorse Gay Marriage," *USA Today,* July 29, 2004.

38. Peter Laslett, Karla Oosterveen, and Richard M. Smith, *Bastardy and Its Comparative History* (London: Edward Arnold, 1980); Jean Rodin, *The Way We Lived Then* (Brookfield, Vt.: Ashgate, 2000); U.S. Census Bureau Public Information Office, CB02-CN173, December 17, 2002.

39. Michelle Conlin, "Unmarried America," *BusinessWeek* (October 20, 2003).

40. Anton Kuijsten, "Changing Family Patterns in Europe," *European Journal of Population* 12 (1996), pp. 140–41.

41. Ulrich Beck and Elizabeth Beck-Gernsheim, *Individualization: Institutionalized Individualism and its Social and Political Consequences* (London: Sage, 2002).

42. Kuijsten, "Changing Family Patterns in Europe"; Katja Boh et al., *Changing Patterns of European Family Life: A Comparative Analysis of 14 European Countries* (New York: Routledge, 1989).

43. McRae, "Introduction," in McCrae, ed., *Changing Britain;* Franz-Xavier Kaufmann et al., eds., *Family Life and Family Policies in Europe* (Oxford, U.K.: Clarendon Press, 1997) vol. 1; Britta Hoem, "Sweden," in Blossfeld, ed., *New Role of Women.*

44. How long that tide can be contained in any direction is an open question. The number of unmarried parents in Japan grew by 85 percent in the last five years of the 1990s, albeit from a very low starting point, and the divorce rate, especially for older people, has also risen significantly. In Ireland, a bastion of sexual conservatism until the 1980s, one-third of all children are now born out of wedlock. Constanza Tobio, "Marriage, Cohabitation and the Residential Independence of Young People in Spain," *International Journal of Law, Policy and the Family* 15 (2001); James Ponzetti, ed., *International Encyclopedia of Marriage and Family* (New York: Macmillan Reference, 2003), p. 966; Gisela Bock, *Women in European History* (Oxford, U.K.: Blackwell Publishers, 2001); Paola Ronfani, "Children, Law and Social Policy in Italy," *International Journal of Law, Policy and the Family* 15 (2001); Rosanna Trifiletti, "Women's Labor Market Participation and the Reconciliation of Work and Family Life in Italy," in Laura den Dulk, Anneke van Doorne-Huiskes, and Joop Schippers, eds., *Work-Family Arrangements in Europe* (Amsterdam: Thela-Thesis, 1999); "The Rise of Cohabitation and Childbearing Outside Marriage in Western Europe," *International Journal of Law, Policy and the Family* 15 (2001); "Sex Taboos on the Way Out, Poll Shows," *Irish Independent,* January, 2001; Dirk Van de Kaa et al., eds., *European Population: Unity in Diversity* (Boston: Kluwer Academic Publishers, 1999). On family changes in Japan, see Yamada Masahiro, *The Japanese Family in Transition* (Tokyo: Foreign Press Center, 1998); Kumiko Fujimura-Fanselow and Atsuko Kameda, eds., *Japanese Women: New Feminist Perspectives on the Past, Present, and Future* (New York: Feminist Press, 1995); Michael Zielenziger, "Shifting Family Values: Fewer Births, Marriages Threaten Japan's Future," *New York Times,* March 13, 2003; John Raymo, "Premarital Living Arrangements and the Transition to First Marriage in Japan," *Journal of Marriage and Family* 65 (2003); Noriko Iawai, "Divorce in Japan," in Robin Miller, ed., *With This Ring: Divorce, Intimacy, and Cohabitation from a Multicultural Perspective* (Stamford, Conn.: JAI Press, 2001); Peter Goodman and Akiko Kashiwagi, "In Japan, Housewives No More," *Washington Post* National Weekly Edition, November 4–10, 2002; Mari Osawa, "Twelve Million Full-time Housewives," in Zunz, Schoppa, and Hiwatari, *Social Contracts Under Stress;* Hiromi Ono, "Women's Economic Standing, Marriage Timing, and Cross-National Contexts of Gender," *Journal of Marriage and Family* 65 (2003); Karen Mason, Noriko Tsuya,

and Manja Choe, *The Changing Family in Comparative Perspective: Asia and the United States* (Honolulu: East-West Center, 1998); Sonni Efron, "Me, Find a Husband?," *Los Angeles Times,* June 26, 2001; Howard French, "As Japan's Women Move Up, Many Are Moving Out," *New York Times,* March 25, 2003; Keiko Tatsuta, "More Women Daring to Be Unmarried Mothers," *Japan Today,* December 29, 2001. My thanks to Liza Rognas, faculty reference librarian at The Evergreen State College, for help finding statistics on falling Japanese birthrates.

45. Paul Wiseman, "In Taiwan, Not Much Ado over Gays Saying 'I Do,'" *USA Today,* February 5, 2004.

46. Ronald Inglehart and Pippa Norris, *Rising Tide: Gender Equality and Cultural Changes Around the World* (New York: Cambridge University Press, 2003); Estelle Freedman, *No Turning Back: The History of Feminism and the Future of Women* (New York: Ballantine Books, 2002).

47. Kevin Kinsella, "Demographic Dimensions of Global Aging," *Journal of Family Issues* 21 (2000); Ben Wattenberg, "It Will Be a Smaller World After All," *New York Times,* March 8, 2003; "Growth Rate Slowing: Global Population in 2002 Tops 6.2 Billion," Census Press Release CB04-48, March 22, 2004.

48. Arland Thornton and Linda Young-DeMarco, "Four Decades of Trends in Attitudes Toward Family Issues in the United States," *Journal of Marriage and Family* 63 (2001).

49. Andrew Cherlin, "The Deinstitutionalization of American Marriage," *Journal of Marriage and Family* 66 (2004); Jane Millar and Andrea Warman, *Family Obligations in Europe* (London: Family Policy Studies Centre, 1996); Harry Willekens, "Is Contemporary Family Law Historically Unique?," *Journal of Family History* 28 (2003); Irène Thery, *Demarriage* (Paris: Édition Odile Jacob, 1994); Nancy Cott, *Public Vows: A History of Marriage and the Nation* (Cambridge, Mass.: Harvard University Press, 2000).

Chapter 17. Uncharted Territory

1. Clifford Adams, "Making Marriage Work," *Ladies' Home Journal* (June 1950), p. 26.

2. Clifford Adams, "Making Marriage Work," *Ladies' Home Journal* (April 1951), p. 28.

3. William Doherty, *The Intentional Family: How to Build Family Ties in Our Modern World* (Reading, Mass.: Addison-Wesley, 1997).

4. There are some outstanding exceptions, of course. Researchers and clinicians at the Council on Contemporary Families and the National Council on Family Relations recommend the following books particularly highly: John Gottman and Nan Silver, *The Seven Principles for Making*

Marriage Work (New York: Crown Publishers, 1999); Andrew Christensen and Neil Jacobson, *Reconcilable Differences* (New York: Guilford Press, 2000); William Doherty, *Take Back Your Marriage* (New York: Guilford Press, 2001). See also Neil Jacobson and Andrew Christensen, *Acceptance and Change in Couples Therapy* (New York: W. W. Norton, 1998); John Gottman and Clifford Notarius, "Marital Research in the 20th Century and a Research Agenda for the 21st Century," *Family Process* 41 (2002); Frank Fincham and Thomas Bradbury, *The Psychology of Marriage* (New York: Guilford Press, 1990).

5. "Too Late for Prince Charming," *Newsweek* (June 2, 1986), p. 55; Sylvia Ann Hewlett, *Creating a Life: Professional Women and the Quest for Children* (New York: TalkMiramax Books, 2002).

6. Barbara Lovenheim, *Beating the Marriage Odds* (New York: William Morrow, 1990), pp. 26–27; Art Levine, "Second Time Around: Realities of Remarriage," *U.S. News & World Report* 108, (January 29, 1990); Felicity Barringer, "Changes in Family Patterns," *New York Times,* June 7, 1991, p. A1; Robert Schoen and Nicola Standish, "The Retrenchment of Marriage," *Population and Development Review* 27 (2001).

7. Gary Becker, *A Treatise on the Family* (Cambridge, Mass.: Harvard University Press, 1981).

8. Andrew Cherlin, *Marriage, Divorce, Remarriage* (Cambridge, Mass.: Harvard University Press, 1992). Interestingly, however, cross-cultural studies show that the independence effect of greater female economic or political influence does not necessarily increase divorce when men and women share responsibility in the home and in the community. Instead, increases in women's power are most likely to produce high divorce rates when there is strict task segregation by sex. Thus the increased specialization that developed with the rise of the male breadwinner marriage may actually have set the stage for the international surge in divorce once women began to earn their own income. See Lewellyn Hendrix and Willie Pearson, "Spousal Interdependence, Female Power and Divorce," *Journal of Comparative Family Studies* 26 (1995).

9. For this and the next paragraph, see Rose Krieder and Jason Fields, "Number, Timing, and Duration of Marriage and Divorce: 1996," *Current Population Reports* P70–80, February 2002, Table 9, p. 14; Joshua Goldstein and Catherine Kenney, "Marriage Delayed or Marriage Foregone?," *American Sociological Review* 66 (2001); Garance Franke-Ruta, "Creating a Lie: Sylvia Ann Hewlett and the Myth of the Baby Bust," *American Prospect* (July 1, 2002); Valerie Oppenheimer, "Women's Employment and the Gains to Marriage," *Annual Review of Sociology* 23 (1997); Hans-Peter Blossfeld, "Changes in the Process of Family Formation and Women's Growing Economic Independence: A Comparison of Nine

Countries," in Hans-Peter Blossfeld, ed., *The New Role of Women: Family Formation in Modern Societies* (Boulder, Colo.: Westview Press, 1995); Noriko Tsuya and Karen Mason, "Changing Gender Roles and Below Replacement Fertility in Japan," in Mason and An-Magritt Jensen, eds., *Gender and Family Change in Industrialized Countries* (Oxford, U.K.: Clarendon Press, 1995).

10. Alice Eagly and Wendy Wolf, "The Origins of Sex Differences in Human Behavior," *American Psychologist* 54 (1999).

11. Rosalind Barnett and Caryl Rivers, *Same Difference: How Gender Myths Are Hurting Our Relationships, Our Children, and Our Jobs* (New York: Basic Books, 2004); Barbara Whitehead and David Popenoe, *The State of Our Unions, 2001* (New Brunswick, N.J.: Rutgers University National Marriage Project, 2001). In 1967, by contrast, three-quarters of college women said they would marry a man they didn't love if he met their other criteria, many of which were connected to his ability to support a family.

12. Scott South, "Sociodemographic Differentials in Mate Selection Processes," *Journal of Marriage and the Family* 53 (1991); Robert Mare, "Five Decades of Educational Assortative Mating," *American Sociological Review* 56 (1991); Pepper Schwartz quoted by Deborah Siegel, "The New Trophy Wife," *Psychology Today* (January 7, 2004).

13. There are even hints that several industrial societies might be experiencing the same kind of reversal in patterns of childbearing that we have already seen in marriage rates: More highly educated women may soon be *more* likely to have children than their less educated counterparts. Steven Martin, "Women's Education and Family Timing," Department of Sociology and Maryland Population Research Center, June 2003; Franke-Ruta, "Creating a Lie"; N. Ahn and P. Mira, "A Note on the Changing Relationship Between Fertility and Female Employment Rates in Developed Countries," *Journal of Population Economics* 15 (2002); M. L. Dewitt and Z. R. Ravanera, "The Changing Impact of Women's Employment and Educational Attainment on the Timing of Births in Canada," *Canadian Studies in Population* 25 (1998); Brigit Hoem, "Entry into Motherhood in Sweden," *Demographic Research* 2 (2000).

14. I discuss this movement and quote its main proponents in *The Way We Really Are: Coming to Terms with America's Changing Families* (New York: Basic Books, 1997). See also Kristin Moore et al., "What Is 'Healthy Marriage'? Defining the Concept," *Child Trends Research Brief,* publication #2004-16, www.childtrends.org.

15. Wendy Carter, "Attitudes Toward Premarital Sex, Non-Marital Childbearing, Cohabitation, and Marriage Among Blacks and Whites," in Robin Miller, ed., *With This Ring: Divorce, Intimacy and Cohabitation from a Multicultural Perspective* (Stamford, Conn.: JAI Press, 2001); Dan

Vergano, "Here Comes the Bride—After College," *USA Today,* August 20, 2002; Megan Sweeney, "Two Decades of Family Change: The Shifting Economic Foundations of Marriage," *American Sociological Review* 67 (2002); Mason and Jensen, "Introduction," in Mason and Jensen, *Gender and Family Change;* "Born Again Christians Just As Likely to Divorce," www.barma.org/Flexpage.aspx?Page=BarmaUpdate&BarmaUpdate10= 170, accessed Oct. 6, 2004; Blaine Harden, "Bible Belt Couples 'Put Asunder' More," *New York Times,* May 21, 2001. This doesn't mean religion is irrelevant to marital stability. Couples who are share religious convictions and are active in church and community associations with like-minded people have more stable marriages than average. But the daily behaviors count much more than the abstract beliefs.

16. Rebekah Coley, "What Mothers Teach, What Daughters Learn: Gender Mistrust and Self-Sufficiency Among Low-Income Women," in Booth and Crouter, *Just Living Together* (see chap. 16, n. 4); Donna Franklin, *What's Love Got to Do with It: Understanding and Healing the Rift Between Black Men and Women* (New York: Simon & Schuster, 2000).

17. Stephanie Coontz and Nancy Folbre, "Marriage, Poverty, and Public Policy," a discussion paper from the Council on Contemporary Families prepared for the Fifth Annual CCF Conference, April 26–28, 2002; Kristin Seefeldt and Pamela Smock, "Marriage on the Public Policy Agenda: What Do Policy Makers Need to Know from Research?," National Poverty Center Working Paper No. 04-2, February 17, 2004, Gerald Ford School of Public Policy, University of Michigan; Daniel Lichter et al., "Is Marriage a Panacea?," *Social Problems* 50 (2003); "Assessing the Importance of Family Structure in Understanding Birth Outcomes," *Journal of Marriage and the Family* 56 (1994); E. Cooksey, "Consequences of Young Mothers' Marital Histories for Children's Cognitive Development," *Journal of Marriage and the Family* 59 (1997).

18. Kathryn Edin, "What Do Low-Income Single Mothers Say About Marriage?," *Social Problems* 47 (2000); Edin, "A Few Good Men: Why Poor Mothers Don't Marry or Remarry," *American Prospect* (January 3, 2000); Edin and Laura Lein, *Making Ends Meet: How Single Mothers Survive Welfare and Low-Wage Work* (New York: Russell Sage, 1998); Wendy Single-Rushton and Sara McLanahan, "For Richer or Poorer?," manuscript, Center for Research on Child Well-Being, Princeton University, July 2001; Michelle Budig and Paula England, "The Wage Penalty for Motherhood," *American Sociological Review* 66 (2001); Heather Joshi, Pierella Paci, and Jane Waldfogel, "The Wages of Motherhood: Better or Worse," *Cambridge Journal of Economics* 23 (1999); Jane Waldfogel, "The Effect of Children on Women's Wages," *American Sociological Review* 62 (1997); Shelly Lundberg, "Nonmarital Fertility: Lessons for Family Economics," in Lawrence Wu

and Barbara Wolfe, eds., *Out of Wedlock: Causes and Consequences of Nonmarital Fertility* (New York: Russell Sage, 2001).

19. Andrew Cherlin, "The Deinstitutionalization of American Marriage," *Journal of Marriage and Family* 66 (2004). See also Kathryn Edin, Maria Kefalas, and Joanna Reed, "A Peek Inside the Black Box," *Journal of Marriage and Family* 66 (2004). The reluctance of low-income women to marry is reinforced by government policies that penalize poor people for marrying by sharply reducing their eligibility for welfare or tax credits when their income rises even by a very small amount. Repealing such policies would be a sensible way to make it easier for low-income couples to wed, but it would not reinstate marriage as the normative behavior for all.

20. Frank Furstenberg, Jr., "The Future of Marriage," *American Demographics* 18 (1996).

21. Pamela Smock, "The Wax and Wane of Marriage," *Journal of Marriage and Family,* 66 (2004) and personal communication, May 3, 2004. For poll on being "set," see Whitehead and Popenoe, *State of Our Unions, 2002.*

22. Seefeldt and Smock, "Marriage on the Public Policy Agenda"; Thomas Bradbury and Benjamin Karney, "Understanding and Altering the Longitudinal Course of Marriage," *Journal of Marriage and Family,* 66 (2004).

23. Seefeldt and Smock, "Marriage on the Public Policy Agenda." For more on why these couples don't wed—and there are often very good reasons for one or the other partner to back away—see Single-Rushton and McLanahan, "For Richer or Poorer?," p. 4; Edin, "What Do Low-Income Single Mothers Say About Marriage?," pp. 112–33. For more information on the Fragile Families study, see http://crcw.princeton.edu/fragilefamilies/national report.pdf.

24. The importance of promoting healthy conflict-solving skills for unmarried and divorced couples, not just couples about to marry, has been shown by Robert Emery's twelve-year follow-up study of high-conflict, low-income couples randomly assigned to mediation and litigation. He found that an average of five hours in mediation resulted in dramatic improvements in nonresidential parent-child relationships twelve years into the future. Emery, *The Truth About Children and Divorce* (New York: Viking, 2004).

25. Andrew Hacker, *Mismatch: The Growing Gulf Between Woman and Men* (New York: Scribner, 2003), p. 29; Elizabeth Enright, "House Divided," *AARP Magazine,* (July/August 2004).

26. Edin, Kefalas, and Reed, "A Peek Inside the Black Box"; Liana Sayer and Suzanne Bianchi, "Women's Economic Independence and the Probability of Divorce," *Journal of Family Issues* 21 (2000); Krieder and Fields, "Number, Timing, and Duration of Marriages," Table 9, p. 14. For international

comparisons of the changing relationship between divorce and education, see Hans-Peter Blossfeld et al., "Education, Modernization, and the Risk of Marriage Disruption in Sweden, West Germany, and Italy," in Mason and Jensen, eds., *Gender and Family Change.*

27. Stacy Rogers, "Wives' Income and Marital Quality," *Journal of Marriage and the Family* 61 (1999).

28. Stacy Rogers and Danielle DeBoer, "Changes in Wives' Income: Effects on Marital Happiness, Psychological Well-Being, and the Risk of Divorce," *Journal of Marriage and Family* 63 (2001); Hiromi Ono, "Husbands' and Wives' Resources and Marital Dissolution," *Journal of Marriage and the Family* 60 (1998); Janice Stiehl, *Marital Equality: Its Relationship to the Well-Being of Husbands and Wives* (Thousand Oaks, Calif.: Sage, 1997); Mary Hicks and Marilyn Platt, "Marital Happiness and Stability: A Review of the Research in the Sixties," *Journal of Marriage and the Family* 32 (1970); Jane Wilkie, Myra Ferree, and Kathryn Ratcliff, "Gender and Fairness: Marital Satisfaction in Two-Earner Couples," *Journal of Marriage and the Family* 60 (1998); Maureen Perry-Jenkins and Elizabeth Turner, "Jobs, Marriage, and Parenting: Working It Out in Dual-Earner Families," in Marilyn Coleman and Larry Ganong, eds., *Handbook of Contemporary Families: Considering the Past, Contemplating the Future* (Thousand Oaks, Calif.: Sage, 2003); Scott Coltrane, *Family Man* (New York: Oxford University Press, 1996); Paul Amato, David Johnson, Alan Booth, and Stacy Rogers, "Continuity and Change in Marital Quality Between 1980 and 2000," *Journal of Marriage and Family* 65 (2003).

29. For this and the next paragraph, see Amato, Johnson, Booth, and Rogers, "Continuity and Change in Marital Quality Between 1980 and 2000"; Matthus Kalmijn, "Father Involvement in Childrearing and the Perceived Stability of Marriage," *Journal of Marriage and Family Life* 16 (1999); Coltrane, *Family Man.*

30. Julie Brines and Kara Joyner, "The Ties that Bind: Principles of Cohesion in Cohabitation and Marriage," *American Sociological Review* 64 (1999); Terry Arendell, "Women and the Economics of Divorce in the Contemporary United States," *Signs* 13 (1987). Interestingly, Brines and Joiner found that some of the things that destabilize marriage work in reverse for cohabiting couples. Unlike married couples, cohabitors whose employment and earnings grew more similar over time had much less chance of breaking up than those whose earnings and work diverged.

31. Karla Hackstaff, *Marriage in a Culture of Divorce* (Philadelphia: Temple University Press, 1999), pp. 177–79.

32. Betsey Stevenson and Justin Wolfers, "'Til Death Do Us Part: Effects of Divorce Laws on Suicide, Domestic Violence and Spousal Murder" and "Bargaining in the Shadow of the Law: Divorce Laws and Family

Distress," NBER Working Paper 10175 (2003), available at http://faculty-gsb.Stanford.edu/Wolfers/Papers/DivorcewebPDF; William Bailey and Ruth Peterson, "Gender Inequality and Violence Against Women," in John Hagan and Ruth Peterson, eds., *Crime and Inequality* (Palo Alto, Calif.: Stanford University Press, 1995); Leonard Paulozzi et al., "Surveillance for Homicide Among Intimate Partners—United States, 1981–1998," Centers for Disease Control, *Morbidity and Mortality Weekly Report* 50 (October 12, 2001); Laura Guan, Daniel Nagin, and Richard Rosenfeld, "Explaining the Decline in Intimate Partner Violence," *Homicide Studies* 3 (1999).

33. For this and the next two paragraphs, see Mavis Hetherington, *For Better or for Worse: Divorce Reconsidered* (New York: W. W. Norton, 2001); Constance Ahrons, *We're Still Family: What Grown Children Have to Say About their Parents' Divorce* (New York: HarperCollins, 2004); Joan Kelly, "Changing Perspectives on Children's Adjustment Following Divorce," *Childhood* 10 (2003); Yongmin Sun and Yuanzhang Li, "Children's Well-Being During Parents' Marital Disruption Process," *Journal of Marriage and Family* 64 (2002); Paul Amato and Alan Booth, "The Legacy of Parents' Marital Discord," *Journal of Personality and Social Psychology* 81 (2001); Abigail Stewart et al., *Separating Together: How Divorce Transforms Families* (New York: Guilford Press, 1997); Ronald Simons and Associates, *Understanding Differences Between Divorced and Intact Families: Stress, Interaction, and Child Outcome* (Thousand Oaks, Calif.: Sage, 1996); Christy Buchanan, Eleanor Maccoby, and Sanford Dornbusch, *Adolescents After Divorce* (Cambridge, Mass.: Harvard University Press, 1996); E. M. Hetherington, M. Bridges, and G. M. Isabella, "What Matters? What Does Not? Five Perspectives on the Associations Between Marital Transitions and Children's Adjustment," *American Psychologist* 58 (1998); Elizabeth Vandewater and Jennifer Lansford, "Influences of Family Structure and Parental Conflict on Children's Well-Being," *Family Relations* 47 (1998); E. M. Hetherington, S. Henderson, and D. Reiss, *Adolescent Siblings in Stepfamilies: Family Functioning and Adolescent Adjustment,* Monographs of the Society for Research in Child Development, Series 259, vol. 64, (Chicago: University of Chicago Press, 1999); National Center on Addiction and Substance Abuse at Columbia University, "Back to School 1999—National Survey of American Attitudes on Substance Abuse," August 1999. Practically the lone dissenter to this scholarly consensus is Judith Wallerstein, whose work has been critically reviewed in depth in a recent issue of *Family Relations* 52 (2003).

34. Paul Amato, "Reconciling Divergent Perspectives: Judith Wallerstein, Quantitative Family Research, and Children of Divorce," *Family Relations* 52 (2003); personal communication, August 20, 2003.

35. These data were generously calculated for me by Paula England of Stanford University. See also Janet C. Gornick, and Marcia K. Meyers, *Families that Work: Policies for Reconciling Parenthood and Employment* (New York: Russell Sage, 2003). Another reversal from the 1950s is that white wives are as likely to work as married black women. Paula England, Carmen Garcia-Beaulieu, and Mary Rose, "Women's Employment Among Blacks, Whites, and Three Groups of Latinas: Do Privileged Women Have Higher Employment?," *Gender & Society* 18 (2004).

36. L. K. Stroh and J. M. Brett, "The Dual Earner Daddy Penalty in Salary Progression," *Human Resource Management Journal* 35 (1996); Gene Koretz, "Why Married Men Earn More," *BusinessWeek* (September 17, 2001).

37. Margaret Nelson and Joan Smith, *Working Hard and Making Do: Surviving in Small Town America* (Berkeley: University of California, 1999).

38. Philip Cowan and Carolyn Pape Cowan, "New Families: Modern Couples as New Pioneers," in Mary Ann Mason, Arlene Skolnick, and Stephen Sugarman, eds., *All Our Families: New Policies for a New Century* (New York: Oxford University Press, 1998).

39. John Leland, "For Better or for Worse: He's Retired, She Works," *New York Times,* March 23, 2004.

40. For this and the following paragraphs, see Kathleen Kiernan, "Cohabitation in Western Europe," *Population Trends* (1990); "The State of the European Unions," in M. Macura and G. Beets, eds., *Dynamics of Fertility and Partnership in Europe,* vol. 1 (Geneva: United Nations, 2002); Judith Seltzer, "Cohabitation and Family Change," in Coleman and Ganong, eds., *Handbook of Contemporary Families;* William Axinn and Arland Thornton, "The Relationship Between Cohabitation and Divorce," *Demography* 29 (1992); Casper and Bianchi, *Continuity and Change;* Booth and Crouter, *Just Living Together;* John Haskey, "Demographic Aspects of Cohabitation in Great Britain," *International Journal of Law, Policy, and the Family* 15 (2001); Pamela Smock, "Cohabitation in the United States," *Annual Review of Sociology* 26 (2000). For a spirited defense of cohabiting relationships formed by choice, see Dorion Solot and Marshall Miller, *Unmarried to Each Other* (New York: Marlowe and Co., 2002).

41. Catherine Kenney and Sara McLanahan, "Are Cohabiting Relationships More Violent than Marriages?," Princeton University Center for Research on Child Wellbeing, Working Paper 01-22, June 1, 2001.

42. Judith Seltzer, "Families Formed Outside of Marriage," *Journal of Marriage and the Family* 62 (2000); Jeanne Batalova and Philip Cohen, "Premarital Cohabitation and Housework: Couples in Cross-National Perspective," *Journal of Marriage and Family* 64 (2002); Patricia Wren, "A Couple's Work," *Boston Globe,* November 9, 2002.

43. Cherlin, "Deinstitutionalization"; Emily Visher, John Visher, and Kay

Pasley, "Remarriage, Families and Stepparenting," in Froma Walsh, ed., *Normal Family Processes* (New York: Guilford, 2003).

44. For this and the next paragraph, see Sharon Sassler and Robert Schoen, "The Effect of Attitudes and Economic Activity on Marriage," *Journal of Marriage and the Family* 61 (1999); Laura Sanchez and Constance Gager, "Hard Living, Perceived Entitlement to a Great Marriage, and Marital Dissolution," *Journal of Marriage and the Family* 62 (2000); Tim Heaton and Ashley Blake, "Gender Differences in Determinants of Marital Disruption," *Journal of Family Issues* 20 (1999); Wilkie, Ferree, and Ratcliff, "Gender and Fairness"; Paul Amato and Alan Booth, "Changes in Gender Role Attitudes and Perceived Marital Quality," *American Sociological Review* 60 (1995); Gayle Kaufman, "Do Gender Role Attitudes Matter?," *Journal of Family Issues* 21 (2000).

45. Hacker, *Mismatch*.

46. Quoted in Ellen Ross, *Love and Toil: Motherhood in Outcast London, 1870–1918* (New York: Oxford University Press, 1993), p. 35. For more on inequities of family life in the past, see Coontz, *The Way We Never Were* (chap. 10, n. 29).

47. *New York Times,* June 10, 1998.

48. Jennifer Flowers, "Mail-Order Brides Give Some Men the 'Traditional' Wife They're Looking For, but There Are Concerns," *Minneapolis Star Tribune,* March 27, 2004.

49. Jonathan Gershuny, Michael Godwin, and Sally Jones, "The Domestic Labour Revolution: A Process of Lagged Adaptation?," in Michael Anderson, Frank Bechhofer, and Jonathan Gershuny, eds., *The Social and Political Economy of the Household* (Oxford, U.K.: Oxford University Press, 1994); "U.S. Husbands Are Doing More Housework," U.S. Census Bureau, Public Information Office, April 12, 2001; Coltrane, *Family Man;* Scott Coltrane and Michele Adams, "Men's Family Work," in Rosanna Hertz and Nancy Marshall, eds., *Working Families: The Transformation of the American Home* (Berkeley: University of California Press, 2001); Scott Coltrane, "Fathering: Paradoxes, Contradictions, and Dilemma," in Coleman and Ganong, eds., *Handbook of Contemporary Families;* Paul Amato, David Johnson, Alan Booth, and Stacy Rogers, "Continuity and Change in Marital Quality between 1980 and 2000," *Journal of Marriage and the Family* 65 (2003); Scott Coltrane, "Research on Household Labor," *Journal of Marriage and the Family* 62 (2000). The likelihood is that men and women will continue to converge, as sons of employed mothers are especially likely to believe that couples should share child care and housework equally. Marilyn Elias, "Working Moms Shape Kids' Family Roles," *USA Today,* August 9, 2004.

50. Kathleen Gerson, "Moral Dilemmas, Moral Strategies, and the Transformation of Gender," *Gender & Society* 16 (2002) and *Children of the Gender Revolution: Growing Up in an Age of Gender and Family Change* (forthcoming). For more on the spread of egalitarian views, despite the fact that women may be changing faster than men, see Arland Thornton and Linda Young-DeMarco, "Four Decades of Trends in Attitudes Toward Family Issues in the United States," *Journal of Marriage and Family* 63 (2001); Karin Brester and Irene Padavic, "Changes in Gender Ideology, 1977–1996," *Journal of Marriage and the Family* 62 (2000); Karen Mason, Noriko Tsuya, and Minja Choe, eds., *The Changing Family in Comparative Perspective: Asia and the United States* (Honolulu: East-West Center, 1998); Rosalind Barnett and Caryl Rivers, *She Works/He Works: How Two-Income Families Are Happier, Healthier, and Better Off* (New York: HarperCollins, 1996).

51. Peggy Orenstein, *Flux: Women on Sex, Work, Kids, Love, and Life in a Half-Changed World* (New York: Doubleday, 2000).

52. Arland Thornton and Linda Young-DeMarco, "Four Decades of Trends in Attitudes Toward Family Issues in the United States: The 1960s through the 1990s," *Journal of Marriage and Family* 63 (2001); Gayle Kaufman, "Do Gender Role Attitudes Matter?" *Journal of Family Issues* 21 (2000); George Gallup, Jr., *The Gallup Poll: Public Opinion 1996* (Wilmington, Del.: Scholarly Resources Inc., 1997); Bruce Chadwick and Tim Heaton, *Statistical Handbook on the American Family* (Phoenix: Oryx Press, 1999); DBB Needham Worldwide Survey; The 1995 Virginia Slims Opinion Poll, Tobacco Documents Online, and John Schulenberg et al., "Historical Trends in Attitudes and Preferences Regarding Family, Work and the Future Among American Adolescents," *Monitoring the Future,* Occasional Paper 37, Institute for Social Research, University of Michigan, 1994. My thanks to Dorion Solot, coauthor, *Unmarried to Each Other,* for directing my attention to many of these sources and compiling other figures indicating that women are becoming more reluctant to enter marriage.

53. Daniel Scott Smith, "A Higher Quality of Life for Whom?," *Journal of Family History* 19 (1994); Michael Young and Peter Willmott, *The Symmetrical Family* (Middlesex, U.K.: Penguin, 1973).

54. Thornton and Young-DeMarco, "Four Decades of Trends."

55. For a discussion of how men tend to see their relations with children as mediated through their wives, see Nicholas Townsend, *"The Package Deal": Marriage, Work and Fatherhood in Men's Lives* (Philadelphia: Temple University Press, 2002).

Conclusion: Better or Worse? . . .

1. For polls showing married people's happiness, see Ronald Inglehart, *Culture Shift in Advanced Industrial Society* (Princeton: Princeton University Press, 1990), Appendix, Table A-17, p. 451. For the most thorough collection of studies showing the benefits of marriage, although it ignores contradictory and conflicting evidence, see Linda Waite and Maggie Gallagher, *The Case for Marriage: Why Married People Are Happier, Healthier and Better Off Financially* (Garden City, N.Y.: Doubleday, 2000).

2. International evidence confirms that we might lose many of the benefits of modern marriage if we try to force it back to its dominating role in social and personal life. Polls taken in the 1980s revealed several exceptions to the general finding that married people were happier than non-married ones. In Ireland, Greece, Spain, Japan, and France, couples living together outside marriage were *more* likely to report themselves very happy than were married couples. Interestingly, in four of these five countries divorce was hard to obtain or highly stigmatized and the pressure to marry was quite high, meaning that there were a lot of people stuck in unhappy marriages. In South Korea, where there are few alternatives to marriage, single women tell pollsters that they would be worse off in several respects if they got married, while married women in South Korea say they would be better off in *most* respects if they were single. A recent poll in Japan, where divorce is still highly stigmatized, found that six times as many Japanese schoolgirls as Americans *disagreed* that everyone ought to get married. Inglehart, *Culture Shift,* Appendix, Table A-17, p. 451; "Introduction, " in Karen Mason, Noriko Tsuya, and Minja Choe, eds., *The Changing Family in Comparative Perspective: Asia and the United States* (Honolulu: East-West Center, 1998); "A New Class of Drifters," *JapanEcho* 10 (2001).

3. Catherine Ross, "Reconceptualizing Marital Status as a Continuum of Social Attachment," *Journal of Marriage and the Family* 57 (1995); Chloe Bird, "Gender Differences in the Social and Economic Burdens of Parenting and Psychological Distress," *Journal of Marriage and the Family* 59 (1997); Brian Baker et al., "The Influence of Marital Adjustment on 3-Year Left Ventricular Mass and Ambulatory Blood Pressure in Mild Hypertension," *Archives of Internal Medicine* 160 (2000); Sharon Lerner, "Good and Bad Marriage," *New York Times,* October 22, 2002; "Marital Stress and the Heart," *Harvard Men's Health Watch* 8 (2004); Marilyn Elias, "Over Time, Bickering Spouses Take a Toll on Well-Being," *USA Today,* August 2, 2004. For a review of other studies of the impact of a bad marriage, see Timothy Loving et al., "Stress Hormone Changes and Marital Conflict," *Journal of Marriage and Family* 66 (2004).

4. Steven Nock, *Marriage in Men's Lives* (New York: Oxford University Press, 1998); Marilyn Elias, "Miserable Marriage Can Make You Sick," *USA Today,* March 12, 2001; Lerner, "Good and Bad Marriage" and "Marriage Taken to Heart," *USA Today,* March 4, 2004; May Blom et al., "Social Relations in Women with Coronary Heart Disease," *Journal of Cardiovascular Risk* 10 (2003); Marilyn Elias, "Marriage Taken to Heart," *USA Today,* March 4, 2004; Mary Duenwald, "Discovering What it Takes to Live to 100," *New York Times,* December 25, 2001; Judith Hibbard and C.R. Pope, "The Quality of Social Roles as Predictors of Morbidity and Mortality," *Social Science and Medicine* 36 (1993).

5. Betty Carter and Joan Peters, *Love, Honor and Negotiate* (New York: Pocket Books, 1996). For other helpful marital advice books, see chap. 17, n. 4.

6. Sanjiv Gupta, "The Effects of Transitions in Marital Status on Men's Performance of Housework," *Journal of Marriage and the Family* 61 (1999); Scott South and Glenna Spitze, "Housework in Marital and Nonmarital Households," *American Sociological Review* 59 (1994); Marbeth Mattingly and Suzanne Bianchi, "Gender Differences in the Quantity and Quality of Free Time," *Social Forces* 81 (2003).

7. John Gottman, James Coan, Sybil Carrere, and Catherine Swanson, "Predicting Marital Happiness and Stability from Newlywed Interactions," *Journal of Marriage and the Family* 60 (1998), p. 6; Esther Kuwer, Jose Heesink, and Evert Van de Vliert, "The Marital Dynamics of Conflict over the Division of Labor," *Journal of Marriage and the Family* 59 (1997), p. 649. Predicting marital success is a tricky endeavor, and researchers have important differences of emphasis. Women have to be open to change too, of course, and that includes giving up the control that comes from being the household "experts" and learning to recognize that men may express their love through practical action rather than intimate talk. To get a flavor for the areas of agreement and disagreement, see John Gottman and Clifford Notarius, "Marital Research in the 20th Century and a Research Agenda for the 21st Century," *Family Process* 41 (2002); Scott Stanley, Thomas Bradbury, and Howard Markman, "Structure Flaws in the Bridge from Basic Research on Marriage to Interventions with Couples," *Journal of Marriage and the Family* 62 (2000); Frank Fincham and Thomas Bradbury, *The Psychology of Marriage* (New York: Guilford Press, 1990).

Index

Index

Index

Index

Index

Index